# Markets and Marketplaces

# in Medieval Italy

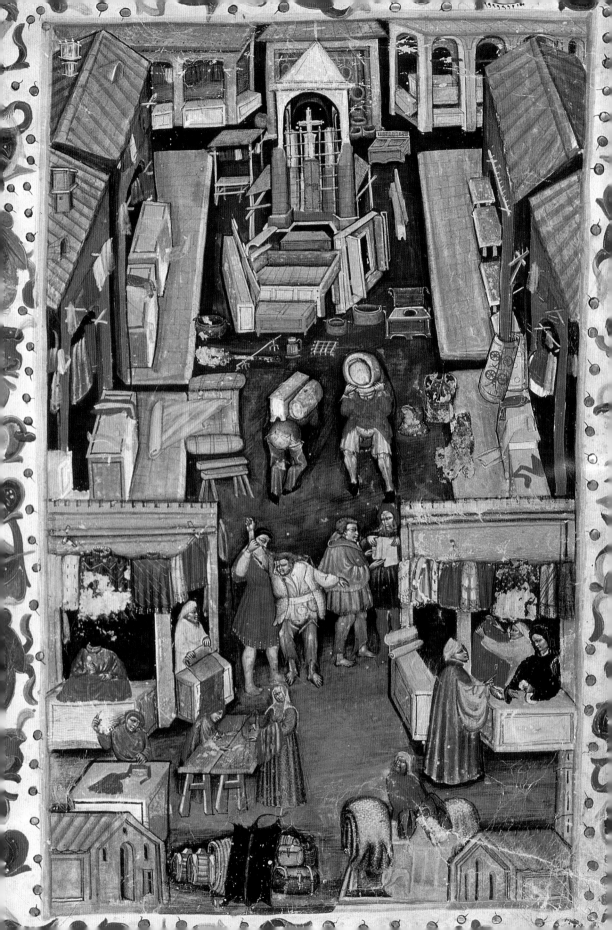

# Markets and Marketplaces in Medieval Italy

## c. 1100 to c. 1440

Dennis Romano

Yale University Press
New Haven & London

For Bob,
and in memory of Carey

*page ii* Detail of fig. 13

Copyright © 2015 by Dennis Romano
Designed by Emily Winter
Printed in China

Library of Congress Control Number: 2014953203
ISBN 978-0-300-16907-2

A catalogue record for this book is available from the British Library

# CONTENTS

Acknowledgments     vii

Introduction     1

**PART ONE: SPACE AND PLACE**     13

1   The Marketplace as Civic Symbol     19

2   The Evolution of Marketplaces     43

3   The Organization of the Marketplace     71

**PART TWO: BUYING AND SELLING**     85

4   Market Infrastructure: Streets, Shops, and Stalls     89

5   The Choreography of Buying and Selling     109

6   Regulating and Controlling the Marketplace     127

**PART THREE: MARKETPLACE ETHICS**     153

7   *Bona fide, sine fraude* (In Good Faith and Without Fraud)     159

8   Combatting Fraud and Promoting Trust:
Embellishing the Marketplace     191

Epilogue: *"È il bene comune nel mercatare"*     221

Notes     228

Bibliography     250

Index     263

Illustration Credits     272

AD honorem et reuerenciam omnipotentis dei et beate marie virginis glorioſe et omnium ſanctorum et ſanctarum
eiuſdem Anno beneuidicam in eo tutte et dii dii Lactiano dei gra hoſtien et [uetienſis] Epi-
neo no Ciuitatis Bon. eiuſque forcie et de ſaluce dni generaliſ epca Roman Felia de etiam dni Bla-
zy de tornaquinco de Flor rectoris et dni thomacie et laranzo de legio Gicecapio et duos prin-
co epal poſt ciuitatis Longa Romana ſelia et ut ſocietaſ mercatas ciuitad Bon ſerp in bono ſtatu debeant
gſuan et de bono innelius omne augmentari Hec ſunt ſtato ord ſocietart pdce ſca epilara et ordinata tpe ſapientium virus dnos Petri adam dni Atreuardini de Johanttis et Johiſ Bertolucy fratre petri griſendini pair
ſocietarin pdce ſca epilara et ordinaria tpe ſapientium virus et pprudenteſ et diſcretoſ viros ad pdca ſpecati-
abſentos ſdicalicat dnni Rolinum de Sabarnio dſo Gerardum de palioттis dſo Placentium de potis dſo
Philippum pauli dſo legnarini Gabios dſo Franciſcum de palioттis dſo Boniim bararenium donis eſelch-
onem adam Sanoy dſo Johem Barctini dſo Graciarium de Caxi dſo Bonfil alexi dſo Bertolinu Blacolini
dſo Johem dni Primirani dſo Sco georgio dſo ſtefan de Bodaldis et dſo Rodulfini de hoſberis. Capienteſ et
ſtatuteſ abſentos pedco pair ad ſtat et ord de ſocietart facienda et ordinata ſebra pime Bertolomei dſo Ber-
tioni Manſonis Augiali ſuede not de oſenſu puduplcate pdcoz generator
De [ratia rededa] 226.

# Acknowledgments

During the course of researching and writing this book, I have incurred, like the medieval producers and consumers studied here, innumerable obligations and debts which I can never fully repay but which I happily acknowledge. I am especially indebted to the Center for Advanced Study in the Visual Arts (CASVA) at the National Gallery of Art in Washington where I was an Ailsa Mellon Bruce Senior Fellow during the academic year 2007–08. Most of the research for this project was carried out in the welcoming and intellectually stimulating atmosphere fostered there by Dean Elizabeth Cropper and Associate Deans Peter Lukehart and Therese O'Malley. They and my fellow fellows, both junior and senior, most especially Beth Holman, Stanko Kokole, and Felipe Pereda, were unfailingly gracious as this "mere" historian ventured tentatively into the methods and approaches of art history. The staff of the Gallery's library, most particularly in the Interlibrary Loan Office, performed veritable miracles in locating many of the published primary source materials on which this study is largely based. The CASVA year remains one of the highlights of my years in academe.

Many institutions in Italy also deserve to be recognized for their generous assistance. I am especially grateful to the staffs of the State Archives of Bologna, Parma, Prato, and Venice, as well as those of the Archivio Municipale di Venezia, the Biblioteca Nazionale Universitaria of Turin, the Biblioteca Medicea Laurenziana, the Biblioteca Riccardiana, the photo archive of the Musei Civici agli Eremitani in Padua, the Società Dantesca Italiana in Florence, and Villa I Tatti, the Harvard University Center for Italian Renaissance Studies. I want especially to thank Elena Gurrieri at the Biblioteca del Seminario Arcivescovile Maggiore of Florence, Graziano Raveggi at the Soprintendenza Speciale per il Patrimonio Storico, Artistico ed Ethnoantropologico per il Polo Museale della Città di Firenze, Cristina Stefani in the Archivio Fotografico of the Museo Civico d'Arte of Modena, and Ambra Tommasi at the Museo Civico Correr in Venice. Closer to home, I happily acknowledge the assistance of librarians at the Library of Congress and the library of Syracuse University. I also wish to thank the Folger Shakespeare Library for the opportunity to participate in the weekend seminar "Connections, Trust, and Causation in Economic History" directed by Craig Muldrew in March 2008.

Detail of fig. 70

The research funds associated with the Dr. Walter G. Montgomery and Marian Gruber Professorship in the History Department at Syracuse University, of which I am honored to be the inaugural incumbent, provided crucial financial support for research trips to Italy and for the acquisition of images and reproduction rights. I am grateful to the creators of the chair for their recognition of the ongoing importance of the historical enterprise.

Additionally, I am obligated to friends and fellow scholars, almost too numerous to enumerate. First, I wish to recognize Caroline Bruzelius, Katherine L. Jansen, Maureen C. Miller, and Juergen Schulz for their early encouragement and support of this project. Along the way, I have benefited from the advice, knowledge, and support, both academic and non-academic, of Karen-edis Barzman, Sarah Rubin Blanshei, Francesco Turio Böhm, Louise Bordua, Molly Bourne, Michela dal Borgo and Sandro Bosato, William Caferro, Sally Cornelison, Janna Israel, Paola Lanaro, Kate Lowe, Sarah Blake McHam, Areli Marina, John Paoletti, Kenneth Pennington, Debra and Joe Pincus, Gary Radke, Michael Rocke, Elaine Ruffolo, Alan Stahl, Kevin Stevens, Helen Tangires, and Barbara Wisch. I apologize to those whom I have inadvertently failed to recall.

A very special debt is owed to Maureen Miller and Duane Osheim who offered extremely careful and insightful readings of an earlier version of this study as well as numerous recommendations for its improvement. It is rare to find colleagues who offer their time and knowledge so graciously and generously. I am sure that Maureen especially will continue to disagree rather vigorously with some of my arguments; and so it is important to state that all errors of both fact and interpretation remain mine alone. At the very least, I hope that this work will generate further research and debate. Frances Andrews and an anonymous reader evaluated the manuscript for Yale University Press. Both also provided extremely valuable suggestions and advice for improving the text, and I thank them wholeheartedly. My editor, Gillian Malpass, has also encouraged this project at every stage; her contributions in sustaining the field of medieval and Renaissance studies are beyond measure. I am grateful as well to Emily Winter for expertly shepherding the book through production.

Finally, I dedicate this study to my partner James Robert (Bob) Vance who makes my life both pleasurable and complete. It is dedicated as well to my niece Rebecca Carey Romano Charland whose tragic loss is tempered only by the way she still shines brightly and lives forever in my memory.

Author's Note

In this book, words for measures (such as pound, mile, foot) are literal translations of the original Italian or Latin. They should not be understood as corresponding to their United States or imperial customary units. Conversions to the metric system are based, unless otherwise noted, on the indications of medieval measures found in Ronald Edward Zupko's *Italian Weights and Measures from the Middle Ages to the Nineteenth Century* (1981).

# Introduction

In June 1425 the Franciscan friar Bernardino da Siena preached a cycle of sermons in his native city (fig. 1). The subject of the very first sermon that Bernardino gave during that preaching cycle was charity, which he compared to merchandise that Christ has for sale. The future saint told his listeners,

> Therefore, Christ Jesus says, come to me you who want this merchandise since there is no other person who sells it in his *buttiga* [*bottega* – shop] . . . And because you are familiar with the shop of this merchant, you know that it has five tall windows and that they spew forth the fire of love. What is this shop? It is the gracious body of Christ on the cross which has five windows which are the wounds on his hands, feet, and breast, from which, out of love for you, blood pours forth in order to wash away your sins. The sign of this shop is the cross . . . at the cross love is for sale![1]

More than a century earlier, in 1304, the Dominican friar Giordano da Pisa gave a series of sermons in the city of Florence for the Advent/Christmas season. In a homily he preached on February 2, the Feast of the Purification of the Virgin, Giordano compared Mary to a merchant who exchanged bad goods for better ones. He proclaimed, "[Mary] gave up earthly delights in order to have eternal ones and profited from everything . . . she profited from everything and extracted benefit just like a wise merchant."[2] In another sermon given earlier that day, Giordano equated the brevity of life on earth to a trade fair where great profits were to be made but which a merchant had neglected to attend. He exhorted his audience, "This stall of the world is like a fair for which the Lord God has established the time and the profit. How long will

1    Sano di Pietro, *San Bernardino Preaching in the Campo of Siena*, c. 1444.
Museo del Opera Metropolitana, Siena.

it last? Only to the end of your life, no longer. Therefore if you made a good profit,
you did well; otherwise you won't be able to return there or trade again."[3]

   These passages from sermons by two of the most popular preachers in late medieval
Italy – passages comparing Jesus and Mary to merchants, Christ's body to a *bottega*, the
cross to a shop-sign, and the fixed span of human life on earth to the duration of a
trade fair – illustrate how profoundly the great revival of trade and business, what
historians refer to as the "commercial revolution" of the Middle Ages, had altered not
only the material life of Western Europeans in the later Middle Ages but their cultural

horizons as well.[4] The habits of buying and selling, going to fairs, and looking to make a profit had become so ubiquitous that preachers could employ them as metaphors for such ineffable things as God's love for humankind and their appointed time on earth.[5] In the economically precocious cities of central and northern Italy especially, a fully fledged commercial economy and society had emerged that profoundly altered how men and women thought about themselves and others, about the virtues and vices, even about life and death.[6]

As this study will show, the development of this market mentality was intimately and inextricably connected to the spaces and places in which those exchanges took place, that is, to the marketplaces themselves. As the Swedish economic historian Odd Langholm has observed in his book *The Merchant in the Confessional*, whereas today the market is generally thought of in abstract terms as, for example, in the expression "market forces," in the Middle Ages, "the market was always a place, the marketplace, where trade in certain commodities was regularly conducted."[7] In this regard, it cannot have been lost on Bernardino's audience that the very spot where they were listening to him compare Jesus's body to a *bottega* was the Campo, Siena's civic square and principal marketplace, itself lined with shops. And Giordano preached one of his sermons during the 1304 Florentine cycle in the Mercato Vecchio, Florence's central marketplace.[8]

This book takes as its subject the markets and marketplaces in the towns of north and central Italy in the period from the beginning of the twelfth century to the mid-fifteenth century, that is, from the height of the commercial revolution when the communes or city-states emerged until the beginnings of the Renaissance when those city-states were consolidated into a set of more or less coherent regional states.[9] Its themes are space, power, and ethics. It seeks to contribute to a better understanding of the economy and culture of medieval Italy, and takes as its primary concern how the layout, organization, architecture, and artistic embellishment of marketplaces, that is the materiality of the marketplaces themselves, influenced and shaped market practices and vice versa. It explores the means by which some of the fundamental ideas associated with the market economy – concepts such as fraud, trust, justice, truth, and the common good (*bonum commune* in Latin, *bene comune* in Italian) – were formulated and negotiated not only in the treatises and sermons of the lawyers and churchmen who constituted the intelligentsia in medieval society but also in the day-to-day operation and organization of the marketplace itself as established by the various coalitions of local aristocrats, great merchants, and small-scale artisans who governed the communes and (in the case of the last two groups) the guilds of north and central Italy. This book prioritizes the quotidian and takes seriously the marketplace both as a place and as a space. The marketplace truly was, as scholars have termed it, "the mirror of the city," reflecting for each individual city its particular politics, social composition, and values.[10]

In recent years, as part of a revival of economic history more generally, a number of historians have turned their attention to the study of the medieval and especially the early modern market economy.[11] As a group, they have systematically dismantled

an older historiographical view which held that, beginning with the commercial revolution and continuing into the Renaissance, there emerged an early form of modern
commercial capitalism that operated by its own values and logic – namely the individual pursuit of profit – and that was largely divorced from the social and moral codes
of the Christian society in which it existed – a view powerfully expressed in Jacques
LeGoff's well-known formulation contrasting church time with merchant time.[12] For
proponents of this position inspired by classical economics, including such distinguished
scholars as Robert S. Lopez, Raymond de Roover, and Frederic C. Lane (to name
only a few of the leading scholars of the Italian economy), the commercial revolution
of the Middle Ages and the emergence of the Italian communes were the products
of a burgeoning new, middle class of merchant-entrepreneurs who bravely forged
not only innovative business practices and instruments and therefore the origins of
modern free-market capitalism but also republicanism.[13] As Philip Jones declared in his
magisterial history of medieval Italian city-states, "the qualities defined as characteristic
of modern capitalism – economic rationalism in the service of profit – were earliest
articulated in medieval Italy."[14] Jones went on to declare that "the theory of *mercatura*"
represented "an undiluted doctrine of economic individualism."[15]

Today, scholars are not so willing to view the medieval market economy as a self-
regulating and morally neutral sphere of activity and the medieval merchant as a
precursor of the modern commercial capitalist. Instead, they have come to understand
that the medieval marketplace was a highly moralized space – one profoundly influenced by the ethics of the Christian church and by such societal values as honor,
esteem, and reputation. As James Davis states in his recent study of market morality in
medieval England, "medieval markets . . . were embedded in social and cultural controls
and thus not self-regulating and driven by maximising self-interest."[16]

The works of Giacomo Todeschini have been especially influential in this more
recent formulation. In a series of articles and books, he has challenged the idea that
market practices and economic thought represented a secular alternative to the prevailing order in the Latin Christian West.[17] Rather, as he cogently illustrates, the economic
language in the Middle Ages was deeply informed by and imbued with Christian
meanings, rendering futile any effort to locate the purely secular origins of the market
economy in this period. As he observes, in Latin Christianity there was a strong connection between the description of the economy and "the definition of a moral-
theological identity."[18] So, for example, usury was condemned because it violated the
Christian values of *caritas* (charity) and *largitio* (largesse).[19] He also argues, as have other
scholars including Langholm, that churchmen were in no way antithetical to commerce
and trade, only to trade that violated the Christian imperative to practice charity toward
the poor. For Todeschini, the key figure is Saint Francis, the *mercator* (merchant) who
practiced poverty and avoided avarice.[20]

Paolo Prodi has also done much to dismantle the older view. In a sweeping survey
covering the period from the late Middle Ages to the Napoleonic era and with even
a brief foray into the nineteenth and twentieth centuries, Prodi reconsiders the relationship between Christianity and economic development and characterizes the

dynamic over this long time as a dialectic among church, state, and market.[21] Prodi accomplishes this through an analysis of the concept of theft, which in his formulation evolved from a sin against ethics, into a violation of market norms, and finally into a crime against the state. He views the fifteenth century, the end-point of this current study, as a moment of crisis in the relationship between the market and the state, since the question emerged as to who could judge the validity of contracts, that is, who could determine when a theft had occurred in the market. In his view, the problem in the late Middle Ages, especially in the Italian cities, was not commerce but the political control of commerce to ensure that it functioned for the *bene comune*.[22]

As a first order of business, it is important to consider precisely what kind of market and economy emerged as a result of the commercial revolution. In this regard, it is still helpful to keep in mind Fernand Braudel's useful distinction between a "market economy" and a "capitalist economy" since the two are often confused or conflated.[23] As Braudel observed, a market economy – the kind examined here – is based on connecting producers and consumers, is fixed on determining "exchange value," and is a "precondition" of capitalism.[24] And whereas the market economy is "down-to-earth . . . and is almost transparent," capitalism is "sophisticated and domineering." Most importantly, the market economy is "based on competition" whereas capitalism, where the truly great profits are to be made, "relies on real or de facto monopolies," monopolies that are bestowed by the state.[25]

In a formulation that in many respects builds on Braudel's work, Martha Howell argues that before capitalism emerged, commercialization characterized the European economy and society in the period from the fourteenth to the sixteenth centuries.[26] In her view, the crucial factor in the emergence of this new form of economy was the legal repositioning of land from the category of immovable to movable property, a development that appears to have occurred much earlier in Italy – well before the fourteenth century – than in northern Europe, which Howell knows best.[27] This profoundly affected all aspects of life, as now virtually anything could be assigned a commercial or monetary value. One consequence was that old markers of status, such as clothing, were monetized and lost their fixed meaning. Anxiety over this particular change prompted the flood of sumptuary laws that swept across Europe in this period. Governments also rushed in to regulate the market, to defuse its dangers, which included hoarding, engrossing, and deceit. And gifts took on a new meaning as they became a means of conferring honor which translated into commercial credit. As Howell observes, the "man of credit had become a man of honor."[28]

In yet another challenge to the position that the late medieval and early modern economy was simply the modern capitalistic economy in embryonic form, several historians, especially Craig Muldrew, have emphasized the complex meaning of trust in this period. The extension of a loan or credit (which involved an assessment of trustworthiness) depended not simply on a lender's evaluation of a borrower's economic standing, that is, on his ability to repay the money, but rather on a complex calculation of the borrower's honor, social status, and reputation for honesty. As Muldrew observes, "credit in this sense became a system of judgements about trustworthiness; and the trustworthiness of neighbours came to be stressed as the paramount communal virtue just as trust in God was stressed as the central religious duty."[29]

Clearly, much more was at play in the marketplace than the mere accumulation of monetary profit. As Anthony Molho and Ronald Weissman have demonstrated, the mutual indebtedness of Quattrocentro Florentines created crisscrossing bonds of obligation that served many purposes that were not tied directly to the marketplace or economic profit.[30] In addition to serving economic ends, market activities such as extending loans and allowing delayed repayment were also aimed at garnering friends and marital allies, securing social and political obligations, even at guaranteeing (or publicizing) one's position as an upright Christian member of the community.[31]

What is also clear is that many marketplace practices, regulatory habits, and ideals knew no national or regional boundaries. For example, the tropes about artisanal and mercantile fraud and deceit found in the sermons of Italian preachers such as Bernardino of Siena are the same ones expressed by preachers and others in England and elsewhere; their origins often can be traced to classical or patristic writers. Similarly, governmental and guild efforts to supervise the marketplace, impose standardized weights and measures, and create an open market were as common in England and the Low Countries as they were in Italy. So why devote a book to markets and marketplaces in medieval Italy? The first and most obvious answer is that there is no full study of the medieval Italian marketplace as a moralized sphere.[32] Such studies as do exist, especially those of Todeschini and Prodi, tend to focus on the writings of intellectuals rather than on how those ideas and ideals were translated into action and policy at ground level, while the studies of actual Italian market organization and practice concentrate almost exclusively on the early modern period.

Second and more importantly, such a study is called for since the older formulation of the medieval Italian marketplace as the birthplace of modern capitalism has been made to carry great interpretive weight. Scholars have, as noted above, related the rise of commercial capitalism not only to the emergence of republicanism but also to the development of humanism. For the French scholar Christian Bec, the businessmen who ruled Florence were, in his words, "merchant-writers" (*marchands écrivains*), much given to introspection.[33] Bec's formulation profoundly influenced Vittore Branca, who argued that these merchant-writers (*mercanti scrittori*) were driven by the imperatives of *ragion di mercatura* (reason of commerce) and *ragion di famiglia* (reason of family), motivations which also included a public element – one that was eventually formulated as *ragion di stato* (reason of state).[34] For the generation of scholars especially active in the years around and following the Second World War, the mercantile world born in the commercial revolution sowed the seeds for the Renaissance of the Quattrocento and beyond. While this study argues that market practices did indeed foster changes in society and culture, including a greater awareness of self, it also contends that merchants and others continued to articulate goals, such as furtherance of the common good, that encompassed more than the mere calculation of economic profit.

Third, although the Italian cities shared a number of commonalities with their northern European counterparts, they also exhibited significant differences. Most significantly, unlike towns in medieval England, France, and the Low Countries, which were subject in one form or another to kings or other great princes and consequently saw greater or lesser degrees of interference in their economic policies, the communes of medieval Italy were, for all intents and purposes, autonomous and independent polities. Although the Holy Roman Emperor and the pope enjoyed theoretical jurisdiction over various cities of north and central Italy, their actual ability to shape policy at the local level was extremely limited and usually met with fierce resistance. Instead, the markets and marketplaces of the medieval Italian cities were arenas for the operation of communal politics. In most towns this involved a contest between the church establishment (the bishop and/or great monasteries); the older established elites, commonly referred to as magnates, comprising the local landowning nobility who also had a foothold in the cities; the greater merchants including money-changers (bankers), traders, and textile manufacturers, with interests in international commerce and wholesale trade, usually called the *popolo grasso*; and small-scale artisans primarily engaged in retail trade and handwork, referred to as the *popolo minuto*.[35] As various coalitions came to power, they took steps to assert their control over the marketplace. In many instances this involved the creation of new market spaces that replaced or competed with older established market sites, while in every instance it led to efforts to establish market policies that favored the interests of the coalitions in power.

The trend throughout the later Middle Ages was toward greater intervention in the marketplace and ever increasing efforts to regulate trade, especially by the popular regimes, usually coalitions of the *popolo grasso* and *minuto* which came to power in the thirteenth century. This effort was framed ideologically by those regimes as a contest between particular interests and the common good, although it masked, as ideologies always do, the special interests of the very groups promoting them, most especially the *popolo grasso*. To this extent, the claim to uphold the common good should be viewed as the slogan that the popular regimes used to pummel their opponents. It is only a slight exaggeration to state that the struggle for power characteristic of the Italian communes was a struggle to control the marketplace. And so, by paying close attention to the marketplace, one gains a fuller appreciation of the play of communal politics.

The Dominican preacher Remigio de' Girolami (1235–1319) wrote that, "the common good is undoubtedly preferable to the good of individuals."[36] Yet, while theologians, preachers, and others continuously railed against those who sought advantage from the misfortune (or, as will be seen, the misinformation) of others, it is also true that wholesale merchants and petty artisans did at times adopt fraudulent or deceptive methods. Fraud was the central preoccupation of the Italian medieval market economy; it was the marketplace manifestation of avarice, judged to be the deadliest sin of the later Middle Ages and one frequently represented in medieval art (fig. 2).[37] Indeed, fraud was a much more ubiquitous marketplace concern than was usury. At the same time, while guild and civic statutes condemned deception, merchants and artisans were motivated at least in part by the desire to make money; and popular literature of the period, especially *novelle* or short stories, frequently celebrated the trickster who deceived and defrauded others and was out for himself.[38]

2   Ambrogio Lorenzetti, *Allegory of Bad Government*, detail showing *Avarice*, 1338–40,
Palazzo Pubblico, Siena.

Exploring this tension, this study will suggest that it was in marketplace practice,
especially in negotiating sales, that a greater appreciation of the complexities of human
personality developed. Thus this study engages the question of selfhood, a subject first
introduced by Jacob Burckhardt in 1860 as central to the Italian urban experience.[39]
Alfred von Martin, in *The Sociology of the Renaissance* (1932, translated 1944), pointed
to developing capitalism as the cause of emerging individualism.[40] In his view, "relations based on cash replaced relations based on personal obligation."[41] Von Martin's
materialist perspective has been challenged on many fronts as scholars have demonstrated how ubiquitous were the many different kinds of ties binding people together.
And Burckhardt's assertion of Renaissance individualism has been challenged by an
ongoing "revolt of the Medievalists."[42] Nevertheless, this study will argue that something important did occur in medieval marketplaces, namely that the need of buyers

and sellers to bargain with one another, to reach a deal, to extend trust, and to weigh their own desire for profit against a Christian imperative toward charity fostered an attentiveness to their own intentions and those of others, and thereby created a deeper appreciation of the self and how it was presented. As Lapo Mazzei (1350–1412), the notary and friend of the Pratese merchant Francesco di Marco Datini, declared, "I look not to a man's semblance or family, but only to his nature."[43]

A crucial factor that appears to have fostered this development, particularly in Italy, was increasing literacy and dependency on the written word, especially in the form of notarized contracts. As Ronald Witt has argued, two book cultures existed in Italy – not only a "traditional" book culture primarily located in cathedrals (and also found in northern Europe) but also a "legal" book culture based on documents and the study of the Justinianic legal corpus.[44] The latter was almost exclusively an Italian phenomenon and developed in tandem with the commercial revolution. Some scholars have characterized the broader transition taking place here as the evolution from a status-based society to a contract-based one, but this distinction is certainly overdrawn since important concepts such as trust continued to depend (despite Mazzei's claim) as much on a person's family and reputation as on legal documents.[45] Nevertheless, an essential advantage of contracts was their verifiability, and in this way writing helped shape market relations, providing, as Brian Stock noted, "the criteria for an agreed meaning" to an exchange.[46] In Italy, literacy became an important component of market practices and served as a safeguard for all sorts of market transactions. And it did more. It offered a vehicle for men (they were almost exclusively men) to begin to record their thoughts and signal events in their lives, interspersing these with their records of transactions in their account books and letters. To this extent then, this book is concerned with the marketplace's role in a growing appreciation of the complexity of human personality and in that sense with the transition to modernity or, more properly, early modernity.

What most distinguishes this study, however, is its approach; it takes space and place as key elements in the analysis of Italian markets and market practices. To be sure, architectural and urban historians have offered broad templates and overviews of market evolution. For instance, in a survey of cities throughout the Mediterranean world in the Middle Ages, Alireza Naser Eslami notes that in the ancient world, markets were secondary elements of the cityscape and that "merchants were prohibited [from playing] any important function in the political and cultural activity [of cities]."[47] But in the Middle Ages the marketplace assumed a major role in the cityscape as economic activities shed their previous isolation and as the figure of the "merchant-citizen" emerged first in Italy and other locales along the western Mediterranean (Barcelona and Marseille), before becoming ubiquitous throughout Europe.[48] Furthermore, in the western Mediterranean, at least, political, economic, and religious spaces often overlapped, particularly in the civic piazza, which with its market space often came to serve as a sort of "shop window" for the display of a city's products.[49]

In a similar vein, Donatella Calabi's *The Market and the City: Square, Street, and Architecture*, first published in Italian in 1993, charts a European-wide movement during the early modern period to impose greater order on the jumble of medieval market-places.[50] She documents an effort to distinguish and separate various kinds of urban spaces according to their uses – administrative, commercial, and religious. But, for all its strengths, her study, like Eslami's, remains firmly fixed on architectural and urban forms and gives little consideration to actual market practices and how those may or may not have influenced the creation of marketplaces and attempts to disentangle them from other kinds of civic centers.

This study takes up a call issued by Peter Arnade, Martha Howell, and Walter Simons more than a decade ago.[51] Noting that space was (and is) "a multivalent concept, a complex product of apprehension, experience, and reification," these historians urged that it be "studied as a multifaceted, multivalenced creation, a social reality that exists both at the discursive and material level."[52] More specifically, they contended that the key question with regard to market space is this: "how ... did the market *place* give birth to market *society*?"[53] Their query can also profitably be reversed to ask how market society gave rise to the marketplace. This book seeks to offer at least partial answers to these questions.[54]

It does so in three parts and an epilogue that strive to keep the spatial, built, and physical aspects of the marketplace firmly in the foreground. Part One examines the marketplace as a whole, both as a space and as a place. It considers the role of the marketplace in the civic imagination; the evolution and development of marketplaces over time, especially as they are related to configurations of power in specific cities; the buildings and structures that were commonly found in them; and, based on the well-documented example of Padua, the topographical distribution of market activities. It examines the central marketplace as a key component of civic identity and as an expression of the *bene comune*. Part Two explores the architecture and arrangement of streets and shops, the practices of buying and selling, and guild and governmental efforts to regulate and control the marketplace. In this section, the focus shifts from the marketplace as a whole to individual shops and stalls and to the persons found in the marketplace, be they civic or guild officials, established shopkeepers, or itinerant hawkers. It accords special attention to the performative aspects of buying and selling as well as to market personnel. The third and final part examines market ethics and values, especially the binary fraud/trust, and how the tension between them fostered introspection. It also investigates how the physical layout and architecture of market-places, as well as their embellishment with statues, paintings, and inscriptions, helped to publicize and reinforce market ideals and to punish (in the case of defaming pictures) those who violated those norms and practices. It is here that the clash between individual interests and the common good becomes most apparent. The study concludes with a brief epilogue that considers one of the most renowned works of art of the period, Ambrogio Lorenzetti's fresco cycle in the Sala dei Nove (Hall of the Nine) in Siena's Palazzo Pubblico from a mercantile or marketplace perspective.

It is important, finally, to offer several caveats about the material presented. First and most importantly, it needs to be emphasized that this is primarily a study of market ideals, as expressed in civic statutes and guild regulations, in various forms of literature, and in the materiality of marketplaces, although it does offer, where possible, evidence of practice. That evidence suggests that the concerns expressed in normative literature and legal codes reflected not only tradition but also the realities of everyday market experience. Rules and regulations continued to appear in successive editions of statutes and codes precisely because they continued to speak to the concerns of those who articulated them. A thorough study of practice, however, would, almost certainly, need to focus on one particular city and require an in-depth investigation of the archival evidence.[55] Specificity would come at the cost of a comparative perspective. Second, this study considers together wholesale and retail trading. Certainly many of the concerns expressed in law about engrossing and forestalling applied more to wholesalers than to retailers, while others, especially about giving proper measure, would have impacted to a greater degree small-scale retailers, who, as will be seen, relied more than did great wholesale merchants on short measure in order to garner a profit. However, examples of a tailor in thirteenth-century Milan, a draper in late fourteenth-century Pinerolo in Piedmont, and a druggist in Quattrocento Florence illustrate just how intertwined were wholesaling and retailing. Accordingly, any absolute distinction between the two would almost certainly apply only at the extremes, with great international merchants at one end and itinerant peddlers and prepared-food sellers at the other.[56] Many of those food-sellers were women and a third caveat to keep in mind is that the laws, regulations, sermons, and other evidence examined here were all created by men. Consequently, what we have is a male perception of the marketplace and its importance. Women's experience of the marketplace was necessarily different. One need only consider how the Florentine widow Alessandra Strozzi, a member of one of the city's most powerful families, was tormented by the demands of a butcher for the payment of her deceased husband's outstanding debt of nine ducats to catch a glimpse of the interplay of gender and class.[57] Unfortunately, though, how women experienced the marketplace and what they thought of it is now almost completely lost from view.

When Bernardino returned to Siena in 1427 to preach again, the future saint directed one of his sermons at merchants. In it Bernardino sanctioned commerce that was conducted honestly and licitly. But he did more than this: he staked out a positive place for commerce in civic life, declaring that "nothing contributes to the Commune so much as the profit of the guilds and of the merchandize that is bought and sold."[58] Yet the collective advantage of which he spoke – the civic prosperity and wealth brought about by trade – was nothing but the cumulative effect of individual buyers and sellers seeking to realize their own interests. Herein lay the energizing dynamic of the marketplace and of the society that produced it.[59] That tension between the common good and individual interest shaped every aspect of life and served in its way to foster a heightened sense of selfhood and of the complexity of human motivations.

# PART ONE

# SPACE AND PLACE

Sometime in the late 1330s the Dominican friar Galvano de la Fiamma began composing his *Chronicon extravagans de antiquitatibus mediolani* (Appended Chronicle Concerning the Antiquities of Milan), a work that complemented his *Chronicon maius* (Great Chronicle), an account of Milanese history. The *Chronicon extravagans* combined a thoroughgoing consideration of the city's topography, population, and major buildings, including ancient Roman ones, with a much briefer exposition of some of the significant events in its more recent past, while the *Chronicon maius* focused on a more detailed history of Milan from 568 CE, when the Lombard king Albuinus entered Italy, to 1342. Fiamma began the *Chronicon extravagans* with a description and list of the lakes and rivers in Milanese territory, followed this with a chapter on the city's riparian ports, and then with a discussion of its principal groups of merchants and the products (arms, horses, cloth, spices, and liquids such as wine and oil) in which they dealt. He devoted individual chapters to various ancient Roman buildings including the hippodrome and amphitheater, as well as to the city's many primary and secondary gates. In only one chapter did he describe Milan's churches. Fiamma dedicated the middle chapters of the chronicle to the inhabitants and various occupations of the city, while the final chapters concerned such topics as the city's *carroccio* (war-wagon) and its victories over the Holy Roman Emperor Frederick Barbarossa, the pope, and Cremona and Pavia.[1]

At some point in the second half of the fourteenth century, a map by Petrus de Guioldis was inserted into a manuscript containing Fiamma's two chronicles (fig. 3).[2] The mapmaker gave priority to the same elements that Fiamma emphasized. Oriented with the south at the top (labeled "Meridies") and hence east to the left (labeled "Oriens"), the map shows the major rivers and bridges of the region, as well as neighboring and more distant cities including Pavia, Cremona, Bergamo, and Verona. Drawn to a different scale from the surrounding territory, Milan itself is depicted by two concentric circles representing the city's two sets of walls: the inner circle indicates the walls built by Maximian Hercules in the late third/early fourth century CE; the outer circle the medieval walls which were begun in the twelfth and finished in the fourteenth century. The city's six principal gates are depicted with two towers (just as they are described in the *Chronicon maius*), while the secondary gates are represented with crenellation, except for that of Sant'Ambrogio which has crenellation and one tower.[3] Moreover, just as in the *Chronicon maius*, the mapmaker has indicated the distance between the various gates.[4]

Although the locations of a few buildings within the walls are identified by labels (for example, the caption "de galarate," at the top of the inner circle and running toward the center, marks the location of the church of the Umiliati), only two buildings are actually indicated by rectangles adorned with dental molding borders to denote crenellation. The smaller rectangle to the upper left, labeled "P" for *palatium*, indicates the location of the court of the Visconti lords of Milan, near what is today the duomo or cathedral. The larger rectangle directly in the center of the map stands for the Broletto Nuovo (or simply the Broletto, as it is known today). It is labeled as measuring 10 perticas. A *pertica* was a unit of linear or, as in this case, surface measure. Ten perticas was approximately 70,450 square feet (c. 6545 square meters).[5]

The Broletto Nuovo was the name given to the communal town hall (the Palazzo della Ragione) that stood (and still stands) in the center of the space, although the name eventually also came to signify the entire enclosed space made up of the palazzo and several other buildings located there (fig. 4). As Fiamma described it, the Broletto was, "a quadrangular building surrounded by a high wall, located in the center of the city, whose surface area encompasses around ten perticas."[6] The surrounding wall was punctuated by six portals which led in turn to the city's six main gates, while the rest of the complex included the palace of the podestà, the chief police official of the city, with a chapel dedicated to Saint Ambrose, the city's patron saint; other "palaces" of unspecified use; a marble loggia and the civic bell tower with four bells. Begun in 1228, the Broletto was the architectural expression of the independent Milanese popular

3   Petrus de Guioldis, *Map of Milan and Surrounding Territory*, second half 14th century, Biblioteca Ambrosiana, Milan, Ms. A 275, fol. 46v.

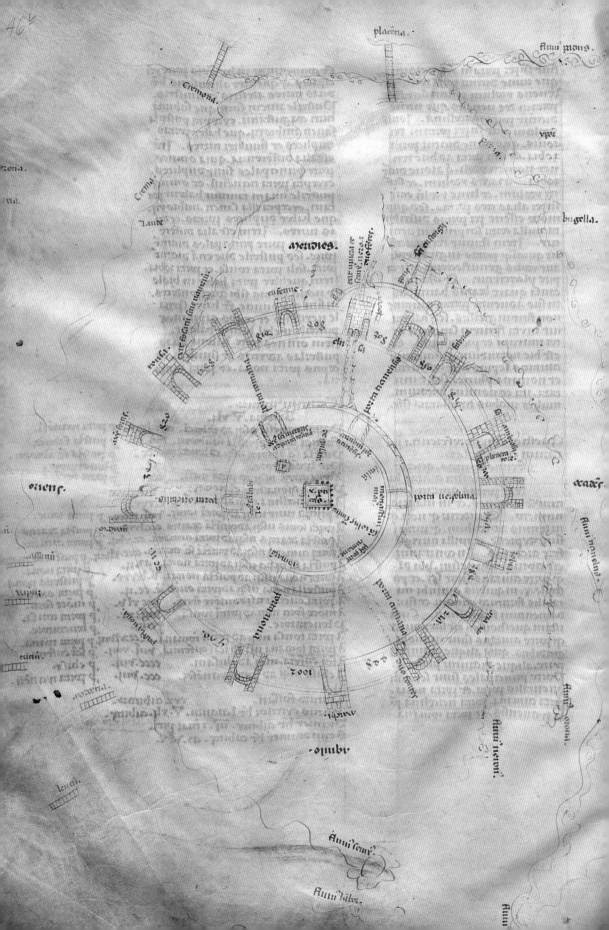

4   Milan, Broletto Nuovo, begun 1228.

commune (the Broletto Vecchio was the precinct of the archbishop), but which had
by Fiamma's time fallen under the control of the Visconti family, the signorial rulers
of the city. Fiamma concluded his discussion this way: "it may be said . . . that that
Broletto is the stronghold [*castrum*] of the city."[7]

It was also Milan's major marketplace. Fiamma singled out three of the economic
activities carried out here: first, the makers of iron weapons, one of Milan's most
important industries, concentrated their shops around the Porta Nuova (New Gate)
also known as the Porta Ferrea (Iron Gate), one of the six entry gates into the Broletto;
second, the fish market was held in the precincts of the Porta Sant'Ambrogio, also
known as the Porta Piscium (Fish Gate); third, in the southern part of the square stood
the marble loggia under which the money-changers had their counting tables.[8] But
Fiamma's list was hardly complete. A meat market was held in the Broletto, notaries
set up their tables here as well, and the city's grain market was situated under the vaults
of the open ground floor of the Palazzo della Ragione itself.[9] The Broletto Nuovo
was the economic heart of the city; indeed it was here that the consuls of the merchants, representatives of the most powerful guilds in the city including the international merchants and money-changers, chose from 1228 onward to hold their meetings;
in fact, it was largely on their initiative that the Broletto Nuovo was constructed.
Previously they had met in a communal palace that had been built early in the twelfth
century on land near the archiepiscopal center.[10]

For the mapmaker de Guioldis, then, as for Fiamma, the Broletto Nuovo was the
very heart not only of the city itself but also of the surrounding Milanese territory.
Indeed, what is striking about the map is its emphasis on both the natural and manmade features that promoted trade and commerce, namely the rivers and canals (and

bridges) by which goods were shipped to and from Milan and the many gates through which merchants and merchandise entered and left the city. By contrast, the city's religious sites receive little attention, just as in Fiamma's chronicle. The perfect circles of the surrounding walls indicate that this is an idealized vision of Milan, and at the center of that ideal city stands not a church but the communal governmental complex and the city's principal marketplace.[11] For de Guioldis, the Broletto Nuovo continued to represent the center of Milan even though, in many respects, the actual center of power had shifted to the palace of the Visconti.

In his book, *The Production of Space*, Henri Lefebvre wrote that "(Social) space is a (social) product." As the influential theorist made clear, every society produces its own distinctive space.[12] Lefebvre identified three components or elements of spatiality: spatial practice, which is made up of the routine and daily activities that occur in a given physical location, particularly as mediated and perceived by the bodily senses; representations of space, including maps, and plans; and representational space or how a space is fully experienced and which, in many respects, offers to those encountering it a sense of their place in the world. These three elements correspond, in Lefebvre's view, to "perceived – conceived – [and] lived" spaces.[13]

Following a materialist narrative and the model of historians like Jacques LeGoff, Lefebvre argued that the commercial revolution of the Middle Ages "brought commerce inside the town and lodged it at the centre of a transformed urban space," although he acknowledged that it still allowed a space for religion. It gave new prominence to exchange, communications, and networks. Nevertheless, in his view, the transition from "feudal" to "capitalistic" space did not fully occur until the sixteenth century.[14] Even so, the Italian Renaissance represented a special moment when the three aspects of space he identified achieved coherence. Specifically, he argued that a new ability to represent space – namely linear perspective – managed to subordinate the earlier "representational space, of religious origin."[15]

While Lefebvre's historical narrative remains overly schematic, his work reminds us that space is neither natural nor neutral; rather, that it is the product of power relations and thus is laden with meaning. Considering the Fiamma chronicle map in the light of his work highlights even more the significance of its double perspective on Milan (both regional and civic) and complicates even further efforts to understand why the mapmaker de Guioldis chose to place the Broletto Nuovo – the communal governmental-market complex – rather than the Visconti palace at the center of the map.

Part One of this study considers markets and other commercial spaces as key components of the medieval Italian physical, social, and political cityscape. Chapter One examines the representation of markets and commercial activities and considers their function as multivalent civic symbols, as bearers of extremely complex meanings. Chapter Two explores the evolution of markets and marketplaces over time and how they both reflected and influenced shifting configurations of power in particular cities. Chapter Three dissects the layout and organization of market space and seeks to understand the meanings that inhered therein.

# I

# THE MARKETPLACE
# AS CIVIC SYMBOL

Galvano de la Fiamma's *Chronicon extravagans* belongs to one of the most distinctive literary forms in medieval Italy, the civic *laus* (pl. *laudes*), a work in verse or prose that offers a celebratory description of a particular city and of the splendors and treasures to be found therein.[1] These works testify to the urbanized character of Italy, something that set the peninsula apart from much of the rest of Europe in the medieval period, and to the intense loyalty and pride that the cities inspired among their inhabitants. This feeling of *campanilismo* (city-state patriotism) found architectural expression in two buildings on which cities lavished their wealth and attention: the duomo and the communal palace, what today would be called the town hall. But, as Fiamma's chronicle and the accompanying map indicate, a third urban feature could evoke similar feelings and also testified to a city's power and reach – namely, the marketplace. Commerce was such a determining factor of urban development that it led Philip Jones to declare that "the Italian city was an emanation of trade."[2] The central marketplace was often either coterminous with or contiguous to the piazzas facing the cathedral and town hall. Together the civic palace, cathedral, and marketplace stood as symbols of the trinity of actors (state, church, and economy) that defined the essence of medieval Italian urban life.

The genre of civic *laudes* includes two extant examples from the eighth century that celebrate Milan and Verona, but these early works appear to have had little influence on later examples of the type that began to flourish from the twelfth century

onward, that is, just as the independent communes began to arise, and that followed
a variety of rhetorical and organizational patterns.[3] The first extant example from this
twelfth-century revival is the *Liber Pergaminus*, a description of Bergamo, written in
Latin hexameters by Moses del Brolo in the third decade of the century, when the city
was under the control of magnate families.[4] It says nothing about the marketplace per
se, although the author praises the countryside surrounding Bergamo for its rivers and
agricultural productivity. Indeed, many of the city panegyrics emphasize the rich provisioning of the cities with food and other goods, which was, needless to say, a function
not only of local agriculture but also of the market and international commerce. In a
poem entitled "On the condition of the city of Genoa, speaking with a certain lord
of Brescia," for example, the thirteenth-century poet known as the Anonimo Genovese
offers a description of the merchandise including spices, precious stones, and furs available in the city, observing that in Genoa, "De queste mercantie fine/ le buteghe ne
stan pinne" (of these kinds of fine goods, the shops are full). Elsewhere he claims that
there is an abundance of goods "from Romania, Beyond-the Sea, and all other places."[5]

Abundance and affluence are also the themes in a celebrated panegyric, Bonvesin
da la Riva's *De magnalibus urbis Mediolani* (On the Marvels of Milan), written in 1288,
nearly a half century before Fiamma's chronicle, when Milan had recently come under
the control of Ottone Visconti.[6] As J.K. Hyde observed, the author's "original contribution" to the genre was his effort not merely to describe Milan but to prove its greatness
by reason of eight qualities including its site, dignity, and freedom.[7] Another was Milan's
"fertility and affluence in all goods" (*fertilitatis et omnium bonorum affluentie*), an affluence
that included not only material goods (the author offers detailed descriptions of various
vegetables and fruits found in the city and countryside) but also spiritual ones, as his
enumeration of the city's churches and bells makes clear. He wrote that God's benignity
had provided the city not only with "an abundance of temporal goods but also spiritual
ones" (*bonorum temporalium sic etiam spiritualium copiam*).[8] A proponent of Milan's popular
regime, Bonvesin condemned in the final part of his work the factional strife, especially
on the part of the magnates, that was tearing Milan apart.[9]

Milan's rival, Pavia, found its literary champion in Opicino de Canistris, a priest
who composed around 1330 a description of his native city while at the papal court
in Avignon.[10] The first sections of the work are taken up with long lists of the churches
in the city and its suburbs, the relics contained in those churches, and the city's hos-
pitals. It then becomes more prolix with discussions of Pavian customs and religiosity
as well as a description of the city itself, including its various markets. Canistris
describes the central piazza, the "platea Atrii" (the Atrio di San Siro, today known as
the Piazza del Duomo), the main market square, in some detail. He observes that, in
addition to various fruits, cheeses, fish, and meats,

> there are for sale ... fine and thick rope, old slippers, woolen cloth, and skins or furs,
> purses and gloves and things of that sort, many wooden utensils and wicker baskets
> and things of that kind ... all around then or near to the same piazza, [there is for
> sale] wine of every sort, cooked foods, spices and pigments, wax and tallow candles,

olive oil for cooking and for church lamps ... various glass vases, and the most beautiful wooden cups, terracotta plates and bowls and almost every kind of wooden container. Here one finds the tables of the money-changers and others.

His description of Pavia's commercial prosperity and trading spaces continues:

> Beyond the fact that almost every article mentioned is available throughout the city or is carried about by ambulatory vendors, on certain days new shoes are sold in the piazza which is called San Savino and on other days used clothes, ironwork, and many other things.
>
> In the piazza of Santa Maria Perone, in front of the Palazzo del Popolo, linen, thread and woolens are for sale; [and] under the said palace fustians.
>
> In the *broglio grande* cattle and beasts of burden.
>
> In the courtyard of the Communal Palace, under two loggias [*pallatiis*] grain and legumes. There in certain spots justice is rendered. Similarly in the lesser Broglio, many things are sold during the fairs.
>
> Within the city are nine meat-markets, which are called *beccarie*, of which the largest, called the greater *beccaria*, is in the center of the city; but in none of them are diseased [meat of] cows or of other animals allowed to be sold, except in the Piazza Atrio to the poor.[11]

Elsewhere in the work, Canistris notes the "abundance" of fish that come from the Po, Ticino, and Gravellone rivers and "from other smaller streams."[12]

Several elements of Canistris's description are worth remark. First, the author emphasizes that commerce is simultaneously centralized and diffused throughout the city. It is clear from his description that the Piazza Atrio is the primary market square – here the diversity of goods available is greatest. But commerce and trade are not confined to that area. Other piazzas, including San Savino and Santa Maria Perone, host commercial activities with some degree of specialization; Santa Maria Perone, in particular, is the center of the textile trades. Even so, goods are available throughout the city by means of itinerant vendors; butcher shops especially are scattered throughout the town. Second, Canistris notes the rhythmic nature of trade: Pavia is host to fairs and certain days of the week are dedicated to the sale and purchase of particular kinds of merchandise. Third, the uses of these spaces overlap – the courtyard of the communal palace hosts the grain market, but it is also where certain forms of justice are meted out. Finally, the author calls attention to the class element of commercial activities: only in the Piazza Atrio is the meat of diseased animals allowed to be sold and then only to the poor. As his description makes clear, there were many spoken and unspoken hierarchies governing commerce and the marketplace.

Like da la Riva, Canistris wishes to convey that his city is blessed both spiritually and materially. His detailed list of the goods for sale testifies not only to God's benefi-cence toward the Pavians but also to the skill of the city's craftsmen who produce many of the goods on offer as well as to the reach of its merchants' trade networks. Also like da la Riva, Canistris overlays his description with a warning about the factional strife and discord that has been brought about, he believes, by the very abundance of material goods (*cunctis humane vite necessariis copiosa/ temporalium mirabilis copia*). But God will right the situation and crown the good.[13]

The moralizing tone and penchant for list-making and for offering statistical proof of a city's greatness found in Canistris and da la Riva is also evident in Giovanni Villani's oft-cited description of Florence in his chronicle of the city, a work composed in the 1330s.[14] As part of his discussion of the war that Florence was waging in the years 1336–38 against Mastino della Scala, the lord of Verona, Villani documented Florence's revenues, which amounted to 300,000 florins annually. But he also offered a cautionary note, writing, "Now, do you [Florentine lords] not know that as large as is the sea, so also is the tempest, and as revenue rises, so [also] bad spending is prepared? Temper, dear ones, inordinate desires and please God, and don't aggravate the innocent *popolo*."[15] After recounting the city's annual expenditures, he added: "it seems right to me to make mention of it [the income and outlays] and of the other great things of our city."[16] What follows is an enumeration of the city's population, its schools and pupils, its churches, wool shops (and their annual production), money-changers, and other professions. Villani claimed that Florence was home to 146 bakeries and that the city consumed 140 *moggia* of grain per day (one *moggia* equaled approximately 24 bushels); 4,000 cattle per year, 60,000 sheep, 20,000 goats, and 30,000 pigs. He enumerated the foreign officials employed in the town and then mentioned the many beautiful buildings of Florence. But he condemned the recent practice of spending magnificently on properties in the countryside, noting that in this "everyone sins, and for these inordinate expenses they are considered mad."[17] His admonitory tone is clear in his condemnation of excessive expenditures by both public officials and private citizens.

Villani sought to prove Florence's greatness with numbers so that, as he said, those who came after could determine whether the status and condition of Florence had diminished or improved, and so that the future rulers of the city, "with the aid of our record and the example of this chronicle, may try to advance the city in condition and in greater power."[18] His statistic-filled account of Florence's greatness is just one part of his lengthy chronicle of Florence; it is not a civic *laus* per se. For this reason, he did not offer a description of the major civic buildings and piazzas. One learns little from his chronicle, for example, about the physical attributes of the Mercato Vecchio, Florence's major market square.

Civic *laudes* continued to be written into the seventeenth century although, according to Hyde, they reached their rhetorical highpoint around 1400/02 in the Aretine Leonardo Bruni's *Laudatio Florentinae urbis* (Panegyric to the City of Florence).[19] However, it is important to consider in this context two other works by Florentine writers. The first falls clearly in the tradition of civic panegyrics. It is Jacopo d'Albizzotto Guidi's poem *El sommo della condizione di Vinegia* (The Summation of the Situation of Venice). The second, Antonio Pucci's poem about the Florentine Mercato Vecchio, is not a civic *descriptio* or *laus*, although it bears certain affinities with them.

Guidi, a Florentine merchant, was born in 1377 and moved to Venice in 1427 where he enrolled in the confraternity of San Cristoforo de' Mercanti. He composed his lengthy poem (it runs to more than 130 pages in a modern edition) in praise of his adopted city in 1442.[20] *El sommo* is written in tercets and is divided into sixteen chapters of nearly 300 verses each. It offers a thorough guide to the city; in the prologue Guidi states that he hopes it will be pleasing to those who have never seen Venice as well as to those who live there.[21] The first chapter covers the city's founding, the Piazza San Marco, and the Ducal Palace. The second discusses the Procurators of San Marco and then follows the main commercial street – the Merceria – to the Rialto market, which is also the subject of the third chapter. Other chapters address such topics as women's dress, churches and confraternities, and the Arsenal, as well as Venice's mainland and overseas possessions. The final chapters consider, among other subjects, the offices in the city, its revenues, as well as Venice's famously intricate method for electing its doge. Guidi ends his work with a prayer asking God to maintain the city in peace until the end of the world.

The poem's scope is panoramic and without apparent plan. This has led Marta Ceci, the poem's modern editor, to suggest that Guidi is viewing the city from a merchant's perspective in that he prioritizes the cost of things above all else.[22] In keeping with this mercantile viewpoint, Guidi devotes considerable attention to Venice's commercial space that runs from San Marco, where victuals are sold, to Rialto by way of the Merceria. Guidi offers a particularly lengthy description of the Rialto market complex: he discusses the merchants' loggia that once stood at the foot of the bridge, the banks, the poulterers, butchers, fishmongers, fruit and vegetable sellers, goldsmiths, drapers, and others (fig. 5). However, he does not mention here or elsewhere the church of San Giacomo di Rialto which stands at the very center of the market and was especially venerated by the Venetians. Instead, he is dazzled by the jewelers' shops ("I know of no other city where one finds so many jewels on one street"), remarks on the public scales and the men who work them and owe their jobs to governmental favors, and comments on the traffic on the Rivi del Ferro and del Vin (the iron and wine embankments), the grain warehouses, and especially the spices (pepper, cinnamon, nutmeg, and cloves) on display.[23] The third chapter ends with a return to San Marco and a discussion of the basilica.

Guidi, like other writers of civic panegyrics, tries throughout *El sommo* to convey the richness and variety of goods available at Rialto. He uses words and phrases like "abondanza" (abundance), "piena" (full), "copiosa" (copious), "gran numer" (great number), and "gran quantità" (great quantity). More than once he laments his inability to put into words what he sees and worries that his readers will either tire of his descriptions or take him for a liar.[24] He states, "I cannot, by God, tell all of the great commodiousness that there is in Venice; it has everything that you can name."[25] If ever there was a celebration of the benefits of commerce, it is Guidi's description of the Rialto market. And, as his discussion of the government's prohibition on German merchants trading with anyone in Venice but Venetians makes clear, it is also an endorsement of Venetian economic protectionism.[26]

5  Venice, Rialto Market, detail from Jacopo de' Barbari, *Woodcut Map of Venice*, 1500.

Unlike Guidi, the Florentine Antonio Pucci never abandoned his native city. Born around 1310, Pucci worked first as a metal-founder, specializing in the manufacture of bells, and later as a *banditore*, or town crier. He was a prolific poet who composed a large number of works, including the *Centiloquio*, a verse reworking of Villani's chronicle. Given his humble social status, Pucci is widely recognized as a poet who captured the spirit of everyday life, especially as it was experienced by the *popolo minuto*. He died in 1388.[27]

Among his many poems is the "Proprietà di Mercato Vecchio," a work in terza rima, celebrating Florence's famous marketplace (fig. 6).[28] The Mercato Vecchio was destroyed in the nineteenth-century's zeal for urban renewal; the Piazza della Repubblica occupies that space today. Like many of the urban *laudes*, Pucci's poem offers a vivid description of the bounty of Florence's commercial center. Pucci begins by stating that he has seen many piazzas in other cities: he judges Perugia's to be especially beautiful and well adorned, while he criticizes that of Florence's rival Siena, claiming that its famous Campo is sweltering in summer and freezing in winter. But none can compare to the Mercato Vecchio, which is better provisioned than all others in the world. Pucci then situates the market, stating that it has a church at each of its four corners, each corner defined by two cross-streets (*'n ogni canto ha due vie manifeste*; 404, line 27). In fact, this oldest part of Florence still retained something of the characteristic grid pattern of towns founded by the Romans. He remarks that all around are the shops of artisans and merchants, including doctors, sellers of linen, grocers, and spice-sellers. Warehouses of all sorts abound, and the Mercato Vecchio contains "to my mind, the most beautiful meat-market that can be, with good meat" (*la più bella beccaria che sia, di buona carne, al mio parere*; 404, lines 38–9). The poulterers' shops are furnished in every season with boar, hare, and deer, as well as pheasants, partridges, and capons. Pucci

6   Florence, Piazza del Mercato Vecchio with Church of
San Tommaso and Column of *Dovizia* (Riches), c. 1880.

seems especially impressed with the variety of fruits and flowers that arrive in the
market in season, exclaiming that "there was never so noble a garden . . . as the Mercato
Vecchio" and that it has no equal in the world (405, lines 73–6). Like the authors of
the *laudes*, Pucci sees the bounty of the market as the material manifestation of the
city's greatness and reach.

Unlike those authors, however, Pucci fills his market not only with goods but also
with people. Indeed, what sets his poem apart from other descriptions of markets is
his animation of the marketplace. Pucci's market is overwhelmingly a lower-class world
populated by countrywomen who come to town to sell fruit and vegetables, carters
and porters who haul goods about, brokers who place servants in households, and
petty artisans such as cobblers, smiths, and key-makers. It is also the site of illicit trade
and activities. Prostitutes frequent the Mercato Vecchio, as do beggars, pimps, gamblers,
and criminals of various sorts. In the marketplace, fights break out and knives are
quickly drawn; and in an attempt to keep order, the city posts patrolmen and uses the
Mercato as the backdrop for the public parading of criminals who are branded and/
or crowned with mitres publicizing their offences. Pucci also reports the cacophony
of sounds in the market: the blaspheming of gamblers when they lose their wagers
and the arguments of the itinerant women fruit sellers who fight and call each other
"whores" (*putte*; 404–5, lines 52–5).

Pucci is especially attuned to the seasonal rhythms of the Mercato Vecchio. At Carnival the market is filled with capons and chickens; during Lent with garlic, onions,
and parsnips (407, lines 139–44). After the austerity of Lent, the market is reborn at
Easter: the shops overflow with lamb, veal, birds of various sorts (including pet birds
to be kept for their song), pigeons, rabbits, and household goods. But Pucci accords
the most space in his poem to an annual event that begins in December when brigades

are formed by the demi-monde regulars of the market. They elect a *signore*, or lord, who is then decked out in finery. On the calends of January, they parade to the Ponte Vecchio where they choose a "cavalier" and throw themselves into the Arno. After drying off and eating watermelon (sic), they parade back to the Mercato Vecchio, feasting on food provided by "gintiluomini." Returning from the river, they do not appear like the low-life habitués of the market they are, but rather like "lords, going to dine in their finery" (409, lines 191–2).[29] But soon the festivities end and misery returns. Quoting Dante's *Comedy* ("Inferno," Canto 5, lines 121–3), Pucci notes: "there is no greater sorrow than to remember happy times in bad ones" (409, lines 208–10), especially as partridge and capon, veal and meat pies give way to leeks and root vegetables. The poem ends on a moralizing note as the great are brought low, and as a diet of stale bread and water elicits sweet memories of draught upon draught of wine. Pucci concludes by asking how many who have been atop the Wheel of Fortune have been similarly reduced, and notes that mad is the man who tries to rule through haughtiness or pride (*Foll'è chi vuole oprar, signor, per boria*; 410, line 226).

The poem is richly multivalent and can be read on many levels. Evelyn Welch has called attention to the danger of the market as brought forth by Pucci and to the sexuality associated with the marketplace – best exemplified by the prostitutes who frequent it.[30] Giovanni Cherubini, by contrast, emphasized the carnivalesque aspects of the poem, especially the temporary role reversals celebrated by the brigades. He reads this, as have other students of Carnival, as a safety-valve mechanism, one that reinforces the social order by allowing the disenfranchised and dispossessed to let off steam periodically.[31] But what comes across most strongly is the temporal aspect of the market: for Pucci, time is measured in the market by the seasonal flow of fruit and other comestibles and by the church-sanctioned contest between Carnival and Lent.[32] The market year moves according to natural and church-inspired cycles, revolutions that are reinforced by the reference to the Wheel of Fortune.

What also stands out is the contrast between abundance and want. Pucci's market, like that of other writers, is a place of plenty – a symbol of Florence's greatness – especially when contrasted with other cities, as he makes clear. The profusion of goods is itself testimony to the fecundity of Florence and its surrounding territories, and implicitly an endorsement of its guild-based political regime. The market even traffics in fertility – as in the pigeons and rabbits sold in the spring expressly for the purpose of reproducing (*per figliare*; 408, line 160). And, as Cherubini noted, the brigade's unusual feasting at the New Year on watermelon (he wonders how it was stored for so long, though perhaps melons were preserved) may itself have been a fertility rite since the watermelon's innumerable seeds may have been viewed, like the modern-day Italian custom of eating lentils on New Year's Day, as ensuring riches and plenty.[33] But dearth is always just around the corner, waiting to humble the contented and proud.

The ever-changing market becomes a metaphor for the vicissitudes of human life, witness to human beings' foolish belief that they are in control of their destiny or fate. In this way, Pucci, like da la Riva and Canistris, subverts or at the least problematizes the apparently self-congratulatory tone of the civic *laudes* and reveals the seductive (and deceptive) allure of the marketplace and its moral connotations. It may well be that Pucci's position as town crier and Canistris's early job as a toll collector at a bridge over the Po at Bassignana made them all too familiar with human foibles and the vagaries of events and thus conditioned their views of humankind's vanity.[34]

Fortune and the changeability of human affairs also form the thematic centerpieces of Domenico Lenzi's *Specchio umano* (more commonly known as the *Libro del biadaiolo* or Book of the Grain Seller). Lenzi was a Florentine grain merchant and for fifteen years between 1320 and 1335 he kept a detailed record of prices in the grain market at Orsanmichele, just a few steps from the Mercato Vecchio. Like many merchants' writings, Lenzi's book is a hybrid. In addition to the running index of grain prices, it includes an extended account of the famine of 1328/29, as well as several sonnets that Lenzi composed. He had his work copied by an amanuensis and then embellished with nine miniatures that relate directly to the text. The modern editor, Giuliano Pinto, dates the manuscript and illustrations to the early 1340s and characterizes the work as a "diary *sui generis* – of the piazza of Orsanmichele."[35]

Two of the miniatures in Lenzi's book depict the grain market at Orsanmichele (figs 7 and 8). Given the centrality of commerce to civic life, images of marketplaces are surprisingly rare in medieval Italian art. Those of individual shops are more common since they are often incorporated into depictions of the lives of the saints, medical tracts, and other works (some of which will be analyzed for what they reveal about shop architecture and fixtures in Chapter Four). But efforts to depict markets as a whole are infrequent, and marketplaces are seldom included in city views. This may be due to the tradition of representing cities by showing only the walls which ringed them.[36] Such visual shorthand failed to capture the markets which were usually located in the center of the cities and whose structures generally were only one or two stories in height. A rare, very late exception is Piero di Jacopo del Massaio's bird's-eye view of Florence dated c. 1470 contained in a manuscript of Ptolemy's *Geography* (fig. 9). The Mercato Vecchio is represented by the *beccaria* surrounded by a rectangular wall, and by its distinctive column of Riches (discussed shortly). Nearby stand the Mercato Nuovo and Orsanmichele. Massaio's image of the Mercato Vecchio as a central building surrounded on all sides by walls recalls Fiamma's description of Milan's Broletto Nuovo.

The images from the Lenzi manuscript show the grain market at Orsanmichele in times of plenty and dearth. That depicting the market in good times faces a page illustrating the harvest in a time of abundance, itself preceded by one of Lenzi's sonnets, which encourages humankind to thank God for his blessings. The illustration of the harvest of plenty shows figures gathering and threshing wheat. From an angel's trumpet sound the words "Con allegrezza ogn'uom canti cho' meco. Or abbondate in fructi e in bene" (With happiness sing everyman with me. Now in the abundance of the fruits of the earth and in goodness), while the voice of God warns: "Posso rimuover tucto, me ringrazia" (I can take it all away, so thank me).[37]

The accompanying image of the market in times of plenty shows it well-stocked. There are twelve large storage bins, all filled with grain, as well as two *staii* (bushels),

7    Anonymous, *Grain Market at Orsanmichele in a Time of Abundance*, in Domenico Lenzi, *Specchio umano*, c. 1335, Biblioteca Medicea Laurenziana, Florence, Ms. Tempi 3, fol. 7r.

8    Anonymous, *Grain Market at Orsanmichele in a Time of Dearth*, in Domenico Lenzi, *Specchio umano*, c. 1335. Biblioteca Medicea Laurenziana, Florence, Ms. Tempi 3, fol. 79r.

the standard unit of measurement for grain. In the foreground people sit and talk on sacks full of wheat, while in the middle ground sales are being negotiated. Behind at left, grain is being poured from one sack into another, while on the far right guards protect the market. In the sky, an angel balances three trumpets which proclaim: "Tropp'aver, ben non ti faccia peggiore" (Too much abundance shouldn't make you worse), "In dovizia fa ben che mal non segua" (In times of riches do good that bad times not follow), and "Chon allegrezza ogn'uom chanti cho'meco" (with happiness sing every man with me). From the angel's hands grain pours down to earth. One man in the back spies the angelic messenger and raises his hands in an attitude of prayer. The angel's words epitomize the author's moralizing message, captured in the sonnet which follows: times of plenty are a gift from God, yet mankind, unlike other creatures, is never content and always craves more.[38]

Indeed mankind does not heed God's warning and a later illustration shows the grain harvest in a time of dearth. A horrible bat-like demon hovers over the

9   Workshop of Piero di Jacopo del Massaio, *Florentia*, from Ptolemy's *Geography*, c. 1470,
Paris, Bibliothèque Nationale, Ms. Lat. 4802, fol. 132v.

harvesters.[39] God (only his hands are visible at the top left of the page) recalls the angel, whose trumpets have shattered into pieces, with the words, "Rivien, ritorna in ciel più netta e pura" (Come back, return to heaven more clean and pure). The angel responds, "Torno e lor lascio in alpeste pasture" (I am returning and leaving them in the rocky field).[40] The facing page illustrates the grain market at Orsanmichele during famine. Anarchy prevails in spite of the efforts by the guardsmen to maintain order. Men and women scramble among the empty storage bins; one lucky couple on the left has managed to secure two sacks of grain, but they are the exception. Elsewhere chaos reigns and the worst in human nature is on display. In one particularly disturbing scene a woman with two small children (all the more visible for spilling out of the painted frame) begs for food, but her entreaties only serve to provoke a man who threatens her with a knife; it calls to mind depictions of the Massacre of the Innocents. In the sky the demon – the malevolent counterpoint to the angel – proclaims that "E io faro come tu m'ài largito. Piangi ch'ài donde, ch'addietro il ben torna. In fame e 'n charo vi farò dolere" (And I will do as you commissioned me. Cry with good reason, that afterwards goodness return. In hunger and in dearth, I will make you grieve). For its part the crowd cries, "Duol sopra duol che dio ci lascia al peggio" (Sorrow upon sorrow that God abandons us to the worst).[41] Indifferent to the shrine of the Madonna, the rioters show by their action that selfishness and greed have replaced charity and concern for the common good.

Fearing just such tumults (in fact, during disturbances, rioters often targeted shops and warehouses),[42] civic governments of all political stripes, but perhaps especially those dominated by the *popolo*, sought to guarantee adequate food supplies since abundant grain was a sign of a government's ability to govern the city well, to marshal the resources of the surrounding *contado* or countryside, and, as Lenzi understood, to garner divine approbation. Civic and guild statutes spoke frequently of the importance of abundance. Statutes of the town of Rieti described "the abundance of victuals in the city" as a "consolation to the citizens, a public gladness, and a comfort of delights," whereas the lack of them induced scandals.[43] The 1318 statutes of the Florentine oil and cheese sellers authorized the guild to appoint men who would go undercover in order to expose fraud; this was to be done "in order that a great abundance of goods be available in the city."[44] And magistracies in many cities operated to guarantee a steady supply of food. In 1282, Florence established the office of the Six of Wheat; these six men were responsible for making sure that the city was well furnished with grain; in 1353 they were replaced by the Offitiales super copia et habundantia grani et bladi et aliorum victualium (Officers in charge of plenty and abundance of grain, wheat and other victuals).[45] Bologna too had a magistracy known as the Uffitio della Biada (Grain Office), later the Ufficio Abbondanza e Grascia (Office of Abundance and Plenty), the former created at an unknown date but certainly by 1259.[46]

Almost every city passed laws offering incentives to import foodstuffs or prohibiting their export. The Perugian statutes of 1279, for example, forbade the exportation of "wheat, flour, or any grains" from the city or its *contado*; conversely, the same statutes declared that anyone wishing to sell fish in the city was allowed to do so in order that

10   Padua, Fondaco delle Biade (Public Granary), begun 1302 (demolished).

"in the city of Perugia a greater abundance of fish may be had."[47] In 1283 the Perugian government even considered punishing with the amputation of a foot those who illegally exported grain, although the measure failed to pass.[48] A law from Venice, dated 1277, prohibited the export of wheat, flour, and legumes; those caught contravening the rule would have the foodstuffs confiscated and suffer a fine of three lire per bushel. Furthermore, those apprehended for trying to contravene these laws would have the boats by which they attempted to export the goods burned.[49] Towns built public granaries to house the communal grain stores, such as that in Padua's market square built in 1302 (now destroyed), the Palazzo della Biada in Bologna's Piazza Maggiore begun around 1287, and those of Venice strategically located near the Ducal Palace and Rialto (fig. 10).[50]

More was at stake, however, than merely the provisioning of food. As one of the rubrics in the 1325 statutes of the Florentine podestà stated, abundance – in this case of horses, donkeys, and mules – contributed to the "ornament and honor of the city" (*decor et honor civitatis*).[51] Plenitude of every sort contributed to a city's reputation, served to advertise the beneficent rule of its governing elite, and demonstrated God's favor. The commune of Parma chose to celebrate in paint its success in 1318 in securing salt wells that were located in the area around Salsomaggiore, Salsominore, Tabiano, and Scipione in a lawsuit that it brought against the marchese of Scipione. Salt was an important source of civic revenue since most communes maintained a monopoly on its sale. The image was painted on the walls of the communal palace and showed the Torello or bull, the symbol of Parma, holding a scroll which explained that the lawsuit had been settled "in favor of the magnificent and glorious *popolo* of the city of Parma." The painting also showed the salt wells for each site. It has been lost; but a miniature was made of it on parchment, probably at the time of the mural's execution, which shows the Torello and the wells, each of which is carefully labeled (fig. 11).[52]

When Lenzi commissioned the miniatures for his account of the grain market at Orsanmichele, he specifically requested that it be adorned with an image of abundance

11   Anonymous, *Salt Deposits Controlled by the Commune of Parma*, after a painting of 1318 on the Palazzo Pubblico of Parma. Archivio di Stato di Parma, Diplomatico, Pergamene Miniate, doc. 50.

(fig. 12). In faint writing just above the female figure who adorns the letter "N" on folio 3 recto, Lenzi advised the illuminator to "fa grano i' mano a la donna e in capo" (show grain in the woman's hands and on her head) and that is exactly what the artist did. A female figure representing abundance holds sprays of grain in her hands and her hair is also adorned with grain.[53] Seated and with outstretched arms that seem to mimic the pans of a balance – a justice motif – she echoes the moral intention of the book's author. Right or just living results in plenitude.

12   Anonymous, *Personification of Abundance*, in Domenico Lenzi, *Specchio umano*, c. 1335, Biblioteca Medicea Laurenziana, Florence, Ms. Tempi 3, fol. 3r.

13   Anonymous, *The Market at Porta Ravegnana*, Matriculation Book of the Bolognese Drapers, 1411,
Museo Civico Medievale, Bologna, Ms. Cod. Min. 641, fol. 1r.

Another rare depiction of a marketplace is that of the Porta Ravegnana market in
Bologna. It comes from an illuminated page in the statutes of the guild of Bolognese
drapers dated 1411 (fig. 13). The anonymous artist shows the street, known at the time
as the Mercato del Mezzo, leading up to the intersection directly in front of the
Garisenda and Asinelli towers, which serve even today as symbols of the city. In front
of the towers stood a tabernacle sheltering a cross (now housed in San Petronio). As

14    Perugia, Fontana Maggiore, 1275–8.

15    Perugia, Fontana Maggiore, *Augusta Perusia,*

16    Perugia, Fontana Maggiore, *Domina Clusii.*

17    Perugia, Fontana Maggiore, *Domina Laci.*

the artist portrays it, this part of the market is occupied by the drapers and the second-
hand dealers. And what he wants to show is a marketplace busy with activity and rich
in commodities. In the foreground a shipment of goods, including some heavily laden
trunks, lies piled on the ground. Immediately behind are the well-stocked shops of
two drapers, their multi-colored wares hanging from ropes. On the left a woman seems

to be negotiating with a shop assistant, perhaps about the length of cloth she is interested in purchasing, while on the right a well-turned-out man in a blue mantle is being shown a fine piece of crimson fabric. Further back are two porters, one coming toward the viewer carrying a large sack, his fellow worker carrying a small bench and a barrel and heading away from the viewer. Although no people appear in the far distance, goods are abundant. Cloth hangs in the shops on the left, while used articles, including a portable toilet, have been haphazardly (and to modern sensibilities somewhat disrespectfully) piled around the tabernacle. The artist created for his patrons, the drapers of Bologna, an image that captured their marketplace and certified their contribution to the material wellbeing and stature of the city.

Yet even in this celebratory image of the drapers' marketplace, the unknown artist has included two moralizing elements. First, in the lower-middle ground he has depicted two vagabonds, one of whom may have stolen something and so is being frisked. The inclusion of these figures reminds the viewer that the licit and the illicit – or at least the winners and losers in society's contest for wealth and status – coexist in the marketplace. Second, the artist has placed a particularly striking detail in the used articles shop on the middle right. Angled so that is easily readable is a shield bearing the coat of the arms of the Carrara family, the former signorial rulers of Padua who had been deposed only six years earlier in 1405. The shield thus serves as another reminder of the vagaries of human existence and of the turn of Fortune's wheel. Overall, then, the artist created for his patrons, the drapers of Bologna, an image that captured their marketplace and certified their contribution to the material wellbeing and stature of the city, but that also contained a subtle warning about the danger of placing too much stock in material riches and worldly power.

For their part, civic governments of various configurations commissioned for their central market squares statues and carvings celebrating abundance and plenitude. Perugia's renowned Fontana Maggiore, completed around 1278 by Nicola and Giovanni Pisano and assistants, includes sculpted personifications of Perugia itself, as well as of Lake Trasimene and Chiusi (the plains lying between the lake and the Chiana river that served as Perugia's granary; figs 14–17). Augusta Perusia, the embodiment of the city, is represented on the fountain as an abundance figure, a seated female holding a cornucopia. Domina Clusii personifies the farming district and so holds ears of grain, while Domina Laci, the representation of Lake Trasimene, clutches a catch of fish.[54] While the attribution of the figures remains uncertain, John Pope-Hennessy attributed Augusta Perusia to Nicola.[55] These figures were particularly appropriate for the fountain, a public works project that was itself a life-sustaining source.

Verona too had a fountain adorned with a female figure, although this one was created at the behest of a signorial regime. In an effort to bolster and legitimize his rule, Cansignorio della Scala, lord of Verona from 1359 to 1375, erected in 1368 a fountain in that city's central square and marketplace, the Piazza delle Erbe. He surmounted the fountain with a damaged Roman statue of a woman, to which a new head and arms were added, and affixed to the statue a bronze banderole with a Latin inscription, "Est iusti latrix urbs haec et laudes Amatrix" (This city is the bearer of

18   Verona, *Madonna Verona*, c. 1368.

19   Modena, *Bonissima*, early to mid-13th century.

justice and the lover of praises; fig. 18). At the statue's base, the fountain itself bears
four inscriptions, one of which reads either "Marmorea Verona" or "Marmorei Verona"
(it remains uncertain). What is clear is that Cansignorio made a concerted effort to
embellish the city with marble, a resource readily available in the surrounding hills. In
this way, he probably hoped to evoke Verona's Roman past. But presiding as it did over
the marketplace, the statue, which came to be referred to as "Madonna Verona," mainly
served as a symbol of abundance and fertility.[56]

In Modena, another female figure, *Bonissima*, dating from the early to mid thirteenth
century, presided over the main marketplace adjacent to the cathedral (fig. 19). Her
principal function was to personify the office of the officials of *bona opinione*, who
were in charge of supervising the marketplace and ensuring fair trade and just measures;
indeed, she probably held a set of scales and the structure on which she originally
stood was carved with various standards for measures. But her "sturdy and healthy"
appearance also embodied the material prosperity and physical wellbeing that were
believed to derive from a well-regulated marketplace.[57]

The most notable example of a public statue celebrating civic plenitude, however,
was Donatello's figure of *Dovizia* (Riches) that once surmounted the column in Florence's Mercato Vecchio (fig. 20). Commissioned by the Florentine commune at a time
when it was firmly under the control of an oligarchy composed of international merchants and bankers, Donatello completed the work around 1430. Exposure to the
elements eventually took its toll on the statue; and it was replaced in the early 1720s
by another abundance figure by Giovanni Battista Foggini, and subsequently lost. But

20    School of Vasari, *The Mercato Vecchio*, Florence, c. 1560,
Sala di Gualdrada, Palazzo Vecchio, Florence.

paintings of the Mercato Vecchio show that Donatello's *Dovizia* was a female figure
who held a cornucopia in her left hand while with her right she steadied a basket of
fruit which she carried on her head. The ancient column on which the statue rested
was erected at or very near the intersection of the ancient Roman *cardo maximus* and
*decumanus maximus*, that is, at the very center of ancient Roman Florence.[58] The statue's
prominent inclusion in Massaio's bird's-eye view of the city (see fig. 9) testifies to its
significance in the Florentine cityscape, both as a symbol of Florence's pride in its
material riches and as a warrant for the city's inhabitants to trust in the ruling regime.[59]

A column also marked an important location in the Paduan market complex, which
was clustered around its communal hall, the Palazzo della Ragione. The northern
section of the market housed a structure known as the Peronio, where fruit was sold.
As will be seen in Chapter Three, the Peronio was razed in 1302 during a thorough
reorganization of the space. All that remains is a column possibly dating from the
twelfth century with a capital carved with various fruits, which is surmounted by a
rectangular block which is in turn surmounted by an obelisk topped with a ball and
pennant (the block and obelisk are clearly later additions; fig. 21). One hypothesis holds
that the column secured an awning that covered the fruit market.[60] But it is more
likely that the column with its carvings served to symbolize the market and to identify
this section of the marketplace as the location of the fruit sellers. In some respects it
is similar to a column that the miniaturist known as the Master of 1328 includes in
his depiction of the sale of a horse, which is discussed in Chapter Five (see fig. 66).

21    Padua, Peronio Column, Piazza della Frutta, 12th century.

Donatello's *Dovizia*, with its sweeping classicizing drapery and positioning on a column in the ancient forum, certainly called to mind the antique world, although the Virgin Mary was also associated with abundance, in particular that of grain.[61] A more direct allusion to the Roman world was the name by which the marketplace in Ravenna was known, the Platea Mercurii, or Piazza of Mercury.[62] Mercury was the Roman god of commerce. He made a later appearance, along with Neptune, god of the sea, in Jacopo de' Barbari's 1500 map of Venice, as well as on that same city's Scala dei Giganti in the ducal palace.

As the Florentine government's decision to adorn the Mercato Vecchio with Donatello's statue makes clear, the central marketplace in many medieval Italian cities stood out (to adapt Lefebvre's terminology) both conceptually and perceptually. It marked in a real sense the center of the city, the hub around which civic life turned, although commerce and trade were not confined to that space. It was the place where all members of society, regardless of their social status, came together and where a city's identity was in large measure formed.

Although the depictions of the grain market at Orsanmichele in times of plenty in the *Libro del biadaiolo* and of the Porta Ravegnana market in the statutes of the Bolognese drapers echo to some degree the sentiments expressed in civic *laudes*, perhaps the closest pictorial parallel is Ambrogio Lorenzetti's painting *The Effects of Good Government in the City and Countryside*, part of his program commissioned in the late 1330s for the Sala dei Nove in the Palazzo Pubblico in Siena by the mercantile elite in control of the city at that time. The entire program is justly famous and is the subject of a vast amount of scholarly commentary.[63]

The city that Lorenzetti depicts in his *Effects of Good Government* fresco is simultaneously an image of Siena and the depiction of every well-governed city (fig. 22). At left, the campanile and, at right, the statue of a she-wolf mounted above the city gate identity the locale as Siena, although these are probably additions painted by Andrea Vanni sometime after 1363. Had Lorenzetti wished the image to be unmistakably identifiable as Siena, he could have depicted the Palazzo Pubblico itself and the surrounding Campo; but he chose not to do so.[64] In this way the work encompassed over time and through alteration both particular and universal meanings.

Although the image is not that of the Campo, Siena's main market square, Lorenzetti clearly intended to demonstrate that commerce and trade were the very lifeblood of the well-governed city, the result of all working together for the common good. Especially when viewed from where the ruling council of Nine sat, that is, directly under the Good Government tribunal, the street that winds through the town, out the city gate, and into the countryside comes sharply into focus; it is a "strada maggiore."[65] Lorenzetti shows the street where it intersects with another major thoroughfare. Both are lined with shops including those of a goldsmith, a cloth merchant, a cobbler, and a seller of earthenware pots. And each of the shops has a variety of goods on display. Woolen cloth manufacturing was a major industry in medieval Italy and so, close by the city gate, Lorenzetti shows men engaged in various stages of cloth manufacturing. The prosperity of this urban emporium is further emphasized by the construction activity taking place. And a different kind of production, biological reproduction, is represented by the bride being led in procession at the bottom left.

The surrounding countryside is similarly prosperous and fertile and is marked by the cultivation of grain (fig. 23). This scene, despite its seeming realism, actually conflates the agricultural year into one image so, while some peasants are engaged in plowing and sowing seed, others are harvesting the fields with scythes and still others

22    Ambrogio Lorenzetti, *Effects of Good Government in the City*, 1338–40, Palazzo Pubblico, Siena.

are threshing the harvested grain.[66] Peasants travel along the well-maintained road with donkeys laden with sacks of grain and a fattened pig, while within the city walls a peasant woman brings two birds to town to sell, a man carries a basket of eggs, and another woman balances a basket on her head, filled with what appears to be bread or fruit. In the far distance Lorenzetti renders Talamone, Siena's fledgling seaport by which it hoped to increase its access to international trade. The painted frieze at the top of the fresco indicates the time of year: good government is shown during summer, the season of productivity and plenty. Here Lorenzetti includes a female personification of summer. With her headdress laden with vegetation and ears of wheat in her hand, she is unmistakably a symbol of abundance.[67] In stark contrast, the fresco showing the effects of bad government includes a personification of winter; and both the city and countryside are barren and given over to violence and rapine. As in Lenzi's marketplace at Orsanmichele in times of dearth, self-interest has replaced the common good.

Lorenzetti's *Effects of Good Government* fresco is in many ways the visual equivalent of a civic *descriptio* or *laus*. Just as Bonvesin da la Riva used words to commend Milan for its location, buildings, inhabitants, and its fertility and material abundance, so Lorenzetti used pigments. This is not to say that a *descriptio* provided the direct model for Lorenzetti's program, merely that the fresco and the genre of city descriptions have a strong affinity in celebrating the materialism of civic life.

23  Ambrogio Lorenzetti, *Effects of Good Government in the Countryside*, with personification of *Summer* in the freize above, 1338–40, Palazzo Pubblico, Siena.

Examining the evidence of *laudes* and other literary works, representations of markets, and the statuary erected in them, it is clear that markets were highly charged civic spaces laden with meaning. Not simply places of (supposedly neutral) commercial exchange, they were moralized spaces that could, depending on circumstances, testify to the citizens' rectitude or sinfulness and to God's benignity (in times of abundance) or anger (in times of dearth); offer a warrant for the ongoing rule of a particular civic regime be it magnatial, popular, or signorial; and embody aspirations either toward the *bene comune* or toward self-interest. The effort especially by popular regimes to guarantee abundance, particularly but not only of food, and the celebration by the writers of civic *laudes* of abundance offer striking evidence of how thoroughly civic identity was tied up with commerce as symbolized by the well-stocked marketplace. For this very reason, markets were also contested spaces where various groups that aspired to power sought to assert their authority and make their presence known. So the next chapter examines how markets evolved in the politically fraught environment of the Italian communes.

# 2

# THE EVOLUTION
# OF MARKETPLACES

Markets were, as has become clear, places laden with meaning. Yet their status as signifiers needed to be constantly reiterated and reinforced. The 1347 statutes of Spoleto,
for example, stated that fines would be doubled for crimes committed "in the marketplace piazza" (in Platea Fori) or on market days (Wednesdays and Saturdays), as well
as during the city's annual fair held in August. Through this law, the government of
Spoleto sought to emphasize the special character of the marketplace and of the commercial activities taking place there; any threat to those activities was a threat to the
city as a whole. The law declared that fines were also to be doubled for infractions
committed in the Palazzo del Popolo and the residence of the podestà, as well as in
all churches in the city and surrounding countryside.[1] It makes clear the point noted
earlier, that marketplaces stood along with churches and public buildings as one part
of a trinity of spaces central to urban life.

Markets were also deeply contested spaces. Control of the markets was essential, and
the ability to maintain that control became an incontrovertible sign of authority and
prestige. As Martha Howell has noted, when urban regimes took command of the
marketplace and regulated the activities taking place there, "they were also establishing
their own authority and ineluctably linking it to a *bien public* that was intimately bound
to the idea of the market."[2]

Tracing the evolution and development of markets and marketplaces in the Italian
city-states over the period from c. 1100 to c. 1440 is a daunting task since every city

was unique, every configuration of political, ecclesiastical, and commercial power different. But, in general, jurisdiction over markets mirrored the political evolution of the communes. As each new group asserted itself, it attempted to make its claim to public authority by putting its stamp on the marketplace in one way or another. In the earlier part of the period under consideration, this contest usually involved communal governments wresting control of markets and fairs from the prevailing ecclesiastical authorities, especially bishops. Later struggles often pitted the aristocratic magnate groups, which first came to prominence as the communes arose in the late eleventh and early twelfth centuries, against the *popolo*, whose own rise to power occurred over the course of the thirteenth century. Marketplaces often reflected these conflicts spatially and architecturally. Sometimes the rise of new groups to power included the creation of new marketplaces; other times it involved efforts to systematize and reorder existing market space or to assert some authority over the market architecturally, through the building and strategic placement of merchant courts and guild headquarters. What is clear is that throughout the period covered by this study and in most cities, political, commercial, and ecclesiastical spaces overlapped promiscuously, unlike in the early modern period when they became segregated one from another, although the beginnings of that trend toward segregation can be observed in the fourteenth century.

The evolution and arrangement of markets and fairs also depended on the economic base and commercial focus of individual towns and cities, factors which were in turn determined to a large degree by natural or geographical factors, including access to the sea and the course of rivers, as well as on manmade features including roads and canals. The organization of market space in a small regional center or one that served as the focus of an agricultural catchment area was necessarily different from a city like Venice that served as a major international emporium or Florence that had an economy focused on banking and manufacturing. Market space itself was also different. Whereas a small town like Prato or Padua might have one primary market center, towns such as Florence and Venice had many market squares. Additionally there is the problem of defining what actually constituted market space, since commercial activities were not confined to those spaces even in small towns. Nevertheless, it is clear that every town had a space that inhabitants recognized as "the marketplace." And so it is there that this investigation of the evolution of marketplaces begins.

Jurisdiction over markets was a legal privilege since it entailed the right to levy duties and other imposts, to determine who could engage in buying and selling and when, to supervise the activities conducted therein, and to establish standards for weights and measures. In the chaotic century following the collapse of the Carolingian Empire, control of the markets in various Italian towns often devolved (or was granted) to local lay or ecclesiastical lords. In 905, for example, Berengario I granted the bishop of Bologna jurisdiction over a port and fair held at Selva Pescarola, close by the river Reno (near present-day Bertalia).[3] And as the Saxon emperors sought to reassert imperial authority, they sometimes tried to legitimate further these arrangements. In 952, Emperor Otto I granted to the monks of Sant'Ambrogio of Milan jurisdiction over land that had originally been part of the royal domain. He donated to them "five contiguous plots of land under the jurisdiction of our kingdom in the city of Milan in the place where the public market is held" (*areas quinque terre iuris regni nostri infra Mediolanensem civitatem in loco ubi publicum mercatum extat coniacentes*) as well as "a hall situated in the established market with stalls therein having counters in front of them" (*salam unam in pretaxato mercato situm cum stationibus inibi banculas ante se habentibus*).[4] In 997 Otto III issued a diploma to Bishop Antonino of Pistoia reaffirming Otto's right to invest the bishop with his office and confirming the bishop's possessions. Among these were various episcopal properties, including the open space that was the site of the city market.[5] As the historian of Pistoia, Natale Rauty, makes clear, during the eleventh century, the bishop exercised effective control over the town.[6]

The urban development of Pistoia and Bologna over this period is particularly well documented and studied, and the cities may serve as examples of two different models of market evolution. In Pistoia, despite shifting configurations of power, the primary ecclesiastical, governmental, and market spaces remained conjoined around the Piazza Maggiore, also known as the Piazza del Duomo. In Bologna, by contrast, three distinct spaces developed: the episcopal center at the cathedral of San Pietro, the communal/governmental center at the Piazza Maggiore, and the mercantile center at the Porta Ravegnana and the Carrobbio, although the Piazza Maggiore also served as market space. Most Italian cities followed one model or the other so it is useful to examine Pistoia and Bologna more closely.

Otto III's 997 diploma granted the bishop of Pistoia control of the "vacant land where the market is [held]" (*terram vacuam ubi mercatum est*). This market space was bordered on the south and west by a public street (*via regis*), on the east by the cathedral of San Zeno and its canonry, and on the north by a tower, known as the Gardingo, that appears to have served as the center for the supervision of fiscal functions. The market was intersected by the ancient Roman *cardo* which ran north–south and that crossed the *via regis* which linked the Porta San Pietro in the east with the Porta Lucensis in the west and which ran roughly parallel to the old Roman *decumanus* farther to the north (fig. 24).[7] In the last quarter of the eleventh century, the bishop erected his palace on the southern part of the *terra vacua*. This reduction of the available market space led to the expansion of market activities into the adjacent Piazza della Sala, which became the center for the sale of fruit and vegetables. The growing power of the bishop, evident in his new palace, stirred resentment among the cathedral canons. Rivalry between the two is evidenced by the fact that the canons created their own measure for grain, which differed from that sanctioned by the bishop.[8]

A third actor soon appeared on the Pistoian stage, namely the commune, controlled by local aristocrats. The first notice of consuls, the executive officers of the communal government, appears in 1105 and the earliest statute of the consuls dates from 1117. This communal government consisted of a *parlamentum* or assembly, a *consiglio* or council, and the consuls themselves. According to Rauty, the early years of the commune saw an alliance of the bishop, the cathedral canons, and the new commune. However, the commune soon reached an agreement with Emperor Henry V which allowed it to contest the bishop's temporal power. The constitutions of 1117 required

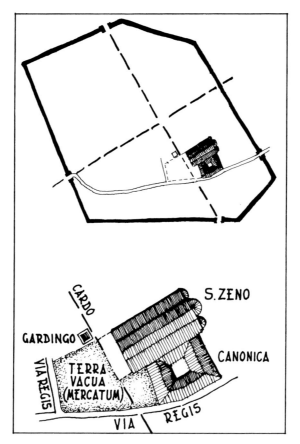

24    Plan of the Cathedral and Market Square in Pistoia and its location within the city walls, late
       10th century. Reproduced from Natale Rauty, *Storia di Pistoia*, 1988, vol. 1, p. 262.

the commune to protect the church and its properties, but subjected the bishop and
clergy to civil law and reduced the bishop's control over the marketplace. By the middle
of the twelfth century, the market was clearly under the jurisdiction of the commune:
the 1180 statutes of the podestà gave him the authority to fix the measure for grain.
The first notice of the podestà himself is dated 1158, making Pistoia the town that
offers the earliest evidence of this office in Tuscany.[9] By 1216 he had emerged as the
chief civic officer.[10]

    It is estimated that by 1219, Pistoia had around 11,000 inhabitants, and by 1244 the
surrounding *contado* had a population of approximately 34,000. This growth spurred
the emergence of the *popolo*, who began to challenge the authority of the magnates.
The *popolo* developed their own institutions, including a *capitano* or captain (first documented in 1263) and an executive of twelve *anziani* (elders), as well as two councils:
the Quaranta (Forty), or Council of the Anziani, and the Council of the Popolo with
200 members. In 1283 the *popolo* enacted anti-magnatial (aristocratic) legislation and
in 1296 created a *gonfaloniere della giustizia* (standard-bearer of justice) to serve as the
head of the commune.[11] During the fourteenth century, factional fighting tore Pistoia

25   Pistoia, Palazzo degli Anziani, begun c. 1294.

apart as the city came increasingly under the domination of nearby Florence. In 1401 Florence subjugated the city.

The political evolution briefly outlined here was accompanied by major alterations to the civic center. It seems to have taken more than a century for the newly formed commune to construct a building for its own use. For a time the different magistracies and councils met in various locales including private homes, the church of San Matteo, and the cathedral. The first evidence of a *palatium comunis* (communal palace) dates from 1211. It is unclear where this communal palace stood, although it has been suggested that it was located on the site of the later Palazzo degli Anziani, which itself was begun sometime near or after 1294, enlarged in the 1330s and 40s, and included an open portico facing the piazza (fig. 25). In this it differed from the usual Tuscan model and resembled more closely the public palaces common in the cities of the Po valley such as Milan's Broletto Nuovo.[12] In 1367 the Council of the Popolo voted to construct directly across the piazza from the Palazzo degli Anziani a building to house the podestà and his staff. In that same year, the office of the Capitano del Popolo was abolished and replaced with a Capitano del Custodia, a Florentine official, further evidence that Pistoia was coming increasingly into the Florentine sphere of influence. It is likely that at that same time the decision was made to build a palace for the Capitano del Custodia on the north side of the civic piazza.[13] With the completion of that edifice, the framing of the piazza was more or less complete (fig. 26). Also during the Trecento, the bishop extended his palace farther into the piazza, by adding a ground-floor arcade.[14]

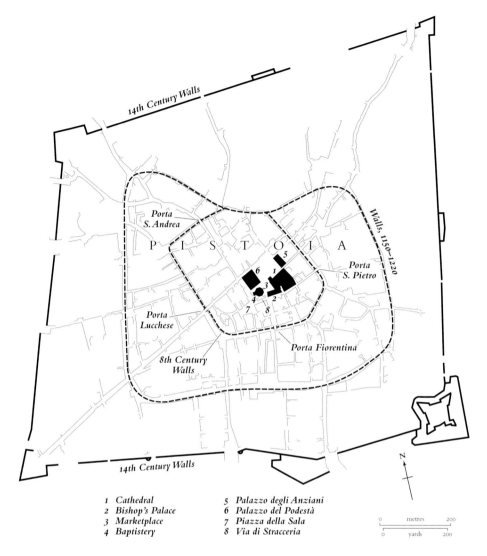

| | | |
|---|---|---|
| 1 | *Cathedral* | |
| 2 | *Bishop's Palace* | |
| 3 | *Marketplace* | |
| 4 | *Baptistery* | |

| | | |
|---|---|---|
| 5 | *Palazzo degli Anziani* | |
| 6 | *Palazzo del Podestà* | |
| 7 | *Piazza della Sala* | |
| 8 | *Via di Stracceria* | |

26   Map of the Pistoia in the mid-14th century.

In Pistoia the market continued to operate in the same location although, as already noted, control passed from the bishop to the commune. The piazza was the site of the weekly market that was held on Saturdays; it included two sessions: the morning session was dedicated to the sale of small barnyard animals, eggs, and cheese; the afternoon market to the sale of grain. At some point, the official (standard) grain measure was sculpted and placed in the piazza. Also, as already noted, the extension of the bishop's palace led to the removal of the fruit and vegetable sellers to the adjacent Piazza della Sala, where a daily market was held. For sanitary reasons, the pig and cattle markets took place elsewhere, in a large piazza to the east of the civic piazza.

As in many Tuscan towns, the woolen cloth industry and banking predominated in Pistoia; indeed the merchant bankers formed the "elemental motor" for the Pistoian economy from the twelfth to the fourteenth centuries.[15] In 1257 there were nineteen shops or benches of money-changers in the piazza near the cathedral. And the notaries, who performed an essential function in the drafting of contracts and other business documents, had their benches or tables next to the baptistery, directly in front of the cathedral.[16] What is clear is that, as the government of Pistoia evolved and as jurisdiction and control over market activities shifted, the marketplace itself, as a civic space, remained fixed, except for its expansion into Piazza della Sala.

This was not the case in Bologna, which has been thoroughly studied by Francesca Bocchi. It is unclear where the marketplace was located in Bologna during the early Middle Ages, although it seems likely that it was in the vicinity of the cathedral of San Pietro. The ancient Roman market was held in this area and in all probability it had not migrated from this space. As such it would have been located within – or at the edge of – the Selenite walls (constructed sometime between the fifth and early eighth centuries) which incorporated about nineteen hectares of land (around 47 acres) and was situated along one of the city's main thoroughfares, the ancient Roman *cardo*, today's Via dell'Indipendenza.[17] When, however, the market reappears in the sources, it had migrated to two sites: near the monastery of Santo Stefano and the eastern gate of the Selenite walls, the Porta Ravegnana, through which passed the ancient Roman *decumanus*, the Via Emilia (the present-day Via Rizzoli). In Bocchi's view, the emergence of the market at the Porta Ravegnana represented a challenge to the bishop and the families which had benefited from episcopal power by new groups with some interest in business.[18] A commune had emerged in Bologna by 1116, as evidenced by a diploma of Henry v; and consuls are first mentioned in 1123. This new communal government pursued a policy of subduing the *contado*, as a way of securing lines of communication as well as taxes and food supplies. But already by this early date, the political and commercial centers had begun to diverge. Whereas the market was concentrated around the Porta Ravegnana, the *arengo*, or communal general assembly, met at the churchyard of Sant'Ambrogio, a church that was later demolished to make way for the construction of San Petronio (fig. 27).[19]

During the rest of the twelfth century, the aristocratic commune continued to pursue projects that promoted trade and commerce. These included the building of the Reno canal, the acquisition of publicly owned flour mills on the Savena canal, and the construction between 1167 and 1176 of a new set of walls, known as the Torresotti ring, which enclosed 113 hectares (279 acres), including the roads which converged at the Porta Ravegnana. And in 1191, the city began to mint coins, a sure sign of Bologna's increasing economic power.

The years around 1200 were busy with building activity. Starting in 1200, the commune began to buy up land to create a new civic square, which was enlarged more and more over time to become the Piazza Maggiore. This opened up space for market activities that had become cramped and crowded at the Porta Ravegnana and had, as a consequence, begun to creep up the old *decumanus*, acquiring the name the Mercato del Mezzo. Also in 1200 construction began on a communal palace, what is today referred to as the Palazzo del Podestà, which faces the Piazza Maggiore. The

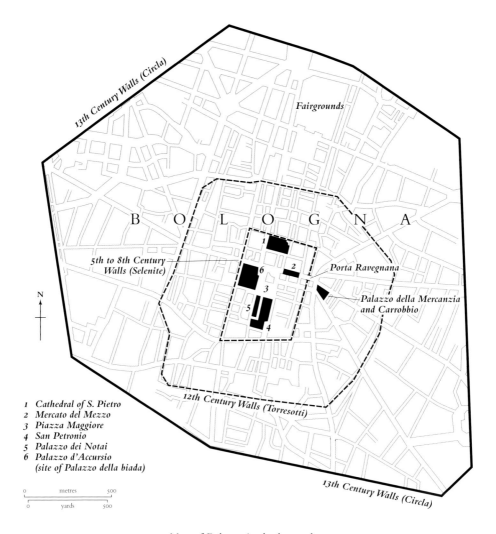

1  Cathedral of S. Pietro
2  Mercato del Mezzo
3  Piazza Maggiore
4  San Petronio
5  Palazzo dei Notai
6  Palazzo d'Accursio
   (site of Palazzo della biada)

27    Map of Bologna in the late 14th century.

building included space for shops that sold salt and oil, both of which may have been
communal monopolies, as well as the headquarters of the offices of the *yscarii*, who
regulated market activities and controlled weights and measures. In Bocchi's view, the
location of shops selling foodstuffs at the communal palace began the process by which
the food market migrated from the Porta Ravegnana toward the Piazza Maggiore.[20]
In 1208 the commune also began to construct yet another canal, the Navile, linking
the city to the Reno.[21] All of this occurred before the guilds – the institutional manifestation of the *popolo* – assumed any direct role in government.

   That assumption commenced in 1217 with the first admission of some guildsmen
(the money-changers and merchants) to the General Council of the commune.[22] A
more thoroughgoing entry of the guilds (*arti*) and of neighborhood associations (the
*armi*) occurred with the revolt of 1228 led by the merchant Giuseppe Toschi and, with
many variations, the popular commune continued to control Bologna until the end of

the thirteenth century. Although the initial entry of guildsmen into the government in 1217 was short-lived (they were excluded again in 1219), those two years saw major innovations in the city's commercial infrastructure. In those years, Bologna created the space for a weekly cattle market at what came to be known as the Campo del Mercato (today Piazzolo) and for annual fairs on land just outside the Porta Govese on the road leading to Galliera (today the Piazza Otto Agosto and Parco della Montagnola). In order to create the latter fairground space, the commune made over 67 individual land purchases and acquired an area encompassing 17 hectares, nearly the surface area enclosed in the old Selenite walls.[23] Clearly, the communal government was supporting even more fully than before the commercial interests of the merchant classes.

From 1228 until the end of the century, the communal government of Bologna was in the hands of the *popolo*, including from 1265 when the 24 *anziani* represented the executive branch. Four of the *anziani* had to come from the money-changers and merchants, the balance from the other *arti* and *armi*. Over the course of these seven decades, the government pursued a variety of measures aimed at taking even firmer control over urban space. These included the construction, beginning in the 1220s, of a third set of walls (the Circla) encompassing 408 hectares (1008 acres); a systematic land survey beginning in 1245; restrictions on the height of residential towers; the requirement that owners build on their private property porticos onto public streets; and, beginning in 1245, the construction of a new communal palace (today referred to as the Palazzo del Re Enzo). In 1257 the serfs in the *contado* were freed, which represented a significant commercialization of rural land, and in the 1270s the commune passed legislation aimed at reining in the magnates.[24]

With specific regard to the markets, the later decades of the thirteenth century in particular saw efforts to systematize even further the market spaces. Between 1244 and 1251 the government constructed the Beccaria Magna, or Great Meat Market, just west of the Porta Ravegnana, along the Mercato del Mezzo. It was strategically located near the Aposa stream, allowing for the easy removal of waste products, but in 1274 the *beccaria* was relocated to the Palazzo del Podesta.[25] Also, the Pescheria or fish-market was torn down. It was at the Piazza Maggiore that the commune situated its grain warehouse, the Palazzo della Biada, which was eventually incorporated into the Palazzo d'Accursio, which from the 1330s on became the permanent home of the Anziani (fig. 28).[26] In the 1280s efforts were made to systematize the Porta Ravegnana market, including the purchase by the commune of property around the two towers, the Garisenda and Asinelli, that dominated the space in the center of the Porta Ravegnana square; it did this, it stated, for "public utility." And in 1290 the commune purchased land at the Carrobbio, the intersection slightly to the south of the Porta Ravegnana square (today's Piazza della Mercanzia).[27] Two objectives motivated these interventions. First, the government clearly wished to facilitate the flow of traffic in the precincts around the Porta Ravegnana and the Carrobbio; second, it sought to create a clearer separation between the food markets (now centered in the Piazza Maggiore) and the higher-end trades (the cloth trade, second-hand dealing, and others) at Porta Ravegnana.[28]

28    Bologna, Palazzo d'Accursio, begun 1287.

In the first three-quarters of the fourteenth century Bologna passed in bewildering succession under the rule, among others, of papal vicars, the Visconti of Milan, and the native Pepoli family.[29] When in 1350 the Visconti took control of the city, they fortified both the Piazza Maggiore and the Two Towers; this must have impeded the movement of traffic to the food market and perhaps explains why in 1354 it was decided that butcher stalls needed to be distributed throughout the four quarters of the city.[30]

Then, between 1373 and 1401, a second popular regime took power; this regime was dominated by the twelve most prestigious guilds of the twenty-six authorized in the city: the twelve, known as the Universitas Mercatorum, were comprised of the money-changers, drapers, second-hand dealers, mercers, spice dealers, silk makers, gold-smiths, cotton cloth makers, makers of fine woolen cloth, butchers, cobblers, and smiths.[31] This period saw further efforts to systematize the area around the Porta Ravegnana and the Carrobbio. In 1380 the commune acquired property near the Car-robbio to build a new office for the gabelles and in 1382 the commune was construct-ing a building on the site which consisted of a two-story vaulted loggia supporting a vaulted room above: the construction documents refer to it as the "loggia delle gabelle" and also as the "loggia del Carrobbio."[32] The loggia was apparently used for off-loading merchandise that needed to be taxed. However, when the building at the rear of the loggia was finished in 1391, it came to house the Foro dei Mercanti, a court established by the Universitas to handle disputes between guilds and other trade matters; mean-while, the room above the loggia was used, for a time at least, as the assembly hall for

29   Bologna, Loggia della Mercanzia, 1380s.

the money-changers' guild.[33] Eventually the entire complex came to be known as the Mercanzia, the name by which it continues to this day (fig. 29). And in 1384 the notaries, whose power had grown at the expense of other professions, completed the expansion of their palace on the Piazza Maggiore, which was itself enlarged so that in 1396 work could begin on the massive new civic church, San Petronio.[34]

Several points should be emphasized from this brief overview of Bolognese urban developments from around 1000 to 1400. First and most obviously, Bologna, unlike Pistoia, developed three distinct urban spaces: the relatively marginalized episcopal center at San Pietro, the commercial center at the Porta Ravegnana and the Carrobbio, and the governmental center at the Piazza Maggiore. With regard to the cathedral complex, although the cathedral itself was relatively underdeveloped as a civic locus, other ecclesiastical centers, most notably Santo Stefano and subsequently the Dominican and Franciscan churches, figured prominently in the cityscape. Second, although Bologna developed differentiated spaces, there was nevertheless some overlap of the activities carried out in them. In particular, the governmental center at Piazza Maggiore was also the primary location of the city's food markets. Third, as Bocchi observes, even before the exclusion of the magnates from power, the communal government had demonstrated a fairly significant interest in urbanistic matters. In other words, it is impossible to establish a simple equation between the emergence of the *popolo* and efforts to promote trade and systematize markets.[35] Nevertheless, it seems clear that the primary force pushing for improvements to increase trade and commerce and to facilitate communication within the city – projects such as the creation of the

fairgrounds, the removal of the food markets to the Piazza Maggiore, and the system-
atization of the Porta Ravegnana/Carrobbio complex – was the guildsmen, in particular the merchants and money-changers. It seems certain as well that Bologna's greater
size, the presence of a large population of students, and its critical location at the
confluence of important river and land routes created a more complex situation than
that found in Pistoia and that together these factors led to greater specialization of
urban space.

Surveying cities across the peninsula, it is clear that many communes adopted the
same urban strategy as Bologna and created civic piazzas (and marketplaces) that were
distinct and physically removed from the older episcopal centers. Siena, Florence, Milan,
Padua, Pavia, Verona, Parma, and Treviso were among those that followed this pattern.
Other communal governments, including those of Brescia, Bergamo, Cremona, Lodi,
San Gimignano, and Modena, followed the same pattern as Pistoia and did not create
new and distinct urban spaces but, rather, developed civic piazzas that housed the
cathedral, communal offices, and the market. Based on her examination of episcopal
palaces in the towns of the Po valley, Maureen Miller has offered an explanation for
these divergent patterns. She argues that in those cities where the bishops enjoyed full
comital rights (such as the authority to levy tolls, to regulate the market, and to appoint
judges), "the period of power sharing between bishop and commune was long and the
communal palace was built very close to the episcopal palace." By contrast, in those
cities where the bishop's jurisdiction was limited, especially by powerful families with
comital rights, "the commune established its dominance early and built its palace distant
from the bishop's."[36] Miller's theory may explain why some cities developed distinctly
different episcopal and communal centers. But the situation with regard to marketplaces
seems more complicated since, as the examples of Pistoia and Bologna demonstrate,
tradition, proprietary rights, geography, and a variety of social and political factors all
conjoined to determine the location of markets and marketplaces.

One deciding factor may have been population size. Indeed, the evidence seems to
suggest that it was the larger cities where the greatest differentiation took place. It may
well be that at some point cities reached a critical mass after which it became impossible, for reasons of accessibility and communication, for episcopal, governmental, and
commercial activities to occupy the same space on a continuing basis. This is not to
say that in the more urbanistically differentiated cities any particular piazza could not
serve on special occasions as the locus of a variety of different activities, only that on
a daily basis differentiation worked better.

Also it appears that in the larger (and therefore more commercially prosperous)
cities, there was greater social differentiation and that this too influenced the location
of different purpose-built spaces. A critical role in Bologna's urban development was
played by men engaged in the most prosperous and advanced sectors of the economy,
namely trade and money-changing. It was when they got their first foothold in government in 1217 that the city built its cattle market and fairgrounds, and it was when
the Universitas Mercatorum took control in the 1370s that the Porta Ravegnana/
Carrobbio complex was further systematized. Evidence from Milan and Piacenza

further supports the idea that merchants and bankers (as well as textile manufacturers) played a critical role in the location of market squares.

Milan was one of the largest cities in Italy and the seat of a prestigious and powerful archbishopric. For several centuries the city's primary markets were under the jurisdiction of the archbishop and other important ecclesiastical establishments. As already noted, in 952 Otto I granted certain market rights to the monks of Sant'Ambrogio. Until the construction of the city's current cathedral began under Giangaleazzo Visconti in 1386, Milan had two cathedral churches: Santa Maria Maggiore or Yemale (the winter cathedral) and Santa Tecla (the summer cathedral). The food markets were located here and in the vicinity of the archiepiscopal palace. For example, the fish market was located in front of the church of Santa Tecla and was the property of the cathedral chapter.[37]

As in Pistoia, the early commune operated as much in cooperation as in opposition to the ecclesiastical establishment. From the beginning of the twelfth century, the commune occupied a building that was located in an enclosed garden (brolum) that belonged to the archbishop and was located near the church of Santa Maria Yemale. By 1162 it was being referred to as the communal palace (palacium comunis).[38] The Universitas Mercatorum, or consuls of the merchants (organized in 1159), met here after 1212.[39] As Enrica Salvatori has observed, as the residence of the bishop and the cathedral clergy, the seat of political power, the meeting place of the merchant consuls, and the marketplace, the piazza of the cathedrals of Santa Maria Yemale and Santa Tecla constituted "the religious, civic and economic heart of Milan."[40]

Relations, however, between the commune and the archbishop grew increasingly rancorous; in 1228 (the same year as the popular revolution in Bologna) the communal government, under the influence of the merchant consuls, made the decision to construct a new palace for itself at some distance from the cathedral complex. The Broletto Nuovo, as it was known to distinguish it from the Broletto Vecchio, symbolized and represented a direct challenge to archiepiscopal authority. As seen in the introduction to this section, the Broletto Nuovo became a crucial urban hub and many of the more important market activities came to be centered here. The market for large fish was transferred here, while that for smaller fish and crustaceans remained at the older archiepiscopal center. The meat market was also located here, as was the grain market; and, as seen earlier, the bankers and notaries were situated around the piazza.[41] Most significantly, the consuls of the merchants, who had formerly met at the Broletto Vecchio, transferred their meetings to the Broletto Nuovo. As representatives of the most powerful guilds in the city, among them the international merchants and money-changers, the Mercanzia had jurisdiction over a variety of issues including supervision of commercial brokers and weights and measures, even though the consuls were not officials of the commune.[42] In Milan, then, the impetus to create a distinct governmental and market space came from its greater merchants.

The pattern in Piacenza is remarkably similar to that of Bologna. In the year 819 Louis the Pious granted the bishop of Piacenza a variety of privileges over markets, river ports, and mills as well as over an annual fair held on the feast of Sant'Antonino.

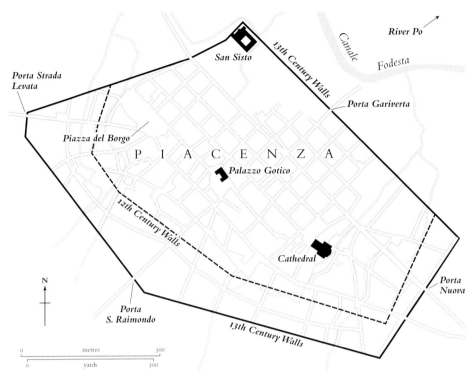

30    Map of Piacenza in the 14th century.

Later in the century, the Benedictine monastery of San Sisto was granted similar rights. Then in 997 the bishop received comital rights.[43] In consequence, the cathedral piazza became an important commercial site where, according to a fourteenth-century law, a Saturday market took place at which a variety of products were sold, including furs, dry goods, cloth, leather, meat, and cheese.[44] As was the case in other cities, the aristocratically based communal government, first documented in 1126, met for a time at the episcopal palace. Only in the early thirteenth century did it construct a communal palace in the vicinity of the cathedral, making the cathedral square the center of political, ecclesiastical, and commercial activities for the town (fig. 30).[45]

With the revival of the economy in the eleventh and twelfth centuries, Piacenza became an important center in the production of textiles, particularly cotton and fustian. Most of this activity was located in the western part of the city known as the Borgo, located just outside the walls of the ancient Roman *castrum* and at the intersection of the Via Francigena and the route leading to the river Po and Milan. It was here that the College of Merchants, known in Piacenza as the Nuxio, built its headquarters, the Palatium Nuxii, probably sometime near the end of the twelfth century.[46] Accordingly, the Piazza del Borgo became the market for cloth and the bankers located to this area as well. A Saturday market for foodstuffs and wood also developed here. But most importantly and as an indication of its growing importance, the College of

31    Piacenza, Palazzo Gotico, begun 1281.

Merchants gained jurisdiction over weights and measures and other aspects of commerce not only at the Piazza del Borgo but also at the market at the cathedral.[47]

Then, in 1281 the popular regime, first instituted in 1250 with the creation of a
captain, constructed a communal palace, now known as the Palazzo Gotico, and created
a surrounding square (the *platea nova comunis*) that stood completely separate and at an
approximately equal distance from the cathedral and Piazza del Borgo, but flanking the
church of San Francesco (fig. 31). This new urban center became the site of a new
market – which, like the market in the Piazza Maggiore of Bologna, seems to have
been dedicated primarily to the sale of foodstuffs. According to the fourteenth-century
statutes, the new Piazza Maggiore was the only place in the city where fresh fish
could be sold. The piazza also housed a meat market, although meat also continued
to be sold in the markets at the Piazza del Borgo and at the cathedral. A late fifteenth-
century law established Wednesday as the day for the market in the Piazza Maggiore.[48]
Finally, when the Visconti of Milan extended their lordship over Piacenza in the
first decades of the fourteenth century, they fortified (as they had done in Bologna at
the Piazza Maggiore) the Palazzo Gotico-San Francesco complex with a wall pierced
by three entry gates and erected a tower, known as the Torrazzo, from which the
authorities could monitor the city. As Anna Zaninoni and Marcello Spigaroli have
observed, the building of these fortifications represented the coup de grace to
Piacenza's civic autonomy.[49]

Even though a relatively small city, Piacenza was strategically located on the Po and along major roads, including the Via Francigena. As the city developed, three different market squares emerged, each simultaneously the product and symbol of the institutions or groups which in various periods determined the political development of the city.[50] The role of the College of Merchants was especially pronounced in the creation of the Piazza del Borgo, a space, like the Bolognese Porta Ravegnana/Carrobbio complex, given over almost entirely to commerce. Again, what Bologna, Milan, and Piacenza all suggest is the role the greater merchants played in shaping market space.

Three additional examples, Venice, Rome, and Florence, further illustrate and indicate in telling ways how unique combinations of power and tradition served to shape particular urban commercial landscapes. Probably no Italian city, with the possible exception of Genoa, had more space dedicated to commerce than did Venice. As Jacopo d'Albizzotto Guidi explained in his *El sommo della condizione di Vinegia* of 1442, Venice's market encompassed the retail market in Piazza San Marco and the predominantly wholesale market at Rialto, as well as the street of mercers (the Merceria) and the bridge linking the two.[51] There was also a retail market in the large Campo San Polo, not far from Rialto.

Venice stood apart from other Italian cities in several respects that conjoined to shape its commercial topography. First, Venice originated as a frontier outpost of the Byzantine Empire; it was not under the jurisdiction of the Holy Roman Emperor. Second, wary of papal interference, Venice marginalized its bishop, whose cathedral was located in the far eastern reaches of the city beyond the Arsenal at San Pietro di Castello. Together these factors guaranteed that control of the market was the prerogative of the doges, the successors of the Byzantine-appointed dukes, although there is some evidence that a market existed in the early centuries of the city's existence at the episcopal stronghold in Castello.[52] Then as the commune developed and, in essence, encompassed or co-opted the doge, transforming the dogeship into the chief office of the commune, it assumed jurisdiction over the markets. Third, the rise of the *popolo* took a unique turn in the lagoon city. On one hand, the newly rich merchants were absorbed into the ranks of the older elites, who were themselves, due to Venice's unique geographic situation, engaged in trade. As Frederic Lane noted, no guild or college of merchants developed in Venice since the government, specifically the Senate – made up as it was of merchants – took it upon itself to protect their interests and to fulfill the other functions that a Universitas Mercatorum or Mercanzia usually assumed. On the other hand, small-scale retailers and artisans, known elsewhere as the *popolo minuto*, were forced into a position of subordination. The guilds had to submit their statutes for approval by governmental officials known as the Giustizieri Vecchi (Old Justices), and guildsmen had to pledge their loyalty to the doge and commune.[53] These factors together meant that the communal government assumed an extraordinary degree of authority and control over Venetian commercial life.

Venetian market space reflected this control. Piazza San Marco was the site of a market, held on Saturdays, and of an annual fair, known as the Sensa, held during the days around the feast of the Ascension. On market days and during the fair, temporary stalls were set up in the piazza.[54] In addition, permanent shops were situated around the piazza's perimeter. These included shops for butchers, fishmongers, and bakers. In the sixteenth century the bakers were relocated to the base of the campanile. And, apparently, certain used–cloth dealers had shops under the portico of San Marco itself.[55] The procurators of San Marco, governmental officials charged with supervision of the basilica, had jurisdiction over the piazza and collected rents from the various shops that lined its perimeter.

The communal government was also the chief proprietor and overseer of the Rialto market complex (see fig. 5). Rialto developed spontaneously in the early history of the city as a market space, probably the result of the ease of navigation there – a consequence of the depth of the Grand Canal at that point – and because of the Rialto island's ready accessibility to the mainland. A crucial moment arrived in 1097 when the brothers Pietro and Tiso, sons of the late Stefano Orio, bequeathed to the doge and nascent commune their property which consisted of a row of shops, "located in the market of Rialto."[56] Soon the government began to locate certain offices here, including the officials in charge of weights and measures and the Mint.[57] As the area took on an increasingly commercial character, other families with property at Rialto either sold it to the government or turned it into private commercial space, so that Rialto retained almost nothing of its earlier residential character. The Querini family was one of the last to hold out; but in the end they too abandoned the area, in part when some members of the family had their share of the family's ancestral home, their Ca' Grande, confiscated by the government and razed as retribution for their participation in the Querini-Tiepolo conspiracy of 1310. Those Querini who were not implicated in the plot eventually sold the remaining portion of the Ca' Grande to the government, and it became in 1339 the site of the new *beccaria*.[58] The *beccaria* at Rialto was under the jurisdiction of the Ufficiali alle Beccarie, who were responsible for assigning stalls to the butchers. In 1408 the Ufficiali also assumed control over the meat market at San Marco when it was removed from that of the Procurators of San Marco.[59] Much of the impetus in the development of Rialto derived from the government, which over the centuries systematized streets and canals, regulated traffic, and built market structures. In turn, the commune derived large revenues from its supervision of Rialto.[60]

The Ufficiali alle Beccarie was just one of many offices that had their headquarters at Rialto. In 1282–3 Doge Giovanni Dandolo formalized a division of governmental offices between San Marco and Rialto. Henceforth, offices located at the Ducal Palace at San Marco dealt with judicial matters, both civil and criminal, while offices located at Rialto had competency over finances, trade, and commerce. Supervision of the Rialto market complex originally was the responsibility of the Visdomini, a magistracy with jurisdiction over fiscal matters. But in the mid-thirteenth century, the government created a new office, the Ufficiali sopra Rialto, specifically to supervise the market.[61] Eventually the Ufficiali were themselves absorbed into the office that evolved into the Provveditori al Sal, the magistracy charged with supervision of the lucrative salt trade.[62] In Venice, then, a combination of factors, including especially a fortuitous early bequest

32　Venice, Rialto Market in the 19th century.

to the doge and community, created a marketplace that was thoroughly under governmental control and that, as will be seen in the introduction to Part Three, was deeply
linked to the Venetians' image of themselves (fig. 32).

　　If Venice exhibited a market characterized by the interventions of a strong central
government that was the exclusive preserve of merchants, the situation in medieval
Rome was very much the opposite. Rome was more like Piacenza but on a larger
scale, in that various institutions had jurisdiction and control over different parts of the

commercial landscape. The markets of medieval and early modern Rome have been thoroughly and expertly studied by Anna Modigliani. According to her, the Campidoglio was the site of a major market in the Middle Ages. It was also the center of Roman communal government (established in 1143) and justice. But the civic government in medieval Rome was less powerful than in most other cities, facing as it did stiff competition from the influential baronial families of the city and from various ecclesiastical entities, including the papacy. Furthermore, the guilds, usually a mainstay of communal governments elsewhere, were, like those of Venice, relatively weak. Unlike in other cities, there is no evidence that the civic government owned or rented out any commercial properties at the Campidoglio. Instead, all of the shops that were located there, even those that are described as "next to the Capitoline palace and in the public market" (*iuxta palatium Capitolii et in foro publico*) were in private hands. And no production was carried out at the Campidoglio; instead, products that were made elsewhere in the city were transported there for sale.[63]

Food markets were scattered throughout the city but the major markets were located in the Campo de' Fiori, in Piazza Santa Maria Rotonda, in Piazza Giudea, and at San Celso, although the last only dated from the second half of the fifteenth century. Santa Maria Rotonda's large projecting portico explains its use as market space (fig. 33). The wholesale fish market was situated under the Portico of Octavian into which had been built the church of Sant'Angelo. Most of the *lapides*, or stone counters, from which the fish was sold were owned by the canons of Sant'Angelo, others by the titular cardinal of Sant'Angelo, and a few by fishmongers themselves. In this, Rome differed dramatically from Venice where the communal government owned and managed the Pescheria at Rialto and from Perugia, Bologna, and Verona where the guilds owned the fishmongers' halls.[64]

As the example of Sant'Angelo in Pescheria indicates, as major property owners in the city, churches often had control over commercial spaces. The chapter of Santa Maria Rotonda had jurisdiction not only over the church itself and its porch but also over the entire piazza in front of the church, and collected rents on shops fronting the piazza.[65] Money-changers occupied the steps and piazza of the Basilica of Saint Peter, while many of the shops around the Vatican catered to the needs of pilgrims. And a special market was held in the Jewish neighborhood every Friday. Known as the Mercatello, it seems to have originated around the year 1400 and was intimately tied to papal authority.[66] Overall, the Roman situation testifies to an extremely diffuse commercial landscape – one characterized by relatively weak civic governmental and guild intervention and by the ongoing importance of ecclesiastical institutions.

In Florence, the city's commercial center was distinct from both its governmental and ecclesiastical centers, and marked by a strong guild presence. The evidence suggests that the Florentine market never migrated away from the site of the old Roman forum.[67] As noted earlier, the symbol of the Mercato Vecchio, Donatello's *Dovizia*, sat atop a column located at the intersection of the ancient Roman *cardo* and *decumanus*. When the first popular regime emerged in Florence in the 1250s, it built a palace for its officials, the Bargello, some distance from the Mercato Vecchio. The Bargello

33   Anonymous, *View of the Pantheon*, 16th century, Paris, Louvre.

subsequently became the residence of the podestà. When the second popular regime arose in 1282, at first it met in various rented properties. It was only in December 1298 that money was authorized for the building of a new palace to house the priors and the standard-bearer of justice. The site chosen was a small open space where the houses of the Ghibelline Uberti family had once stood – again, some distance from the Mercato Vecchio. Work on the new communal palace proceeded fairly quickly, since by March 1302 the priors were already in the new palace, known most commonly today as the Palazzo Vecchio but more accurately at the time as the Palazzo dei Priori or Palazzo della Signoria. Over the course of the fourteenth century, the surrounding area was cleared to create an imposing piazza and the palace itself was reoriented so that its western façade replaced the northern one as the primary entrance.[68] Also in the 1290s work began on the new cathedral of Florence. Thus by the beginning of the fourteenth century, Florence had developed three distinct urban spaces: an ecclesiastical center focused on the Duomo and baptistery; a governmental center located around the Palazzo and Piazza della Signoria; and a commercial district that encompassed not only the Mercato Vecchio but also the Mercato Nuovo, the grain market at Orsanmichele, and the surrounding streets and alleys (fig. 34). The Mercato Vecchio was the major food market; in the middle of the central square stood the *beccaria*, constructed in the fourteenth century.[69] By contrast, the Mercato Nuovo was the center of international trade; bankers set up their shops there especially but also in the Mercato Vecchio.[70]

The division of activities among the political, ecclesiastical, and commercial zones seems to have been especially distinct in Florence.[71] Although some shops were located

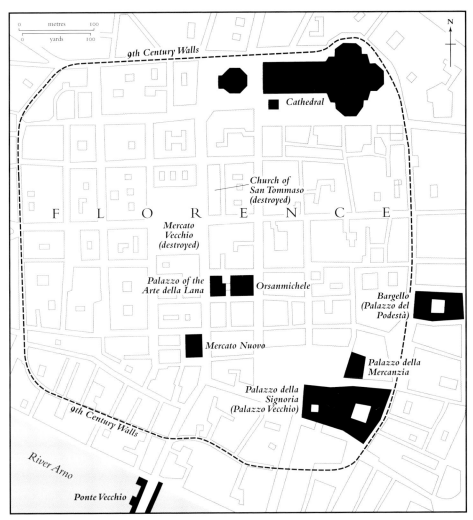

34 Map of the civic center of Florence in the 14th century.

around the periphery of the Piazza della Signoria and woolen cloth was displayed there as part of an annual fair held on the feast of Saint Martin, the piazza, unlike Piazza San Marco in Venice, appears to have served few commercial purposes.[72] Similarly, there is little evidence of concentrated market activities around the cathedral, although the archiepiscopal palace facing the baptistery included ground-floor shops that were rented to drapers and shoemakers.[73]

What also distinguished Florence from both Venice and Rome, at least until the end of the fourteenth century, was the power of its guilds, especially those engaged in international trade and manufacturing. The guild of wool merchants (known as the Calimala) was already in existence in the 1180s; other guilds developed thereafter.[74] With the Ordinances of Justice in 1293, the *popolo* were able to bring a change in government that made guild membership the basis for Florentine political enfranchisement. Also with time, the number of guilds was fixed at twenty-one, although

individual guilds often included several distinct occupational groups. But power lay
primarily with what came to be known as the seven greater guilds: the Calimala (the
importers of semi-finished cloth), the Lana (the manufacturers of woolen cloth), the
Cambio (the money-changers), Por Santa Maria (cloth retailers and silk manufacturers),
the Medici e Speziali (physicians, apothecaries, and spice dealers), the Vaiai e Pellicciai
(furriers), and the Giudici e Notai (judges and notaries).[75]

Early on, many of the guilds held their meetings in churches, cloisters, even cemeter-
ies, until this was forbidden by law in 1335. Eventually, most of the guilds built their
own guildhalls. The powerful Lana guild was perhaps the first to do so; in 1308 it
strategically situated its headquarters close to the Mercato Vecchio and the Mercato
Nuovo on a strip of land between the Via Calimala and the piazza of Orsanmichele.[76]
Por Santa Maria began in 1377 to build a new guildhall near the Mercato Nuovo and
next to the hall of the powerful interest group known as the Parte Guelfa.[77] The
bankers' hall was located near the Piazza della Signoria and that of the Calimala first
at the Mercato Nuovo and then on the Via Calimala.[78] As Richard Goldthwaite
observes, these four guilds of "merchant capitalists" constructed guildhalls that had "a
monumental presence on the urban scene in the immediate vicinity of the Mercato
Nuovo, the banking center of the city."[79] The Medici e Speziali located their guildhall
in the precincts of the Mercato Vecchio, as did the guilds of the second-hand dealers,
the linen workers and tailors, the hostel keepers, and the oil and cheese-mongers, while
the butchers, the most important of the five so-called middle guilds, constructed a
guildhall across from Orsanmichele.[80] Their individual guildhalls underscored the
importance of these occupations to the Florentine economy. But an even more significant architectural statement was made in 1339 when Por Santa Maria petitioned to
have thirteen of the fourteen external piers of the grain loggia at Orsanmichele orna-
mented with tabernacles; the plan was for each of the twelve greater and middle guilds,
as well as the Parte Guelfa, to decorate a pier (fig. 35).

The grain market at Orsanmichele itself had a long and complex history. In 1240
the communal government took over the site, which became the only location where
grain could legally be sold in the city. In 1284 the commune decided to build a loggia
to house the market which until that time had been conducted in the open air. A few
years later a confraternity was founded to sing lauds to an image of the Virgin Mary
painted on one of the internal piers of the loggia, and in 1292 the image began to
perform miracles. By 1336 the old loggia was dilapidated and so construction began
on a replacement. The new building consisted of an open six-bay loggia on the ground
floor with an enclosed granary above. One of the six bays was reserved for an oratory
to the miraculous image of the Virgin, and in 1352 Orcagna was entrusted with the
task of building a new tabernacle dedicated to Mary. Just five years later, in 1357, the
Florentine government decided to remove the grain market from Orsanmichele and
the building became an oratory. Accordingly, the ground-floor arches were enclosed
and the grain market moved to a location to the south-east of the Piazza della Signoria.
In 1619 the new location was embellished with Giulio Parigi's Loggia del Grano.
Despite the move, the upper-floor granary at Orsanmichele continued in use until

35   Florence, Orsanmichele, mid-14th century.

1414.[81] Over time, the twelve proprietary guilds commissioned various artists to create works to fill the ground-floor tabernacles and the building became a showcase for some of Florence's great sculptors, including Donatello and Andrea del Verrocchio. In this way, the public grain market evolved into a symbol of Florence's guild-based republican regime.

With the rise of the Medici family to prominence after 1434, the Parte Guelfa went into serious decline. And so, during the 1450s its statue of Saint Louis of Toulouse was removed from its tabernacle at Orsanmichele and the rights to the niche were sold to the Mercanzia or merchants' union, which commissioned from Verrocchio a statue of Christ and Saint Thomas to fill the space (see Chapter Eight).[82] The Mercanzia had been established in 1308 on the initiative of the five guilds most involved in international trade and banking (Calimala, Lana, Por Santa Maria, Cambio, and Medici e Speziali) in an apparent effort to create a kind of overarching guild of merchants. It consisted of a foreign officer and a council of five, one from each of the constituent guilds and functioned as a pressure group promoting the interests of the great merchants in Florentine policy; from 1318 its decrees carried the force of law, although its primary role was judicial rather than legislative.[83] The Mercanzia concerned itself with such matters as reprisals against Florentine merchants by foreign governments, trade accords, and transportation security. Over time it became less an independent body and more an instrument of the government. It also came to serve as a court handling disputes between creditors and debtors and as a court of appeals against judgments rendered by guild tribunals.

For the first fifty years of its existence, the Mercanzia met in the church of Santa Cecilia east of the Palazzo della Signoria, in private residences, or at various governmental properties.[84] Then in 1359 the communal government leased to the Mercanzia a piece of property located to the left of what is now the main entrance to the Palazzo della Signoria, but which at the time was in front of the Palazzo's main entrance. Construction began on the building under the supervision of Giovanni di Lapo Ghini (fig. 36). Originally three stories in height, in the 1390s it was joined to a smaller building on the left that housed the governmental office that handled contracts with the city's mercenary armies. The ground floor included an audience hall where judicial cases were heard. On the second floor was a larger hall for the Mercanzia council to meet, as well as living space for the foreign officer and his staff. The 1390s rebuilding campaign adorned the second-story hall with an unusual vaulted ceiling and the exterior with the shields of the commune and the city's twenty-one guilds.[85] This palace has been described as "a dignified structure that speaks for the stature of its occupant and makes an important contribution to the square in front of the city's town hall."[86] Writing in the early fifteenth century, Goro Dati described the Mercanzia as "a very large, ornate, and magnificent palace."[87] As a sign of the importance of the five constituent guilds, the government awarded them a palace in a conspicuous location not in the marketplace but next to the Palazzo della Signoria. Massaio included the building in his bird's-eye view of the city (see fig. 9). The Palazzo della Mercanzia's location thus suitably symbolized the power of the great guilds of international merchants and manufacturers within the Florentine government. In this, Florence differed from both Venice and Rome.

Despite all the variations examined here, one generalization holds, namely the determinative role played in most cities by merchants, bankers, and textile manufacturers in shaping commercial space. Indeed, Rome is the most notable exception: there banking and trade were underdeveloped and ecclesiastical rights to markets continued to predominate; but in other cities, together those elements created a particularly diffuse commercial landscape. What is also clear is that many cities made some effort to differentiate the food market from other commercial activities, although this division was by no means clear-cut or absolute.

36   Florence, Palazzo della Mercanzia, begun c. 1359.

Additionally, although communal and commercial centers developed in opposition to the bishops especially in the larger cities, marketplaces themselves were dotted by and sometimes even focused on churches. Florence's Mercato Vecchio included several churches and tabernacles; in his poem Antonio Pucci pointed out that each of the market's four "corners" was defined by a church.[88] Venice's Rialto market complex encompassed several churches including San Bartolomeo, San Giovanni Elemosinario, San Matteo, and especially San Giacomo di Rialto, whose piazza constituted the very heart of the market complex. In Bologna, before transferring their guild meetings to the Mercanzia, the money-changers met at the church of Santa Maria di Porta Ravegnana, and in their new headquarters at the Mercanzia they maintained a chapel dedicated to Saint Matthew and the Archangel Michael. And the merchants and money-changers even built a church at the Reno fairgrounds, known as San Bartolomeo "in insula fori Reni."[89] In Piacenza, the Piazza del Borgo developed near the monastery of Santa Brigida and the Nuxio built a church at the piazza dedicated to Saint Andrew.[90] Thus, even though many marketplaces developed in opposition to episcopal power, contemporaries saw no incompatibility between commerce and religion; indeed, they believed the two to be intimately connected.

In the cities of medieval Italy, then, governmental, ecclesiastical, and commercial spaces and interests intersected and overlapped in myriad ways. As noted in the Introduction, Donatella Calabi contends that the effort to disentangle these uses dates to the urban renewal projects of the sixteenth century when governments made a concerted effort to create distinct urban zones defined by their uses. Yet, there is evidence that much earlier civic regimes were already beginning to make some effort to define space more pronouncedly. Jürgen Paul argued that the Palazzo della Signoria of Florence and the Palazzo dei Consoli of Gubbio, neither of which accommodated any commercial space, were "the first examples of political architecture in the modern sense" in that there was a "separation of political life from the daily life of the market."[91] Certainly by the early fifteenth century a new sensibility was emerging. In 1431, the Consiglio degli Anziani of Brescia, by that time under the rule of Venice, stated that "a good city should have two piazzas, that is, one for assemblies of the populace, the other indeed for holding the market . . ."[92]

Both Paul and Modigliani see this transformation as driven by political change. Paul argued that the separation of political life from the market represented "the defeat of democratic forces and the end of the town hall as an important building type in Italy"; while Modigliani attributes the change to the end of communal autonomy brought about by the rise of signorial regimes regardless of whether they were homegrown or foreign.[93] Certainly, in Verona, Padua, and Milan, the lords of those cities, respectively the Della Scala, the Carrara, and the Visconti, established new spaces of power – fortified palaces – that stood separate from the old communal/market centers. In their native Verona, the Della Scala even monopolized the office of podestà of the Domus Mercatorum (that city's Mercanzia) and used it as one of the bases of their power.[94] In Bologna and Piacenza, as has been seen, as well as in Parma and elsewhere, the Visconti appropriated and militarized the old communal/market squares in towns that had come under their domination.[95]

Even in those cities that retained either the substance or semblance of communal/republican government, elites began to emphasize their distinction (and separation from the bulk of the *popolo*) through architectural interventions. One guild that firmly established itself in Bologna's Piazza Maggiore was that of the notaries (fig. 37). It was especially influential in Bologna which was famous for its university and in particular for its law school. Already by the end of the thirteenth century, the guild had a *domus magna*, located on the Piazza Maggiore. Starting in 1288, the guild embarked on a campaign to acquire various properties including another building that was separated from the *domus magna* by an alley or passageway (*androna*) that belonged to the commune. One hundred years later, the guild undertook a rebuilding program designed to bring unity to the structures that had been joined together.[96] Rather than situating themselves at or near the Carrobbio, the major business district, the notaries asserted their status by building their guildhall on the piazza housing the communal palaces and San Petronio.

In Perugia two guilds, the merchants (the Collegio della Mercanzia) and the money-changers (the Collegio del Cambio) enjoyed a particularly close relationship to the civic government. From the early fourteenth century, the merchants held two of the ten positions in the priorate, the city's top executive body; the money-changers usually occupied one post. Both guilds had significant influence over Perugia's trade and monetary policy, enjoying, in the words of Tiziana Biganti and Clara Cutini, "a position of clear preeminence over the other guild associations [and] . . . a privileged role

37　Bologna, Palazzo dei Notai, begun late 13th century.

in the structure of the government."[97] This preeminence found architectural expression when they were granted meeting halls within the Palazzo dei Priori itself. The Palazzo faces the Piazza Maggiore, which along with the Piazza Piccola (or Sopramuro) served as the city's commercial center. Before the ground-floor loggia of the palace was walled up (the side facing the present-day Corso Vannucci), it housed shops.[98]

On February 29, 1390, the five Conservatori della Libertà e della Pace (three of whom belonged to the merchant guild) ceded to the Mercanzia two rooms on the ground floor of the Palazzo dei Priori, next to the main entrance, and granted the guild the right to reconfigure the rooms as its headquarters. In return the Mercanzia paid the government 1,400 gold florins. Before this, the Mercanzia did not have a fixed seat, although it met from time to time in the church of Santa Maria del Mercato, where it maintained a chapel. Work on restructuring and decorating the newly granted space proceeded over the next decade so that by 1403 the Mercanzia was definitively established in its new audience hall. As Biganti and Cutini observe, the "installation in the Palazzo formally sanctioned the position of clear economic and political preeminence of the Mercanzia."[99] In the mid-fifteenth century, the Collegio del Cambio received similar recognition when it too was granted meeting space within the palace. The creation of these two guildhalls within the confines of the civic palace rather than as freestanding halls testifies to the close relationship between these guilds and the government.

The building of the Bolognese Mercanzia in the 1390s, the addition of a vaulted second story to the Florentine Mercanzia also in the 1390s (probably based on the Bolognese model), and the rebuilding of the Siena's Mercanzia (1417–48) all bespeak the prestige of the elite professions which they represented. David Friedman has argued, based on the iconographical programs of the Sienese and Bolognese Mercanzie (considered in Chapter Eight), that these buildings do not celebrate "the institutions from which they are made but the community, the regime, and the city itself." He refers to them as "hybrids" that served various purposes.[100] As he notes, the Bolognese Mercanzia was built first to house the office of the gabelles and was originally referred to, as noted earlier, as both the "loggia delle gabelle" and the "loggia del Carrobbio."[101] But, in my view, Friedman underestimates these buildings' mercantile and elite guild associations. Located as they were in the heart of the business districts, they offered a place where merchants engaged in international trade and commerce could gather, discuss the latest news, make connections, and arrange deals. Already by 1400 the Bolognese building was being referred to as the "loggia dei mercadanti."[102] When these buildings were constructed, the merchant oligarchs were firmly in control. Especially in Bologna, which had only recently (in 1376) freed itself from papal authority and where memories of the 1378 Ciompi Revolt in Florence were certainly still fresh, it was logical for merchants to downplay their popular roots. Perhaps the inspiration for both of these buildings was the loggia for merchants at the foot of the Rialto Bridge, a building with no popular associations.

To politics, then, can be added an additional factor effecting this change, namely, ideology. In the later fourteenth and fifteenth centuries, the idea of the *bene comune* became more difficult to sustain as regimes (both those that remained republican-leaning communes and those that fell under *signori*) became more elitist and oligarchic and pursued policies clearly geared to the advantage of a privileged few. As such, the civic marketplace, one of the hallmarks of the age of the popular communes, came to serve less well as the symbol of communal pride, the locus of political practice, and as the embodiment of the common good. A work that looks back nostalgically to that communal past is Giovanni da Nono's *Visio Egidii*, written in praise of Padua, which by the time he was writing had fallen under the lordship of the Carrara family. It includes a particularly rich description of Padua's central marketplace, and thereby allows a close analysis of the layout and organization of market space. It is those concerns that the next chapter considers.

# 3

# THE ORGANIZATION
# OF THE MARKETPLACE

The cities and towns of medieval Italy had widely diffuse commercial landscapes. Market squares were not the only places in cities where buying and selling occurred. Commercial activities could take place almost anywhere. For example, Stefano di Cecco, a grain seller in Prato who was active in the late fourteenth century, recorded in his account book where those who owed him money made payments on their debts. He received payments at, among other places, his debtors' homes and their shops, in taverns, at the Porta Serraglio, one of the city gates, and frequently "in the communal piazza" (*in piaçça del chomune*).[1] Similarly, buying and selling might or might not be associated with the place where the goods were actually produced. Niccolò di Martino di Pietro, a tanner or dealer in leather in Perugia, rented property owned by the church of San Fiorenzo in a part of the city given over to the noxious activities of tanning, but kept a shop for selling his goods in the Rimbocco della Salsa, close to the city's central square.[2] In all cities, arteries that connected city gates with the major piazzas were lined with workshops from which goods could sometimes be purchased, although certain restrictions applied. In Florence, for example, grain could only be sold at Orsanmichele and money-changers were supposed to practice their trade only at their designated tables.[3] In Venice, goldsmiths were prohibited from carrying out their craft and selling their wares anywhere except at Rialto.[4] But in every city, itinerant hawkers, selling a variety of goods, especially foodstuffs, made their way through the streets, turning, in a sense, the entire city into a marketplace.

38    Florence, Lana Guildhall, begun 1308.

One of the more extraordinary examples of the diffuse nature of buying and selling is provided by the Lana guild of Florence. Adrienne Atwell has reconstructed the procedure that foreign merchants had to follow during the middle decades of the fourteenth century when purchasing woolen cloth of Florentine manufacture. On arrival in the city, these merchants made their way to the Lana guildhall next to Orsanmichele (fig. 38) where they were paired with brokers employed by the guild. The brokers then accompanied the merchants on four different itineraries to each of the city's four wool manufacturing "conventi" or districts: Oltrarno, San Pancrazio, Por San Piero, and San Piero a Scheraggio. Depending on the distribution of shops along the route, brokers were told to take their clients either to every shop on one side of a street before proceeding down the other side or to zigzag from one side of the street to the other and visit each shop. The broker had to take his client to every shop sanctioned by the guild. Based on the evidence from Giovanni Villani's chronicle, Atwell estimates that merchants visited "somewhere between two- and three-hundred shops."[5] Brokers were assigned to merchants for a fifteen-day period (excluding Sundays and holidays), an indication of how thorough and time-consuming the process was. After visiting the shops, purchase agreements were made, again with the help of the brokers. Atwell notes that these itineraries, all emanating from the Lana guildhall and fanning out into different parts of the city, reflected the centrality of ritual in Florentine life and served to celebrate Florence itself, since they took visiting merchants past important civic buildings and spaces.[6]

The marketing tours organized by the Florentine Lana guild were perhaps unusual, although it is not known how foreign merchants did their purchasing in other textile-producing towns such as Verona. Florence's tours were also relatively short-lived, being discontinued around the time of the Ciompi Revolt of 1378, but they indicate that commercial transactions were not confined to market squares. Nevertheless, as noted before, every city had places specifically dedicated to commerce. Some of these were created to accommodate activities or commodities that could not easily or conveniently be housed in the central marketplace. This was especially true of cattle and horse markets, which required a large amount of space both for the animals and their feed and which produced a quantity of refuse in the form of manure. In Florence, for example, the cattle market was held in the undeveloped area of the city beyond the orchard of Santa Croce; in Verona it was held in the large Piazza Bra, near the old Roman colosseum and some distance from Piazza delle Erbe.[7] In Perugia, the weekly horse market took place in front of the church of San Domenico near Porta San Pietro; during the fair of All Saints, animals were traded in the Borgo San Pietro whereas other fair activities took place in the city's main square.[8] Hay, wood, and charcoal were other commodities that were often sold in specialized and distinct marketplaces due to their bulkiness and the difficulty of transporting them into city centers.[9]

Markets operated not only in a spatial but also in a temporal dimension.[10] In most cities, there was a market that specialized in foodstuffs that needed to be purchased every day. There was also a more important weekly market when products from the surrounding countryside were brought to town. Saturday was commonly the market day, as was the case in Assisi and Piacenza.[11] In some instances, larger towns coordinated the weekly markets of smaller towns under their dominion so that these markets were staggered over the week. Bergamo, for example, decreed that the weekly market be held on Sundays in Palosco, on Wednesdays in Martinengo, and on Fridays in Gisalba.[12] In Florence the cattle market was originally on Mondays but was changed to Fridays; it was held on Thursdays and Saturdays in Treviso.[13] Still other markets were held on a monthly basis; Pisa held a market on the first Sunday of each month.[14] Additionally, cities hosted annual or biannual fairs that tended to draw from a much wider geographical range and that offered opportunities for major sales, both wholesale and retail. Several towns, including Pisa and Assisi, held fairs during August; Pisa's horse fair was held during the first two weeks of October.[15] Bologna held fairs in May and August, including an August cattle market.[16] Venice's Sensa Fair depended on the movable feast of the Ascension.

The daily and weekly markets took place within city walls but, especially for the large annual events, cities created special fairgrounds outside the walls. Partly this was done in order to accommodate the crowds of buyers and sellers and to provide ease of transportation. Bologna, for example, created its fairground (today's Piazza VIII Agosto) to the north of the city. The site offered easy access to the canal linked to the Reno river and helped to balance the natural expansion of the city to the south and east.[17] Pisa held its August fair in fields located to the north of the city.[18] Padua's fairs took place in the Prato della Valle (fig. 39). Already in the eleventh century the nascent comune was seeking to wrest jurisdictional control over the area, then called the Valle del Mercato, from the church of Santa Giustina and the bishop of Padua.[19]

39   Francesco Piranesi, *Prato della Valle*, 1786. Padua, Musei Civici agli Eremitani.

Another reason for locating fairs at separate fairgrounds was that while they were in session, the usual rules of trade were suspended or at least modified, and this was much easier to manage in a location outside the city walls. For example, merchants attending fairs were usually exempt from gabelles and other duties that applied when products entered the city gates. Cities also appointed special officers and judges to coordinate affairs and to handle disputes between buyers and sellers as expeditiously as possible.[20] In most cases, temporary wooden stalls at the fairgrounds were constructed. Given the transitory nature of fairs, most of the infrastructure associated with them has disappeared. One rare extant remnant is a stone boundary marker that was used in Verona's Campo Marzo for the Fair of Saints Michael and Giustina that took place there between September 27 and October 7 each year (fig. 40). Dated 1335, it was designed to delimit the area of the fairground assigned to the shoemakers. It bears the names of the two wardens (*gastaldi*) of the guild as well as of the podestà and is adorned, perhaps as a concession to those who were illiterate, with sculpted renderings of a boot and two shoes.[21]

It remains unclear whether or not most cities assigned areas in the fairgrounds on an annual basis or whether tradition or legal rights determined where different occupational groups set up their stalls. Certainly, in the permanent city marketplaces, positions were more fixed and changed only slowly with time, usually as a consequence of governmental action. As noted earlier, in 1357 the Florentine government decided to remove the grain market from Orsanmichele; and in 1339, the Venetian government had completed the construction of the new meat market, moving the butchers from near the church of San Giovanni to a location more peripheral to the Rialto market complex but with the advantage of easier access to the Grand Canal and hence to the mainland whence the animals came.

Two of the most difficult issues to reconstruct in an examination of marketplaces are the arrangement of various shops and stalls and the relationship of one occupational group or kind of commodity to another. Fortunately, one of the more unusual examples of a civic *laus*, Giovanni da Nono's *Visio Egidii regis Patavie* (Vision of Egidius,

40  Verona, marker delimiting the area reserved for the
shoemakers in the Campo Marzo fairground, 1335.
Verona, Museo di Castelvecchio.

king of Patavium [Padua]), allows for a remarkably complete reconstruction of Padua's
commercial and political center.

Giovanni da Nono (c. 1276–1346), a Paduan who held many judicial posts, composed
a trilogy of works about his native city. The first, *De hedificatione urbis Patholomie* (On
the building of the city of Padua), deals with Padua's legendary origins by Trojan refugees. The last, *De generatione aliquorum civium urbis Padue tam nobilium quam ignobilium*
(On the families of some citizens of the city of Padua, both noble and ignoble), is an
account of Padua's notable families. The middle work, the *Visio Egidii*, purports to be
the account that an angel offered to Egidius, a mythical king of Padua who fled to
Rimini in order to avoid the depredations of Attila. In it the angel consoles Egidius
by recounting the greatness of the city to come and does so by offering a tour of the
future city. Da Nono completed the entire trilogy, it is thought, sometime in the 1330s,
while the *Visio* was probably written between 1314 and 1318, that is, before the rule
of the Carrara family, since the author was an "ardent supporter of the popular party
[in Padua] and of communal liberty."[22]

The *Visio Egidii* begins by establishing the premise for the work – the encounter
between the angel and Egidius. Once the more recent history of Padua has been
outlined, including the terrible years under the tyranny of Ezzelino da Romano, the
angelic tour of the city commences. It starts with a discussion of the city's "most
beautiful walls" (4) and its four principal gates and the routes leading from them into
the surrounding territory and to neighboring cities. Near the Porta Altinate, for
example, are the waterways leading to Venice and Chioggia. From this gate, the angel
observes, many merchants and others, both Paduans and foreigners, will "secretly and
unjustly" export foodstuffs to Venice (6–7). Also close by this gate is the piazza where

wood is sold. The angel then names the city's fifteen minor gates, including the Porta Contarini whence arrives the "greatest abundance" of herbs, fruits, and vegetables from the district known as Porciglia (10).

After being instructed about the contours of the future city, Egidius asks the angel to tell him about its "communal buildings" (*domus communes*). The angel responds that the Paduans will build fourteen "communal palaces" (*palacia communia*), both before the time of Ezzelino and after and that some will be destroyed and others transformed (11). The fourteen are comprised of the four principal public buildings – the Palacium Regale or Comune (the Palazzo della Ragione), the Palacium Consilii (the Palazzo del Consiglio), the Palacium Potestatis (the Palazzo del Podestà), and the Palacium Senatorum (the Palazzo degli Anziani) – and ten other "palacia" (palaces) surrounding the Palazzo della Ragione from which various goods will be sold. J.K. Hyde argued that Da Nono elevated these ten simple market structures to the status of "palaces" in order to have Padua compare favorably with Rome, since Da Nono's literary model is likely to have been the *Mirabilia urbis Romae*, a work composed around 1143 by a canon of Saint Peter's basilica.[23]

The angel's tour then continues with a lengthy discussion of the Palazzo della Ragione, including, as befitted the jurist Da Nono, a consideration of the various courts that met there. One, the tribunal of Victuals and the Unicorn (the various tribunals were named after animals), handled cases involving the illegal exportation of food and the use of false weights and measures (16).[24] The angel also names the four staircases and the goods that are sold by them, and then discusses the merchandise that is available in the middle of the two piazzas formed by the building. His tour concludes with a consideration of some changes made to the complex, including the construction of the public granary, and a brief mention of the decoration of the walls of the Palazzo della Ragione, painted with the twelve signs of the Zodiac and the seven planets by the "greatest of painters," Giotto (20).

According to Hyde, the theme that knits Da Nono's trilogy together is the play of Fortune, as reflected in the title assigned to it in some manuscripts, the *Liber ludi fortunae* (The Book of the Play of Fortune). In this respect it shares an affinity with Lenzi's *Specchio umano* and Pucci's "Proprietà del Mercato Vecchio." The story of Padua's ever changing fortunes serves as a warning to the Paduans to mend their ways, especially their predilection for usury. In Hyde's opinion, the *Visio Egidii* offers "a baffling combination of commonplace convention and startling originality." He judged it noteworthy for "the impression of the world as it must have appeared to many of the citizens of the communes," namely of their particular city as the center of the world – a point of view emphasized by envisioning the world from the perspective of the city gates; and for the "particularly detailed" description of the law courts and markets.[25] According to Elisa Occhipinti, Da Nono offers to his readers "the real city, realistically perceived by the eyes of the observer." Given to neither hyperbole nor idealization, Da Nono's viewpoint is that of a layman, whose interest is juridical and civic rather than religious.[26] Certainly, the thoroughness of his description of the layout of the marketplace is unparalleled in other civic *laudes*.

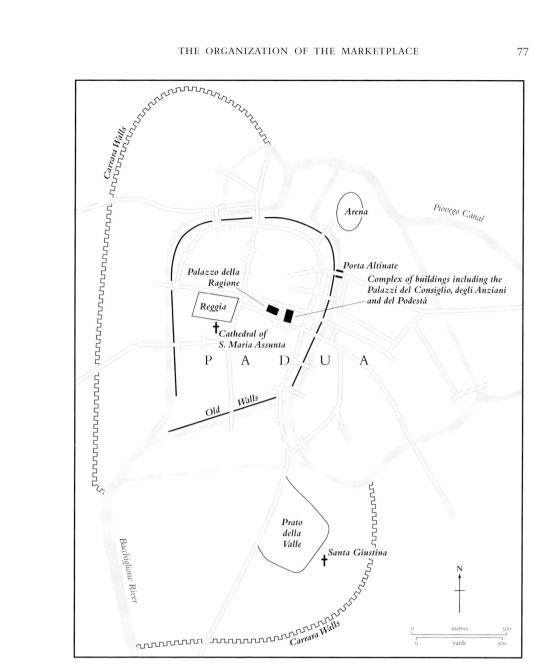

41   Map of Padua in the 14th century.

In order to understand the organization of the Paduan marketplace, it is first necessary to consider and situate the buildings that formed the civic center. As in many
other cities, jurisdiction over the Paduan market passed from the bishop to the
commune and led to the creation of a market square near the first communal palace.[27]
This first palace, referred to in the early documents as the "Domus Communis," was
probably built in the mid-twelfth century; it was replaced by the Palazzo della Ragione
which was built on the same site in the years 1218–19.[28] The new market area included
the structure known as the Peronio where fruit was sold (of which the column examined in Chapter One appears to be a remnant), another known as the Alodio, dedicated

to gambling and where brassware and bread were sold, and various shops housing tanners, leather workers, and mercers.[29] With the revival of communal liberty after Ezzelino da Romano's defeat in 1256 and the growing strength of the *popolo*, the commune embarked in the 1280s on an ambitious building program. The Palazzo del Podestà was built in 1281; the Palazzo del Consiglio in 1284, and the Palazzo degli Anziani in 1285/6.[30] These buildings located to the east of the Palazzo della Ragione were connected to one another and incorporated two towers: the Torre Rossa and the Torre Bianca (fig. 41).

The centerpiece of the entire complex was the Palazzo della Ragione itself, which was connected by a bridge to the Palazzo del Podestà (fig. 42). As originally built in the early thirteenth century, it consisted of a ground floor dedicated to shops, a mezzanine with some artisan workshops and governmental offices, and a second floor (partitioned into several spaces) where most of the city's courts, including the tribunal of the podestà, and a chapel were located. Four exterior staircases offered access to the mezzanine and upper story.[31] Then in the first decade of the fourteenth century Fra Giovanni degli Eremitani was entrusted with the task of remodeling the building (fig. 43). He kept the footprint of the exterior walls and maintained the external staircases but raised the walls of the second story and topped it with an inverted ship's-hull ceiling. It was this heightened second-story hall that Giotto decorated (Giotto's and subsequent decorative programs are considered in Chapter Eight). Shortly thereafter, Fra Giovanni also added two-story loggias on the long sides of the building. These loggias increased considerably the amount of covered commercial space around the exterior of the palace (fig. 44).[32] It was also almost certainly this expansion into the surrounding piazza and the need to disencumber that space that prompted Fra Giovanni to demolish the Peronio and Alodio (14).[33] But he also added the new vaulted public granary, the Fondaco delle Biade, to the south of the Palazzo del Podestà (see fig. 10).[34]

A serious fire in 1420 led to further changes in the Palazzo della Ragione. The mezzanine was removed (the fire had started there), which allowed for the vaulting of the ground floor. Also at this time the partitions dividing the upper story were removed, thereby creating one huge hall known, appropriately enough, as the Salone (fig. 45).[35] Later in the century, two one-story loggias were added to the two long sides of the building; these created yet more covered commercial space but partially obscured Fra Giovanni's original loggias.[36] The palazzo was not the only governmental palace with space dedicated to commerce: the other principal public buildings around the piazza – the Palazzi del Podestà, degli Anziani, and del Consiglio – all incorporated shops into their ground-floor spaces as well.

As noted earlier, Da Nono claimed that ten other "palaces" (*palacia*) surrounded the Palazzo della Ragione on the east, north, and west. Apparently, this number did not include either the New Prison or the Granary, although some shops selling goods other than grain were located at the Granary. Perhaps, these buildings were colonnaded structures. It remains unclear whether or not they had usable space on a second floor (Hyde, for one, believed they did) or whether they were simply one-story vaulted loggias.[37] In Rome's Campo de' Fiori there stood a colonnaded house known as

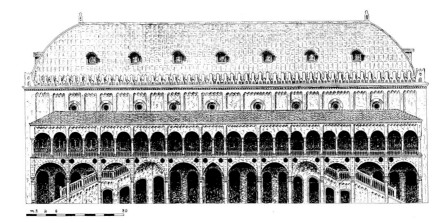

42  Padua, Palazzo della Ragione, begun 1218/19.

43  Moschetti, reconstruction of the Palazzo della Ragione as it appeared between 1306 and 1318.

44  Moschetti, reconstruction of the Palazzo della Ragione as it appeared between 1318 and 1420.

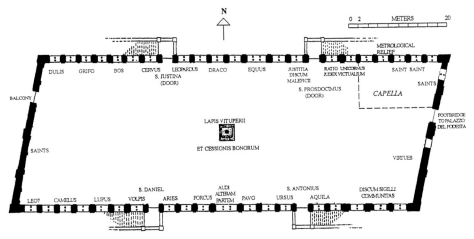

45   Plan of the Salone in the early 15th century, Palazzo della Ragione, Padua.
Courtesy of Eva Frojmovič.

L'Abbondanza that was owned by the chapter of St Peter's. According to Modigliani, this house was also referred to as a *palatium*.[38] Especially in the towns of the Po valley, communes built communal palaces in which the ground floor was opened up to include a covered and (sometimes) vaulted arcade. Milan's Broletto Nuovo is exemplary. It is possible that what qualified the ten structures as palaces in Da Nono's mind was their loggia-like or vaulted effect. In almost every case, Da Nono stated that goods were sold "under" (*sub*) these palaces. But they seem to have been more than mere porticoes, as were famously to be found in Bologna. Further evidence that this was the case is that in one instance, Da Nono actually mentioned a portico. Referring of one of these buildings, he wrote that "under this palace will be sold the hides of animals and on the side [of this palace] toward the west, there will be a portico [*porticus*], in which communal bread will be sold" (13). The entire complex of buildings may have called to mind an ancient Roman forum.[39]

As Da Nono described the fourteen palaces, he was careful to detail the products sold under them. He also included, as noted, two separate sections entitled "Concerning the names of the staircases of the Palace of the Commune of Padua and the items that will be sold next to them" (De nominibus scalarum communis palacii Padue et de rebus que vendentur iuxta illas) and "Concerning the items that will be sold in the piazzas of the city of Padua" (De rebus que vendentur super plateas urbis Padue). Taken together, this information allows for a fairly accurate reconstruction of Padua's market. What follows draws in part on Da Nono and in part on modern-day reconstructions of the entire complex (fig. 46).

According to Da Nono, Veronese and other cloth of little value was sold under the Palazzo del Consiglio. Under the adjoining Palazzo del Podestà, shopkeepers marketed both worked and unworked iron, as well as waste cotton and "cotton cloth of every kind" (11). The Palazzo degli Anziani housed the offices of gabelles and tolls and the sellers of salt (12). On the northern side of the piazza were two buildings where belts, gloves, and silk goods were sold. Sellers of pork occupied a third building on the northwest, with sellers of oil and cheese occupying another there. Also to the west stood the communal jail, as well as buildings devoted to the sale of footwear and the meat-market. In the middle of the piazza on the north was the site of the former Alodio where, as noted earlier, brassware and communally baked bread had been sold. Around the Peronio was the fruit market. In yet another building to the north and west of the Alodio, Da Nono states that brass and old ironware were sold. On the eastern side, cloth and linen were sold as well as knives.

The arcades of the ground floor of the Palazzo della Ragione housed many different shops, including those of makers of fine cloth, furriers, gold- and silversmiths, and money-changers. Combs, for example, were sold at the eastern end of the building. As for the four staircases: at the one to the northeast (known as the Staircase of the Birds), birds, game, and fish were sold; at the one to the northwest (the Staircase of Vegetables) vegetables, as well as roasted pork and cooked ox feet. The staircase on the southwest was called the Staircase of Wine, while the fourth staircase, known as the Staircase of Iron, took its name from the ironware sold at the nearby Palazzo del Podestà. Around 1277, the government had the official units of measurement, including the *brazzolaro*

46  Distribution of market activities around Padua's Palazzo della Ragione and surrounding
buildings according to Giovanni da Nono. Reproduced from C. Cunningham,
"For the Honour and Beauty of the City: The Design of Town Halls,"
in D. Norman, ed., *Siena, Florence, and Padua*, 1995, vol. II, p. 51 (pl. 60).

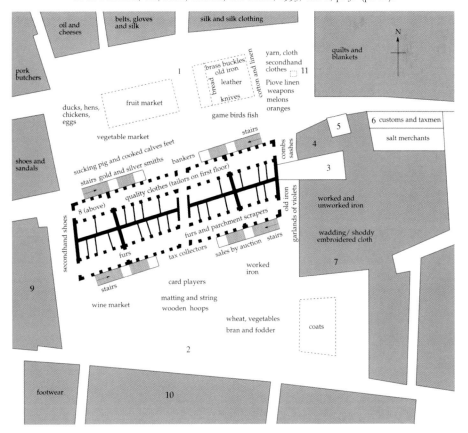

47    Padua, Palazzo della Ragione, standards carved at the
Staircase of the Birds, c. 1277.

or the measure for cloth, carved on a pilaster near the Staircase of the Birds (fig. 47).[40]
In the piazzas around the Palazzo, cereals, dishware and wooden implements, wine,
clogs, used clothing, poultry, eggs, linen, old cloth, and fruit were among the diverse
items on offer.

It is clear from Da Nono's description that it was possible to purchase almost everything that was necessary or desirable for life around Padua's main market square. The
only significant lacuna in the list of commodities and professions mentioned by Da
Nono is a reference to apothecaries or spice dealers. At the same time, there appears
to be no discernible pattern to the way in which goods were organized around the
market center: linen and old cloth were sold next to fish, salami near leather goods,
shoes near the shops selling wine. The one exception concerns the commodities that
were for sale in the arcades directly under the main body of the Palazzo della Ragione
itself. Here members of the most prestigious professions – money-changers, merchants
of high-quality cloth, goldsmiths, and furriers – had their stalls.[41] Their placement here
was surely no accident since it benefited both the merchants themselves and the government. The merchants drew advantage since their shops were secure and well protected; the government could exact higher rents for these locales and gained in prestige
when visitors to the palace saw the quality and luxury of goods for sale under their
rule.[42] Otherwise, there is no indication that the communal authorities sought to
arrange the professions in any particular way.

From the limited evidence available, it appears that the same was true in other cities.
Although Opicino de Canistris's intention was to list the goods available in the Piazza
Atrio, Pavia's main market square, rather than to provide a plan of the market itself,
his enumeration of items for sale considered in Chapter One suggests a hodgepodge.
In Verona, the organization of the market displayed the same apparent randomness as

in Padua: vegetable sellers set up their stalls in front of the money-changers' tables; tailors and poulterers had their stalls near the Domus Mercatorum.[43] The anthropologist Cliffort Geertz's map of the permanent markets held in Sefrou, Morocco in the mid-twentieth century indicates something similar: while the proximity of certain stalls to one another seems logical (vegetable and fruit sellers near butchers, tailors near the market for silk, and saddle-makers and farriers near blacksmiths), others are less obviously connected (tinsmiths proximate to sellers of cooked food, and barbers near sellers of flour, bread, and sweet rolls).[44]

As the boundary marker from the Veronese fairground indicates, governments, under pressure from the guilds, made a concerted effort to keep various sets of merchants and their goods carefully delineated. In 1300 the government of Siena, for example, charged the Justice of the Divieto (the official charged with ensuring that foodstuffs were not exported) and the Executors of the Gabelles with organizing and setting up "distinct and separate places in which the various trades may be exercised in the Campo market [campo fori]."[45] Except for their concern with trades that created a lot of refuse or whose bulky items impeded the flow of traffic, however, there is little to suggest that communal authorities were interested in arranging or rearranging trades to any prescribed pattern. The Florentine guild of bankers (the Cambio) included in its statutes a rule that members were not to set up counters from which fishmongers could sell their goods within six braccia ("arms"; approximately 11½ feet or 350 centimeters) of money-changing tables. Apparently, members of the guild were allowing fishmongers to do so in return, no doubt, for some kind of rent or portion of the profits. But the guild's concern was not that the sale of fish was somehow incongruous with the business of banking (after all, it simply established a minimum distance); rather, the worry was that fish stalls set up any closer would occupy the space of or impede traffic to the tables of neighboring bankers.[46] Otherwise, fishmongers and bankers could happily coexist. And, as the miniaturist who painted the image of the Porta Ravegnana market for the Bolognese drapers' guild understood it, used goods, including portable toilets, could be placed for sale in some proximity to religious tabernacles without causing any consternation.

In the centuries before governments sought to create distinct religious, political, and commercial spaces, market squares were lively, polyvalent spaces, as Antonio Pucci's poem about the Mercato Vecchio suggests. To judge such spaces as simply chaotic is to misapprehend how they were understood by contemporaries. What to today's sensibilities may appear disorderly – the sight of row upon row of merchandise arranged without any plan or logic, the sound of sales being negotiated in local accents and foreign tongues, the fragrant odor of exotic spices mixing with the noxious stench of rotting fruit and vegetables, the hard feel of stone and wood counters and the soft touch of fabrics and ribbons, the sweet taste of honeyed fritters and the acrid and gritty sensation created on the tongue by dust kicked up by passing carts – spoke instead, as the civic laudes make clear, to the wealth, prosperity, and the power of the cities, and to their concern for godliness, abundance, and the bene comune. There was meaning, in other words, in all the seeming disorder.

martius

# PART TWO

---

# BUYING AND SELLING

In his chronicle written in the 1280s, the Franciscan friar Salimbene de Adam of Parma reported an episode from the nearby city of Reggio under the rubric, "Concerning the statute against the fishmongers of Reggio enacted on account of their foolishness." It reads:

> In that same year [1285], it was decreed by the full council of Reggio that fishmongers would not be permitted to sell fish from the beginning of Lent until Easter, under penalty of twenty-five Bolognese pounds, and that no one would be permitted to buy their fish, under penalty of ten Bolognese pounds. And this law was observed scrupulously. The reason for the law was as follows: whenever a knight or judge asked any fishmonger, "For what price will you give me this fish?" he would not deign to answer, even though he was asked two or three times. Far from it, he would look away and say to his partner, "Comrade [*compater*], put the basket away." Thus the passage in Proverbs 29 [verse 19]: "A slave will not be corrected by words: because he understandeth what thou sayest, and will not answer." Furthermore, they were asking three and four grossi for a small tench or eel. When the fishermen and fishmongers, however, saw how strictly the law was being applied and how much

they were hurt by it – for a record of each man's catch was made and the fish were put in a fish-pond until after Easter – they went to the Friars Minor and begged them to request the podestà, the captain, the anziani, and the entire council to relax the law. For their part the fishermen promised that they would sell their fish reasonably, discreetly, and courteously [*curialiter*] to all comers, at a reasonable price [*pro bono mercato*]. But even so, the rule was not relaxed, in keeping with the words of the Apostle about Esau in Hebrews 12 [verse 17]: "For he found no place of repentance, although with tears he has sought it." The citizens of Reggio threatened to treat the butchers in the same way at Easter, unless they too agreed to sell their wares in a courteous and reasonable manner. When they heard this, the butchers behaved in accordance with the words of the Wise Man in Proverbs 19 [verse 25]: "The wicked man being scourged, the fool shall be wiser: but if thou rebuke a wise man he will understand discipline." The man who brought the foolishness of the fishermen to the attention of the council was a judge in Reggio, Lord Gherardo Varolo, who was, in fact, the one who drew up the law. He did what the Wise Man teaches in Proverbs 26 [verse 5]: "Answer a fool according to his folly, lest he imagine himself to be wise."[1]

As reported by Salimbene, it is clear that the marketplace in Reggio had become a battleground between the city's elites (knights and judges) and some portion of the *popolo*, as represented by the fishmongers (fig. 48). The fishmongers knew that during Lent they had power over consumers since the sale of meat was forbidden. Accordingly, using what the anthropologist James Scott described as "weapons of the weak," they harassed the elites by refusing even to answer their queries as to the price of their goods.[2] For their part, the elites struck back with what amounted to a government-sanctioned boycott. All sales of fish during Lent were outlawed, thereby depriving the fishmongers (and fishermen) of the opportunity to sell their wares during their most profitable season. Under economic pressure, the fishmongers appealed for a relaxation of the law by promising to sell their products courteously and at reasonable prices; but the authorities refused to relent. The elites also threatened the butchers, who were soon to enter one of their highly profitable seasons, the period following Lent. Recognizing the threat to their earnings, the butchers wisely, according to Salimbene, also agreed to sell their meat in a friendly and courteous manner.

It is no coincidence that this episode took place during Lent, when fishmongers had consumers over a barrel, nor that it was in the food trades where these tensions surfaced. As noted in Chapter One, civic regimes were assiduous in trying to ensure that their cities were well supplied with food as a way to quell popular unrest. In this instance, the fishmongers used their control of food as a way to hassle the elites.

As this example from Reggio makes abundantly clear, markets could be agonistic spaces and arenas for conflict. And these conflicts were played out on many different levels. First and most fundamentally, they pitted individual buyers against individual sellers. Indeed, the very nature of the medieval Italian marketplace served to increase the potential for conflict since, unlike in the modern marketplace, the vast majority of goods in it were not standardized. Even seemingly similar items, such as manufactured woolen cloth or unprocessed grains, could vary widely in quality and quantity. For this reason, there was, just as Clifford Geertz recognized in the Moroccan suq, an information asymmetry between the buyer and seller: the seller knew the quality of the goods on offer while the buyer did not. The burden of overcoming that imbalance rested on the purchaser, who had to assess for him- or herself the quality of the goods and then make a determination as to how much they were worth and what he or she was willing to pay for them.[3] As will be seen in a later chapter, concern with establishing the fair or just price was a preoccupation of the schoolmen intellectuals of the period.

In his study of the market in a town in north India, the anthropologist Frank Fanselow distinguishes the highly substitutable, standardized goods characteristic of the modern marketplace from non-substitutable, non-standardized goods found in the bazaar (and in the medieval marketplace). In his view, Geertz's information asymmetry logically followed from non-standardization and became "the distinguishing feature of the bazaar."[4] Moreover, that imbalance has "important structural implications for the organization of trade," influencing everything from the operation of the price mechanism, to relations between buyers and sellers, and even "the spatial aggregation of businesses dealing in the same kinds of commodities."[5]

Second, as the conflict involving the fishmongers of Reggio also makes clear, the marketplace was an arena where conflicts between groups were played out. These could take a variety of forms. Sometimes, as in disputes over the allocation of market stalls, they pitted guildsmen against their guildsmen brothers; but they could also involve contests between guilds, especially regarding the right to sell certain wares. Additionally, established guildsmen and shopkeepers with fixed shops constantly struggled with itinerant hawkers, peasants who came to town to sell their products, and others with no fixed establishment. On a broader level, as in the Reggio case, the marketplace was at times the scene of class tensions, especially as various coalitions sought to establish the terms for buying and selling to their own advantage and even to shape market space according to their own vision of the well-organized marketplace.

Finally, the marketplace was an arena of ideological conflict in which those with power sought to frame the policies they favored as fostering the common good, while those who opposed those policies were accused of pursuing their private interests. The perceived conflict between private interest and the common good animated discussion of the marketplace and explains why, as will be shown in Part Three, fraud and right-dealing, trust and mistrust were seen to be the qualities dominating the operation of the marketplace.[6]

The focus in this section shifts, then, to the very purpose of the market, that is, to buying and selling and to the conflicts inherent therein. Chapter Four considers the architecture and arrangement of individual commercial spaces (shops, stalls, and other retail environments), the methods employed by sellers to organize and display their goods, and the disputes that arose as a consequence. Chapter Five examines the often fraught act of buying and selling, a highly choreographed and ritualized activity, in which the goal was to complete a sale by overcoming the mistrust that existed between

buyer and seller. Chapter Six is concerned with efforts to regulate and control the
marketplace. These included such policies as requiring the use of standardized weights
and measures, establishing legitimate hours of operation, appointing overseers, hiring
personnel to keep the marketplace clean, and protecting the public space of the market
from encroachment by private individuals. These issues concerned civic authorities
since poorly regulated markets reflected badly on cities' reputations and could adversely
affect trade. As Salimbene's account of the Reggio fishmongers' actions makes clear,
many of these market concerns encompassed a class dimension, making the marketplace, along with the council hall, a locus in the constant struggle for power and for
the ability to frame policies as serving the common good.

# 4

# Market Infrastructure:
# Streets, Shops and Stalls

On 17 December 1364 the Great Council of Venice considered a petition from a butcher named Zaneto for a *grazia*, or special favor. According to Zaneto, his brother Franceschino had been operating one of the state-owned butcher stalls in Piazza San Marco on behalf of a certain Lucia. But Lucia had died, and rights to the stall had devolved to the commune. In his supplication, Zaneto requested that his brother Franceschino be granted the stall on the grounds that he would maintain it and keep it well stocked. Consulted for their opinion on the matter, the Ufficiali alla Beccaria declared Franceschino worthy of the favor. They went on to state that, in their view, he and Zaneto would continue to keep the stall well furnished with meat (*illam* [*tenebunt*] *bene fulcitam*) and that this would redound to the "great benefit to the commune" (*magnum utile Communis*). Considering all this, the Great Council approved the favor (fig. 49).[1]

This special favor to a Venetian butcher offers further evidence that governmental authorities in medieval Italian cities saw an essential connection between the well-provisioned marketplace and their own security, which they framed as a concern with the *bene comune*. In the view of the Ufficiali alla Beccaria (and the Great Council), a well-supplied butcher stall would be beneficial (*utile*) to the commune of Venice. Certainly, the noblemen who approved this petition understood that utility in a practical sense: consumers coming to the market at Piazza San Marco would find their need and desire for meat satisfied. Yet, their assessment of its usefulness encompassed other considerations as well: shops like this one well supplied with food would help guarantee the contentment (and quiescence) of the disempowered *popolo* of Venice, and would impress visitors to Piazza San Marco – be they pilgrims, foreign merchants, or

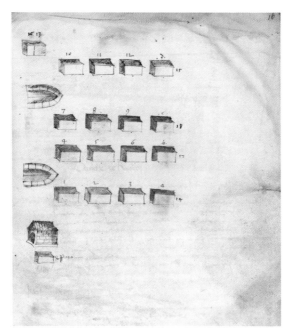

49    Floor plan of the 15th-century Beccaria (meat market)
of San Marco, Venice, Archivio di Stato di Venezia,
Provveditori alle Beccarie, b. 5, reg. 1, fol. 16r.

diplomats – with the wealth and power of the Venetian regime. It also allowed the
Ufficiali an opportunity to exercise patronage. For their part, Zaneto and his brother
Franceschino had a strong economic interest in maintaining their control over one of
the limited number of government-owned butcher stalls in a prime retail location, the
Piazza San Marco. Their success depended, as it did for all merchants, not only on
their ability as salesmen but also on their legal right to space in the marketplace. This
chapter examines the architecture, layout, and distribution of streets, shops, and stalls
and the struggles that developed as vendors sought access to the marketplace.

Generally speaking but with numerous variations and many exceptions, producers
and sellers of the same kinds of wares tended to concentrate in particular areas, such
as streets or sections of the market. This is apparent, for example, in Padua where, as
seen in the previous chapter, the vendors of various kinds of items had prescribed
locations in the marketplace allocated to them. The situation in Padua, although particularly well documented, was not unique. In Venice and many other cities, street
names record for posterity where various groups of merchants or tradesmen were
concentrated. One of the important streets at the Rialto market, for example, was the
Ruga dei Oresi, or Street of the Goldsmiths (fig. 50). And the now destroyed Florentine
Mercato Vecchio included, among others, streets designated the Via degli Spadai for
the sword and cuirass makers whose shops were located there, and the Via degli Speziali
Grossi or Street of the Wholesale Spice Dealers.[2]

Although the designation of particular streets or parts of the market for specific
trades may have originated spontaneously through voluntary action on the part of

50  Giovanni Battista Brustoloni, *Campo San Giacomo di Rialto/Ruga dei Oresi*, 18th century.

vendors – that is, they may simply have begun congregating there – it seems more likely that the impetus to cluster together came from civic and guild authorities who viewed concentration as useful since it facilitated regulation and supervision; and so they made it a requirement. The goldsmiths of Venice, to take just one example, were required to practice their trade on the Ruga dei Oresi, although the government occasionally granted exemptions and eventually had to change the rule because respectable women would not venture to Rialto to shop.[3] At the same time, individual vendors would have seen no particular liability in this practice. In fact, it may even have helped sales, since buyers knew where they needed to go to find particular kinds of goods.

Usually shops were concentrated along a *bina*, or street. As the word (as in "binary") suggests, the shops were placed facing one another along opposite sides of a thoroughfare.[4] This was especially true during trade fairs when temporary stalls were erected. The grouping of shops by guild and along opposite sides of a street or aisle facilitated trade since buyers could easily and expeditiously survey the various shops, comparing quality and prices. As noted in the previous chapter, the grouping of woolen cloth shops in four zones of Florence allowed buyers of cloth, accompanied by brokers, systematically to make their way up and down the streets and visit all of the shops. Such an arrangement of shops also served to set (and perhaps equalize) prices and to discourage fraud since vendors were constantly under the watchful eyes of competitors.[5] A clause in the statutes of the Venetian vair furriers' guild forbade members to sell outside of their *ruga*; in this way, the statute proclaimed, "every man being in the aforesaid street and acting in the way prescribed above, the easier it will be to see that

51    Ambrogio Lorenzetti, *Effects of Good Government in the City*,
detail showing a cloth seller eyeing the competition,
1338–40, Palazzo Pubblico, Siena.

each properly follows the rules or improperly does so."[6] A detail in Lorenzetti's
*Effects of Good Government in the City and Countryside* fresco illustrates this competitive
surveillance or what Giacomo Todeschini has called "a collective enterprise of watchfulness."[7] In the image, a vendor sitting in front of his stack of folded cloth surreptitiously watches and eavesdrops on the transaction taking place at the booth next to
his (fig. 51).

Such arrangements of shops facilitated supervision and inspection by guild and civic
authorities. When attending various markets and fairs, the linen sellers of Verona, for
example, had to have their shops "in the *bina* with the other linen-sellers of this guild"
and were required to follow all of the other guild regulations concerning such matters
as the hour when trading could begin.[8] The same was true for the drapers selling in
the fairs at Piacenza.[9]

These arrangements also served to reduce tension between guilds, especially those
selling similar products. In Venice, rules were put in place demarcating the space in
Piazza San Marco where furriers specializing in vair furs could locate their stalls, and
where furriers specializing in lambskins could locate theirs: the vair furriers were to
occupy that part of the piazza nearest the campanile, the lambskin furriers near the

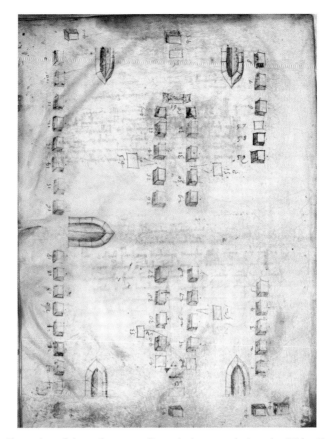

52   Floor plan of the 15th-century Beccaria (meat market) at the Rialto, Venice,
Archivio di Stato di Venezia, Provveditori alle Beccarie, b. 5, reg. 1, fol. 70v.

church of San Geminiano; the Venetian cobblers (*cerdones*) and clog makers were also allotted specific (and separate) spaces in the piazza.[10]

For individual vendors, the particular location of their shops or stalls was a matter of singular importance since certain spots were more advantageous than others, even along the same street or section of the market. The fourteenth-century Florentine merchant writer Paolo da Certaldo knew this when he wrote in his *Libro di buoni costumi* (Book of Good Practices), his book of advice: "Always, if you wish to set up a shop or a warehouse in your own city or in a foreign city, take the house in the best spot in the city or [the best] spot belonging to the guild that you can possibly have . . ."[11] In 1366 the bakers with shops at Venice's Rialto complained that the "darkness" (*obscuritatem*) of their location hindered sales and were assigned instead a new site under the portico of the Beccaria of Rialto (fig. 52).[12]

Given the importance of location, the assignment of stalls was, in most cities, the responsibility of either governmental or guild officials; and in order to guarantee equity and minimize conflicts, many relied on lotteries to make the allocations. In Piacenza, for example, when fairs and markets took place and several guilds wanted space, a lottery first was held to determine which guilds would be assigned which venues within the market or fairground; once that was established, each guild then held its own lottery to assign individual stations for stalls.[13] Also in Piacenza, when money-changers wished to practice their trade at the bishop's market, a lottery was to be organized. According to the rules, each money-changer was to be "quiet and content" with the spot which he drew in the lottery; otherwise he would face a fine of five soldi.[14] The statutes of the Veronese tanners prohibited members from turning in more than one ticket for the lottery of stalls at fairs or from selling, trading, or exchanging the stalls once they had been assigned. Failure to observe these rules would result in a fine and loss of the stall.[15] However, the ironmongers of Verona allowed members to occupy the stalls of their closest neighbors if those neighbors failed to take possession of the stalls that had been allotted to them.[16]

In Bologna, too, some guilds were responsible for assigning stalls at fairs and markets to their members by lot.[17] But this could lead to complaints of favoritism or that the lotteries were rigged. Accordingly, some guilds placed supervision of the lottery in the hands of persons not associated with the guild. The 1256 statutes of the drapers, for instance, stated that two men who were not guild members were to draw the tickets, while the 1293 statutes of the butchers assigned that task to a boy who was not associated with the guild.[18] Boys were sometimes given official roles in lotteries and elections since they were believed to embody purity and innocence and not yet be tainted by the corruptions of adulthood.[19]

As has been seen, in Venice the government owned and controlled most of the market space at Rialto and San Marco. It held periodic auctions in which interested parties bid on the right to these spaces for set periods of time. But this led to its own problems, as when the government complained in 1355 that groups were colluding to control the bidding for various "counters, warehouses, and shops." Several decades earlier, the government had discovered that some vendors, especially the drapers, had been conspiring among themselves to limit the bids in an auction of shops at Rialto.[20] In at least two instances, money-changers in Piazza San Marco resorted to violence when they failed to secure the tables they were after in the governmental auction of stalls.[21]

The Venetian government also used the assignment of publicly owned stalls as a way to reward the loyalty and reduce the hardships of deserving subjects. In 1364, for example, a fishmonger named Ermolino Bono from the fishermen's parish San Nicolò dei Mendicoli was granted for two years the right to use "a wicker basket at Rialto towards the office of the Camerlenghi" from which he could sell fish. The government granted this favor since Ermolino along with two of his brothers, two of his cousins, and two of his nephews had served on the galley of Stefano Contarini in the recent war of Candia. Ermolino had been wounded and his cousins and nephews killed. Additionally, Ermolino noted his great need in that he had a marriageable daughter and another eight years old and that he was "most poor." The Ufficiali sopra Rialto, who concurred with the award, observed that it was a pious act on the part of the government to make this grant, one that was justified by Ermolino's and his brothers' "good deportment" and service in the navy.[22] A year later, in 1365, the government granted the right to sell from a wicker basket to a fishmonger named Zanino, son of the late Checho de Vendramela. Zanino claimed that his father and grandfather before him had had a fixed counter (*bancham*) at Rialto. But his father had died while traveling with the Romania-line merchant galleys, the galleys that traveled to Constantinople and ports on the Black Sea, leaving Zanino to take care of a sister and his mother. In response to Zanino's petition, the Ufficiali sopra Rialto investigated their records and found that indeed his grandfather had been granted a counter by *grazia*, but that his father had retained it without legal authorization. In their view and in light of Zanino's "poverty and youth," they decided that he should be granted "a wicker basket not fixed to the ground" rather than a fixed counter since all the other *grazie* granted to his relatives spoke of wicker baskets rather than counters.[23]

Stalls and shops proved to be an endless source of controversy and bother and prompted a torrent of regulations by guilds and governments. The statutes of the Veronese fishmongers, for example, contained several clauses aimed at solving various problems that had arisen. First, unlike in many places where retail locations were assigned on a monthly or a yearly basis, in Verona the designated locations where fish could be sold were assigned by tickets every day that fish could legally be marketed. It was the duty of the guild officers – the *gastaldus* (warden) and his *fideiussor* (bailiff) – to make these assignments, although it is unclear whether this was done by lottery, rotation, or some other method. But it appears that guild members were often unhappy with the posts they were assigned, since the guild's statutes stated that they had to be "content" with their assignments and sell from those posts; otherwise they were subject to a ten-soldi fine. Any fishmonger who mislaid the ticket he was given was subject to a five-soldi fine; the same penalty was to be levied on anyone who forged a ticket. Judging by a clause written into the statutes, fishmongers sometimes tried to prevent their fellow fishmongers from taking up the spots they had been assigned, while others left their counters fouled and dirty. Additionally, the statutes warned that any fishmonger who stood outside his stall or counter for the purpose of selling fish was to be fined twenty soldi for every infraction.[24]

Vendors also disputed the boundaries between stalls. In Florence a clause in the statutes of the oil and cheese sellers warned against "bad neighborliness" (*malam vicinanciam*) among members with contiguous shops, particularly cautioning them against occupying neighboring shops. Evidently, shopkeepers were encroaching on the space of those next to them. In an effort to minimize such conflicts, the same clause allowed members to place boards as boundary markers between their shops and those of their neighbors without penalty.[25]

Much more common, though, were rules seeking to establish uniform dimensions for shops and counters. In Treviso, for example, the communal statutes dating from the 1280s stated that all counters from which fish and crabs were sold in the communal market had to be precisely the same length and height, while a rule from Piacenza required all stalls at fairs to be 7 *braccia* (212 centimeters) in length and no more; in Florence the butcher's counters (*dischi*) were to be 3 *braccia* in length and 1½ in width (1 *braccio* was nearly 2 feet or 58.4 centimeters).[26] Sellers were constantly trying to expand their space (and thereby attract more customers) by extending their shops into the streets. The 1296 statutes of the podestà of Pistoia prohibited anyone in the "old city" from extending a counter beyond the walls or columns of his house by more than a foot (approximately 32 centimeters).[27] Members of the Florentine guild of Por Santa Maria were similarly prohibited from expanding their shops into the market space by more than a foot or displaying goods outside their shops.[28]

Two concerns prompted these rules. First, from the point of view of the guilds, vendors who increased their sales space gained an unfair advantage over their fellow guildsmen. Such prohibitions thus sought to preserve the equality of guild members. Second, for the civic authorities, such extensions represented an encroachment onto public land and hence a challenge to civic authority. In Pistoia, the podestà ordered the money-changers who had counters around the door of the communal palace to clear a space so that those wishing to access the stairs of the palace could easily make their way between the counters. In this case, the concern was clearly with traffic.[29] However, in another clause from the same statutes, the civic authorities complained about the awnings (tende) that cloth merchants and indeed other merchants were hanging in front of their shops in the marketplace and around the communal piazza. These awnings were not, as in "other cities," flush with the doors of the shops but instead extended beyond the doors and were suspended "under supports" (sub taulitiis). In the view of the authorities, they were "ugly and unattractive" (turpe et indecens) and impeded the way. To make matters even worse, they left a bad impression on foreigners and ambassadors coming to Pistoia, since when they were making their way "under these supports" they got hit in the face by the awnings. In this case, the shopkeepers' encroachment into public space impeded traffic, marred the city's beauty, and even threatened its foreign relations.[30]

Stalls and shops were the subject of still other kinds of abuses. In some instances, shopkeepers sought to take over more than one shop; this was expressly prohibited in Pistoia, where a vendor could only have one "counter" (banchus) in the marketplace.[31] The opposite problem worried the Florentine authorities. They prohibited any company (societas) of men from selling salted fish from a single stall; instead, each counter (disco) or bench had to be operated by a single vendor only. In this case the authorities were motivated by the desire to prevent "monopolies" (monopolia) or agreements among the vendors that would artificially affect the price, quality, and quantity of salted fish available in the market. The officials in charge of abundance were authorized to make inquiries both openly and secretly to see that this rule was being observed.[32]

In still other instances, vendors procured the rights to shops and stalls and then sublet them to others. The statutes of the Bolognese butchers contained several prohibitions against this sort of abuse.[33] In Venice, however, the authorities on occasion granted concessions allowing shopkeepers to take on associates in order to help run their establishments. In 1368, for example, the Great Council approved a grazia allowing Donato Aguia, a retailer (compravendi) who was too infirm to carry out his trade, to take on someone to run his shop. Two years earlier the council had made a similar concession to the dyer Pietro who likewise was too debilitated to run his dye-shop at

Rialto. The Giustizieri Vecchi endorsed Pietro's petition on the grounds that he had to support not only his own family but also that of his deceased brother.[34]

All in all, the distribution of shops and stalls in marketplaces and fairs created endless problems as vendors sought to gain advantage over their competitors by expanding their shop space. For their part, guild authorities tried to ensure basic equality and equal access to the market among their members, while civic officials sought to protect public space against encroachment and to promote the smooth operation of the market in general.

The actual construction or composition of trading spaces varied widely, from permanent stone or brick shops built into the fabric of other buildings, to temporary wooden stalls set up for the duration of fairs or assembled and disassembled on market days, to simple crates and wicker baskets from which sellers hawked their wares.[35] Much of the information about medieval shops derives from images found in paintings and manuscripts and from archeological evidence.[36]

The most substantial retail spaces were those shops built into the ground floor of other buildings. As a way to generate income from rent and promote trade, communal authorities often built fixed shops into their governmental palaces. This was especially true in the cities of the Po valley where communes adopted the Ottonian imperial palace hall for their communal palaces. The palace hall type consisted of a two-story oblong building, with a ground floor that was often divided into smaller rooms and an upper story comprising one great hall. As Jürgen Paul, who examined medieval Italian town halls, observed, when the communes built their governmental palaces, they modified the imperial type by opening up the ground floor to accommodate a loggia or arcade. This ground floor loggia, "served as a covered market hall and housed all institutions essential for commercial life – control boards, judges, money changers,

53   Verona, Domus Mercatorum, 1301.

54    Padua, shops on the ground floor of the Palazzo della Ragione, 20th century.

notaries, appraisers, the public scales and standards office."[37] There were many local variations, but Milan's Broletto Nuovo, Piacenza's Palazzo Gotico, Padua's Palazzo della Ragione, and Verona's Domus Mercatorum are all examples (fig. 53). In Milan, as noted earlier, the grain market was conducted under the vaults of the Broletto Nuovo, while in Bologna linen was sold at the staircase or under the portico of the communal palace. For a time at the beginning of the fourteenth century there were butcher shops at the communal palace of Bologna as well.[38] The commune of Treviso, which controlled the town of Castelfranco, required that shops be built in Castelfranco "under the palace of the comune of Treviso" (*sub domo comunis Tervisii*) and that the income generated from them be forwarded to Treviso.[39]

This style of communal palace was less common in central Italy. The Palazzo Pubblico of Siena included no commercial space on the side facing the Campo (although there was some built into the supporting structure at the rear); the Palazzo della Signoria of Florence included none at all and was, as Paul noted, intentionally built "far from the Mercato Vecchio."[40] But generalizations based on geography are risky since exceptions can be found. In Pistoia, for example, the commune built eleven shops into the walls of the Palazzo del Podestà. In 1382 these were being rented to, among others, used-goods dealers, money-changers, a silk manufacturer, a surveyor, and two notaries.[41] And even though the bishop of Pistoia had lost jurisdiction over the market, he too continued to profit from it. The addition to the episcopal palace, in the fourteenth century, of a first-floor loggia facing the piazza created space for several counters (*banchi*) and shops (*botteghe*). In 1411, these were being rented to, among others, a silk manufacturer, two mercers, and a cobbler.[42] In Assisi, there were shops on the ground

55 Anonymous, *Cheese-Monger*, from the *Tacuinum sanitatis*, Verona, late 14th century,
Österreichische Nationalbibliotek, Vienna, Codex, s.n. 2644, fol. 60v.

floor of both the Palazzo del Capitano and the Palazzo dei Priori.[43] And in Orvieto,
butchers had shops at the communal palace.[44]

As for the shops themselves, those on the ground floor of Padua's Palazzo della
Ragione are fairly typical (fig. 54). Such shops usually consisted of a square or rectangular space with an entryway at the front; they might be vaulted or not (fig. 55).
They were often poorly lit since usually there was only once source of natural
light – that coming from the street – although there might be a small window or
grate or even a smaller subsidiary door in the back of the shop if a passage- or alley-
way ran along the back.

Space within shops was extremely cramped. The plan for the shops on Florence's Ponte Vecchio which were built sometime after 1345, for example, called for them to be 8 *braccia* square (approximately 15 feet, 4 inches or 4.6 meters square).[45] But spaciousness was not a major concern since in most cases it would have been unusual for the customer to step behind the counter and enter the shop proper. The exception was for shops such as those of the Florentine textile industry: the statutes of Por Santa Maria stated that when tailors took customers on tours of the shops, they should "enter and circulate" but that was clearly not the case for the Bolognese drapers, at least not according to the depiction of the Porta Ravegnana market (see fig. 13).[46] In most establishments, customers would have stood outside and spied goods displayed on the counter, hanging on hooks above it, or arranged on shelves attached to the walls of the shop.

Contemporaries used a variety of terms to describe the counter, including *bancum*, *dischum*, and *tabula*. It constituted the most important element of any retail space since it was where buyer and seller literally came face to face, with the goods strategically placed between them, and across which the negotiations of the transaction proceeded, as in a carving from c. 1160–70, a capital in Modena showing the three Maries purchasing spices with which to anoint Jesus's body. The spice merchant places his right hand protectively on his stock while with his left he weighs the purchase (fig. 56). For their part, the Maries keep their eyes firmly fixed on the proceedings. Given how important counters were, it is understandable that vendors were constantly seeking to extend them farther and farther into the streets in front of their shops, and that the civic authorities were constantly on guard against such encroachments into public space.

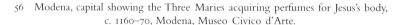

56   Modena, capital showing the Three Maries acquiring perfumes for Jesus's body,
c. 1160–70, Modena, Museo Civico d'Arte.

57    Pistoia, medieval shops on Via di Stracceria.

58    Bologna, modern-day shops with fold-down counters.

Some counters were built directly into the fabric of the building, as some of the shops on and adjacent to Pistoia's Piazza della Sala illustrate (fig. 57). Stone counters (*lapides*) also suited certain types of goods, such as fish, since their relatively nonporous surfaces made them easier to wash and clean than wood.[47] In other cases, as in the present-day shops around the base of the Garisenda and Asinelli towers of Bologna and on Florence's Ponte Vecchio, the counters were made of wood and were attached with hinges; they were folded down when the shops were open for business and then folded up and locked when they were not (fig. 58).

Given the limited space in shops (and perhaps for reasons of security), merchants often stored their stock elsewhere, in underground storage rooms, vaults, and other warehouse spaces. The vendor would fetch this stock as needed. In Venice, for example, the brother cheese-mongers Andreolo, Pietro, Checho, and Lio Rosso maintained a shop in the cheese market at Rialto, but stored cheese, oil, salami, and other items in a storage space located on the nearby Ruga dei Oresi. All of it was destroyed in 1364 when a fire broke out on the *ruga*; the brothers estimated their loss at 400 ducats or more.[48] Storing goods off premises may also have suited vendors since they could first try to unload inferior merchandise, unless pressed by discerning buyers for better ones, and could conceal the quantity and value of their stock from both competitors and civil authorities to whom it might be subject to various imposts and surcharges.[49] Some towns and major guilds maintained *fondachi* or warehouses that combined both storage and selling space, and in some instances living quarters for visiting merchants. The best

59   Venice, Fondaco dei Tedeschi, labeled "Fontico dalamani,"
detail from Jacopo de' Barbari, *Woodcut Map of Venice*, 1500.

known is the Fondaco dei Tedeschi, or German merchants' warehouse, in Venice. Sales within the Fondaco were almost exclusively of a wholesale nature and were mediated by brokers, who were appointed by the government and spoke German (fig. 59).[50]

Few of the permanent shops and stalls arranged around the urban market squares appear to have had names, marked by shop signs affixed to them.[51] In Florence every baker and seller of bread was supposed to display in front of his establishment a panel with the fleur-de-lys, the city's symbol, painted on it. But such panels did not serve to identify particular shops; instead they simply let passersby know that bread was available at that location and that it was expected to meet official standards.[52] Also in Florence it appears that a blue cloth identified the shops of Jewish pawnbrokers while red cloths identified shops run by Christians.[53] In this case as well, the purpose of these markers was not to identify particular bankers but, rather, to let potential custom-ers know whether or not they would be dealing with their co-religionists – another indication of the moral calculation that went into market transactions. Certainly, some establishments, especially taverns and hostels, were identified by particular names, but in most market squares, customers would have simply identified the stalls they were trying to locate by the seeking out the shopkeepers themselves.[54] Shop signs may have become more common in the Renaissance as consumer demand grew, the range of items available for consumption multiplied, and as markets were displaced from the political and ecclesiastical centers of town.[55]

While the most substantial shops were the ones permanently built into the fabric of other buildings, many vendors operated out of temporary and movable structures

60    Gabriele Bella, *The Sensa Fair in Piazza San Marco*, second half of the 18th century, Fondazione Querini Stampalia, Venice.

that were assembled and disassembled on a regular basis. Usually, as in the case of Siena's Campo, vendors were required to remove these fixtures every evening. As Maurizio Tuliani notes, this forced removal protected against any "pretense" to a legal claim to public land.[56] The temporary booths set up for fairs were allowed to stand for the duration of the event but were closed, guarded, and sometimes even lit at night.[57] Judging by images of such fairs created during the Renaissance and even later, it appears that some effort was made to replicate in wood the appearance of streets of shops, as one would find in the city centers themselves. This is certainly what one sees in Gabriele Bella's eighteenth-century image of the Sensa fair in Venice (fig. 60).

Unlike the fixed shops in buildings made of brick or stone, the structures assembled for daily or weekly markets were fashioned from lumber and consisted of little more than wide wooden planks placed atop sawhorses (as seen in the foreground of the image of Bologna's Porta Ravegnana market [see fig. 13] and in a detail in Giotto's image of Justice in the Scrovegni Chapel in Padua) or lean-to structures. The more elaborate ones had canvas awnings secured by ropes, which protected both vendors and their goods from the elements. They were affixed to poles stuck in the ground or anchored into stone bases.

A good deal of selling, especially of foodstuffs, required nothing more than a wicker basket or wooden crate on which the items could be displayed and behind which the vendor sat or knelt. As examined earlier, the Venetian fishmonger Zanino was granted the right to sell from a basket "not fixed to the ground," although his father had, apparently without authorization, retained control over one of the fixed fishmongers'

61    Ambrogio Lorenzetti, *Effects of Good Government in the City*, detail showing peasant woman vendors, 1338–40, Palazzo Pubblico, Siena.

counters. In Lorenzetti's *Effects of Good Government in the City*, a woman is seen coming into town with a basket balanced on her head (fig. 61 and see fig. 22). Like the other peasant men and women who came to market regularly to sell agricultural products, all this woman would have had to do was find a spot to situate herself and begin hawking her goods, much like the "vù comprà" (immigrant sellers) whom one sees in Italy today. As will be seen later, these itinerants were a constant source of irritation to guild and governmental officials and were subject to much regulation and control.

There were distinct hierarchies among vendors based in no small measure on the permanence or impermanence of their stalls. More will be said about this in Chapter Six in the consideration of rents paid for the privilege of selling in Siena's Campo. At the same time, it is clear that it was considered perfectly acceptable to display wares on the ground. Again, in the image of the Porta Ravegnana market, the seller of used items has simply arranged many of his goods around the tabernacle that marks the intersection (see fig. 13). Finally, itinerant vendors and hawkers did not confine themselves to the market squares but wandered about the cities selling their goods. They carried these objects in baskets, on poles, or even on their person. The statutes of the Bolognese drapers specifically forbade those who sold cloth "off their backs" from entering the drapers' *bina* during fairs.[58]

Given that customers were not usually expected to go behind the counter, the task of attracting buyers depended in large measure on the way goods were displayed to passersby. As noted earlier, the visual evidence suggests that shopkeepers arranged

62   Maestro della Madonna della Misericordia (formerly attributed to Taddeo Gaddi),
*Saint Eligius as Goldsmith*, c. 1370, Madrid, Museo del Prado.

objects on shelves behind the counters, hung them from rafters, beams, and on hooks, set them on the counters, and, where allowed, placed them on crates and boxes in front of their shops. In a scene from the *Storia di Sant'Eligio*, the patron saint of goldsmiths (attributed to the Maestro della Madonna della Misericordia), gold chains of various sorts hang safely attached to the support beam over the head of the saint and his assistants (fig. 62). In Venice, due to the danger of fire, glassmaking had been confined since the late thirteenth century to the island of Murano. But a Muranese glassmaker named Martino for years in the mid-fourteenth century maintained a stall at Rialto which he kept, according to the records, "almost as a display of glasswork" (*quasi pro una monstra laboreria vitrea*).[59]

These *mostre* or displays too were the subject of regulation by both guilds and governments. Civic authorities actually required some forms of display. In Florence, for example, butchers selling buffalo meat had to display the heads of the animals on their counters as a way of signaling to customers what kind of meat it was. Similarly, in order to protect consumers, Florentine butchers were prohibited from displaying the heads of any kinds of animals whose meat they did *not* have for sale.[60] In Siena, bakers were required to produce bread abundantly and display it openly on their window sills in baskets; the bread was to be covered with a napkin or other type of cloth. According to the authorities, these requirements would guarantee plenty (*ubertas*) to both citizens and foreigners.[61]

63   Anonymous, *Seller of Dried Meat*, from the *Tacuinum sanitatis*, French, 15th century,
Paris, Bibliothèque Nationale, Ms. Lat. 1673, fol. 39.

In most instances, however, vendors of their own volition created displays as a way
to attract customers and increase sales. Guilds sometimes regulated these displays in
order to guarantee a degree of equality among members. The drapers and linen sellers
of Bologna, for example, limited the number of cloths that their guild members could
display to two.[62] (This is not, however, what one sees in the image of the Porta

64   Matteo di Ser Cambio, *Calling of Saint Matthew*, 1377, Perugia,
Archivio del Collegio del Cambio, Ms. 1, fol. 27r.

Ravegnana market from their matriculation book – another indication that the artist
wished to convey an impression of abundance.) Other officials were more concerned
with encroachments on public land and with allowing traffic to flow unimpeded. The
statutes of the merchants of Piacenza of 1321 prohibited merchants subject to their
jurisdiction from attaching objects in such a way that the goods hung in front of their

counters and so blocked the street or caused annoyance to their neighbors. And additions to the Piacentine statutes dated 1326 contained a clause forbidding used-article dealers from hanging from their establishments any baskets or crates that impeded traffic in the Piazza del Borgo.[63] The statutes of Por Santa Maria likewise prohibited members from displaying objects anywhere except within the confines of their shops or on the counters.[64]

Most shops were furnished only with the most basic implements needed to transact business. In the typical fixed shop, these would have included plain wooden shelves for displaying merchandise along with such objects as a strongbox for money, a ladder for fetching stock from upper shelves, a desk and bench for recording transactions in account books, pens and ink, candles and lanterns, and scales and/or measuring sticks (fig. 63). Other equipment would have depended on the particular kind of merchandise in which the vendor specialized: for example, scissors and snips, needles and thread for tailors; knives and cleavers for butchers; jars and mortars and pestles for apothecaries. The wool shop on Florence's Via Calimala (which also gave onto Piazza Orsanmichele), opened by Francesco del Bene and Company in 1319, was simply furnished, although it included a mattress and linens since a shop-boy was required by the Calimala guild to sleep in the shop at night.[65] In certain high-end trades such as money-changing, an important piece of shop equipment was the carpet that was laid over the counter and that served, according to Richard Goldthwaite, as the "public sign of the moneychanger."[66] The statutes of the Bolognese money-changers required them to furnish their shops with "a carpet [*tapetum*] of woolen cloth or similar fabric." Such a cloth is visible in an image of the calling of Saint Matthew in a manuscript of the Perugian money-changers' guild: a decorated carpet with a fringe is draped over the entire carved stone counter (fig. 64). There also seems to be a smaller, solid-dark cloth or tray on top of the larger cloth; it may well be a counting board, a device used to tally amounts. The darkness and solidity of the color would have facilitated the counting of shiny coins and helped to guarantee that all were safely gathered up when transactions were complete.[67] But even in these special cases, the furnishings of shops were surprisingly spare.

The evidence for the construction, layout, and infrastructure of commercial establishments indicates that most shops were extremely modest affairs. Location counted for much more than either size or the refinement of furnishings, since it was the frontage of shops on public streets or piazzas that attracted customers. For this reason, shopkeepers constantly sought to increase their visibility and attract customers by extending their shops beyond the legal limits and by mounting displays of their goods which encroached on public land. The counter was a liminal space between the private confines of the shop and public space, as well as between buyer and seller. Across the counter, goods changed ownership. Successfully completing sales often involved elaborate negotiations that resembled nothing so much as a dance between partners. And the choreography of that dance, as will be seen in the next chapter, constituted the essential activity of the marketplace.

# 5

# THE CHOREOGRAPHY

# OF BUYING AND SELLING

In a fourteenth-century manuscript of Accursius's *Ordinary Gloss of Justinian's Digest*, the anonymous Bolognese illuminator known as the Master of 1328 has depicted a market scene (fig. 65).[1] In it, four separate transactions are taking place: money is being changed, wine poured, ironware weighed, and a horse traded. Two of the four take place on carved stone counters that are raised one step off the street. All of the sales occur in front of a fantastical building or complex of buildings that includes two open loggias with upper-story rooms on both ends, two large arches with pediments that connect the loggias to the central building, which consists of projecting balconies with additional covered stories above, and a central tower with a niche and a tabernacle-like story on top. This tower breaks through the imaginary frame of the picture and divides the two columns of text at the top of the page. The image includes sixteen male figures at the street level, some engaged directly in transactions, others acting as witnesses to them. And two figures (a man and a woman) survey the entire marketplace from the vantage point of the rooms above the loggias, while an angel hovers in the niche. The illuminator selected this scene to illustrate the beginning of Book Twelve of the *Digest*, which commences with a discussion of credit and loans; that context certainly helped determine the illuminator's choice of subject matter. This is not, however, the depiction of an actual market, as is the case in the image of the Porta Ravegnana market of Bologna (see fig. 13). Nevertheless, the miniaturist included such architectural elements as loggias, a tower, and built-in counters to indicate this as a market square. Just as importantly, he managed to capture several of the steps in virtually every commercial transaction, namely negotiating terms, weighing and transferring goods, and settling accounts.

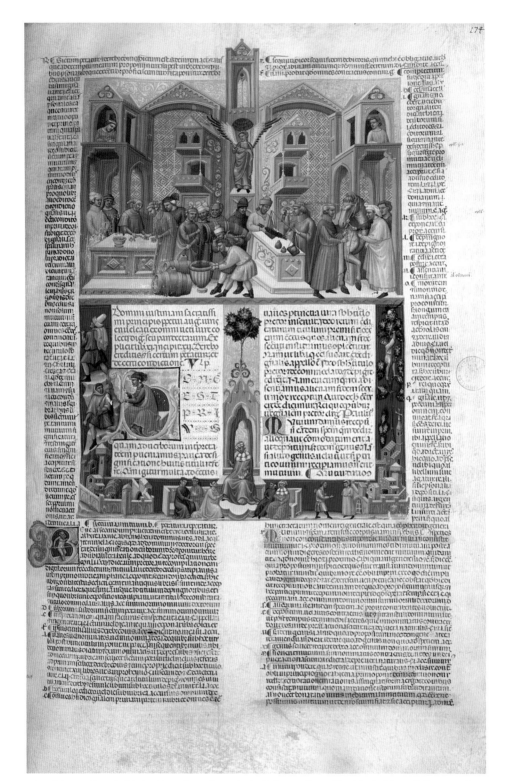

65   Master of 1328, *Market Scene*, from Accursius's *Ordinary Gloss of Justinian's Digest*, Bolognese, first
half 14th century, Turin, Biblioteca Nazionale Universitaria di Torino, Ms. E I.1, fol. 174r.

In medieval Italy, as elsewhere, the acts of buying and selling were governed by a set of unspoken rules that informed and shaped the behavior of the parties involved. Like prayer and other commonplace behaviors, they were highly ritualized activities requiring those engaged in them to know and perform certain predetermined roles and to act out prescribed behaviors. Any significant deviation from those roles and behaviors could disrupt the exchange. Judging by the evidence found in statutes and other sources, the stages of the typical transaction included approach, inspection, negotiation, agreement on terms, measurement, and exchange. However, there could be endless variations. Philippe Braunstein has analyzed the sample dialogues of sales included in a Venetian–German dictionary/grammar book that was composed in 1424 by Maestro Zorzi da Norimburgo, a Venetian of German origin, in order to instruct Venetians, especially those wishing to work as brokers at the Fondaco dei Tedeschi, in the German language (see fig. 59). Braunstein divides these imaginary conversations into nine steps: salutations, invitations, exchange of courtesies, proposals, counterproposals, negotiation, feigned anger, appeasement, agreement, and settlement of accounts.[2] Of course, most transactions concluded in the Fondaco dei Tedeschi were wholesale sales and hence required more time and effort than simple retail sales of such items as food that were carried out during weekly or daily markets. Nevertheless in all transactions, both parties, but especially the buyer, had to draw on as many of the five senses as possible in order to assess the goods on offer. And each ritualized stage of the transaction contained potential pitfalls that could delay or even undermine the deal. Trading truly was an art.

The first step in any transaction was the approach. It has already been seen how sellers used visual stimuli to attract customers by creating tantalizing displays of their goods. Vocal cues were important as well. Vendors called out to customers, extolling the quality of their goods and enticing them to inspect their wares.[3] These attempts to hawk their goods and lure customers to their shops were the subject of rules and regulations in cities across the peninsula. The temptation for many vendors was to stand in front of their stalls and nab passing shoppers. But in Verona butchers and fishmongers were expressly prohibited from standing in front of their shops for the purpose of selling; infractions incurred a fine of 20 soldi. And during fairs in Piacenza, all vendors were warned to remain behind their counters.[4] Florentine butchers were forbidden altogether from calling out what they were selling.[5]

Even more problematic was the vendors' habit of trying to lure in customers when they were still at the stalls of competitors. In some cases there were strict rules about when it was permissible to call out to potential customers. The statutes of the Bolognese butchers' and cheese-mongers' guilds contained clauses that forbade members to call buyers who were at the stands of their competitors until they had moved away from those stands.[6] The statutes of the butchers of Viterbo prohibited the same.[7] And in Bologna and Verona, rules forbade the furriers and ironmongers respectively from calling out to customers unless they were directly in front of their shops.[8] In Florence, belt-makers could speak to customers or signal to them only when they were in the street or piazza in front of their shops and only in that half of the street closest to their shops.[9] Similarly, the members of the guild of Por Santa Maria could try to lure potential customers only if they were directly in front of their shops and in the part of the street between the gutter and their shops.[10] The statutes of the Mercanzia of Perugia allowed merchants to inquire of customers who had exited the shops of competitors and who were in the street or piazza, "What do you desire?" (*quod vis?*), but only as long as the merchants making the inquiries remained inside their own shops.[11] Furthermore, there is some evidence of enforcement of such rules. In 1322 the Florentine firm Francesco del Bene and Company had to pay a fine to the treasurer of the Calimala guild when members of the firm were found to have called out to potential buyers.[12]

Worse still was criticism of a competitor or the claim that a customer had gotten a bad deal in another's shop. In Verona, both the linen scutchers (beaters) and sellers were prohibited from criticizing deals that had already been sealed. The statutes of the beaters forbade them from saying to a customer, "You made a bad deal, I will make you a better one" (*tu fecisti malum mercatum, ego facerem melius forum*).[13] And the linen sellers were prohibited from saying in criticism of others' merchandise, "I will give you good [that is, better cloth]" (*ego dabo vobis bonum*).[14]

Once the initial contact had been made, the parties exchanged pleasantries. In one of Zorzi da Norimburgo's sample dialogues the conversation involves Bartolamio, the son of a Venetian cloth seller, and an unnamed German merchant.[15] They begin with phrases such as "It's been a long time since I've seen you" and "How are things in Germany?" (239). With the niceties out of the way, the most important part of the transaction, namely the inspection of the goods, could begin. At this stage the potential buyer had to overcome the imbalance in information characteristic of the market in non-standardized goods – that is, he had to examine the goods and make as informed a decision as possible about their quality and value. The owner, by contrast, had an interest in hiding any defects in his products and in showing them in the best possible light in the hope of securing the highest possible price.

It was this stage of the process that the Master of 1328 captured in another miniature in the same manuscript of Accursius's gloss on the *Digest*. The image appears at the beginning of the Book 18 of the *Digest*, which concerns contracts of purchase, and it depicts the sale of a horse (fig. 66). The potential buyer and his assistant or servant are seeking information; the buyer is trying to determine the age of the horse by examining its teeth while his helper is feeling the horse's left foreleg for possible defects such as lameness. The seller, who stands somewhat defensively behind the steed, tries to steady it to show it to best effect. Five witnesses follow the inspection, and the entire scene takes place in an undefined space meant perhaps to suggest a cattle or livestock market that is distinguished only by a column. As noted before, horse and other livestock sales usually took place in open spaces on the periphery of cities, so the absence of an architectural backdrop is appropriate, although, as also noted in Chapter One, columns often served as defining elements of marketplaces (see fig. 21).

A discerning customer knew to ask questions. The fourteenth-century statutes of the city of Rome required butchers, if asked, to tell honestly (*fideliter*) the kind of

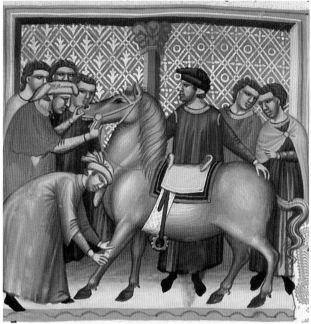

66a and b    Master of 1328, *Sale of a Horse*, from Accursius's *Ordinary Gloss of Justinian's Digest*,
Bolognese, first half 14th century, Turin, Biblioteca Nazionale Universitaria di Torino,
Ms. E I.1, fol. 242v.

meat they had on offer.[16] In Venice, by contrast, the guild of furriers of vair skins
required members, even when not asked, to tell potential customers about the type of
pelts used in their wares.[17] In addition to asking questions as a way of garnering
information, the astute customer inspected the goods carefully by marshaling as many
of his senses as possible. Merchants' manuals offer evidence of this. The fourteenth-
century *Zibaldone da Canal*, a merchant manual composed in Venetian dialect, includes
a chapter entitled "These are the characteristics of spices and how to recognize them
as each is written singly below." Among the entries are the following, which relate
respectively to sound, touch, sight, smell, and taste:

> Also, the reeds of cassia ought to be whole and big and heavy, and they should
> not make a sound when a man shakes them...
> Also, the characteristics of ginger are that it should appear long, and that it not
> be rough ...
> Also, the characteristics of cloves are that they ought to be black and red within,
> tending more toward black ...
> Also, the characteristics of galangal: it ought to be a large, firm root ... and there
> should be nothing gamey about it. Gaminess [is acceptable] if it is ... slight, and no
> one can detect any sharp odor ...
> Also, the characteristics of cinnamon are these: it ought to be reddish color, and
> it ought to be light and strong to the taste, and the good kind is a little sweet ...[18]

It is not difficult to imagine the conscientious customer running his fingers over furs and woolen cloth to detect their thickness and quality; smelling fish and meat for freshness; holding up rock crystal, amber, and precious stones to the light to search for imperfections, striking swords, hammers, and other metal tools and listening for the ring, and tasting spices, wines, and other foodstuffs. Sight was by far the most important of the senses; and people seem to have been especially alert to color. The *Zibaldone da Canal*'s description of spices alone includes the following hues: white, gray, black, shiny pitch black, blackish, red, brilliant red, bright red, reddish brown, reddish yellow, yellowish, gold, and violet.[19] In Padua, cloth merchants were required to carry their cloth to the entrance of their shops so that customers could examine it in the light.[20]

However, some guilds and merchants' associations dealing in textiles discouraged side by side comparisons of the goods of different vendors. In Florence, for example, in a reform of the statutes completed in 1411, the retail cloth dealers of Por Santa Maria were forbidden to "compare" (*paragonare*) different items of merchandise one with another, except when the pieces belonged to the same merchant. Otherwise the offending merchant faced a fine of five *lire di piccoli*; in 1418 the guild increased the fine to 25 *lire di piccoli*.[21] The early fourteenth-century statutes of the merchants of Rome prohibited merchants from showing cloth to customers except in their shops or in their stalls at the marketplace. They were also forbidden to take cloth out of their shops to show to potential customers, although exceptions were made for the pope, cardinals, senators, and certain nobles. But another clause in the statutes stated that even when merchants took their cloth to such dignitaries for demonstration, any direct comparison between the merchandise of different merchants was forbidden. Once a merchant had shown his stock, he was required to gather it up and retie it before the next merchant could show his, so that "by no means can one cloth be seen near to another."[22] The motivation for these rules seems to have been to preserve guild solidarity (and price stability) by offering members a chance to show their goods to best effect. This also seems to have been the motive behind the requirement of the Florentine Lana guild that cloth traders visit all shops of members, and of Por Santa Maria that tailors take their clients to all shops belonging to the guild. Guilds wanted customers to examine the goods of all guild members but not to make direct comparisons between them.[23]

During the examination of goods, the seller cooperated as little or as much as possible, depending on his confidence in the quality of his merchandise or in his skill as a salesman. If he was certain of the quality of his goods (or even if he was trying to pass off inferior goods), he showed them off with pride. In the sample dialogue in the Venetian shop, after Bartolamio says that he has the best merchandise in the city (*No ve loio ditto eho el mior che sia in questa terra*; 240), the German buyer tries to dampen his enthusiasm (and lower the asking price) by exclaiming: "you really know how to praise your stock" (*Tu sa ben loldar la to roba*; 240). To this Bartolamio responds: "And I praise it with truth, as God knows, as does his mother" (*Ela lolda Cola Veritade / Questo sa ben dio / El sa anche so mare*; 241).

67 Workshop of Boccardino il Vecchio, *Bartering/Bargaining*, from Filippo Calandri, *Trattato di Aritmetica*, late 15th century, Florence, Biblioteca Ricciardiana, Ms. Ricc. 2669, fol. 66r.

As the inspection progressed, the process of negotiating a price began (fig. 67). This involved offers and counter-offers. In the Venetian dialogue the potential buyer finally asks, "how much do you want per piece [of cloth]" (*Per quanto me vuostu dar per peza*), to which Bartolamio responds, "Do you want me to tell you in a word or in a hundred words?" (*Voliuui che vel digo in una parola o czento*; 241). Bartolamio tells him that the price is 4½ ducats per piece of fustian, to which the German replies, "I can get it from others for less" (*Ello posso ben aver in altru per meno*). Bartolamio retorts, "I'd be pleased [surprised] if it is as good as this" (*El me piase sele chossi bon como questo*; 241). Prices are floated and rejected. In the dialogue, negotiations break off, only to resume another day with the assistance of a broker. At one point an exasperated Bartolamio exclaims to the broker, "he [the German buyer] never knows how to deal with me except as if in battle" (*El no sa mai far marcha chom mi seno chom bataia*; 246). But eventually the parties agree on a price of 4¼ ducats per piece.[24]

For some items, such as bread, the civic authorities set the price. In those cases, it was simply a question of the buyer selecting particular items for purchase. In Florence, customers were not allowed to touch the bread that bakers had for sale. Instead, bakers had to keep a stick in their shops which they handed to customers so that they could point to the loaves they wanted saying, "I want this one and this one" (*hunc et hunc volo*).[25]

Once the parties agreed on a price, the next step was the weighing or measuring of the items to be exchanged.[26] This was another critical stage since at this point the seller could potentially add to his profit by giving short measure.[27] In the dialogue, the German buyer supervises the weighing of the cotton (certain products could be sold by weight rather than length) he has bought with great care, and even asks for a "zonta" or bonus amount, the equivalent of today's baker's dozen (250–51), which Bartolamio gives with some reluctance. While the fustian is being weighed, Bartolamio admonishes the scales themselves, saying "give me good measure" (*fame bon peso*; 250).[28]

Weighing and measuring too were the subjects of nearly endless rules and regulations. As seen in Chapter Two, one of the most important gauges of public authority was the right to establish the standards for weights and measures. These were often inscribed on public buildings such as the cathedral (as in Pisa and Reggio), other churches often directly associated with the commune (as in Bergamo on Santa Maria, the "chapel of the city" and as in Bologna), on civic palaces (as in Padua), or on market structures, such as the Capitello in Verona's Piazza delle Erbe (figs 68 and 69).[29] In Florence an authorized example of each official weight and measure, tellingly referred to in the statutes as the "iudex" (judge), was to be placed in the treasury (*camera comunis Florentie*), at Orsanmichele, and everywhere else deemed necessary.[30] As will be seen in the next chapter, most cities maintained public scales where wholesale purchases were weighed, and appointed weighers to operate them. In individual shops, merchants were expected to keep measuring rods or scales that were calibrated to accord with the official standards and subject to regular inspection by guild or civic authorities for accuracy.

68   Verona, Capitello with incised standards, Piazza delle Erbe, late 14th century.

Cities and guilds established strict procedures for measuring. Textiles, by far the most important manufactured product in medieval Italy, were often sold by length using measuring sticks made of wood. Por Santa Maria required that the sticks be fitted with metal tips at both ends; this prevented merchants from intentionally shortening them and from their being shortened by wear and tear. The members of the guild who sold cloth at retail had to maintain two measuring rods, a *canna* of four *braccia* and a *passetto* of two. The guild's rules explained precisely how the cloth was to be laid out on the counter and measured.[31] Similar rules existed in Rome and elsewhere; and in Piacenza and Reggio vendors were warned not to pull or stretch cloth as it was being measured.[32] An image from the Bolognese 1329 statutes of the merchants shows cloth being

69   Bologna, incised standards on the Palazzo d'Accursio,
early 13th century, relocated to present location c. 1574.

70   Anonymous, *Measuring Cloth*, Statuti dei Mercanti del 1329, c. 1329,
Archivio di Stato di Bologna, Cod. Min. 9, fol. 1r.

measured (fig. 70). Two figures, presumably the buyer and seller, hold a piece of cloth
between them. The figure on the left measures the cloth with a measuring stick, while
the other counts along. Both lean inward over the merchandize and concentrate
intently on the proceedings. As an object, this depiction would have served as an image
of the guild's fair dealing and equity.

Other items were sold by weight or volume. Merchants had available two different
sorts of scales for weighing: the familiar balance with two pans in which the items to
be weighed were placed in one pan and weights in the other until the two sides balanced, and the steelyard, which consisted of a calibrated arm suspended off center, with
a hook at the short end on which the object to be weighed was hung, and a coun-
terbalance at the longer end which could be moved to determine the weight. The
figure selling ironware in the Turin manuscript of Accursius's gloss holds a balance (see
fig. 65). The less familiar steelyard is shown being held by a draper weighing wool in

71   Anonymous, *Weighing Wool with a Steelyard*, Statutes of the Venetian Arte della
Lana, c. 1386, Venice, Museo Civico Correr, Correr Codex, cl. IV, 129, fol. 20r.

Qui comença la secõda parte dequisto libro çoe capitulare enlo
qual se contene lenfrascripte cose.—

Larubrica de tucti quilli liqli e enladicta arte çoe marego
la. possa lauorare secõdo se cõtene qui de socto :—

Ancora ordena τ licencia de açadauno laquale
scripto e. o plo tempo sera scripto enla enfrascrip
ta margola dela dicta arte τ no altri chelli possa
lauorare τ far lauorare boldõne e lane perxice τ
de uendere τ stamen da uendere τ perxicone de fare o de far
fare panni tucta lana τ meçça lana τ tucte et çascaune la
ne sole et mesele alo so arbitrio τ uoluntate bene τ hal
mente τ ad bona fede secondo lo modo delli lombardi
deli toscani τ deli oltramontani salue lenfrascripte la
ne uerde τ enfrascripti modi et maneire:

Larubrica che nexuio ardisca lauorare lenfrascripte lane :—

Ancora ordena che alguno della dicta arte nel alguna al
tra psona ardisca o presoma lauorare ne far lauora
re p erxion deuen̄te lane ostame pagni ne meçça lana
tucta lana algune lane marçe ostarde lancecta olana depetu
gacçe depelliçarie ragusine ne pelo debo de becho de cau
ra o de camoçça pelo de foligno torrdella de panni bam
baxo de sfilato. En pã de soldi. uinti degrossi τ plu τ meno
en arbitrio delli dicta segnori consoli açascauno che cõ
trafacesse τ p çascauna fiada laquale lo contrafara et
çascauno possa accusare denuntiare τ notificare τ se tã
tengnuto de credença τ ad ueir debia lo terço della dicta
condannatione laquale se fesse τ sco desse se p erxione
de quella. cotale accusa denuntiatione τ notificatione

a miniature from the statutes of the Venetian wool guild, an image that appears near the clause regulating the weight requirements for spun wool (fig. 71).[33]

Cities also established official standards for liquid and dry volume. As the statutes of the podestà of Pistoia observed, the measures known as quartines, used to measure grain, had to be of equal size so that "no one may deceive or be deceived" (*ita quod nullus decipiat vel decipiatur*).[34]

Some items were sold without weighing them. In Treviso, certain varieties of fish could be sold without being weighed but only if they were sold whole.[35] In Pisa, the customer could determine whether he wanted to buy meat by weight or "by sight" (*per vistam*). The same rule specifically noted that vendors should not weigh intestines, heads, feet, or shanks, but instead should sell them by sight.[36] By contrast, because of the many "frauds and deceits" that had been committed in the sale of wood, the Venetian government prohibited the sale of wood at Rialto *ad ochio* (sic; "by eye," as in eyeing something to measure it). Instead it had to be sold by the "cord or by number, or by count."[37]

As noted earlier, Por Santa Maria prescribed how cloth sold at retail should be measured and then sealed. The guild also provided a remedy for those who believed they had not gotten that for which they had paid. All the buyer had to do was take an oath and say that there was "bad measure" (*mala misura*), and his word was to be accepted. The seller then had to give him all that he had paid for and pay a fine. In addition, in these instances, the guild authorized the appointment of two of its members to re-measure the cloth and fine the seller even more if bad measuring had indeed occurred.[38] In this case, the guild intentionally gave the benefit of the doubt to the buyer. It did so to protect its reputation and that of the city as a whole, especially since it dealt in one of Florence's premiere products, silks. A different motive seems be have been behind a provision in the statutes of the Florentine wine sellers. The prologue to their rule requiring guild leaders to ensure the accuracy of barrel measures stated that this was necessary "since equality of measures is of the greatest necessity to the people [*a' popoli*]." In this case, the goals of fair measures were social harmony and the prevention of civil unrest.[39]

After the terms had been reached and the items measured or weighed, the deal was often sealed with a handshake or a glass of wine. A fourteenth-century French manuscript of Aristotle's *Politics* shows two merchants shaking hands; and in the Venetian dialogue, after reaching an accord, the parties agree to have a glass of wine together with Bartolamio proclaiming "Wait, we need to drink to the sale" (*Aspete nuj devemo beuere del marcado*; 251).[40] Such signals that a sale had been completed applied to larger transactions. These sales also required payment of earnest money, known as the *denarius dei*, or God's penny, which was usually paid to the broker. In Rome, when this payment was made the deal was considered complete and legally binding; the same was true for the Florentine Lana and Calimala guilds.[41] While intended as an alm, the *denarius dei's* real import seems to have been its role in sealing transactions. In Piacenza and Verona a deal was considered complete either when the parties shook hands on it or the *denarius dei* was paid.[42] In the imaginary dialogue, the German buyer offers a deposit of ten ducats and advises Bartolomeo to "write it down so that you won't forget it" (*Escrivellj che tu no li desmentigy*; 250).

Even when a deposit had been made, however, it could be difficult to complete the sale. Por Santa Maria included several clauses in its statutes concerning how payments were to be made. The guild stated that if a buyer did not pay the seller within ten days of the sale, then the seller was free to resell the merchandise to another buyer; it also laid out the cases in which credit could be extended.[43] In Rome, merchants had to hold merchandise for which a deposit had been made for two months before it could put it up for sale again.[44] They also had to accept all currency legally in circulation in the city and to accept it at its current value.[45] As the need to include this rule suggests, there were various means by which merchants could speculate and profit by taking into account the changing value of different currencies. They could also sell on credit and make a profit on the interest charged. In the sample dialogue, the German buyer pays Bartolamio in cash but then Bartolamio asks him if he also wishes to purchase some cotton cloth, to which the German responds that he does not have any more money (*Eno ho piu dinari*). Bartolamio, however, is ready to sell it to him on credit, all it will require is a note written in the merchant's hand (*de me pur una scritta de vostra man cho*[m] *el vostro segno*); but the German replies, "I do not know how to buy on credit, it isn't my custom" (*Eno so chomprare incredenza/ El no e mia usanza*; 252).

Certainly, many of the small transactions in the marketplace for everyday goods relied on the petty coins that cities minted to facilitate these kinds of purchases. But even the market in everyday products relied to a great extent on credit. Richard Marshall investigated the "local merchants" of Prato such as druggists, cheese-mongers, tailors, and the like, in other words those not engaged in large-scale international business, and concluded that "credit – short-term and long-term – was a way of life in fourteenth-century Prato." And, while many debts were not paid on time, Marshall found, nevertheless, that the ultimate collection rate was very good.[46] Many of the customers in Giovanni Canale's wool shop in Pinerolo also bought on credit.[47] With final payment made or accounts credited and the merchandise exchanged or delivered, a sale was complete.

Buyers and sellers were not always, however, the only ones involved in sales. As the Master of 1328's images indicate, witnesses often played a role in marketplace transactions as well (see fig. 66). Indeed, their role was crucial since they could offer testimony in court if disputes arose. The presence of witnesses was sometimes recorded in account books.[48] Rome's 1363 statutes actually required the presence of witnesses when dealers in used clothing were purchasing items worked with silver or gold thread from "infamous persons." In those circumstances, two men who were not members of the guild but who knew both the buyer and seller had to be present in order to witness the transaction. Clearly, the intention here was to prevent used-item dealers from serving as fences for stolen property. Witnesses helped to instill the trust that was required for the marketplace to function properly; notaries, who are considered later in this study, played a similar role.[49]

For many wholesale transactions, like the one in the imaginary dialogue, brokers served as intermediaries between buyers and sellers.[50] As discussed in Chapter Three, the Florentine Lana guild assigned brokers to foreign merchants who came to the city to buy cloth, while the Venetian Fondaco dei Tedeschi had a group of officially appointed brokers who knew the German language and facilitated trade between visiting German merchants and resident Venetian traders. Indeed, the government forbade Venetians from dealing with Germans without the mediation of one of the licensed brokers.[51] In Verona, foreigners could not, with few exceptions, make deals valued at more than ten Veronese lire without the assistance of a broker.[52] In Pisa, the number of brokers was set at one-hundred; they had to be natives of Pisa or its district (or residents of Pisa for ten years who paid taxes) and were required to wear a ring marked with a seal.[53] In Florence, the Lana guild authorized forty-four brokers, each of whom also had to have ring with a seal with which he was required to mark the cloth whose sale he had mediated.[54] The Calimala firm of Francesco del Bene and Company had to pay a fine for showing a tailor some cloth without the mediation of a broker.[55] And individual merchants sometimes took on informally the task of mediating sales. The accounts of the Milanese merchant Marco Serraineri (d. 1407) indicate that in some years he earned up to a quarter of his income from his role as an intermediary.[56]

Professional brokers enjoyed a knowledge of the marketplace that few others did since their job allowed them to compare the merchandise of various merchants, see what clients were willing to pay, and know how well goods were selling and at what price. With this insider knowledge, they also represented a potential threat to the integrity of the marketplace. As the prologue to a change in the statutes of Por Santa Maria observed, brokers were often at the root of "dishonest contracts."[57] In Boccaccio's tale of Salabaetto and Jancofiore in the *Decameron*, Jancofiore is in league with a broker who helps her to trick Salabaetto.[58] In their oath, the brokers of the Bolognese guild of *lana bisella* (coarse woolen cloth) swore, among other things, to treat fairly both buyers and sellers and not to speak badly of one to the other.[59] To prevent abuses, officials made a concerted effort to regulate brokers' activities. In many instances they were not allowed to trade in goods themselves: the Venetian vair furriers prohibited their brokers from maintaining shops in the trade, while the Veronese brokers were forbidden to take part in any deal that they had mediated; this rule also applied to their wives, sons, others who lived under their care, and their business partners.[60] In Florence, the Lana brokers had to inform the merchants they were escorting around the city if they were about to enter shops owned by their fathers, sons, or brothers.[61] And, despite the Calimala's statutes prohibiting members of the guild from making loans to brokers, the firm of Francesco del Bene and Company defied the rules and made loans to a broker named Manno Saragoni.[62]

Brokers worked on commission, and the rates that they received were officially set; in the Florentine Lana guild the brokers pooled and divided equally among themselves the commissions they received.[63] Brokers were enjoined to keep good written records of the sales they had mediated and were forbidden from accepting any gifts from those

72   Anonymous Genoese, *Dickering in the Pawnbroker's Shop*, from the *Cocharelli Treatise*, c. 1330,
London, British Library, Add. Ms. 27695, fol. 7v.

whose sales they had arranged.[64] Despite all the fear of abuses on brokers' part, guilds
and cities licensed them since they were viewed as crucial facilitators.[65] Indeed, the
Florentine Lana guild stated that if questions arose concerning a sale of wool or other
merchandise, the word of the broker was to be accepted with regard to the price and
merchandise agreed, while that of the official weigher was to be taken as true regarding the measure.[66]

The elaborate choreography of sales, whether mediated by a broker or not, facilitated
trade. It smoothed the way for exchange by allowing buyers and sellers to interact
with one another in routinized, largely predictable ways that overcame such obstacles
as language and social position.[67] Yet, even without the assistance of a broker, a foreign
buyer could make his wishes known by going through the various steps characteristic
of sales and using a pantomime of hand and facial gestures, as the image of a cheese
seller shows in which the customer indicates with his hand the amount of cheese he
wishes to buy (see fig. 55) or in the image of a pawnshop (the illustration of the vice
of avarice in the *Cocharelli Treatise on the Virtues and Vices* from Genoa dated c. 1330)
in which the pawnbroker and his client appear to be using their hands to signal their
offers and counteroffers (fig. 72).[68] After all, Zorzi da Norimburgo did not have to
explain to his readers *how* to negotiate a deal, he only had to give them the linguistic
tools to do so. Because buyer and seller both knew the steps in advance, they could
assume the roles with relative ease.

What this routine also did, though less successfully, was instill confidence in the
integrity of sales and of the marketplace more generally. Certainly, going through the
various parts of the dance went some way toward generating trust, since it offered
buyers the opportunity to overcome the information imbalance of the market: they

Ome pui ueramente si manifesta

73   Anonymous, *Measuring Grain and the Grain Merchant in his Office*
*Surrounded by Sieves and Measures*, in Domenico Lenzi, *Specchio umano*, c. 1335,
Florence, Biblioteca Medicea Laurenziana, Ms. Tempi 3, fol. 2r.

could ask questions and examine the goods using as many of the five senses as they deemed necessary, while sellers could reach better judgments as to the credit-worthiness of buyers. Nevertheless, doubts lingered and uncertainty remained since, even when buyers believed that they had accurately assessed the quality of the goods and judged their value, they could not be sure that they had actually gotten what they had paid for, given that sellers could increase their profit by giving short measure.

This was not an idle fear, as evidenced by the advice that Paolo da Certaldo offered in his commonplace book. A conventionally moral man, Certaldo roundly condemned usury and cupidity. In one of his maxims, for example, he wrote: "To flee cupidity is to acquire every treasure."[69] But Certaldo also understood the marketplace (and society more generally) as an arena of conflict where trust was scarce and one had to test one's friends a hundred times.[70] Nevertheless, even the morally conventional Certaldo advised one small trick or deception (fig. 73): "when you buy grain, look to see that the measure isn't filled in one pour, since you will always miss two or three percent; and when you sell it, do it [in one pour] and you will gain from it."[71] Pouring the grain in one pour did not allow the kernels to settle. For this very reason, the statutes of the podestà of Pistoia enjoined customers buying grain to hit the measure twice with their hands or feet so that the grain would settle and they would get their full amount; only then could the seller use a stick to level off the top of the measure.[72] Certaldo thus advised a little trick that would bring a gain of two or three percent.[73]

Two or three percent is a modest advantage, but the meager information available to us regarding profit margins suggests that this was not outside the norm. Marshall found that the local merchants of Prato would add a few soldi to what a customer owed and pad their accounts.[74] Even the international merchants of the period, men like Francesco di Marco Datini of Prato and Andrea Barbarigo of Venice, made their fortunes slowly and steadily over their lifetimes by trading in an astonishingly wide array of goods. As Iris Origo wrote of Datini, he "made his fortune, not so much by a series of brilliant *coups*, as by an infinitely patient accumulation of small profits – an avoidance of dangers, quite as much as a seizure of opportunities."[75] The wool shop of Giovanni Canale in Pinerolo saw profits that varied widely between one and forty percent on single pieces of cloth, but averaged about eleven percent.[76] This is close to the amount that Armando Sapori calculated for Francesco del Bene and Company, which made a profit of 11.9 percent on some of its cloth sales.[77] In his family diary, Giovanni di Pagolo Morelli, who was a member of the Florentine Lana guild, wrote: "if you take up the trade in wool or in *panni franceschi* [high-quality woolen cloth from northern Europe], do it yourself and don't try to enrich yourself in two days ..."[78] This is in keeping with Fernand Braudel's distinction between the market economy and the capitalist economy. In his view, the great profits of capitalism can only be made under monopoly conditions authorized by political authorities, but few such conditions existed in medieval Italy, governmental monopolies on the sale of salt being a notable exception.[79]

Indeed, cities discouraged efforts by merchants to hoard or corner the market. The statutes of Florence, for example, prohibited any associations or "monopolies" among sellers of salted fish; this was to ensure that there would be an abundance of fish in the city.[80] Perugia forbade pacts among fishmongers, fearing that they would make fish costlier.[81] Florence also prohibited monopolies in the grain trade.[82] For their part, guilds sought to protect the exclusive right of their members to engage in their particular trade, while, at the same time, making it illegal for members to gain an unfair advantage over other members. In Bologna, the sellers of swords forbade members from buying wholesale quantities of swords during fairs unless they were buying for the entire guild – that is, making them available to their fellow guildsmen – while the smiths prohibited any agreements aimed at monopoly.[83] Por Santa Maria proclaimed that monopolies went against the Christian doctrine of brotherhood and against "dearest charity."[84] Guilds sought, at least in theory, to guarantee that all their members would enjoy an equitable share of the association's business.

All this is in keeping with the nature of markets in non-standardized goods. As Fanselow articulated in his analysis of the bazaar economy in modern India, competition takes different forms in the markets for standardized and non-standardized goods. In the market for standardized goods, that is, in which goods are prepackaged and in which quality and quantity are fixed, the seller can only make a profit by adjusting the price. In such a market, sellers compete against other sellers. But in the non-standardized market, like that in medieval Italy, the seller relies on the frequency of sales and adjustments of quantity (that is, short measure) to make a profit. In this kind of market, buyers compete against sellers.[85]

This explains the agonistic nature of the marketplace at the interpersonal level in medieval Italy. Every transaction was a contest (a "battle," as Bartolamio would have it in the Fondaco dei Tedeschi dialogue) between buyer and seller in which the goal was to get the better of the other.[86] The Dominican preacher Giordano da Pisa (d. 1311) also saw economic activities in these terms. As he explained, "everyone wishing to enrich himself, each is against the other; for whatever you want, I want it too, and it cannot be possessed by all. And thus there are contentions and battles because each man is against the other."[87] As noted above, the expected profits were often small (in Certaldo's case only two or three percent). What mattered was success in pulling it off. To make a profit by giving short measure or to bargain for a particularly advantageous price was not only a material gain but also a demonstration of one's business acumen – even, it can be said, an affirmation of one's selfhood.[88] In the event, a fraudulent act such as giving short measure was an act of self-interest and against the interests of the commonality – be it a guild or the city at large. In his translation of the *Moralia* of Gregory the Great, the fourteenth-century Florentine Zanobi da Strata wrote that fraud "proceeds from a private love, which man often has for himself."[89] The next chapter examines the ways in which buying and selling also formed part of the larger "battle" between various social groups and political blocs, to use their domination to control markets and to establish policies regarding the marketplace that worked to their own advantage. It also considers the myriad personnel who were employed to enforce those policies.

# 6

# REGULATING AND CONTROLLING THE MARKETPLACE

As the dispute reported by Salimbene between the fishmongers and elites of Reggio makes clear, much was at stake in the marketplace.[1] Indeed, a case can be made that it was there that civic politics were played out most fully, since laws and policies concerning buying and selling had the capacity to touch the entire populace, including residents of the *contado*. This chapter examines efforts and policies to regulate and control the marketplace and the personnel who were entrusted with that task. What it illustrates is that over the course of the centuries considered in this study, efforts by civic authorities to regulate the marketplace grew more comprehensive and far-reaching. Some of this is attributable, no doubt, to population pressure, that is to the growth of cities during this period, since an ever increasing populace (at least until the Black Death) necessitated more and more rules to keep the market operating smoothly. Revenue was a factor as well, given that communal governments made money by renting commercial space both in the buildings they constructed and the piazzas over which they extended their control. But there were also political and social components to governmental involvement. The impetus for greater market regulation and control came primarily from the *popolo*, although they did not speak with one voice – the interests of merchants and bankers often differed from those of humble artisans, and individual guilds had necessarily specific agendas. Nevertheless, the overall trend was toward greater and greater regulation aimed almost always at standardization, greater market efficiency, and minimizing fraud.

Pistoia is the centerpiece for this analysis of market control because its unusually complete series of civic statutes offers the opportunity to trace efforts to regulate the marketplace over the course of the twelfth and thirteenth centuries. They consist of the following: a fragment of the statutes of the consuls dated 1117; the *breve* or oath of the consuls, which consists of a redaction of statutes dated 1140 with additions and modifications made between 1177 and 1180; the statutes of the podestà, with an initial section dated 1162 and additions up to 1180; the oath and ordinances of the *popolo* of Pistoia redacted around 1267–8 with additions to 1284; and the statutes of the podestà of the commune of Pistoia of 1296.[2] Although these statutes offer for the most part snapshots of the city at particular moments in time, rather than a continuously running picture from 1117 to 1296, they are nevertheless extremely valuable not only because they include some of the earliest extant statutes for any Italian commune, but also because they make it possible at least in part to view the city and its policies toward markets when it was under regimes dominated by the magnates and later by the *popolo*.[3] The evidence from Pistoia is then supplemented with examples and evidence from other cities and towns.

The twelfth-century statutes of the consuls and those of the podestà indicate that Pistoia's magnate-controlled commune had wrested control of the marketplace from the bishop and was taking a role in promoting commerce and regulating the market. Already by 1117, as evidenced by the fragment of the statutes of the consuls of that year, the commune had assumed a position of preeminence. Indeed, the very first clause stated that the consuls were responsible for protecting the cathedral church of San Zeno, and all other churches within the city and its district, which it defined as encompassing an area that extended four miles beyond the city walls. That early fragment also made clear that the consuls were to guarantee the safety of the "citizens *and their goods*" (my emphasis) traveling the roads to and from the city. Additional clauses established the maximum wages to be paid to agricultural workers, mule-drivers, carpenters, stonemasons, and farriers, all occupations for which the magnates would have had an interest in keeping wages under control.[4]

Later in the century, the statutes of the consuls and podestà show the government more actively seeking to regulate the market. By this point the commune had taken steps to ensure adequate supplies of bread in the city by prohibiting the exportation of grain and chestnuts (which were also used to make flour) to any lands with which Pistoia was at war.[5] Also the commune had by then taken on the responsibility for grain measures. According to one of the clauses in the podestà's statutes, both he and the consuls had to have an official *staio* or bushel measure for grain made for every parish in the city. This was to be done "so that the cereals taken to the mills [for milling] are measured with the same *staio* when it is consigned [to the mills] as when it is returned."[6] Another clause stated that the podestà had to make sure that all bushels used for grain corresponded to the standard measure as it was carved in the main piazza.[7] By assuming this responsibility, the podestà and consuls were trying to guarantee the integrity of grain sales and milling services by making sure that buyers got that for which they paid.

By the late twelfth century, the communal government was also seeking to protect certain streets within the city from encroachment by private interests and was taking the first steps toward regulating actual market infrastructure. One clause in the statutes declared that the podestà was to raze all structures described as "balcos" that impinged on designated "public streets." Almost certainly, the term refers to out-jutting structures that were added to the upper floors of buildings and that were supported with pillars or posts. The podestà was also enjoined to make sure that after their destruction, these additions were not reconstructed so that they could again impede traffic. The same clause went on to declare that the podestà was to see to it that all "fixed counters" (*bancis fixis*) found around the marketplace (*circum forum*) and in public streets were removed. Anyone who tried to set them up again once they had been removed was to be fined five soldi.[8] Clearly, the communal government was concerned in both these instances that private individuals were appropriating public space (streets and market space) for their private use and advantage.[9] At the same time, the removal of the offending balconies and counters allowed the market to operate more efficiently by facilitating the movement of goods and people; the statutes also included rules establishing the minimum width of streets in the city itself, the outlying *borghi* and within a radius of two miles of the city walls, and called for the appointment of officials to guarantee that this rule was observed.[10]

By 1138 the commune had also taken over control of the cathedral campanile. This too was an important piece of civic/market infrastructure since the ringing of the bells determined among other things when buying and selling could commence on market days. The consuls also used a ground-floor store room (*apoteca*) in the campanile as a makeshift communal treasury since there was as yet no communal palace. In return for the use of the space, the consuls made an annual contribution of 40 soldi for the illumination of altars in the church (fig. 74).[11]

What the twelfth-century statutes indicate is that the magnate-controlled commune was acting in some measure to regulate the market and was defending what it considered communal or public property. What is unclear is whether or not they took these actions on account of increasing pressure from merchants and other elements of the *popolo*. There is evidence by the late twelfth century for the existence of guild and neighborhood organizations in Pistoia; these were commonly vehicles of popular power; and certainly by the end of the century, the *popolo* or, more precisely, the merchants had attained not only the right to be consuls but also the requirement that the numerical majority of consuls be from the *popolo*. In addition, the consuls of the merchant guild were regularly meeting with the Consiglio Comune, the commune's chief legislative body.[12] It may well be that, as in Bologna in the late twelfth and early thirteenth centuries, the magnates and merchants of Pistoia were acting together to create a more efficient marketplace.

By the 1260s, the *popolo* were firmly in control of Pistoia: the consulate had been suppressed in 1216, and by 1263 the office of captain of the people had emerged along

74    Pistoia, entrance to ground-floor *apoteca* (shop)
of the bell tower of San Zeno, 12th century.

with twelve *anziani*, although the captain was still subordinate to the podestà.[13] In the late 1260s a new executive body, the *anziani* (elders), gained power, but artisans had only limited representation among them.[14] Then in 1291–2, Pistoia passed anti-magnate legislation and in 1294, Giano della Bella, a central figure in the creation of the guild-based regime in Florence, was podestà. In that same year, work began on the new public palace, the present-day Palazzo degli Anziani (see fig. 25).

The *breve* and ordinances of the *popolo* dated 1284, but with large sections from 1267 to 1271 (shortly after the popular takeover of power), and the statutes of the podestà dated 1296 show a much transformed situation, with the communal government intervening in virtually all aspects of the marketplace. It regulated who could participate in selling and also determined where, when, and how certain vendors could sell their goods. It enacted even stricter measures to protect public market space, charged fees for the right to use that space, and passed laws affecting individual trades. And it employed men who had responsibilities and/or jurisdiction over the marketplace and the trades practiced therein. What follows offers a summary of these interventions.

Many of the rules included in the late thirteenth-century statutes regulated the most basic activity of the marketplace – buying and selling. First and foremost, the commune was determining, at least in some circumstances, who could actually participate in the marketplace on market days. For example, a clause written into the *breve* and ordinances of the *popolo* in July 1271 forbade bread and wine sellers, as well as tavern-keepers and itinerant food-sellers – people who normally sold chickens, eggs, cheese and "similar items" – from buying such items on Saturdays, the day when the weekly market was held in Pistoia. They were even forbidden to enter the marketplace on market days under risk of a 40-soldi fine. When the same law was written into the 1296 statutes of the podestà, it was amended to prohibit the purchase by the same persons of fresh fish or meat worth more than 18 denarii, a very small amount of money, and hence a small amount of meat or fish. Clearly, the authorities were concerned that those engaged in these occupations – who were essentially prepared-food vendors – would regrate, that is, buy up the available stock of these items and then resell it at a higher price. A law from the *breve* specifically forbade the purchase of fish for the purpose of reselling it.[15] Another clause in those same statutes forbade fruit vendors from selling in the Piazza della Sala or the Piazza del Duomo before noon, although an exception was made for those selling leeks, onions, and the like.[16]

In addition to regulating who could sell and when, the commune also regulated where things could be sold and sometimes even how vendors should conduct their business. The same groups that were prohibited from entering the market on market days – that is, bread and wine sellers and tavern-keepers – were forbidden to receive customers in their private homes or other properties, but had to sell to them only in "public" streets; otherwise they would pay a fine of 100 soldi. Customers caught consuming food in the prohibited locales would themselves be subject to a fine of 40 soldi.[17] For their part, butchers were required to kill and skin animals which they wished to sell "openly" (*palam*) in the shops where the meat would actually be sold. This law was prompted, the preamble stated, by the desire to obviate the "evils of the butchers" and the "great and many frauds" which they committed in selling meat from diseased animals.[18] A similar concern prompted another rule which required any butcher or tavern-keeper who had bought an animal from a person "not well known and of good reputation" (*non sit bene nota et bone fame*) to keep openly (*palam*) the animal in the abattoir for one day "so that it can be seen by passersby" (*ut a transuentibus possit videri*).[19] In this way, customers could determine for themselves the state of the animal's health. Another law forbade sellers of cooked food from putting towels over the items they were selling unless the towels were "well washed and white and clean"; they were also forbidden to throw water on the food. This may have been a trick either to make stale food seem fresh or to increase its weight.[20]

In some instances, the government also set the price at which items could be sold. This was most commonly the case with bread and wine. A law in the statutes of the podestà established the amount of profit wine sellers could garner: those selling wine at retail were allowed a profit of four soldi per *congio* (1 *congio* was about 456 liters or 100 gallons); those selling in bulk could make two soldi per *congio* "and not more."[21] The commune also established the required weight and price of bread; anyone producing bread that did not correspond to the standard was to be fined five soldi for each loaf and have the loaves confiscated.[22] Moreover, anyone found to have produced more than twenty "false loaves" was prohibited from making bread for the entire term of the podestà during whose mandate the counterfeit bread was discovered. Malefactors could be easily traced since bakers were required to mark their loaves with identifying seals.[23]

The reader will no doubt have noticed by now that all of the laws discussed so far involved the food trades.[24] As noted in Chapter One, from the earliest days of their development, communal governments had shown an interest in guaranteeing that their towns were well supplied with food, especially grain. Partially this was done to stave off the possibility of popular unrest. But it appears that regimes dominated by the *popolo*, like that of thirteenth-century Pistoia, went even further in seeking to set the price at which the basics, bread and wine, could be sold.[25] Generally speaking, historians have interpreted this as part of an effort by these more broadly based regimes to care for the lower classes, the *popolo minuto*, those who were most vulnerable to high prices and the danger of hunger.[26] And certainly, there is some evidence to support this point of view. As seen in the last chapter, a clause in the statutes of the Florentine wine sellers' guild stated explicitly that "equality of measure is of the greatest necessity to the popolo."[27]

There is another possible interpretation, however. It may be that the greater merchants and guildsmen, those usually identified as the *popolo grasso*, pushed for such measures not out of concern for the poor or to prevent public disorder but in order to protect themselves against what they perceived as price gouging by the food vendors. The tension between the elites and fishmongers of Reggio suggests as much; and a rule written into the 1296 statutes of the podestà offers some evidence of class-based tension involving the food trades in Pistoia as well. It stated that those who sold wine at retail had to sell to it to everyone who requested it; otherwise they would face a twenty-soldi fine. The very fact that this statute was enacted suggests that, like the fishmongers of Reggio, the wine sellers of Pistoia were at times refusing to sell to certain customers.[28] What is more, the statutes of the podestà granted anyone who wished to do so the right to practice the art of butchering in the city of Pistoia and forbade the formation of a butchers' guild. The same prohibition applied to the fishmongers. The podestà had to protect anyone who wished to practice the trade of butchering from retaliation; and anyone who tried to prevent someone from engaging in the trade faced a stiff ten-lire fine.[29] What is notable here is that these were the same occupations – butchering and fishmongering – as had caused concern in Reggio. While popular regimes, like that in Pistoia in the late thirteenth century, were much concerned with food policies, then, it is not clear that the goal of those policies was always to aid the poor. It seems just as likely that they were designed to protect the interests of the greater guildsmen, such as merchants and bankers.[30]

Furthermore, while the popular regime in Pistoia showed a special concern with the food trades, it intervened at times in the affairs of other professions, including the most prestigious ones. A clause in the 1296 statutes, for example, stated that if anyone wanted to buy more than twelve pounds of *lana de Garbo* (a mixture of wool and linen or hemp), he had to buy it "openly and from a public merchant." In other words, the regime was seeking to prevent clandestine deals; the law went on to state that anyone wishing to practice the wool trade had to submit to the jurisdiction of the Lana guild of Pistoia. At the time, persons engaged in the wool trade were moving to Pistoia from Verona and Lombardy; and, while the commune was actively encouraging such immigration, some members of the Lana guild clearly feared that they would be undersold by persons who were practicing the trade but not submitting to the rules, requirements, and obligations of the guild.[31] In another clause from the same statutes, money-changers were required to put up security or a pledge of 2,000 lire, guaranteeing that they would "exercise the said art of money-changing faithfully and restitute deposits made to them."[32] Both of these rules were designed to protect specific trades and prestigious ones at that. In the first instance, the law protected wool manufacturers from unlicensed competitors; in the second, it protected money-changers, as well as others, from those who did not have enough money properly to capitalize and guarantee their business.

Under the popular regime, the communal government also expanded its supervision of weights and measures. This was already a concern in the twelfth-century statutes, as has been noted, especially in the creation of an official standard for the grain *staio*. But the number of laws regarding standards increased substantially in the later collections of statutes. Again, many of these involved the measures used for bread and wine. One stated that the keepers of hostels had to sell items to foreigners with the same weights and measures as those used for residents of the city, while another emphasized that residents of the *contado* had to use the same weights and measures as those used in the city.[33] As seen in the last chapter, another Pistoiese statute required those buying grain to hit the measure twice with their hands or feet so that the grain would settle and buyers would get the amount of grain for which they had paid.[34] But such concerns with standards and measuring were not confined to the food trades. A law in the statutes of the podestà allowed those who sold ironwork (an important industry in Pistoia) and cheese to maintain steelyards that could weigh items up to 50 pounds (around 16 kilos) in their shops. Presumably, items weighing more than that had to be taken to the public scales in the marketplace for weighing.[35] Another law stated that in all transactions involving items weighing less than 12 pounds (slightly less than 4 kilos), the items were to be weighed with a balance using weights established by the Opera di San Jacopo, an institution honoring Saint James, who in the mid-twelfth century became co-patron with San Zeno of Pistoia, and to whom a chapel was dedicated within the cathedral. According to Rauty, the entrusting of standards to the Opera may have represented a compromise between the commune and the church (which had once controlled weights and measures), even though members of the Opera were laymen and were required to mark the weights with the seal of the commune. The law went on to state specifically that every person buying and selling in the "communal marketplace [the Piazza del Duomo] or in the Piazza della Sala" had to use the measures established by the Opera.[36]

Also by the thirteenth century, the government was appointing men with some responsibility for the supervision and smooth operation of the market. One of the most important of these was the keeper of the communal scales. It is not known if this post was held by one man or shared among many. But a clause written into the statutes of the *popolo* in July 1271 required the keeper to maintain complete records of every weighing he conducted. He had to record the names of both buyers and sellers, the items exchanged in transactions, and their weight and price. If he failed to do so, he would face a fine of 100 soldi.[37] It is unclear if the keeper of the scales was the same person as the "mensurator" who worked for the Opera di San Jacopo "in mercato," or whether one maintained the steelyard while the other kept the official standards of weights and measures.[38] Another official, the *iudex de dannis datis* ("judge on damage caused") – part of the podestà's staff – was required twice a week along with two of his notaries to check the weight of bread that was available for sale. Also twice a week he or one of his notaries had to inspect the measures used by those selling wine at retail. A clause warned that the staff were not to alert sellers that the inspections were about to take place.[39]

The commune also appointed custodians responsible for the security and cleanliness of the marketplace. According to the statutes of the podestà, the city appointed twelve custodians or guards for each of the city's four quarters: their job was to gather each evening at the sounding of the third bell in the Piazza del Duomo and then to patrol the city until morning. They were especially to be on the lookout for thefts and property damage.[40] Four of them were assigned to guard the Piazza del Duomo, where they were responsible for investigating anyone who broke the nighttime curfew and for removing the rubbish.[41] However, the piazza needed more regular and systematic cleaning and maintenance than the guards were able to supply and so, in another statute, the communal treasurer was enjoined to auction off the right to sweep and clean the Piazza del Duomo as well as the Piazza della Sala (fig. 75), site of the daily fruit and vegetable market.[42] The winning bidder could keep the refuse, which had

75    Pistoia, Piazza della Sala.

some value since it could be used either as green manure or as feed for pigs and other animals. The winner was enjoined to keep the piazzas "well cleaned and swept."[43]

This concern with the cleanliness of the two market squares was just one part of a greater concern expressed by the popular government with market infrastructure. As noted earlier, already in the twelfth century the government was trying to rid public streets of overhanging balconies or jetty floors and the marketplace of fixed counters. Both rules were repeated in the 1296 statutes with some amendments: one specifically accused the drapers of placing counters in front of their shops.[44] The drapers were also singled out in the law (discussed in Chapter Four) that forbade the hanging of awnings which extended out into the space of the market and which were considered both "ugly and indecorous."[45] Such efforts to protect public space only increased. A rule in the 1296 statutes of the podestà stated that nowhere within the old city, by which they meant within the first circuit of walls, was any counter to extend more than one foot (approximately 32 centimeters) beyond the walls of the building; while another stated that neither mercers nor grocers (*pizzicarie*) were to have counters that extended beyond the windows of their shops, by which they presumably meant beyond the sill.[46] Clearly, this was an ongoing problem that resisted a permanent solution; a rule from 1296 required the podestà to call a council to discuss the removal of illegal counters in the marketplace.[47] Other rules prohibited the drying of grain and the tethering of beasts of burden within the market areas since these practices too could impede the movement of people and goods and create refuse.[48]

The government also concerned itself with the allotment and organization of market stalls. It declared that no one could have more than one stall or counter in the marketplace and ordered the rearrangement of the stalls occupied by the money-changers near the staircase of the communal palace so that a pathway would be created between them and hence easier access afforded to the staircase. Furthermore, it declared that counters could be no more than seven half-feet (*semisses*) in length and that the seats behind the counters could not be wider than a foot.[49]

By the late thirteenth century the communal government was charging for the privilege of using public space for business. It established, in a clause in the 1296 statutes, a sliding scale based in part on the occupation of the vendor and in part on the kind of space being utilized. The clause began by declaring that all money-changers who had counters in the Piazza del Duomo (*in foro*) were to pay 40 soldi annually to the commune. (A different law established the same fee for butchers and fishmongers with counters in the piazza).[50] Cheese-mongers and others having counters or tents (*tendam*) in either the Piazza del Duomo or the Piazza della Sala were to pay 20 soldi. The same annual fee of 20 soldi applied to anyone within the new city walls and in the suburbs who maintained a counter that extended beyond the doorway of his house, as well as to everyone who maintained a counter in the Piazza del Duomo or the Piazza della Sala or who had a counter extending three feet (96 centimeters) beyond his house. The seeming redundancy of these last two stipulations suggests that the legislators were trying to encompass all possible definitions of commercial space. They went on to declare that anyone who set up a counter or tent in the Piazza del Duomo outside the portico (*extra portico*), by which they presumably meant the portico of the Palazzo degli Anziani, on Saturdays was to pay 10 soldi annually. This rule seems to have been aimed at those whose retail space did not enjoy the privileged position near the building but who occupied space in the center of the piazza on market days only. The final clause extended this fee of 10 soldi to encompass "those who maintain a *sextorium* [awning?] or counter or *pannum* [cloth spread on the ground?] of any sort [*aliquo modo*]."[51] As will shortly be seen, the government of Siena likewise distinguished between those who had shops on the periphery of the Campo and those who traded from the unpaved inner portion of the square.

Finally, the statutes of popular commune included a variety of clauses regulating credit and contracts and otherwise promoting commerce. To cite only two examples, one law required creditors to surrender promissory notes once debts had been repaid and to record the same in their private account books; the same law required notaries either to record in their protocols when debts had been repaid to creditors or to give to debtors receipts acknowledging that their obligations had been fulfilled.[52] Another prohibited anyone who was in the marketplace on Fridays or Saturdays or who was making his way to the marketplace on those days from being detained unless he was wanted for theft or counterfeiting or was an exile or otherwise an "enemy" of the commune of Pistoia. The same applied during the fairs held to honor the city's patron saints and other special market occasions.[53] Clearly, the regime wanted to promote commerce by guaranteeing that merchants and others could travel to Pistoia's market without fear of being apprehended for crimes that did not threaten directly either business or the regime itself. And in another effort to guarantee Pistoia's concern for honest business dealings and its good reputation, a clause in the 1296 statutes stated simply, "No public usurer may be in the city of Pistoia or its diocese and no one may offer to him a place to live either for rent or by any other means."[54]

The language that the commune used to explain or justify its action regarding standards and infrastructure is illuminating. Most commonly it used the word "benefit" (*utilitas*), combining that word with others that explained more precisely who would benefit. When in 1271, for example, the popular commune established the weight of bread, the government stated that it was ordering this standard weight "for the common benefit of the men and persons of the city of Pistoia and the district" (*pro comuni utilitate hominum et personarum civitatis Pistorii et districtus*); and the law explaining how grain was to be measured stated that this was being done "for the evident benefit of the men and persons of the city of Pistoia and the district and to avoid the evils of false measurings of grain" (*pro evidenti utilitate hominum et personarum civitatis Pistorii et districtus et pro evitandis maleficiis falsorum mensuratorum blavi*).[55] When it ordered that a city street running by the home of the sons of a certain Bonato remain open and unobstructed, it declared that this was to be done "for the evident benefit of the commune and of the Parte Guelfa of the city of Pistoia" (*pro evidenti utilitate comunis et partis Guelfe civitatis Pistorii*); and when it required that the road leading to the Lucchese gate be paved with "well fired bricks," it stated that this was being undertaken "for the benefit of the commune of Pistoia and the betterment of all persons" (*pro utilitate comunis*

*Pistorii et mellioramento omnium personarum*). It also emphasized that it was important to pave the road, "since the said Lucchese Gate is more beautiful [*pulcrior*] than all the other gates of the entire city of Pistoia."[56]

Civic officials understood "benefit" primarily in a material sense; and the popular government saw as its job not only the maintenance but also the improvement of the material wellbeing of the city's inhabitants, as the word "betterment" in the law just cited indicates. The law requiring the appointment of four gatekeepers and four notaries for each of the city's four gates stated that this was to be done "for the greater conservation of the profit and other things of the citizens and the churches" (*ad maiorem conservationem fructuum et aliarum rerum civium et ecclesiarum*), while a law calling for improvement of the port of Brugnano allowing for more commerce with Pisa declared that it would redound "to the evident benefit and condition of the commune and *popolo* of Pistoia and the district" since there would be "greater plenty, and fertility and abundance" of merchandise and goods in the city and the *contado*.[57]

Material benefits were not the popular government's only concerns, however. It justified a law forbidding the tethering of pack animals near the grain market held in the Piazza del Duomo not on the grounds that the manure created by these animals would foul the grain market but instead "out of reverence for Saint James the Apostle and Saint Zeno the Confessor." And when it did pass a law against the encumbering or fouling of any piazza in front of any church in the city, it stated that this was done "to the honor of omnipotent God and of his saints."[58]

As the reference to the Lucchese Gate's beauty suggests, aesthetics were also a concern. The law discussed in Chapter Four forbidding the extension of awnings beyond the doorways of drapers' shops in the communal market stated that this was being enacted "for the benefit and beauty of the piazza and the communal market" (*pro utilitate et venustate platee et mercati comunis*) and that awnings that did extend out from shops were "ugly and indecent and rustic practice" (*turpe et indecens et res castellana*). The legislators also believed, as seen, that the awnings damaged Pistoia's reputation since foreigners and ambassadors often were struck in the face by them.[59]

The popular commune, then, had a wide-ranging and multivalent notion of utility and the common good. It encompassed not only material benefits but also reverence for God and a concern with beauty and the city's reputation among foreigners.[60] The laws promulgated in the twelfth century, when Pistoia was dominated by the magnates, also used the word "benefit" but there were several significant differences. First, the term was usually employed generically, especially in oaths and the appointment of officials. For example, the consuls and the city treasurer promised to act for the "benefit" of the city.[61] Second, it was not used in the rules regarding the private appropriation of public space, although it was used in a law authorizing the survey for new city walls and the maintenance of castles in the *contado*.[62] Third and most significantly, in almost every instance under the magnate regime, benefit or utility was linked with honor, as when the communal treasurer pledged to act "for the common honor and benefit of the Pistoian people" (*ad comunem honorem et utilitatem Pistoriensis populi*).[63] In none of the justifications for laws passed by the popular commune examined here was *utilitas* paired with *honor*. It seems reasonable to suggest that honor was a value deeply revered by the magnates; for this reason, it served to justify their governmental actions. By contrast, the *popolo*, at least in these statutes, avoided the word, justifying their actions instead with different, more mercantile values.

From the early and somewhat tentative efforts by the magnate-dominated govern- ment to regulate market space and control the market, then, there emerged under the Pistoian popular regime a full range of laws and statutes aimed at supervising the market, generating income, and protecting the reputation of the city. The unavoidable conclusion is that this government dominated by mercantile interests, especially the interests of merchants and bankers, saw as its job the protection and promotion of commerce, the honoring of God and the saints, and the fostering of Pistoia's reputation and beauty.

The trends attested to in Pistoia are evident in Pisa as well, another city for which statutes from both the mid-twelfth century and the later thirteenth century are extant.[64] Like the statutes from Pistoia, those from Pisa evidence ever greater efforts by the commune to regulate commerce and the marketplace. While the twelfth-century Pisan statutes demonstrate a concern with such issues as maintenance of streets and canals, standard measures, and the smooth administration of the annual fair held in August, those of the late thirteenth century, when the regime was dominated by a captain and *anziani*, are more far-reaching and cover a range of occupations, products, personnel, and business practices.[65] There are also differences in the experience of the two cities: for one thing, Pisa was a major international port and commercial space was more diffused and less concentrated than in Pistoia; it appears more similar in some respects to Venice.[66] For another, the difference in vocabulary noted in Pistoia is not evident in Pisa: the 1286 Pisan statutes include a promise by the representatives of the *popolo* to do everything "for the honor and benefit of the said-same city with justice and equality." In this case, they did not shy away from the word honor, although the word equality again suggests a different emphasis from that of the earlier magnate regime.[67]

Evidence from towns across the peninsula demonstrates that the concerns and poli- cies addressed by the communes of Pistoia and Pisa in the thirteenth century were shared not only by other popular-based communal regimes but also by individual guilds – yet another indication that these policies were promoted first and foremost by the *popolo*.[68] One of the common issues was the tension between the more estab- lished shopkeepers and itinerant vendors with no fixed establishment. Already consid- ered were the 1265 statutes of the Bolognese drapers that forbade men who sold cloth off their backs from entering the drapers' *bina* during fairs.[69] Similarly, the 1335 statutes of Por Santa Maria included a clause prohibiting itinerant hawkers from going about Florence selling a variety of items, including purses, veils, and cloth that pertained to the guild. These ambulatory sellers, according to the guild, committed "frauds, falsities, and thefts" and other depravities that caused "damage and shame."[70] The vehemence of this language indicates that itinerants struck a particularly sensitive nerve in guild and civic authorities, a reaction provoked by their ability to undersell those with fixed establishments as well as by their very mobility. As itinerants, they were harder to control and tax. The 1317 statutes of the mercers of Rome stated that those who wished to go about the city selling mercery out of baskets had to pay an annual fee to the guild; the same statutes prohibited members of the guild with shops from doing any ambulant selling within twelve miles of the city's officially recognized district.[71]

Many of the rules against itinerants were aimed at the poor peasant men and women who came to the cities from the countryside to sell a variety of foodstuffs including fruit, vegetables, fish, fowl, and game. The Florentine civic authorities imposed a number of regulations on them: they were enjoined to sell their products at officially established prices and to sell "publicly and openly in public places;" they were not allowed to sell their products before nones; they were forbidden to sell mushrooms, cheese, fowl, and game of various sorts along the roads within six miles (9.9 kilometers) of the city walls; and they could not sell green or unripened nuts. In addition, they were not to sell in the Mercato Vecchio or occupy and clog the area around the grain market at Orsanmichele.[72] The latter rules seem to have been prompted at least in part by concern for the efficient movement of traffic and civic decorum, since itinerant vendors clogging public streets created an image that displeased the civic authorities. The Venetian Ufficiali sopra Rialto faced similar problems and tried to stop the encumbering of the Rialto Bridge and other areas around the main square at the Rialto market. In Bologna, the court under the jurisdiction of the podestà responsible for streets, bridges, and other public works fined a number of food sellers who were caught illegally hawking their wares at the Porta Ravegnana.[73]

At the same time, peasant sellers performed an important function by augmenting the available stock of fresh fruit, vegetables and other products. Indeed, the Florentine authorities exempted from the gabelles the sellers who came from the surrounding countryside to sell fruit, herbs, and straw, claiming that earlier efforts to impose these taxes had caused a "dearth" of these products in the city; while for their part, the Ufficiali sopra Rialto removed their earlier restrictions on itinerants when they realized that their efforts to limit sales hurt the city as well as the poor who came to Venice to sell their wares. The Ufficiali continued to insist, however, that these "foreigners" not clog the Rialto Bridge or market with their cages and baskets.[74]

As in Pistoia, popular regimes elsewhere tried to regulate where and when goods could be sold. First and foremost, the authorities sought to control who could and could not trade in the marketplace, and what they could sell. Guilds, of course, tried to guarantee that only their members could deal in the products in which they specialized. To cite but two examples among many, the Venetian goldsmiths forbade any foreigners from working gold or silver unless they had a stall on the Ruga dei Oresi at Rialto (and presumably had been granted some sort of Venetian citizenship rights), while the furriers who worked with sheepskins and dormice pelts were prohibited from working with the pelts of vair (there were three distinct guilds of furriers in Venice, each specializing in a particular kind of fur).[75] For their part, governments usually restricted the right of foreign merchants to sell goods in their city. Only during fairs, which as has been seen were often held outside city walls, did communes suspend the normal rules against trading by foreigners and lift the usual trade imposts and bans.

The Florentine civic authorities declared that the only place where grain could be sold within the city and within four miles (6.6 kilometers) of the city was in the piazza of Orsanmichele; likewise they restricted the sale of live sheep and mouton to a designated location that they identified as outside the "ghirlanda" or ring of the Mercato Vecchio.[76] As for the guilds, the linen sellers of Bologna in their statutes of 1307 forbade retail sales anywhere except in the Mercato del Mezzo, while the Florentine money-changers had to swear not to go about the city but only to conduct business at their established tables.[77]

Civic authorities also set the days on which buying and selling could take place and the hours of operation. The 1325 statutes of the merchants of Piacenza offered a list of days on which the drapers were forbidden to sell or even to make their wares available for inspection. In addition to Sundays, they had to close their shops on "the feasts of our Lord Jesus Christ and of his mother, and on the feasts of the Apostles."[78] For their part, the Venetian rock-crystal carvers celebrated the following holidays: Christmas and the two successive days, Easter and the two successive days, the Epiphany, Ascension Day, Pentecost and the two successive days, All Saints, the four feast days of Mary, the four feast days of Saint Mark, the feast days of each of the twelve Apostles, the feast of the Holy Saviour, and the feast days of Saints Michael, Nicholas, Lawrence, Luke, John the Baptist, Martin, and Blaise.[79] In one case that seems to echo the Franciscan abhorrence of money, as well as the sense of brotherly love that was to guide members of the guild, the 1317 statutes of the Florentine oil and cheese sellers forbade members from trying to collect debts from other members of the guild, "on Sundays, Easter, Christmas, and other feast days."[80]

As for market hours, various limits were imposed. In Piacenza, guilds could not set up their stalls in the Piazza del Duomo until the bells of the church signaling Mass rang.[81] In Venice, mercers and all other vendors had to stop selling in Piazza San Marco by noon and to remove their portable stalls by that hour as well.[82] Officials were especially concerned to prevent sales or work activities at night. In Rome, wholesalers of fish were forbidden to operate by candlelight, while Venetian shopkeepers who rented shops at Rialto from the commune were prohibited from having lanterns, candles, or fires lit after the third ringing of San Marco's bells. An exception was made for those who not only worked but also lived in their shops.[83] Two motives prompted these prohibitions on nocturnal activity: first, darkness concealed fraud and other illegal activities; second, the use of candles and lamps significantly increased the danger of fire.

Yet it is unclear how strictly these rules (and many others) were observed and enforced. Certainly, the draper Giovanni Canale of Pinerolo abided by the restrictions: only one of his many transactions took place on a Sunday.[84] But the small-scale merchants of Prato often conducted business of Sundays and other holidays.[85] And in his *ricordanza*, or diary, Goro Dati, a member of Florence's Por Santa Maria, resolved in 1404 to mend his ways and "refrain from going to the shop or conducting business on solemn Church holidays, or from permitting others to work for me or seek temporal gain on such days." However, he also conceded that whenever he made "exceptions in cases of extreme necessity," he would donate a florin to the poor.[86] Moreover, the authorities themselves granted exemptions from various restrictions. The Perugian Mercanzia allowed shops to open on feast days when fairs were in progress.[87] And in Venice, the mercers, whose shops normally had to close on Sundays and various feast days, were permitted to keep them open on the Sunday closest to the feast of the Holy Apostles, which fell on May 1, when large numbers of pilgrims who were heading to Rome were in the city, and on other feast days (as well as their vigils) if the merchant fleets were about to set sail. Although they were permitted to keep their shops open under these circumstances, the mercers were not allowed to set up displays outside their shops, suggesting that the Venetian authorities did not want unduly to publicize the exemption they were granting.[88] But such exemptions did benefit fair-goers, pilgrims, and others including the vendors and the cities themselves.

Strict or not, the enforcement of these and numerous other regulations governing the marketplace required significant manpower. Safety and security were major concerns since a sizable portion of any city's wealth in movable goods was concentrated in the marketplace. In Venice, for example, the criminal records contain many cases of theft around the money-changers' tables at Rialto and San Marco.[89] In order to provide protection, cities employed police and watchmen of various sorts. The 1262 statutes of Siena called for the appointment of two custodians whose job it was to supervise the Saturday market held in the Campo. They were to be on watch for thieves operating in the market and for gamblers.[90] Given the crowds, it was easy for thieves to move about unnoticed. Domenico Lenzi noted in his *Specchio umano* that on May 24, 1329 a large crowd gathered in Florence's piazza of Orsanmichele to buy grain and that on that day, "many men and women had their purses cut."[91]

Break-ins were more likely to occur at night when the marketplace was deserted. Accordingly, as in Pistoia, so in Verona, four night-watchmen were charged with patrolling the market and the communal palace: they were to take turns, with two serving one night, the other two the next.[92] In Pisa, the bridge-keeper of the Ponte Vecchio as well as those who maintained shops on it had to pay the stipends of two guards who patrolled the bridge at night.[93] And in Florence, members of Por Santa Maria paid an impost that went toward the salary of guards who were stationed nightly in the Via Calimala and at Porta Santa Maria.[94] In Venice, policing of Rialto was the responsibility of the Signori di Notte (Lords of the Night), who were obligated to loan patrolmen to the Ufficiali sopra Rialto for this purpose. The policemen working at Rialto during the night had the right to search men passing through the marketplace and sequester any arms that they were found to be carrying.[95]

Gambling was another serious concern, and many cities sought to control it.[96] In 1304, for example, a shearer named Benvenuto was fined 25 lire for gambling at Rialto; his infraction was especially egregious since it occurred after dark on Maundy Thursday.[97] But in many respects, gambling resembled buying and selling since players had to evaluate their competitors' competence and be on the lookout for cheating and other dishonest behaviors; it fueled mistrust. In another respect as well, it mirrored the activity of the market. As the diary of the Florentine nobleman Buonaccorso Pitti indicates, gambling was a way to make money – in Pitti's case significant amounts of money. However, as his diary also illustrates, gambling often led to fights in which slurs were hurled about and matters easily escalated into violence or threats of violence.[98]

More serious still were the riots that erupted and that had the marketplace as one of their targets. Caused by dearth, disease, factionalism, or political powerlessness, they could result in looting, injury, or even death. In his *Specchio umano*, Lenzi reports that when in April 1329, the crowd that had come to Orsanmichele to purchase grain discovered that there was not enough to go around, people began to cry out, "Thus is the city badly governed, that we can't have any grain! And one should like to go to the houses of these thieves who have grain, and set them on fire and burn them alive [in their houses] since they keep us in this famine."[99] In response to this and similar threats, the Six of Grain and the podestà dispatched Ser Villano da Gubbio (a notary with the title of "knight" on the podestà's staff) along with his patrolmen to Orsanmichele on several occasions, where they ruthlessly cleared the piazza, seized control of the entrances to it, and subdued the crowds.[100] They brought with them an axe and chopping block and threatened to cut off the hands or feet of those who stole or rioted.[101] As noted in Chapter One, Lenzi's book includes an image of Orsanmichele in a time of dearth (see fig. 8). It captures the chaos of a tumult, in which Villano and his heavily armed patrolmen, visible in the background, wield halberds and pikes and struggle to restore order (fig. 76).

As the threats of the crowd on that April 1329 day indicate, rioters set homes, shops, and warehouses on fire, leading to devastating financial losses. Regardless of their cause, fires were another serious threat to the marketplace. The sixteenth-century reorganization of the Rialto market was prompted by a fire that broke out in the night of January 9–10, 1514 and destroyed much of the mercantile complex. Earlier centuries saw their share of conflagrations as well. In 1361 the *casaria* (cheese market) at Rialto burned; in 1486 it was the turn of the Ruga dei Barileri (street of the barrel-makers), and in 1505 flames consumed the Fondaco dei Tedeschi.[102] In Florence, fire swept through the area around the Mercato Vecchio in 1117, twice in 1177, in 1232, 1284, and 1304. The last, intentionally set during the factional fighting that ravaged the city, was particularly destructive, consuming more than 1,900 warehouses, shops, and houses.[103] Looting accompanied the 1304 fire. According to the chronicler Dino Compagni, "thieves brazenly went into the fire to steal and carry off whatever they could grab, and nothing was said to them. Even someone who saw his own goods being carried off did not ask for them, because the city was in bad shape in every way."[104] Many cities, including Pistoia and Treviso, organized fire brigades.[105]

Like Pistoia, other cities appointed officials responsible for the general maintenance and upkeep of the marketplace. The constant influx of people, pack animals, and goods created significant quantities of refuse. Perugia's 1279 statutes called for the employment

76    Anonymous, *Grain Market at Orsanmichele in a Time of Dearth*,
detail showing Ser Villano da Gubbio and his patrolmen, in Domenico Lenzi,
*Specchio umano*, c. 1335. Florence, Biblioteca Medicea Laurenziana, Ms. Tempi 3, fol. 79r.

of two men who would sweep the marketplace and communal square.[106] Much of the refuse was generated by greengrocers, fishmongers, and butchers who were regularly reminded in various rules and regulations to keep their stalls clean and not to discard rubbish in the streets. In Florence, officials of the butchers' guild were responsible for ensuring that the stalls and market area occupied by their members were clean and swept, and kept "well purged and without putrefying matter." For their part, the butchers were forbidden to slaughter animals in the Mercato Vecchio, the Mercato Nuovo, the piazza at the foot of the Ponte Vecchio, or in their shops.[107] The 1321 statutes of the merchants of Piacenza required the resellers of fruit and chickens to sweep the Piazza del Borgo every month during the winter. A 1328 addition to the same statutes required the annual appointment of a custodian (*massarius*) who would oversee the cleaning and maintenance of Piazza del Borgo and Via Santa Brigida.[108]

In addition to cleaning, marketplaces required periodic maintenance and improvements, such as paving and furnishing with gutters.[109] Streets and piazzas had to be open, clean, and free of all encumbrances that could obscure vision and hinder traffic and thus harm commerce. The Sienese authorities were much concerned with keeping the Campo unobstructed, while the Florentines worried about lumber, stones, and other material that might clog the piazza at Orsanmichele, the Mercato Vecchio, and Mercato Nuovo.[110] For its part, in 1343, the Venetian Council of Forty forbade the auctioning of large objects in the square known as Rialto Vecchio, located in front of the church of San Giacomo di Rialto, insisting that they be auctioned instead in the more commodious nearby piazza known as Rialto Nuovo.[111]

Additionally, most cities spent significant amounts of treasure and energy paving streets and piazzas and otherwise maintaining them.[112] Such projects were seen as contributing to cities in both tangible and intangible ways. Unimpeded and well-paved streets and piazzas improved traffic flow. They also added, as the statute of Verona calling for the paving of that city's marketplace and several major streets, observed, "to the ornament of the city and the common benefit" (*ad decorum civitatis et comunem utilitatem*).[113]

While the regulations and personnel discussed heretofore had as their mission the overall supervision, management, maintenance, and improvement of the marketplace, other rules and regulations were intended, wherever possible, to impose standards on both the production and selling of goods, and their enforcement required the service of still more officials and staff. Much of the responsibility for this fell not to civic officials but to officers of particular guilds whose job it was to make sure that merchandise was made and sold according to guild-approved standards and practices. In Rome, the mercers worried that members of the guild were not following the rules regarding when shops should be closed. Accordingly, their statutes called for the appointment of secret "accusers" who would report members of the guild who failed to obey the rules prohibiting work on Sundays and feast days. In Florence, the oil and cheese sellers were concerned that candles were not always made to the requisite norms. (It was not uncommon for chandlers to mix old wax with new or to use tallow rather than wax, or poor-quality cotton for the wicks). In order to prevent this, the rectors of the guild were authorized to appoint *cercatori secreti* (secret inspectors) whose job it would be to uncover, "the aforesaid evil [practices]."[114] In Piacenza as well, two men who knew the trade were to go about and make sure that candles were made "with pure wax and pure cotton [wicks]," according to the standards of Genoese candles.[115]

As in Pistoia, foodstuffs were subject to especially rigorous inspection. In Florence, for example, the butchers' guild allowed for "spies" who would be on the lookout for meat that had been altered by various tricks in order to make it appear something it was not.[116] And in Lucca, saffron could not be sold until it had been inspected by the "proveditors of saffron" who were to determine whether it was "real or counterfeit" (*rectum vel falsum*).[117] Given its centrality in the diet of both rich and poor, bread was subject to numerous regulations and inspections overseen by various officials. Both Lucca and Siena appointed examiners and inspectors of bread.[118] Since bread could be made from various kinds of flour, the authorities wanted to make sure that customers got what they paid for and that the loaves met the officially established weight and ingredient requirements. Pistoia was not the only city to require bakers to mark their loaves with a seal, which allowed the authorities to track the loaves back to their makers if they were found deficient. As the early thirteenth-century statutes of Treviso stated, these marks were designed to prevent bakers from concealing their fraudulent practices.[119]

Seals were used to authenticate other products as well. In Florence, once woolen cloth was sold, measured and cut, brokers affixed a metal seal to it by means of a rivet. Extant examples show the Lana guild's symbol, the lamb, on the obverse with the inscription "FLORENTIA," and the city's symbol, the fleur-de-lys, on the reverse.[120] A fragment of a stone seal for the same guild also shows the lamb surrounded by the fleur-de-lys (fig. 77). The city of Rome required all objects worked from silver to be marked either with the letters "SP" or "SPR" in order to certify the purity of the silver used.[121] These seals and marks served as proof that the products met quality and production standards. In that sense they helped to protect buyers who, as noted in the previous chapter, had to try to determine for themselves the quality and value of the goods they were purchasing. They also served as a form of advertising and as a warrant carried far and wide for the reputation of the cities whence the objects derived.[122]

To reduce the endemic problem of short measure, cities, like Pistoia, appointed various officials to inspect weights and measures, man the public scales, and serve as official measurers. Given the importance of the textile industry to Florence, it is not surprising that the Lana guild strictly regulated the measuring of its cloth. The guild required its consuls to appoint official measurers within a month of entering office. The measurers (there were 72 of them, 18 for each of the city's four wool manufacturing *conventi*, or districts) had to be at least twenty years old, not directly involved in woolen cloth manufacture, and swear an oath that they would measure "well and legally." Three measurers had to participate in sales of four bolts of cloth or more: two measured while the third prepared the cloth. For sales of less than four bolts, two measurers were sufficient. In all cases, a broker had to be present. In return for their

77   Seal of the Florentine Lana Guild, 14th century.

service, the measurers received a fee of two soldi for each piece of cloth measured, one from the buyer, and one from the seller.[123] In Piacenza, the merchants' association maintained two public "stretchers," one at the cathedral and the other at the church of Sant'Andrea. Certain cloths had to be measured at these stations.[124] The association also called for the appointment every year at the time of the annual fair of two men who would patrol the fair and report any drapers (Piacentine or foreign) who falsely measured cloth.[125] And the 1287 statutes of Pisa required merchants buying all kinds of cloth except *panni franceschi* to have them measured by the official measurers of the court of merchants with the measuring stick maintained by that court.[126]

For bulk items sold by weight, cities erected public scales that were manned by official keepers and weighers, like the one in Pistoia's Piazza del Duomo. The city of Florence employed communal weighers whose word was to be accepted in disputes over the weight of items exchanged in a transaction.[127] The keepers of the communal scales were also obliged to deputize four weighers to serve in each of the Lana guild's four manufacturing districts and to supply them with four "good and true scales." These four weighers were authorized to weigh only items pertaining to the guild and had to record "distinctly and singularly" every operation they performed.[128]

When the Venetian Marino Dandolo was serving as podestà of Treviso in the early thirteenth century, he established a new set of official weights and measures for that city.[129] Thereafter, at least four times a month, men appointed by the podestà had to make unannounced inspections in order to see if the official standards were being used. The statutes of the city also called for the placement of three official scales, one in

78    Dubrovnik (Ragusa), inscription over the arcade that housed the public scales, Customs House (Sponza Palace), 16th century.

the Carubio (the intersection of four main roads at what is today the Piazza dei Signori), one in the piazza of the Duomo (*curia maiori*), and one in the Piazza San Leonardo, each of which was to be manned by a "good and legal man" who had to swear to weigh all meat, cheese, and other items brought to the scales "with purity and truth."[130] The weigher at the scales used at the Beccaria was required to do his weighing before allowing anyone to ask how much the meat (or other goods) weighed or how much it ought to weigh. The authorities were concerned that the weigher would make sure that the merchandise corresponded to the amount that he had been told in advance that it should weigh.[131]

In Piacenza, the scales were located at the cathedral, "near the market" (*propter mercatum*).[132] In Venice, the steelyard was located under a portico along the Riva del Vin, close by the Rialto Bridge and easily accessed from both the Campo of San Giacomo di Rialto (Rialto Vecchio) and the Campo of Rialto Nuovo. Situated next to the Grand Canal, the scales facilitated the weighing of items being loaded on or off ships.[133] To my knowledge, none of the actual scales is extant. However, an early sixteenth-century inscription over the public scales in the customs house of Dubrovnik/Ragusa, a city that shared many characteristics with its Italian counterparts, is still visible. The inscription, which seems to be written as if the scales themselves are speaking, says, "FALLERE NOSTRA VETANT ET FALLI PONDERA — MEQUE PONDERO CUM MERCES PONDERAT IPSE DEUS" (Our weights neither deceive nor are deceived. When I weigh merchandize, God also weighs me; fig. 78).[134] Yet again, the commercial and the spiritual intertwine.

In addition to the officials and their assistants employed by governments or guilds to supervise and run the market, many other people made their living by providing support services for the marketplace, including tavern-keepers, operators of hostels, and notaries. Balers and porters were among the most important. Balers wrapped and tied wholesale purchases and prepared them for shipping. Porters, like the two visible in the Porta Ravegnana image (see fig. 13), hauled goods to and from warehouses and shops. In Venice, porters traditionally congregated in the Campo of San Giacomo di Rialto, where they waited for work, but they too tended to impede traffic. Consequently, in November 1326, the Council of Forty required them to vacate the square and station themselves instead at a portico near where the vegetable sellers set up their stalls, that is, in an area near both Rialto Vecchio and Rialto Nuovo.[135] In Treviso, the statutes established the rates that porters of wine were allowed to charge.[136] Porters provided much of the back-breaking labor that the market required and were just one of many occupational groups and sets of officials whose livelihoods derived from the marketplace.

As the economic heart of the city, the marketplace was also the source of significant revenue from duties levied on various items that made their way there for sale. In some instances, cities assigned responsibility for collecting duties and imposts to designated officials; in other cases, they auctioned off the right to collect gabelles to private citizens. A full consideration of the various officials whose financial jurisdiction touched on the activities carried out in the marketplace would lead too far from the central concerns of this study and into an analysis of civic administration more generally. Among the Venetian magistracies with some competence over market activities were the officers in charge of the wine gabelles, the gold estimators, the supervisors of the Fondaco dei Tedeschi, the supervisors of gold cloth, of fustian, of gold, and of pepper, and the officials in charge of brokers, to name only a few.[137] All of these magistracies had their offices at Rialto. Venice, of course, was a major international entrepôt with many specialized offices. Nevertheless, even small cities employed gatekeepers, bridge-keepers, guardians of ports (both maritime and riparian), customs and tax officials, and others who performed functions that touched on the marketplace. As has been seen, the 1284 statutes of the *popolo* of Pistoia called for the appointment of four gatekeepers, one for each of the city's four gates; each was to be assisted by a notary.[138] Pistoia likewise selected officials to supervise the collection of the salt tax.[139] All of these officials had especially to be on the lookout for contraband.

As in Pistoia, most governments also generated income by renting out space within the marketplace. In their push to garner income, communal authorities often built, as noted earlier, fixed shops into their governmental palaces and other public buildings; and many cities adopted the Ottonian imperial palace hall as the model for their communal palaces and adapted the model to include commercial space. In other cases, communal governments built distinct market structures which they then rented out to various merchants and artisans. This was particularly true in Venice where space was rented (or awarded free as a governmental favor) at the Fondaco della Farina, the Pescheria, the Beccarie of Rialto and San Marco, and elsewhere.[140] Rents were due

79　Siena, Campo (location of the marketplace in the Middle Ages).

twice a year, on the feast of Saint Martin (November 11) and of Saint Peter (June 29).[141] In Pisa, the government assigned its bridge-keepers the task of renting out the shops located on its Ponte Vecchio.[142] In Treviso, the fish market was communal property; in Padua, the meat market.[143] According to the chronicler Giovanni Villani, the 43 shops planned for Florence's Ponte Vecchio were expected to generate 80 or more florins in rent per year. In the end, however, the number of shops was increased by three, perhaps in order to garner even more revenue for the city.[144]

Fixed shops were not the only source of income. Communes also charged fees for use of space in the market squares where sellers could set up and dismantle temporary market stalls. The Campo of Siena, which has been thoroughly studied by Maurizio Tuliani, offers an especially well-documented example of this (fig. 79). The 1291 volume of the Gabella indicates that 113 different persons, dealing in everything from shoes to food, cloth to candles, paid for the privilege of selling on a daily basis, either from posts on the paved periphery or in the unpaved center of the Campo. This figure does not include either the peasants, who came to town with farm produce or others who sold items on a seasonal basis, or the fishmongers who were authorized to sell only on Thursdays and Fridays, except during Lent when they could do business every day.[145] In addition, many of the buildings that surrounded and formed the boundary of the Campo included shops with counters from which goods were sold. By law these counters could not extend more than approximately a meter into the piazza. According to the 1291 Gabella, there were 88 such shops. Even more sellers participated in the larger market held on Saturdays and paid for the privilege of doing so.[146]

As in Pistoia, the fees paid to the Sienese commune varied according to the location of the retail space and the merchandise on offer. Higher fees were paid for space on the paved perimeter of the Campo than on the unpaved interior. For much of the fourteenth century, second-hand dealers with fixed positions on the paved perimeter paid an annual fee of either 100 or 80 soldi, depending on their classification as sellers of used items.[147] The fishmongers paid unusually high fees (70 lire), based, in all likelihood, on the volume of business that they did. Rental of space in the unpaved interior ranged from 10 to 20 soldi annually, depending in part on the kind of items sold and in part on whether or not the selling space was protected by a tent or awning. And shops throughout the city whose counters extended into the street were also required to pay a fee. Those fees were assessed on a graduated basis, with shops located on the Campo paying the most (10 soldi annually).[148] Tuliani has calculated that all of the fees that the government assessed on the commercial uses of the Campo generated between 2,000 and 2,400 lire annually. In 1305, it received 2,400 lire, most of which derived from the rental of market space, the rest from fees for weighing and measuring and other expenses.[149]

The myriad rules and regulations examined here had many aims. Those involving food were designed to guarantee that adequate supplies were available in the cities, that they were safe, and that consumers received that for which they paid. Other rules sought to prevent guild members from undercutting their fellow guildsmen by taking production shortcuts, selling at night or on holidays, or using substandard materials. Still others sought to protect the products of guilds as a whole by guarding against counterfeit goods. Many rules were put in place to protect buyers against one of the more common forms of fraudulent selling, the giving of short measure. And still others sought to promote the hygiene, safety, and even the beauty of the marketplace. The impulse behind all of these rules was the desire to systematize, organize, standardize. In a marketplace dominated by non-standardized goods, in which the buyer was at a disadvantage, these rules and regulations sought to create an orderly environment in which the buyer could place some trust. They also sought to protect a city's reputation for fair trade. A 1408 law passed by the Venetian Council of Forty made clear that the "falsities" committed in the production of cotton cloth caused "great damage and shame" (*grando dano e vergogna*) not only to the guild but also to the merchants who sold it.[150] And a clause added in 1400 to the capitulary of the Venetian vair furriers' guild decreed that no production was to be undertaken outside of the street assigned to the guild at Rialto, since fraudulently produced goods would bring "infamy" on the city and cause people to say, "they were cheated on a grand scale in Venice" (*lor fi inganati granmente in Veniesia*).[151]

In spite of their best efforts, people did say just that. The Lucchese druggist, chronicler, and storyteller, Giovanni Sercambi (1348–1424), held the Venetians in particularly low repute. He began one of the stories in his *Novelle* (1390–1402), entitled "De falsatore: Di Basino da Trieste, mercadante di perle," with the line, "in the city of Venice, where they are masters of every sort of evil . . ." and another with the words, "In the city of Venice, more full of deceptions [*inganni*] than of love or charity [*amore o carità*] . . ."[152] But the Venetians were not alone in suffering from a bad reputation. Indeed, Sercambi borrowed the second line almost verbatim from Boccaccio, except that Boccaccio leveled the charge not against Venice but against his native city, claiming that Florence was more filled with deceit than with love or trust (*amore o di fede*).[153]

In the end, what the rules and regulations examined in this chapter most testify to, in fact, is the atmosphere of conflict and mistrust (and the accompanying need for watchfulness) that dominated the medieval Italian marketplace, where, again to cite Paolo da Certaldo, one had to test even one's friends a hundred times.[154] Despite all the claims of Christian brotherhood by guilds and invocations of the common benefit and good by popular governments, as individuals, buyers and sellers were out to take advantage of one another. They sought to do so not through outright competition as it is understood in the modern marketplace, but through trickery. This conflict between private advantage and the common good dominated the medieval Italian marketplace and framed relations there. And, as the next section will show, it also determined market values and shaped the very layout and adornment of the marketplace.

# PART THREE

---

# MARKETPLACE ETHICS

On August 3, 1387 a member of the Venetian cotton beaters' guild named Zanin di Gabriel, who went by the nickname Spina, was publicly humiliated when it was discovered that the beaten cotton that he had been producing or selling was deemed to be "false" (*falso*). It is unclear from the cryptic records of this case what the authorities meant by the term; but it seems likely that Spina, who could have been either a beater himself or a merchant member of the guild of beaters, was making or marketing beaten cotton that did not meet requisite quality standards: perhaps impurities had not been properly removed from the cotton or, more likely, the beaten cotton did not contain the prescribed number of beaten bolls per unit of weight. In one way or another it was "badly worked"; and the Giustizieri Vecchi and the three wardens of the cotton beaters' guild – Ser Bortolamio Celsi, Ser Nicoleto of San Vidal, and Antonio di Francesco of Santa Fosca – considered it not up to standard. Accordingly, they gave Spina "a demerit" (.1. *ponto*) and had the offending cloth publicly burned, "in the middle of the Rialto" (*in mezo de Rialto*).[1]

Spina was not the only member of the guild to be prosecuted for illicit activities. Two years earlier, in August 1385, Cristofalo of San Salvador had been found guilty by the Giustizieri Vecchi and a different set of guild wardens – Ser Cabrin di Ziliulo, Ser Zanin di Verdili, and Ser Piero Bon – of "falsifying the craft." He too was given a demerit. But this was not Cristofalo's first offense. In December 1384 and again in May 1385 he had been given demerits for the same reason. With three strikes against him, Cristofalo was out. The authorities expelled him from the guild and ordered him not to practice the trade again. Furthermore, the cloth that he had falsified was burned "in the Fondaco dei Tedeschi."[2]

Venice was by no means the only city where counterfeit or shoddily made goods were destroyed in a public way. In Lucca, badly made silk cloth was burned, as was counterfeit saffron.[3] In Piacenza, it was candles and combs for looms.[4] In Verona, counterfeit drugs (syrups, and so on) were tossed into the street; while in Pisa, imitation saffron was burned at the foot of that city's Ponte Vecchio.[5] In Florence, tainted meat, deceitfully baled hay and straw, and badly dyed silk cloth all were burned.[6]

The authorities who authorized these punishments carefully selected the sites for the destruction. In some instances, the offending items were burned in front of the shops where they were discovered. Thus in Florence, tainted meat could be burned in front of the stall of the butcher who was trading in it, while Por Santa Maria allowed for the burning of poorly dyed silk cloth in the street leading to Porta Santa Maria.[7] In these cases the intention was not only to maximize the humiliation for the merchant or craftsman who traded in such goods but also to warn others in the same profession of the consequences of engaging in similar activities. In other cases, officers chose the sites in order to publicize the crimes themselves. In Pisa, for example, the government forbade the unauthorized selling of goods on bridges; if it was discovered to be happening, the goods were confiscated from the vendor and thrown into the Arno.[8]

In still other instances and apparently most frequently, the preferred location for ritualized destruction was the central marketplace. In Florence, for example, if tainted meat was not burned in front of the offending butcher's stall and ill-dyed cloth in the street leading to Porta Santa Maria, then they were burned in the Mercato Vecchio. Counterfeit cloth was immolated in Verona's market square; counterfeit candles in Piacenza's Piazza del Borgo, while in Venice, as noted earlier, the preferred locations were the main square at Rialto and the courtyard of the Fondaco dei Tedeschi.[9] By burning tainted goods in these places, the authorities gained maximum publicity and sent a warning to all vendors and producers that counterfeit or fraudulent goods would not be tolerated. At the same time, they announced to buyers, particularly foreign customers, that their cities guaranteed the quality of goods on offer. After all, the primary audience for the burning of goods in the Fondaco dei Tedeschi was the German merchants doing business in Venice. In this way, the public destruction of tainted goods served, like the placement of seals on cloth by the Florentine Lana guild, as a way to publicize and certify the reputation of a city for honest trading and high-quality products.

Through their actions, the authorities were also seeking to extirpate evil. As in the razing of enemies' houses (a common practice in the faction-ridden cities of medieval Italy) and the burning of heretics and sodomites, the idea pertained that the community

80   Venice, Pietra di Bando (Proclamation Stone)
with the 16th-century Gobbo di Rialto (Rialto
Hunchback), Campo San Giacomo di Rialto.

could be made whole once again through an act of purification – in most cases
through purification by fire.[10] Evil inhered in the tainted goods and thus had to be
removed. Similarly, the marketplace itself had been befouled, and so it too had to be
purified. Just as the execution of conspirators against the regime in the communal
center restored a polity to peace and concord and the burning of heretics the community to orthodoxy, so the destruction of counterfeit goods in the marketplace
returned the market itself to equity and honesty.

These ritual acts underlined the centrality of the marketplace as an urban space.
Like the communal palace and the cathedral, the marketplace served many different
purposes. In addition to being the locus of commerce, it was a prime location for the
dissemination of news. Merchants and craftsmen gathered in the marketplace to glean
what information they could of such events as droughts, famines, shipwrecks, rebellions,
and wars, all of which could affect commerce and trade.[11] And, not surprisingly, civic
regimes viewed marketplaces as ideal sites at which to make public announcements,
given the confluence of people who gathered in them. The Florentine government
required its criers to make certain announcements in the piazza in front of the Baptistery, at Orsanmichele, in the Mercato Vecchio and Mercato Nuovo, as well as to post
notices on the door of the Palazzo della Signoria.[12] In Venice, public decrees were
proclaimed from the two proclamation columns, one of which stood (and still stands)
at Rialto in Campo San Giacomo (fig. 80), the other at San Marco.[13] Preachers also,
like Bernardino of Siena, sometimes chose market squares, such as Siena's Campo and
Florence's Mercato Vecchio, as the sites for their sermonizing.[14]

This same potential for publicity made markets ideal locales at which to punish
criminals, especially those who had committed market-related crimes. In Padua, bankrupts were publicly humiliated when, stripped to their underclothes, they had to circle

81    Padua, Stone of Vituperation in the Salone, Palazzo della Ragione.

the Stone of Vituperation in the Salone three times while proclaiming the words "Cedo bonis" (I give up my goods; fig. 81).[15] But those who had violated market norms were not the only ones punished in market squares. Near the Peronio in Padua's market square stood a pillory at which persons convicted of various crimes were subject to public humiliation; in Florence, the pillory was located in the Mercato Nuovo.[16] And in Verona, blasphemers who were unable to pay the fines imposed on them for their offenses against God and the saints were to be dunked three times in water if it was wintertime and whipped three times around the column in that city's marketplace if it was summertime.[17] In Bologna, the government executed many but not all criminals at the city's fairgrounds, which stood outside the city walls.[18]

Marketplaces also figured in various civic processional routes. In Florence, a footrace held to celebrate the feast of Santa Reparata made its way to the Mercato Vecchio. The *palii*, or horse races, of Florence traversed the Mercato Vecchio on a course that went from near the church of Ognisanti to San Piero Maggiore, while Siena's famous Palio took place in that city's market and political center, the Campo.[19] Such ritual occasions tied the marketplace to the symbolic systems that governed civic life. Florence, for instance, required the residents of Firenzuola, a town under Florentine jurisdiction, to gather in Firenzuola's major square to celebrate the feast of Florence's patron saint.[20]

Although most Venetian civic processions did not include Rialto in their itineraries, the marketplace held especially deep significance for inhabitants of that city.[21] Legends affirmed that the island of Rialto was where refugees fleeing Attila's predations first established the settlement that later became Venice, and where they founded the city's first church, San Giacomo di Rialto. Furthermore, astrologers determined the precise date and time of the city's founding – noon on March 25, 421 – a date that associated the city's establishment with the Annunciation and thereby endowed Venice with a Christian destiny.[22] It was also at Rialto that the Venetians chose to erect a clock

82  Venice, Campo San Giacomo di Rialto (Rialto Vecchio).

on the campanile of San Giacomo.[23] Together, the clock and the bell known as the Realtina opened and closed the market day.[24] For the Venetians, Rialto became the *umbilicus mundi* (the navel of the world).[25] It was where time and space took on meaning (fig. 82).

Rialto was also the place where in 1322 the Venetians had a *mappamondo* (world map) painted, along with various scenes from Venetian history, including one that depicted the defeat of Pepin in 810 — the event that led to the moving of the "capital" of Venice from Malamocco on the Lido to the settlement that went by the name Rialto.[26] This map — about which little is known — probably served various functions. Although it was unsuitable for actual navigation or travel, it nonetheless offered merchants a reference point for their business deals. Additionally, it celebrated the "global" reach of Venetian trade, as may have a copy of Marco Polo's famous book of travels, which, according to some accounts, was secured on a chain and displayed at Rialto.[27] Like Polo's book, the *mappamondo* emphasized Venice's central location (at least from the Venetian point of view) in the medieval world-system.

Thus the ritualized destruction of fraudulent goods, while certainly dramatic, was just one of many ways in which authorities in different cities sought to inscribe meaning and moral order on the marketplace — an order that vilified self-interest and the vices associated with it and lauded the common good and its accompanying virtues, and that was summed up in the phrase ubiquitously used in laws, statutes, and contracts, *bona fide*, *sine fraude* (in good faith and without fraud). This section explores the ethics of the marketplace and the ways in which architecture and urban form, the keeping of written records, literature, sermons, and works of painting and sculpture instilled those values. The marketplace was where society's often conflicted and conflicting attitudes toward religion, the economy, and even the self were most prominently on display and where questions of the moral order played out. Much more was at stake in the marketplace than merely buying and selling.

# 7

# *BONA FIDE, SINE FRAUDE*
# (IN GOOD FAITH AND
# WITHOUT FRAUD)

Reading the medieval intellectuals, commonly known as the scholastics, and reading guild and civic statutes from medieval Italy is to be confronted by a startling disjuncture. While the scholastics wrote at great length about usury, civic and guild leaders seldom addressed that issue, except to include rather formulaic exclusions of known usurers in their statutes.[1] They were obsessed instead with the problem of fraud in the marketplace. Statutes from cities across the Italian peninsula and guild regulations from every conceivable occupational group contain law after law, clause after clause outlining fraudulent practices and establishing penalties for those who committed them.

Modern scholarship contains a concomitant disjuncture. While there is a rich and sophisticated literature on the scholastic analysis of usury, scholarly consideration of fraud remains neglected, although this is beginning to change.[2] To be sure, the scholastics were not completely silent on the subject; and when they discussed fraud, they generally did so in the context of buying and selling. The Dominican Roland of Cremona (d. 1259), for example, who preached and lectured in Bologna, stated in his commentary on Peter Lombard's *Sentences*, "a thing is worth as much as it can be sold for – it being understood that it is sold without any fraud" (*Res tantum valet quantum vendi potest – intelligendum est: si vendatur sine aliqua fraude*).[3]

Thomas Aquinas devoted considerable attention to fraud in Question 77 of the Second Part of Part Two in his *Summa Theologica*, entitled "Of Cheating, which is committed in Buying and Selling," and encompassing four questions or articles. To the first question, whether or not it is sinful to sell a thing for more than the just price, Aquinas answers that "it is altogether sinful to have recourse to deceit in order to sell a thing for more than its just price." To the second as to "whether a sale is rendered unlawful through a fault in the thing sold," he replies by quoting Ambrose: "It is manifestly a rule of justice that a good man should not depart from the truth, nor inflict an unjust injury on anyone, nor have any connection with fraud." Aquinas further elaborates that the falsification of goods can be due to their substance (the products are counterfeit), quantity (they are not sold according to publicly established weights and measures), or quality (the usefulness of the product is undiscoverable).[4] In answer to the third question, "Whether the seller is bound to state the defects of the thing sold," Aquinas replies that if the defect is manifest (for example, a horse has only one eye), the seller is not obligated to reveal it to the buyer, although he is obliged to ask a lower price. In cases of possible loss or danger to the buyer, however, he must reveal the defects; otherwise, "the sale will be illicit and fraudulent." To the fourth and final question ("Whether, in trading, it is lawful to sell a thing for a higher price than was paid for it"), Aquinas affirms the prevailing argument of the period that a "moderate" gain is permissible, "as payment for his [the trader's] labor."[5] Odd Langholm summarized Aquinas's view as follows: "the right of buyers and sellers to outwit or 'deceive' (decipere) one another granted them by Roman law, does not amount to a license to commit fraud."[6]

Nevertheless, in spite of the influence of Roman law and Aristotle's *Nicomachaean Ethics* in establishing the concept of justice as central to economic exchange, scholastic writers also continued to understand fraud in a highly moralized way, as a threat to the soul of its perpetrator. According to Bonaventura of Bagnoregio (Saint Bonaventure), rare indeed was the merchant who was able to avoid fraudulent practices (*rarissime evandunt mercatores*), including the use of false weights and measures.[7] As Aquinas himself stated, it was sinful to resort to deception in sales, "because this is to deceive one's neighbor so as to injure him."[8] Aquinas and his fellow scholastics understood fraud to be inherently dyadic: it requires a minimum of two persons, the deceiver and the deceived. As the Franciscan Gerald Odonis wrote, "no one is defrauded knowingly and willingly" (*nullus enim fraudatur sciens et consentiens*).[9] In this way, fraud was (and is still) a quintessentially social practice.

First and foremost, though, as the French scholar Anne Montenach observes, fraud is a discourse.[10] For this reason, one has to be particularly attentive to who is calling something fraud. Put differently: fraud is in the eye of the beholder. So, for instance, what an established artisan may perceive as fraud – the use, for example, by a competitor of a new and unauthorized material in the creation of a product – can, from the perspective of the competitor, be viewed as technological innovation.[11] As Montenach notes, fraud is an "eminently supple and adaptable response to the needs of a heterogeneous population."[12] By its very nature, then, talking about fraud is a way of talking about social relations, society, and the self.

The characteristics of medieval manufacturing and marketing themselves contributed powerfully to the preoccupation with fraud. As discussed in the preceding section, in an age of non-standardized goods, items in the market varied radically in the quality of materials contained within them and the workmanship involved in producing them, as well as in size and quantity. And, although popular governments and guilds made a concerted effort to promote standardization (that was, after all, the purpose of their myriad regulations), they could not guarantee the legitimacy of all of the goods found in the marketplace and hence engender trust in them. The onus of responsibility for determining the quality and value of the goods for sale in the market still rested with the buyer.

Civic statutes and guild regulations offer a veritable catalog of the tricks that manufacturers and sellers used to deceive their customers. Much of this fraud (accepting that the authorities considered it as such and not as innovation) occurred during the manufacturing process and thus qualified as counterfeiting. Venetian rock-crystal carvers, for example, substituted colored glass for precious stones in their wares; Florentine chandlers combined old wax with new in their candles, and goldsmiths used "counterfeit" stones rather than "precious stones" in the jewelry they created.[13] In Rome, furriers passed off one kind of pelt for another, while Veronese metalworkers coated their wares with oil to hide defects.[14] In Treviso, those found to have mixed different sorts of thread into their cloth had it confiscated. In that case, rather than being burned, the cloth was put to good use: it was given to the poor of Treviso's civic hospital.[15]

Other kinds of fraud occurred in the marketplace itself, in the display and presentation of goods on offer. Butchers had a variety of tricks at hand. They mixed different varieties of meat together and masked old or tainted meat by inflating it or dabbing it with blood in order to make it appear fresh. Other times they sold sick animals – the authorities in Pistoia have already been noted as describing this as a particularly "great fraud."[16] Fishmongers also used blood for fraudulent purposes by smearing it on the gills of fish that was no longer fresh.[17] Hiding poorer quality goods under better ones was another trick. Florentine sellers of hay and straw used high-quality materials on the outside of their bales to hide inferior ones on the inside, while the fishmongers of Rome who sold at wholesale were warned to make sure that the fish in the bottom of containers were the same as those on the top.[18] In Florence, members of the Lana guild sometimes showed potential customers samples of better cloth than that which they were actually selling.[19] And, according to a sermon by Bernardino of Siena aimed specifically at merchants, some vendors, when asked, told outright lies about their goods.[20]

Opportunities for fraud also presented themselves at the conclusion of sales during measuring and settling of accounts. As noted in the previous chapter, guild and governmental authorities were preoccupied with the use of fraudulent weights and measures. In the same sermon to merchants, Bernardino noted that some of them used one set of weights and measures when buying and another set when selling and profited from the difference. Likewise drapers pulled cloth so tightly when measuring that it tore, while vendors moistened merchandise sold by weight in order to make it

heavier.[21] Some merchants, again according to the preacher, counted out their customers' change quickly in order to cheat them of the correct amount.[22]

These preoccupations were not idle fantasies of preachers and governmental officials,
as some actual cases of vendors accused of giving false measure indicate. In 1304, the
Bolognese notary Gulielmo who had been charged with the task of inspecting the
measures used in the city's taverns discovered that Pietro Alegri, who sold wine out
of his house near the Porta Ravegnana, was using false measures.[23] And in 1365 in
Chioggia, the Venetian podestà fined a butcher named Provinciale for short-changing
a customer of the meat he had purchased. The podestà fined Provinciale ten lire and,
since this was his third offense, banned him in perpetuity from the meat market as the
law required, "if any butcher will be found to give bad weight [three times]." But
Provinciale petitioned for clemency, claiming that because of the "crush of people"
(*tumultum gentium*) he had inadvertently given the short measure. In the end, the Venetian government, on the advice of the podestà himself, granted him a pardon that
required him to pay the fine but expunged the third offense. The podestà supported
the petition, arguing that Provinciale was very adept at his trade and useful to Chioggia
since he helped to bring "plenty" to the town.[24]

Contemporaries used a variety of words to describe various fraudulent practices.
The word fraud itself (*fraude*, *frode*) was most commonly used, followed by *inganno*
(deceit), although one rule from the statutes of Por Santa Maria sought to emphasize
the despicable nature of the deceptions by referring to them as "secret deceits" (*inganni
segreti*).[25] Additionally, officials often paired fraud with other words that reveal its various
connotations and meanings and indicate why it cut so deeply. Some of these terms
further defined fraud itself: hence fraud was *falsità* (the opposite of truth), *malizia*
(malice, directed at others), *dolo* (guile, the characteristic of its perpetrator), and in some
instances simply evil itself (*male*).[26]

In other cases, the synonyms emphasize the social threat posed by fraud: the word
was paired with *danno* (damage) and *vergogna* (shame). The city or guild that allowed
fraud in its marketplace suffered damage to its reputation and therefore shame.[27] In at
least one case from Venice, religious language seeped into guild statutes. The Venetian
cotton-cloth makers' guild referred in their capitulary to "fraud or sin" (*frolda overo
pecha*) and to its practitioners as "perpetrators of fraud or sinners" (*fraudantes vel pec-
cantes*).[28] The 1287 statutes of Pisa used four different verbs to describe the act of
counterfeiting saffron: *falsificare*, *corrumpere*, *vitiare*, and *sophisticare*. These verbs captured
the active intervention of the producer: the saffron itself was passive and morally neutral
while its seller falsified, corrupted, vitiated, and adulterated it.[29] The Sienese statutes of
1262 referred to the perpetrator of fraud as a "committer of fraud and a concealer"
(*fraudator vel celator*).[30] And a clause in the statutes of Por Santa Maria spoke of "frauds,
falsities, and thefts" (*fraudes, falsitates, et furta*).[31]

Equally revealing are the terms contemporaries used to describe items that were not
judged to be fraudulent. Most referred to goods made or sold according to guild or
civic standards. Such authorized goods were referred to as "good and qualified" (*bonas
et idoneas*), "legitimate" (*legitimas*), "exact" or "precise" (*rectum*), "genuine" (*sinceram*), and,

in the case of spices, "fresh" (*recentes*), and "pure and true" (*pura et vera*).[32] A clause in the statutes of the Venetian comb-makers spoke of "good and lawful work" (*bonum opus et legale*), while a rule concerning the wool merchants of Rome required them to do what was "good and legal" (*bonitatem et legalitatem*).[33] As for the maker of lawful goods, he pledged to act with an "honest soul" (*puro animo*) and, in the case of the Florentine butchers, even was expected to exhibit a certain "sympathy" (*simpatia*).[34]

As the terms "secret deceits" (*inganni segreti*) and "concealer" (*celator*) make especially clear, contemporaries understood fraud to occur in places that were private, secret, and beyond public view. The layout of the marketplace and the architecture of shops could facilitate fraud. Some shopkeepers arranged their stalls in such a way as to hide illicit activities. The Dominican friar Henry of Rimini, who was the prior of the Venetian monastery of Santi Giovanni e Paolo in 1304, claimed that certain drapers selected shops that were "dark and gloomy" and then hung cloth over the windows to make them darker still so that the defects in their merchandise could not easily be perceived.[35] The statutes of Verona prohibited tavern-keepers from placing counters or other "obstacles" in front of their shop doors in order to prevent customers from being able to see the wine as it was being extracted from barrels. In so doing the tavern-keepers were able to give short measure, water down the wine, or replace it with another of lesser quality.[36] Similarly, merchandise had to be placed on open display, not concealed. A Florentine rule stated that sellers of clogs were not to keep their goods "hidden" (*absconsos*) either by keeping them at their home or by placing them in boxes, but instead were to display them "openly" for anyone wishing to purchase them.[37]

Many of the rules discussed in the previous chapter – prohibiting selling or working at night (darkness was believed to breed fraud), requiring that sales be conducted only in approved locations, and authorizing inspections of shops – were designed to combat fraud. A clause in the statutes of Por Santa Maria pertaining to the goldsmiths' branch of the guild made this clear. Entitled "Concerning not working in secret places or at night," it stated that in order to remove the opportunity for those wishing to perpetrate "fraud and falsity," no master goldsmith or his assistants were to do work "in any secret place . . . in order that he cannot be seen," or at night, or in any place that was not "open to passersby and on public streets." It went on to declare that no work was to be done in any loft or basement but only in what amounted to the ground floor of the shop.[38] Clearly, the cramped shops and dark and narrow streets of many marketplaces bred corruption (or at the least the fear of corruption).

Contemporaries also understood fraud's effects to be wide-ranging. First and foremost, fraud hurt the buyer, although the warning *caveat emptor* certainly pertained. It also injured its perpetrator by placing him in legal jeopardy and threatening his or her soul. Yet fraud's effects went further still, since they threatened the common good in a variety of ways. The wellbeing and reputation of an entire guild, industry, or city could be injured by such practices. The preface to the statutes of the Bolognese druggists noted that members of that profession were especially obliged not to commit fraud but rather were to operate "legitimately and legally," since their profession dealt with the "health of the human body and the conservation of wellness and the removal of illness."[39] Por Santa Maria's statutes warned those engaged in particular branches of the guild (for example, the silk trade or goldsmithing) not to trade in items that did not pertain to that branch. Otherwise they would be engaging in fraud that would hurt buyers and bring "infamy" on the guild and on Florence generally. An earlier clause in the same statutes stated that using poorer quality dyes for silk cloth would result in the "vituperation" of all merchants and redound to the "perpetual infamy" of the guild and the "danger of souls."[40] As noted in the previous chapter, the Venetians too feared that fraudulent practices would bring "infamy" on the city and contribute to the reputation of Venetians as deceivers.[41]

A clause in the 1318 statutes of the Florentine oil and cheese sellers, pertaining to the use of standard measures, captured many of these aspects of fraud and the danger it posed. The rule required the rectors of the guild to make inquiries about any guildsman who was suspected of committing fraud, "in selling or buying or marketing goods – goods and merchandise pertaining to this guild – and especially [to inquire] against those, who not openly in their shops, but in hidden and secluded things keep measures and produce various merchandise, or who in various parts of the city [sell] with their illicit measures which they carry with them ..." The preface to the rule stated that these inspections would contribute to the "common good of the guild" (*il comune bene de l'università*).[42] Thus officials viewed fraud – the perversion of the marketplace – in terms of a conflict between the private interest of the perpetrator and the common good, in this case the common good of the guild, but by extension of the city more generally.[43]

While statutes and rule books elaborate on specific kinds of fraud and various fraudulent practices, theological tracts, confessional manuals, sermons, poems, and stories present a fuller view of its relationship to the broader moral economy. First and foremost, theologians emphasized that fraud was one aspect of the especially deadly sin of avarice. As Johann Huizinga first observed and as later elaborated by Lester Little, as the commercial revolution of the Middle Ages advanced and money and movable goods came to rival land as sources of wealth, avarice challenged pride's status as the deadliest of the deadly sins. This change reflected a shift (at least in part) from social relations based primarily on hierarchy and personal status (whether feudal- or kinship-based) to ones grounded in commercial relations and contracts.[44] Accordingly, theologians subjected avarice to an elaborate dissection. As Carla Casagrande and Silvana Vecchio note, avarice was, "one of the vices, if not the vice, about which the most was written throughout the Middle Ages."[45] And in the visual arts, avarice enjoyed primacy of representation among the vices (see fig. 2).[46]

As Casagrande and Vecchio also observe, avarice was understood both narrowly and broadly. In its narrower sense, avarice was an excessive love of money or, as Augustine said, of "all things that we are able to possess, give and sell." More generally, however, avarice encompassed an unregulated desire to possess, regardless of whether the things coveted were material, such as goods or money, or immaterial, such as power and knowledge.[47] Avarice was also deemed analogous to, if not identical with, idolatry, with

money replacing God as the object of worship.[48] And it had important social dimensions in that the avaricious man's hoarding of goods left others indigent.[49]

Medieval theologians also were convinced that vice generated vice. According to a
genealogy of the cardinal sins elaborated by Gregory the Great, pride gave birth to
vainglory, vainglory to envy, envy to anger, and so on. For its part, avarice was, in
Gregory's schema, the child of sadness (*tristitia*) since, "when the heart, is confused,
losing the good of interior happiness, it seeks external modes of consolation, and not
being able to return to interior joy, it desires all the more ardently to possess exterior
goods."[50] The cardinal sins had, in turn, the capacity to generate their own offspring.
In the eighth question or article of Question 118 of the Second Part of Part Two of
the *Summa Theologica*, Aquinas enumerates avarice's seven "daughters," namely, "treachery, fraud, falsehood, perjury, restlessness, violence, and insensibility to mercy." One of
the objections to the article is that Isidore of Seville articulated nine, rather than seven,
daughters of avarice: lying, fraud, theft, perjury, greed of filthy lucre, false witnessing,
violence, inhumanity, and rapacity. But Aquinas replies that the nine are reducible to
seven since lying and false witnessing are encompassed under his category of falsehood,
theft under fraud, and so forth, and furthermore that the seven as he articulates them
are the same as those listed by Gregory the Great in his *Moralia*. Despite Aquinas's
authority, other articulations of avarice's progeny remained in circulation. Usury, for
example, was often included among its misbegotten offspring.[51]

Theologians frequently utilized the metaphor of a tree to convey this idea of filia-
tion: just as large limbs emerge from the trunk of a tree and then produce smaller
branches and leaves, so various sins emerge from the root stock of pride. John Rigaud,
Franciscan confessor to Clement v, wrote that fraud in business deals was one branch
of the tree of avarice, as was usury.[52] In the same way, theologians also crafted a tree
of the virtues that they juxtaposed to that of the vices. Miniaturists often rendered the
trees of vice and virtue in their illuminations.[53] One image of a tree of vice comes
from the fourteenth-century psalter of Robert de Lisle. In this image by an artist
whom Lucy Freeman Sandler identifies as the Madonna Master and an anonymous
second illuminator, the "branch" of Avarice supports seven "leaves" comprising Fraud,
Theft, Perjury, Rapine, Treachery, Usury, and Simony (fig. 83).[54]

Theologians and others also utilized another metaphor – that of a battle between
the virtues and vices. Derived from Prudentius's *Psychomachia* of the late fourth/early
fifth century CE, the idea of a contest enjoyed lasting popularity throughout the Middle
Ages. It found its way into the vernacular in various works, including the Florentine
jurist Bono Giamboni's *Libro de' vizî e delle virtudi* composed in the mid-thirteenth
century, a work also heavily influenced by Boethius's *Consolation of Philosophy*.[55] In
Giambono's work, Philosophy comforts the author who is mourning the loss of earthly
goods; she convinces him to seek instead the path to heaven. He is granted a vision
of the battle between the virtues and vices, including the vices' allies Judaism and Islam.
Avarice is the fifth of the vices to appear on the battlefield, accompanied by its twelve
"captains": simony, usury, robbery, perjury, theft, lying, plundering, forced injury, moles-
tation, misuse of justice, deceit, and desire for honor ("Simonia, Usura, Ladorneccio,

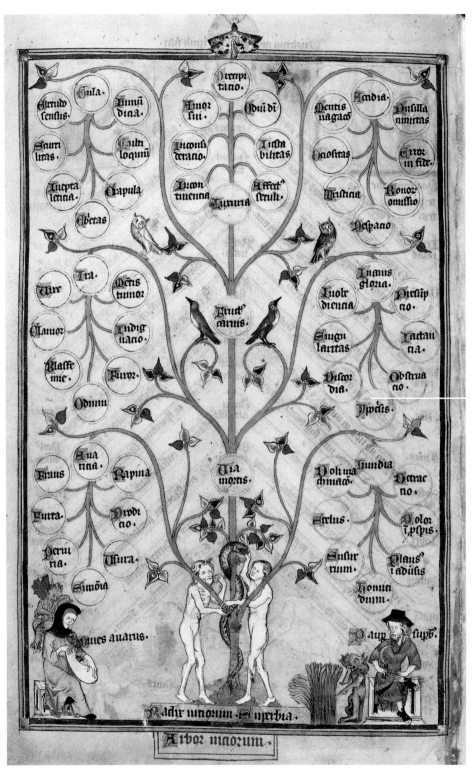

83   Madonna Master and unknown miniaturist, *Tree of Vices*, from the Psalter of Robert de Lisle, c. 1310, London, British Library, Arundel Ms. 83/II, fol. 128v.

84   Anonymous, *The Fox and the Crow*, c. 1297, Sala dei Notari, Palazzo dei Priori, Perugia.

Pergiurio, Furto, Bugia, Rapina, Forza, Inquietare, Mal giudicare, Ingannare e Onor desiderare").[56] In a passage taken nearly wholesale from Prudentius, while Faith, Hope, and Charity repose, the other virtues prepare to return to the field of battle. But under the cover of darkness, "a terrible vice, named Fraud, very astute and ingenious in the evils of the world," sneaks onto the battlefield and digs a deep ditch in the area that the virtues will need to cross, and then covers it over with grass so that it cannot be detected. "And when it had completed this task, it [Fraud] departed secretly so that no one was aware [of it]."[57] But when the battle resumes, the virtues' troops are able to avoid Fraud's ditch. In the end, they triumph, and the author is admitted to the ranks of the faithful.

The animal kingdom too supplied nearly endless possibilities for symbolizing the vices.[58] Sometimes the seven-headed beast mentioned in the Book of the Apocalypse was understood to signify the seven capital vices. Alternatively, various species of animals could symbolize particular vices. Avarice was sometimes rendered as a serpent, frog, mole, hedgehog, or wolf, while fraud was most commonly symbolized by the fox, known for its cunning and deceit.[59] For example, an illustration in the *Hortus deliciarum* of Herrad of Hohenbourg (d. 1195) shows the chariot of Avarice being drawn by a lion symbolizing cruelty and a fox symbolizing fraud. Next to the fox are the words "Fraus est vulpus" (Fraud is the fox).[60]

These associations reached a wide audience through retellings of the *Roman de Renart*, some originating in Italy, and through Aesop's fables.[61] One Tuscan version of Aesop, dating to the second half of the fourteenth century, clearly reflects the mercantile and political environment of the Italian city states, especially in the "temporal" morals which the author draws at the end of each fable (each fable also has a "spiritual" moral).[62] Thus in the story of the fox and the crow, the crow symbolizes the "simple man" who is taken in by the deceiver's flattery.[63] It was one of several fables illustrated in Perugia's Palazzo dei Priori, where its message about extending trust cautiously would have resonated widely (fig. 84).[64] In the fable of the fox and the stork, the fox stands for "every deceiver who is the cause of the breaking of loyalty and faith [fede] . . ."[65] And in the fable of the fox, the wolf, and the sheep-fold, "we should understand [the fox to represent]," the author claims, "every false artisan who through envy of great profits accuses his neighbor."[66] But other animals and objects could also stand for fraud. In the fable of the wolf that finds a decapitated human head, the head symbolizes "those who abandon right and legal business practices and pursue bad contracts and false operations."[67] And in the fable of the wolf who tries to convince a pregnant pig that he is willing to serve as her midwife, the wolf represents "poor and false merchants who adorn their person with beautiful clothes and speak high-sounding words of great business deals and of [their] loyalty, and who adorn their warehouses and shops with fake and dissembling (aparenti) merchandise so that by such means they can trick the simple folk, promising good and doing evil." The astute sow, by contrast, stands for those who judge others not by their words but by their deeds.[68]

Other works of literature also conveyed the message about fraud and its dangers. In the interlude known as "La Penetanza," within Brunetto Latini's *Tesoretto*, a philosophical poem that served in some respects as a model for Dante's *Comedy*, the author tells that he has confessed his sins to a friar of Montpellier and advises his unnamed friend, the dedicatee, to do the same. This offers Latini the opportunity to enumerate and characterize the sins to which humans are vulnerable so that his friend may examine his conscience as a prelude to his own confession. Among the sins that Latini presents in his catalogue of vices is avarice. In Latini's formulation, avarice derives originally from negligence. He describes the avaricious man as follows:

> For he does not spend what he ought,
> And does not give to any other;
> Instead, he fears greatly
> That before he comes to death
> His possessions will decrease,
> And he further tightens the reins.
> And so he grasps and rages,
> And gives false measure
> And fraudulent weight
> And deceitful amounts;
> And he does not fear the sin
> Of overpricing his merchandise
> Or committing fraud;
> Instead he considers this praise;

He is accustomed to deceive,
And through pure words
He cheats others often,
And very generously
Promises to give
When he does not believe he can.

[Ché dovere non spende,
Né già l'altrui non rende;
Ançi a paura forte
C'ançi che vegna a morte
L'aver li vengna meno,
E pu'ristringe'l freno.
Così rapisce e fura,
E dà falsa misura
E peso frodolente
E novero fallente;
E non teme peccato
D'avistar suo mercato
Né di commetter frode;
Ançi 'l si tiene in lode;
Di nasconder lo sòle,
E per bianche parole
Inganna altrui sovente,
E molto largamente
Promette di donare
Quando no'l crede fare.][69]

As Latini's words clearly convey, he viewed merchants as especially susceptible to avarice and its companion fraud.

Dante, Latini's fellow poet and possibly his student, offers his own vision of the avaricious and the perpetrators of fraud in the *Comedy*. In Canto 11 of "Inferno," Virgil and Dante pause at the sixth circle of Hell while Virgil explains to Dante what they have witnessed so far and what they have yet to encounter. Virgil makes clear that the circles of Hell correspond to a hierarchy of sin and that the lower one descends, the more serious are the crimes and the more harrowing the punishments. Circles Two through Six (Circle One is Limbo) are reserved for the incontinent, including the gluttonous and the lustful. The worst sinners are relegated to Circles Seven through Nine. As Dante explains (Canto 11, lines 22–7):

Of every malice that earns hate in heaven
injustice is the end; and each such end
by force or fraud brings harm.
However, fraud is man's peculiar vice,
God finds it more displeasing and therefore
the fraudulent are lower, suffering more.

> [D'ogne malizia, ch'odio in cielo acquista,
> ingiuria è 'l fine, ed ogne fin cotale
> o con forza o con frode altrui constrista.
> Ma perché frode è de l'uom proprio male,
> più spiace a Dio; e però stan di sotto
> li frodolenti, e più dolor li assale][70]

The violent – those who use force against others, themselves, or God – are punished in the seventh circle. Among those suffering here are the usurers for their offense against both art and nature – hence their pairing with other sinners against nature, the Sodomites (Canto 17, lines 58–73).[71]

In lines 52–66 of Canto 11, Virgil explains to Dante that the perpetrators of fraud and treachery inhabit the deepest circles of Hell:

> Now fraud, that eats away at every conscience,
> is practiced by a man against another
> who trusts in him, or one who has no trust.
> This latter way seems only to cut off
> the bond of love that nature forges; thus,
> nestled within the second circle are:
> hypocrisy and flattery, sorcerers,
> and falsifiers, simony and theft,
> and barrators, and panderers and like trash.
> But in the former way of fraud, not only
> the love that nature forges is forgotten, but
> added love that builds a special trust;
> thus, in the tightest circle, where there is
> the universe's center, the seat of Dis,
> all traitors are consumed eternally.

> [La frode, ond'ogne coscienza è morsa,
> può l'omo ursare in colui che 'n lui fida,
> e in quel che fidanza non imborsa.
> Questo modo di retro par ch'incida
> pur lo vinco d'amor che fa natura;
> onde nel cerchio secondo s'annida
> iposcresia, lusinghe e chi affattura,
> falsità, ladroneccio e simonia,
> ruffian, baratti e simile lordura.
> Per l'altro modo quell'amor s'oblia
> che fa natura, e quel ch'è poi aggiunto,
> di che la fede spezial si cria;
> Onde nel cerchio minore, ov'è 'l punto
> de l'universo in su che Dite siede,
> qualunque trade in etterno è consunto.]

In the ten pockets of Malbolge (the name of Circle Eight) and in the four rounds of Circle Nine, Dante enumerates no less than fourteen different forms of fraud, many of which touch only tangentially, if at all, on the marketplace. However, what they have in common is that they constitute a betrayal of trust, that most essential element of commercial transactions in particular and of society more generally.[72]

Dante and Virgil descend into those final two circles of Hell, where the perpetrators of fraud and betrayers of trust suffer their everlasting punishments, on the back of the Geryon, a creature which Virgil has fished up from the depths with the cord taken from around Dante's waist. Dante's describes the Geryon in this way (Canto 17, lines 10–12):

> The face he wore was that of a just man,
> so gracious were his features' outer semblance;
> and all his trunk, the body of a serpent.
>
> [La faccia sua era faccia d'uom giusto,
> Tanto benigna avea di fuor la pelle,
> e d'un serpente tutto l'altro fusto.]

Indeed, the reader learns in the very first line of the canto that the Geryon has a "pointed tail" (*coda aguzza*), which is further described in lines 26 and 27 as "poisonous" (*venenosa*) and "like that of a scorpion" (*a guisa di scorpion*). The Geryon is, in Dante's words (line 7), the "filthy image of fraud" (*sozza imagine di froda*) since, when he first appeared, he showed his benign face but kept his deadly tail concealed in the water.[73] Sometimes depicted with wings, as in a late fourteenth-century illustrated manuscript of the *Comedy* (fig. 85), the Geryon calls to mind other winged creatures, including the demon in the illustration of the *Grain Market in a Time of Dearth* in Lenzi's *Specchio umano* (see fig. 8), and thus adds further meanings to that depiction of a marketplace gone awry.[74]

As all this evidence indicates, medieval Italians were obsessed with fraud, especially in the marketplace. It is difficult to determine how justified their concerns were. But the actual prevalence of fraud was, in many respects, irrelevant or beside the point. It was the fear of being defrauded and the mistrust that that fear generated that mattered. The discourse of fraud in medieval Italy located it squarely in the marketplace and framed its practitioners as enemies of their fellow men and of God and as threats to the community as a whole.

Fraud's opposite, as the phrase *bona fide sine fraude* denotes, was good faith or trust. For the marketplace to function properly, both buyers and sellers had to have faith or trust in one another and thus in their exchange.[75] After all, if buyers did not believe that they had been dealt with fairly, then they were unlikely to return. Although on an individual level this could hurt a particular vendor, the repercussions could be much greater if a guild or city gained a reputation for unfair trade. As the statutes of Rieti emphasized, the "greatest trust" (*fides magna*) was required of merchants and

85   Anonymous Florentine, *Geryon*, from Dante's *Comedy*, c. 1390–1400,
Vatican City, Biblioteca Apostolica Vaticana, Lat. 4776, fol. 60r.

money-changers (*mercatores et campsores*) since they dealt with coins, which could easily
be counterfeit.[76]

It is not easy, however, to determine what precisely was meant by trust. With their
preoccupation with illegal behavior and violation of accepted norms, guild statues and
civic regulations tend to offer a much clearer picture of how contemporaries understood fraud than of how they conceived of trust or faith.[77] Fortunately, Brunetto Latini's
treatise *La rettorica* (c. 1260–61) – intended as a translation and commentary on Cicero's
*De inventione* and the *Rhetorica ad Herennium* – offers a guide.[78] Latini writes of faith
or trust (*fede*):

86   Anonymous, *The Fox and the Stork*, late 14th/early 15th century,
Campiello dei Guardiani, Venice.

by this word I mean that they have faith that they do not deceive others and that
they do not want either conflicts or discord in the cities; and if there are [conflicts
and discord], they settle them in peace. And trust, as a wise man says, is hope in a
thing promised; and the law says that trust is that which one person promises and
the other expects. But Cicero himself says in another book on duties that trust is
the foundation of justice, truth in speaking, and the keeping of promises, and this
is the virtue that is called loyalty.[79]

Trust, then, encompassed keeping one's word, truthfulness, loyalty, and justice.[80] And
indeed these elements are echoed in a variety of writings of the period.

The idea of keeping one's word, of honoring one's contracts and obligations, was
crucial to the success of the marketplace. This is clear from the prologue to a law in
the statutes of Treviso issued by the Carrara in 1385 concerning earnest money – the
money paid to secure a deal. The prologue stated: "we decree that among themselves
merchants are required and ought to observe pacts, and since in deals the greatest and
much trust [*fides*] should be had and should be kept between contracting parties one
toward the other...." The final clause of the law stated that this concept extended also
to those who were not merchants.[81]

Trust linked persons together and so, in less legalistic or contractual terms, it also
encompassed the idea of fair play (of not cheating others) and more broadly of loyalty.
This is apparent in the anonymous Tuscan author's retelling of two of Aesop's fables.
In the fable of the fox and the stork, the fox invites the stork to enjoy a delicious
soup which the stork is unable to eat because it is served in a wide and shallow bowl.
The stork gets his revenge, however, when he invites the fox to dine on an elixir
served in a vessel with a long and deep neck, which the stork's beak can reach into
but which the fox's tongue cannot. According to the author, the fox symbolizes those

who "are the cause of breaking loyalty and faith" and who seek to deceive others and then are deceived themselves, while the stork represents those who having suffered deceits and "grave injuries" seek to avenge themselves.[82] A late fourteenth- or early fifteenth-century sculpted plaque illustrating the fable still adorns a small courtyard in Venice (fig. 86).[83]

In the second fable, that of the goat, sheep, heifer, and lion, the four animals form a company (*compagnia*), swearing faith (*fede*) and agreeing to divide equally all that will come to these "loyal companions." However, when they must divide the prey that they have killed into four parts, the lion takes all four shares for himself. For the author, the lion represents "the false merchant and every one of his station, who through insolence of power breaks faith and pacts with his inferiors and robs them."[84] By its very nature, trust was fragile and easily broken.[85]

For this reason, trust had to be extended cautiously and warily. Paolo da Certaldo advised: "do not entrust [*fidare*] your goods or your affairs to a person who does not love your soul, because he who does not love your soul, will not love your affairs and will not treat you with good faith [*fede*]." Rather, such a person will try to deprive you of your goods and your money. This is especially true, he noted, of usurers and the avaricious.[86] One of the proverbs included in a German–Italian lexicon of the period (not the one compiled by Zorzi da Norimburgo) advised: "Trust in no one so that no one can cheat you" (*Chonfidate in nesun, adoncha nesun no te pò jnganare*).[87] And in another piece of advice, Certaldo warned: "it is the greatest foolishness and stupidity when a man trusts in that person by whom he was deceived many times." He then quotes an unnamed "wise man" who states, "He who tricks you [once], God damns him; he who tricks you twice, God damns him and you; he who tricks you three times, God damns only you."[88]

As Latini's definition further indicates, trust also encompassed the idea of truthfulness. The fourteenth-century statutes of the city of Rome, as noted in Chapter Six, required butchers, if asked, to tell honestly (*fideliter*) the kind of meat they had on offer.[89] And according to the statutes of the Venetian furriers of sheepskins, all guild masters were, if asked, required "by faith" (*per fidanciam*) to tell buyers the provenance of the skins they were selling, that is, whether they came from Romania (the Venetian term for the Byzantine empire) or elsewhere. As the rule stated, "they must tell him [the buyer] the truth."[90] Only truthfulness would engender trust.

Finally, the statutes of the butchers' guild of Padua echo in many ways the complex meaning of trust elaborated by Latini. According to the prologue, the members had come together to form the "congregation" not in order to achieve worldly desires but spiritual ones; and they promised to love and honor one another and to respect the various requirements and rules of the corporation. They agreed, with the help of God to place trust in one another, "in order that all are as truest brothers showing one toward the other trust, truth, and love" (*fede, verità e amore*).[91] Truthfulness and love would serve to foster the trust of which merchants were so uncertain.[92]

It was not easy, however, to determine who was actually worthy of trust. Caution and testing were essential. One had constantly to assess the trustworthiness of others, especially business partners.[93] Several pieces of advice offered by Certaldo reiterate this point. In one, he advocated going slowly:

> And again, I tell you that you should always retain a bit of restraint, and even though you trust yourself, don't trust yourself in everything, as there are many examples of those who trusted and they found themselves to be deceived . . . "He who doesn't trust, isn't deceived": I don't say this because you should be wary of everything, but that all things require measure . . .[94]

The Florentine Giovanni di Pagolo Morelli, who was inscribed in the Arte della Lana and also practiced money-changing, offered similar advice in his *Ricordi*, composed between 1393 and 1411. He wrote, "Test your friend a hundred times, or rather he whom you consider a friend, before you trust him once, and never trust anyone so much that he can bring you to ruin. Go slowly in extending trust and don't dupe yourself."[95]

Giovanni Sercambi wrote a *novella* entitled "De amicitia probata; di Lommoro e Fruosino" (Concerning friendship tested: of Lommoro and Fruosino) that offered a similar message. In the tale, the father Lommoro worries that his son Fruosino is being taken advantage of by false friends. When he asks his son how many friends he has, Fruosino replies that he has fifty, while his father replies that, even at his advanced age, he himself has only one true friend. The two agree to a test. They kill a pig that they have been intending to slaughter, place it in a bag, and then Fruosino goes to his friends, telling them that he has killed a man and needs their help disposing of the body. All fifty refuse to aid him. But when he goes to Taddeo, his father's friend, Taddeo agrees without hesitation to help the son. As Fruosino learns, his own friends are "worth nothing" (*esser da nulla*).[96] Fruosino exemplifies Certaldo's claim that "every man is deceived by himself."[97]

Certainly, while the commercial environment of the marketplace heightened the importance of such advice, it had deep roots in religious thought as well. In his chronicle, Salimbene included a chapter entitled "On good and bad friends," which quoted several verses from Ecclesiasticus, including Chapter 6, verses 6–7 which advise: "Be in peace with many, but let one of a thousand be thy counsellor. If thou wouldst get a friend, try him before you takest him, and do not credit him easily"; and Chapter 12, verse 8 which states: "A friend shall not be known in prosperity, and an enemy shall not be hidden in adversity."[98]

For the individual participant in the medieval moral marketplace, success depended on his good name, on his reputation for trustworthiness.[99] As an anonymous Florentine advisor on business conduct wrote, a man could have no greater or "dearer" friend than "a shining reputation" (*la chiara fama*).[100] Such a reputation fostered more business. As Morelli wrote, "above all else, make licit contracts; from this you will acquire a good reputation [*fama*]."[101] He also advised: "conduct your affairs with trusted persons [*persone fidate*], who have a good reputation [*buona fama*] and who are creditable [*sieno creduti*]."[102] Much went into the acquisition of a good reputation, including social standing, family connections, and, above all else, according to the recent analyses of

87   Vanni di Baldolo, *Procession of the Notaries*, Matriculation Book of the Perugian Notaries, c. 1333,
Perugia, Biblioteca Comunale Augusta, Ms. 973, fol. 2r.

Giacomo Todeschini, active membership in the Christian community.[103] As for one's
personal characteristics, Certaldo enumerated these as follows: "the man who wishes
to do well in his affairs, must have within himself six qualities, which are these: foresight
[*provedenza*], steadfastness, loyalty, industriousness, orderliness, and humility; therefore
try always to be astute [*avveduto*] in these things and you will never fail."[104] Loyalty
was a synonym for trustworthiness.

  While the individual buyer or seller had to judge for himself the trustworthiness of
others and to protect his own reputation for the same, civic and guild authorities made
a concerted effort to combat fraud and thus to instill trust in the marketplace and to
protect their own collective reputations. Many of the ways in which they sought to

do this have already been considered, including policing the marketplace, creating and enforcing standard weights and measures, and determining who could trade in the marketplace and when.

Keeping written records was another important tool for combatting fraud and inspiring trust. A full consideration of the revival of literacy among the laity of medieval Europe and Italy in particular is beyond the scope of this study, yet it is worth noting that the "scribalization of hitherto oral judiciary procedures" occurred almost contemporaneously with the revival of trade and the emergence of the Italian communes.[105] As Brian Stock remarked, "Literacy, like the market, insured that an entity external to the parties in a grain exchange – the text – would ultimately provide the criteria for an agreed meaning." At the same time, "the agreement of both parties in a single written transcription . . . if sworn before a notarial tribunal, became an *instrumentum publicum*."[106]

Given this, notaries became powerful and respected figures in the marketplace and society more generally, as Vanni di Baldolo sought to convey in his image created for the Perugian notaries' matriculation book of the notaries processing into, as Marina Subbioni hypothesizes, Perugia's Palazzo dei Priori (fig. 87).[107] In Treviso, the college of notaries was so concerned with its exalted place in society that it forbade its members to wear clothes that did not extend at least as far as their knees – short tunics implied lower-class status. As they stated, their clothing should "accord with their dignity" (*cum ipsorum dignitate concordet*).[108] Some reacted against notaries' pretensions; the writer Franco Sacchetti (c. 1335–c. 1400) complained of notaries who acquired the status of knights and for whom "the quill case turns into a gilded sheath."[109] Notaries' physical location in the marketplace also signaled their importance. In Bologna, notaries stationed themselves at the head of the *bina* of the money-changers in the Porta Ravegnana market.[110] And as their corporate power increased in the city, they built, as noted in Chapter Two, their meeting hall in the Piazza Maggiore (see fig. 37). In Milan, notaries and money-changers together occupied the piazza around the Broletto Nuovo.[111]

Given their importance, when notaries broke the public trust, the prescribed penalties were severe. In Pisa, any notary who drew up a "false charter" was to be beheaded, as was anyone who had a notary produce such a charter.[112] In Rome, a fraudulent charter would cost a notary 500 lire if the person who had requested it was a member of the *popolo*, 1,000 lire if he was a knight, and 4,000 if he was a magnate baron. Furthermore, the notary was prohibited from again practicing the notarial art; and failure to pay the fine within ten days would result in amputation of his right hand.[113] Amputation of the right hand was the punishment in Treviso, as it was in Venice where in 1407 the notary Masio da Fano suffered such a fate for recording something that was patently false in his protocol. In the small town of Frignano, any notary who produced falsified instruments and was a fugitive from justice was to have his image painted on the walls of the communal palace. He was to be "depicted writing the false instrument" (*pi[n]gatur scribens falsum instrumentum*).[114] Corrupt

88   Anonymous, *The Public Treasurer and his Scribe in their Office*, 1328,
cover of a register from the *biccherna* (tax office), Archivio di Stato di Siena.

notaries were viewed as a particular threat because they violated the public trust and endangered commerce.[115]

With time and the spread of literacy to ever greater numbers of people, written documents of many sorts, not only those drafted by notaries, gained legal standing and could be entered as evidence in court proceedings. Observing, for example, that "trust must be protected between contracting parties," the statutes of Treviso stated that any notice of a debt written (either by the creditor or the debtor) in an account book or in a promissory note had the force of a *publicum instrumentum*.[116]

Accordingly, guild and civic authorities increasingly insisted that transactions be set down in writing. This requirement applied particularly to trades in the leading sectors of the economy such as textile manufacturing and money-changing (banking; fig. 88).

The Lana guild of Florence, for example, required each of its members "to have and maintain" what it referred to as "public books" (*publicos libros*) in which they were to record all transactions. This requirement would allow the "truth" to be manifest by inhibiting illicit sales completed without the assistance of a broker or without the merchandise being weighed at the guild-supervised scales.[117] The money-changers' guild of Bologna established strict guidelines as to what its members had to record about transactions in their personal account books: they were to record both the first and family names of persons with whom they dealt, as well as the day, month, and year of the transaction. Furthermore, they were to write all of this out "clearly and distinctly, so that it can be read by anyone."[118] Brokers and operators of public scales likewise had to record transactions in writing. The brokers who worked for Por Santa Maria in Florence were told to record in their books "all and every single deal they mediate and the family names and first names of the buyers and sellers and the year of the Lord and the day, and the weight and quantity and prices and measures and lengths," while, as already seen, the keepers of the communal scales in Pistoia were required to record the names of the buyers and sellers of the objects weighed, the merchandise sold or weighed, and the weight or price.[119]

Similarly, various groups of guildsmen were enjoined to record immediately payments in their account books, cancel records of debt that had been repaid, and not make erasures in their books.[120] In some instances, the authorities even dictated the form of writing. In both Bologna and Florence, money-changers were forbidden to record figures in their account books in Arabic numerals or, as the Bolognese rule put it, in *figure de labacho*. Rather, they were to write the numbers out in letters; the exact phrase in the Florentine case was "aperte et extense scribat per licteram" (openly and extensively with letters).[121] The goal was clarity since, while the interpretation or deciphering of numerals could be disputed (Arabic numerals could easily be mistaken one for another), that of written out numbers could not. In these ways, then, writing offered legally valid proof of transactions and helped to instill trust. As the rule requiring members of Por Santa Maria to record all transactions proclaimed, "trust is dear indeed and especially that [trust] which is comprised of true evidence" (*Kara est fides quidem et maxime que veris constitit inditiis*).[122]

Like the use of notaries, reliance on witnesses and guarantors also served to generate trust. As noted earlier, the Master of 1328 was careful to include them in his depictions of sales in Accursius's gloss (see figs 65 and 66). And, like the penalties meted out to corrupt notaries, those levied against persons who offered false testimony were harsh. The statutes of both Rome and Pisa called for those giving false testimony to have their tongues cut out, so that, as the Roman statute proclaimed, "[they are] no longer able to speak."[123] Such a fate befell a certain Tommaso, resident of Bologna and the son of the late Martino de Galegata, as it did the men whom he convinced to perjure themselves.[124] Finally, guild tribunals and various civic courts, particularly those charged with jurisdiction over commercial matters, served the marketplace by offering those who believed that they had been wronged avenues by which to pursue their claims legally. In all these ways, the judicial apparatus and the culture of the written word generated confidence in the marketplace, by signaling to both buyers and sellers that justice would be observed.

In sum, market relations involved much more than the mere exchange of goods, services, and cash. Every transaction involved a complicated calculus on the part of both buyer and seller as they tried to determine whether or not they were being defrauded and if they should extend (on this specific occasion) the trust necessary to bring the deal to a conclusion. Much went into that calculation, making the market-place not, as classical economists would have it, an equilibrium mechanism bringing supply and demand together to determine the market price but, rather, a highly social-ized and moralized space in which status, reputation (fama), membership in the city or community and other factors determined who would trade with whom and the kind of deal they would reach. As Philippe Braunstein notes, for Zorzi of Nuremburg, bargaining itself was "the perfect expression of an urban, that is, a civilized, society."[125]

The constant need to be on guard, the prevailing fear of being defrauded, balanced by the desire to bring a deal to a conclusion and to make a profit, came to life in the trickster, one of the most common figures in the novelle of the period. It contributed as well to a heightened awareness of individual motivations, and to a greater apprecia-tion of the self. The trickster, the wily deceiver both admired and despised, personified the ambivalence that people felt toward the marketplace. As Wayne Rebhorn observed in his study of "confidence men" in Machiavelli's thought, the figure of the confidence man or trickster allowed Renaissance writers (and the same was certainly true of their medieval predecessors) to "clarify, reflect on, and respond to concerns of enormous significance for their culture."[126] As he further noted, tricksters are "ideal versions of what most people wish to be: absolutely free, egocentric individuals . . . who frankly rejoice in their pleasures and their triumphs over others," and who also have no concern with the "public interest."[127]

In an extraordinary example of collective admiration, the Venetians commemorated one of the more celebrated instances of mercantile fraud on the façade of the church of San Marco itself. According to the story of the translation of the relics of Saint Mark from Alexandria to Venice, two Venetian merchants (Buono da Malamocco and Rustico da Torcello) were blown off course and landed in Alexandria, where they were befriended by the monk Staurizio and the priest Theodore who were worried that the Muslims might destroy Mark's tomb, along with other Christian shrines. The solu-tion was to rescue the saint by smuggling his body out of Egypt. In order to get their precious cargo past Muslim customs officers, Buono and Rustico relied on a common trade deception, one that was, as has been seen, condemned in statutes and regulations, namely, the placing of one kind or quality of goods on the top or outside of a con-tainer and those of a different kind or quality on the bottom or inside: in this particular case they covered the saint's body with pork. Repelled by the sight and smell of the pork, the Muslim guards let the merchants pass without further inspecting their cargo. In this way, the saint began the journey to his predestined resting place in Venice.[128]

The Venetians retold and commemorated the story of Mark's translation in mosaics installed in the 1260s in the lunettes above the four secondary portals on the west

89   Gentile Bellini, *Procession in Piazza San Marco*, detail showing *Saint Mark's Relics Taken from his Tomb*, 1496, Venice, Gallerie dell'Accademia.

façade of San Marco. The first stage of the story, the smuggling of Mark's body out of Egypt, adorned the lunette and barrel vault above the far right door. The original mosaic was replaced in the eighteenth century, but some sense of how it appeared can be gleaned from Gentile Bellini's well-known image of a procession in Piazza San Marco (fig. 89). Four of the five episodes depicted above the door are readable from Bellini's painting. The first scene (which occupied the right half of the barrel vault) depicted the removal of Mark's body from its tomb in Alexandria, the next scene (on the right of the lunette) showed the placing of the saint's body in a basket by Theodore and Staurizio, while Rustico and Buono stood at the ready with branches and the carcass of a pig. In the next scene in the middle of the lunette, the merchants carry the basket away. The deception of the Muslim guards is barely visible on the far left of the lunette. As Otto Demus described it, "the two figures are turned toward each other, disputing with gesticulating hands." Demus also suggested that the inscription (nonsensical in Bellini's painting) originally read "Kanzir, Kanzir" (Pork, Pork), since that is what is shown on another depiction of the deception in the chapel of San Clemente within the basilica. The final scene over this door, the loading of the relics onto a boat, adorned the left half of the barrel vault but is invisible given the perspective of Bellini's painting.[129]

While the Venetians were the first to condemn theft and smuggling in general, they justified this act of deceit because it was in fact a "sacred theft." A greater purpose, namely the fulfillment of Mark's predetermined destiny, justified this brazen act of trickery on the part of the merchants.[130] Moreover, this celebrated act of deception contributed to the public interest or common good by fostering the installation of Venice's patron within the city's precincts.

Tricksters with less noble goals appeared repeatedly in the *novelle*.[131] Writers such as Giovanni Boccaccio, Franco Sacchetti, and Giovanni Sercambi – to name only the best-known – filled their collections of stories with tales of conmen and deceivers, of men and women who achieve their desires by means of fraud and deception. In most cases, the clever trickster is the protagonist of the story and those he deceives his hapless and often dimwitted antagonists. He is always covetous, he wants something that it is not rightfully his to have, and for that reason he must employ guile and deception.[132] Often the trickster is after sex; many of the *novelle* are stories of young men who wish to sleep with the wives of other men (the women are often complicit in the deception), or hypocritical friars and priests who lust after the female members of their flock, or wayward women, including nuns, who find a way to take lovers.[133] These stories usually end with the trickster achieving his goal.

Such stories were entertaining and offered a pleasurable escape. Indeed, both Boccaccio and Sercambi created the framing premise that such stories were told as a way to pass time while fleeing the ravages of the plague. This is not to deny, of course, that these stories also offered a commentary on and critique of the prevailing mores of the time concerning marriage patterns, female honor, and so on. But in many of these stories, the deceiver is portrayed as relatively benign, and the lies, deceits, and counterfeits he employs to achieve his goals are portrayed not for what they really are – assaults on the truth and subversions of the law, social customs, or justice – but merely as cunning words, quick wit, and the humorous use of disguises, frequently to gain sexual pleasure. A mistaken identity is often simply a means to an end – not a more troubling investigation of the relationship of appearances to reality, although such a meaning can and should also be read into these stories. The deceiver is after all the protagonist of the tale, and the reader or listener expects him to achieve his goal. These stories idealized trickery, fraud, and deceit, and the audience was expected to admire the trickster for his chicanery.[134]

A good example of trickery used to achieve sexual gratification is the tale of Gulfardo and Madonna Ambruogia, the wife of the merchant Guasparuolo. It is the first story told on the eighth day in Boccaccio's *Decameron*. In the story, Gulfardo is a soldier who has a reputation for always paying his debts. He falls in love with Madonna Ambruogia, the wife of Guasparuolo. After many entreaties on his part, she agrees to take Gulfardo as her lover but on two conditions: first, that he never reveal the affair to anyone, and second, that he give her 200 florins in order to purchase something she wants to buy. But Gulfardo is so disgusted by Ambruogia's "greediness" that he determines to humiliate her. Before her husband leaves on a business trip to Genoa, Gulfardo borrows 200 florins from him. After Guasparuolo departs on his trip, Gulfardo proceeds with a friend to see Madonna Ambruogia, gives her the money, and says to her, "My lady, take this money and give it to your husband when he returns." The avaricious Madonna Ambruogia carefully counts out the money to make sure that it is all there, and then beds Gulfardo many times while her husband is away. On his return, Gulfardo and his friend go to Guasparuolo's house and, in the lady's presence, Gulfardo declares to Guasparuolo that he did not need the loan after all and that he returned it immediately to Madonna Ambruogia. Seeing Gulfardo's friend, who witnessed the conveyance of the money, Ambruogia is forced to go along and declares to her husband, "Of course, I received it, but I forgot to tell you about it." Boccaccio concludes the tale in this way: "Gulfardo left, while the woman who had been made a fool of returned to her husband the dishonest price of her wickedness; and thus the clever lover had enjoyed his greedy lady free of charge."[135]

Neifile, the narrator of this tale, begins it by telling the other members of the party that "since we have said a great deal about the tricks played by wives on their husbands, I should like to tell you about a trick played by a man on a woman."[136] But, although the story is one of trickery used to achieve sexual gratification, it is also deeply embedded in the mercantile practices of the period. It is, after all, a story about loans and their repayment. What is more, Gulfardo's friend (who witnesses Gulfardo paying Ambruogia the 200 florins) plays a crucial role since his presence deprives Ambruogia of the opportunity to deny the payment. Most importantly, as Neifile explains at the beginning, the story is ultimately about trust. As he states, he intends "to show that men also know how to play tricks on those who trust [*crede*] them, just as much as they are tricked by those whom they trust [*credono*]."[137] In the tale, Gasparuolo is conned by Gulfardo who turns him into a cuckold; and Gulfardo tricks Madonna Ambruogia, who set the events in motion when she fooled Gulfardo into believing her to be a virtuous rather than a greedy woman. Misplaced trust is at the center of the story.

The commercial aspects of the tale of Gulfardo and Madonna Ambruogia are emphasized in an illustration in a late fourteenth-century manuscript of the *Decameron* produced in Florence (fig. 90). Like several other illustrations in the manuscript, it is divided into three separate scenes that, when read sequentially, convey the key elements of the narrative.[138] The first takes place in Gasparuolo's shop where he is counting out the money that he is lending to Gulfardo. True to the form of a commercial transaction, the two men stand on opposite sides of the *banco* (counter). The cloth covering the counter suggests that Gasparuolo is a money-changer (or even a usurer), although Boccaccio says only that he is a merchant. In the second scene, Gulfardo is handing over the money to Madonna Ambruogia while his friend witnesses the event. This too has all the hallmarks of a commercial transaction, which indeed it is, since in reality Madonna Ambruogia is selling her body. Again, the figures stand on opposite sides of the table, which consists of little more than a broad plank spread across sawhorses. The final scene takes place in Madonna Ambruogia's richly appointed bedroom. With the transaction complete, the couple embraces, as now literally nothing stands between

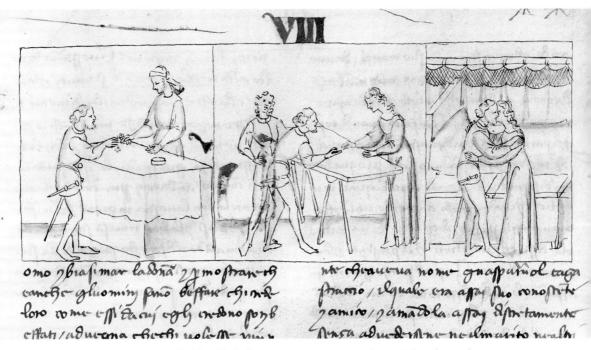

90 Anonymous, *La Beffa del Gulfardo*, from Boccaccio, *Decameron*, Day 8, Tale 1, late 14th century, Paris, Bibliothèque Nationale, Ms. Ital. 482, fol. 151r.

them. The illustrator understood the story in the mercantile context of lending, buying and selling, and repayment.

In this tale, Gulfardo shames the lady for her covetousness. In other stories, however, it is the trickster who is avaricious and who employs guile to cheat others of their goods and money. Again, some stories have an unambiguously (to medieval Italian males, at least) happy ending; for example, the peasant or simpleton is tricked by erstwhile friends.[139] In these cases, the urban and class prejudices of the *novellisti*'s intended audience are apparent. In still other stories, it is clear that although the trickster is the protagonist of the tale, he is not necessarily the hero; he is not to be emulated or admired. These stories reveal deep anxiety about being defrauded and tricked, especially in the marketplace.

Several of the stories recounted by the druggist or spice dealer Sercambi illustrate this point.[140] In this regard, Sercambi's modern-day editor contends that his *novelle*, more than Boccaccio's, accurately reflect "actual life in the medieval city."[141] The story entitled "De Falsario: Di Guida d'Ascoli, ladro per inganno" (On the counterfeiter: of Guida d'Ascoli, thief by means of deception) revolves around the covetousness first of Turello, a resident of Misigliano, and then of Pitullo, a Sienese.[142] In the first instance, the trickster Guida buries a large plate which he has covered with gold leaf in a field owned by Turello; he then goes into town, finds Turello, and convinces him to pay him 400 florins in return for helping him locate the buried treasure, which they do by the light of the moon. Returning home, Turello goes off happily to bed, believing himself to be suddenly rich, while Guida, unbeknownst to him, escapes to Siena. Only in the morning when he tests the plate does Turello discover that he has been deceived and defrauded of 400 florins. He is so distraught that he goes crazy and eventually commits suicide.

In the meantime, Guida, who has changed his name to Zaccagna, tricks Pitullo of Siena into thinking that he can help him find a mine of gold; Guida has secretly buried some ochre with veins of what appears to be gold in the earth. After they extract some of the mineral, Guida surreptitiously adds some real gold during the refining process, so that when Pitullo goes to sell it, he is convinced that they really have discovered gold. Eventually, Pitullo gives Guida 1,000 florins for exclusive rights to the mine; and Guida departs. But when Pitullo tries to extract the gold on his own, he discovers the deception. Fortunately for him, Guida has not yet left Siena, so Pitullo denounces him to the podestà who investigates the case, finds Guida guilty, and has him burned at the stake for his crime. And Pitullo gets his 1,000 florins back.

Guida's story is one of counterfeiting and covetousness; the gold plate is counterfeit, as is the gold mine; even Guida changes into something he is not, namely Zaccagna.[143] But the story has a happy resolution in that justice is served since Guida pays for his deceitfulness with his life. And although the moral of the story is a warning about greed that leads to gullibility, it also reveals the more general anxiety about counterfeiting, one of the primary methods of fraud.

In the next story, "De inganno et falsitate: di Ghisello da Racanati, ladro, vendendo certe anella contrafatte" (On deception and falsity: of Ghisello da Racanati, thief selling certain counterfeit rings), the protagonist, Ghisello da Racanati (Recanati) engages in two forms of counterfeiting.[144] In the first instance, Ghisello arrives in Lucca dressed in silk (his appearance seems to indicate his high social standing, moral rectitude, and trustworthiness) and inquires as to who are the best appraisers of precious stones in the city, since he has the "most beautiful rings" which he wishes to sell. He is told that the best estimators are Tomasino and Petro. Ghisello negotiates separately with each man but in neither instance are the parties able to agree on a price and reach an accord. After this, Tomasino approaches Petro and asks him what he thought of the rings. He responds that he liked them but felt that the asking price was too high. Tomasino then suggests that together they buy the rings and that between them they will make a profit of 250 florins. Petro and Ghisello negotiate again (without Tomasino present) and agree on a price. Ghisello then reaches into his pouch and, unbeknownst to Petro (the text says he did not estimate the falsehood – *non stimando falsità*), hands him a ring that appears identical but is in fact made of glass. Petro pays him and Ghisello rides out of town. However, when Petro shows the ring to Tomasino, he instantly recognizes it as a fake and exclaims, "this merchandise is yours alone, because these are not the stones which I saw." Petro realizes his error too late; Ghisello has fled Lucca. As the narrator explains, Petro passed the rest of his life impoverished and in difficulty.

Ghisello's tricks are not finished, though, since he has made his way to Venice and in the meantime has managed to counterfeit a "large quantity" of gold ducats. He goes to a woman who manufactures embroidery shot through with gold thread and agrees to purchase a thousand ducats' worth of her wares. The two proceed to the stall of a banker where the ducats are carefully counted out, placed in a red purse, and the purse secured with a wax seal. They then return to the workshop of the woman, where she hands over the embroidered cloth, and Ghisello entrusts to her a pouch identical to the one they had gotten from the banker but filled with Ghisello's counterfeit coins. The woman is properly wary; she takes the trouble to open the pouch but judges the ducats to be "new and good." But when the woman's son comes home, he assays one of the ducats and finds it to be false. His mother is distraught, but her son tells her, "Mother, leave it to me." He takes the coins immediately to the "Signoria;" they advise him to keep quiet about the affair. More than a year passes. Having heard no repercussions of the case, Ghisello returns to the woman to strike another deal. When her son learns this, he immediately goes again to the Signoria which sends its police to arrest Ghisello. Brought before the doge and the Lords of the Night, he is found to be in possession of a large quantity of counterfeit ducats as well as real ones, the latter of which are used to compensate the defrauded woman. Ghisello confesses his "sin" (*peccato*) and the false coins are sewn into a cloak which he is made to wear as he is burned at the stake. "And in this way," the reader is told, "Ghisello ended [his life]."

In this story, Ghisello employs two forms of fraud: he passes off fake goods as real ones and pays for other goods with counterfeit coins. But his victims are more sympathetic than were Guida's; they are less clearly avaricious; they are not blinded by an uncontrolled desire for gold; instead, after a set of negotiations, they get what they believe to be good bargains. In another nearly identical iteration of the story, except that the protagonist is named Fiordo and his victims a woman and her son who lose 500 rather than 1,000 ducats, Sercambi ends the tale by explaining that the victims learned their lesson and that from then on they lived "with their eyes more open" (*con li occhi piú apertì*).[145]

While primarily a tale about fraud, the story of Ghisello also offers a cautionary lesson about business partners. Because the agreement between Tomasino and Petro to buy the rings was informal, verbal rather than written, Petro alone suffered the loss and ended his life in poverty. Tomasino, whom the narrator suggests was the more savvy of the two (he was described as "the best appraiser [of jewels] in Lucca"), suffered no financial loss. And in this case as well, there is a happy ending: the perpetrator of the fraud is executed and the defrauded woman and her son get their money. Justice triumphs in the marketplace. Nevertheless, in both the tale of Guida and that of Ghisello, there are victims who never recover: Torello who committed suicide and Petro who ended his life in poverty.

Even with these supposedly happy endings, however, anxiety about being the victim of a trickster remained; and in Sercambi's fourth iteration of the bait-and-switch technique, there is no happy ending. In this version, the trickster is a certain Basino da Trieste who has come to Venice and also feigns the appearance of a well-to-do merchant (*come mercadante si dimostrava per tutta la terra* – "he presented himself as a merchant throughout the city").[146] As part of his plan, Basino has filled bags with various quantities and qualities of pearls. But he has also filled identical bags with chickpeas. He goes to a merchant (whom Sercambi also describes as a usurer – *mercadante o vero usurieri*) and asks to borrow 1,000 ducats, for which he will put up as security a bag of pearls. The merchant is pleased with the deal, but as any cautious merchant should, he carefully records Basino's name, the number of pearls in the bag, their weight, the amount of the loan, the time in which it is to be repaid, and the interest rate. But, of course, when the time comes for the actual exchange, Basino switches the bags, leaving the merchant with a bag full of chickpeas. He makes similar deals with many other "Venetians, and Jews, and other foreigners," and for two years he is careful to make both his principal and interest payments on time. To all appearances, he is doing well in business and is "leading the life of a lord" (*tenendo vita di signore*). Soon his reputation for making his payments on schedule is such that many loan him money without taking any precautions. Executing his final, big scam, Basino collects another 40,000 ducats from his current creditors – who now trust him so much that he does not have to put up more pearls as security – and another 20,000 from other customers, including a certain Jew. With all this money in hand, Basino puts "oars in the water," and flees Venice.

Soon the term of the loan from the Jew is up (he had extended his loan for a shorter period of time than the other merchants), and he wants to sell the pearls in order to recoup the money he had loaned. But when he opens the bag, he discovers that it is filled with chickpeas. When other merchants hear this story, they remain convinced that they are more astute judges of character and that they have not been defrauded by as respectable a merchant as Basino and that their bags contain "only pearls and not chickpeas." But gradually, as the terms of other loans come due, and various merchants learn that they too have been defrauded, word spreads to the Signoria, which orders all the bags opened. All are found to be fraudulent. As a result, many are ruined; and Basino is never heard from again.

The moral of the tale of Basino was a sobering one indeed. It revealed that reputations could be unwarranted, appearances false, and that sometimes the perpetrators of great frauds were not caught. All sorts of merchants were victims of Basino's deceit: both the simpletons who trusted him so much that they loaned him money without requiring pearls as collateral, as well as his first victim, the cautious merchant who was careful to record the precise details of the loan in writing. In other words, everyone – even the most wary and astute – was vulnerable to deceit.

So, while the stories of tricksters who used their wits to gain sexual satisfaction surely garnered (or were expected to garner) laughter and admiration for the tricksters' fast talk, quick wittedness, and ability to think on their feet, the stories of fraud in the marketplace tapped into deep anxieties, since everyone in the marketplace was a potential trickster as well as a possible victim of one. And, indeed, records of the acts of the Florentine podestà and *capitano* contain cases in which the same tricks recounted in these tales, including feigning the identity of a great merchant and switching receptacles, were used to deceive the unsuspecting.[147] People saw the trickster in themselves and in others and understood that his (and indeed their own wiles) threatened to turn

the marketplace on its head by allowing private interest, motivated by avarice, to overcome the impulse toward the common good, as manifest through an honest marketplace. Both feared and emulated, the trickster, the perpetrator of fraud, was deeply
embedded in the view of the marketplace.

The tension between the common good and individual interest, epitomized (but
also exaggerated) in the figure of the trickster, suggests just how thoroughly medieval
Italian society was in conflict with itself. It was a society in which corporate forms of
organization governed political, economic, social, and religious life (through commit-
tees, guilds, confraternities, and so on) and in which the communitarian ideals of those
institutions clashed with the values of the individual, even while the individual was
simultaneously enmeshed in those very institutions.[148] In this rapidly evolving market
economy, social status and reputation were two important indicators of trustworthiness
but, as the *novelle* reveal, were imperfect signifiers at best. Consequently, the cautious
merchant took advantage of the panoply of devices characteristic of a contract-based
society (account books, access to notaries, employment of witnesses) to secure his
interests, although as seen in the case of Basino, these too could fail.[149]

Perhaps most significantly, it appears that the ambiguities in the marketplace served
as a powerful motor driving the development of a more acute sense of selfhood. As
noted in the Introduction, the rise of the individual is a mainstay of the modern
conception of the Italian Renaissance, a vision of the period first formulated by Jacob
Burckhardt.[150] And, while numerous scholars have with good reason and from many
different vantage points challenged Burckhardt's interpretation, others continue to
maintain that something significant occurred in Italy between the fourteenth and
sixteenth centuries – that a new awareness of selfhood did indeed take hold. According
to recent formulations, the development that occurred at least in the last century and
a half of the period that is covered by this book (that is, c. 1300 to c. 1440) encompassed the emergence of what has been termed the "social" or "communal" self, namely,
a sense of selfhood derived from the push and pull of contrasting identities and obligations – to family, neighborhood, friends, polity, guild, church – under which urban
dwellers lived. That rich embeddedness, that "social ambiguity," as Ronald Weissman
put it, fostered a more acute sense of the self as an autonomous if deeply enmeshed
entity.[151] Then, in the later fifteenth and early sixteenth centuries, steps were taken
toward a more fully conscious sense of personhood, particularly of the ability to fashion
an identity.[152]

The findings of this study of the market suggest a possible first cause for the development of a new sense of interiority – the necessity to judge the character and trustworthiness of those with whom one wished to engage in commercial exchanges.[153]
This stands in contrast to the explanation offered by Colin Morris, whereby the chief
impetus toward "the discovery of the individual" – to borrow the title of his book – was
inward self-inspection.[154] What is more, it appears likely that this development began
as early as the eleventh and twelfth centuries as a consequence of the commercial
revolution, although it was only in the late thirteenth and early fourteenth century
that the written evidence for this change becomes substantial. Put simply, the skills

required to negotiate a sale, namely the need on the part of the buyer to read the seller and of the seller to discern the position of the buyer, fostered a deeper awareness of the masks, covers, and tricks that might be deployed to hide the interior self. The necessity in the end to overcome doubt, to extend trust, and to reach a deal fostered this awareness. Such conditions especially pertained in the kind of market characteristic of medieval Italy – one in which goods were not standardized and where information was scarce. The processes and discourses of negotiating were central to the formation of the modern subject, and the proclivity of medieval Italians to commit their thoughts and actions to writing certainly contributed to this development as well.[155]

The importance of negotiations as an arena for discerning the intentions of others is made clear in Edward T. Hall's study, *The Silent Language*, where he analyzes the sale of a squash in a twentieth-century Damascus market: "negotiation . . . swings around a central pivot. Ignorance of the position of the pivot opens one up to the worst type of exploitation, as well as loss of face."[156] In the extended example he offers of negotiations over the squash, the pivot point in the bargaining between the buyer and seller is 6 piasters. Accordingly, an asking price of 12 piasters or more indicates "complete ignorance on the part of the seller [of the conditions of the market];" of 10 means "an insult . . . the seller doesn't want to sell." A price of 8 signifies "will sell, but let's continue bargaining," while 7 means "will sell under the market." In the same way, an offer by the buyer of 1 piaster indicates "ignorance of the value of the item on the part of the buyer," of 2 means "arguments and fighting, buyer doesn't want to buy," of 4 means "will buy," while 5 signifies that the "buyer really wants the squash, [and] will pay over the market."[157]

This same dynamic is discernible in Zorzi da Norimburgo's sample dialogue examined earlier, as well as in the account of negotiations contained in Sercambi's tale of Ghisello. In the latter, Petro begins the negotiations badly by appearing too anxious and saying "Pray, sell me those rings." Ghisello then lures him in by taking the rings out of their pouch and displaying them to him. He also states that they are worth 1,000 florins but that he is in need of money in order to buy some cloth. In this way, he is signaling that he is interested (and perhaps needs) to sell them. Petro then makes an offer of 700 florins, but Ghisello counters that he can accept no less than 800. He puts the rings back in their pouch and begins to walk away. At that point, Petro offers 750 florins. Ghisello responds, "because you are such an agreeable buyer, I'm content," and the deal is complete. A subtle psychological contest has taken place here as the parties have sought to size one another up and to judge the discernment or ignorance of the other.[158]

In transactions such as this, the parties had to read the intentions of the other and try to keep their own intentions secret. Every sale became a contest in which one individual measured himself against another as to which would get the better of the deal.[159] Although we do not know the dynamics underlying them, we do know that Giovanni Canale, a wool merchant from the small town of Pinerolo in Piedmont, sold four identically sized pieces of cloth cut from the same lot for prices ranging from 35 soldi, 11 denarii to 42 soldi. As the editor of Canale's extant account book notes, the variation in prices must be due to bargaining.[160] For this reason, Certaldo offered his advice: "be on guard against those who keep things hidden more than those who are transparent" (*Dagli occulti uomini ti guarda piu tosto che da' palesi*).[161] Or, as the victims of Sercambi's trickster Fiordo learned, one had to have one's eyes wide open. In the last tale told on the eighth day of Boccaccio's *Decameron*, the trickster Jancofiore is herself tricked and learns the lesson, "if with a Tuscan you would deal, be sure to keep your eyes well peeled."[162] And in the tale of Ghisello, Petro's flaw is that despite being one of the two best appraisers of jewels in Lucca, he fails to "estimate the falsehood" of Ghisello. The fictional narrator of the tale of Basino da Trieste prefaced his story by addressing directly "deceivers and falsifiers" (*ingannatori e falsatori*), explaining to them that he was going to relate the story so that people could be on the lookout for "you and for your likes."[163] Finally, as the Venetian merchant manual known as the *Zibaldone da Canal* warned, "Smooth talk and evil deeds deceive both the foolish and the wise."[164] In other words, everyone was vulnerable to fraud.

The need to detect genuine from counterfeit goods was another aspect of the search for what was real in an exchange, although in that case, the concern extended well beyond the self. According to the recent formulation of Martha Howell, the late medieval and early modern period witnessed a "cultural crisis" when the very relationship of the material and immaterial was itself undergoing a profound crisis and transformation.[165] The same was true of the increasing awareness of the potential appearances of the human personality.

In sum, there were winners and losers in the medieval Italian marketplace, and fraud was such a preoccupation because the person who perpetrated it was acting in his self-interest and against the trust and faith of the community. Again, as Zanobi da Strata worded it in his translation of Gregory the Great's *Moralia*, fraud "proceeds from a private love, which man often has for himself."[166] This conflict between private interest and the common good characterized not only the marketplace but also the politics of the city-states. The binary of trust/fraud (*bona fide sine fraude*) captured the tension between the individual and the community, between self-interest and the common good, between Christian charity and personal cupidity that animated both markets and politics throughout the Middle Ages in urban Italy. This was indeed a world in which the Christian values of charity and largesse were mainstays of economic ethics. But it was also a society in which individuals with an ever keener sense of self and of the human capacity to deceive, who were bent on the pursuit of profit, were rapidly emerging. The marketplace as the locus of exchange simultaneously created and mirrored the life of the city. But popular civic and guild regimes had one further set of weapons in their war on fraud and their effort to foster trust, and they are the subject of the next and final chapter of this study.

# 8

# COMBATTING FRAUD AND PROMOTING TRUST: EMBELLISHING THE MARKETPLACE

While individual buyers and sellers had to judge for themselves the trustworthiness of others and to protect their own trustworthiness, popular civic regimes and guild authorities made a concerted effort to combat fraud more generally and thus to instill trust in the market and protect their own collective reputations. Many of the ways in which they sought to do this have been considered, including policing the marketplace, creating and enforcing standard weights and measures, and determining who could engage in commerce and when they could do so. But efforts to protect the integrity of the market extended beyond these measures, to encompass concern for the layout of streets and squares and arrangement of shops, and the strategic deployment of paintings, inscriptions, and sculptures to reinforce proper market values and warn transgressors of the consequences of failure to live up to them. Since fraud has, by its very nature, to be hidden and secret, these efforts to combat it and instill trust focused in one way or another on openness and transparency.[1] In a particularly telling iteration of this belief, the Florentine government complained in 1410 that the practice of painting defamatory pictures (*pitture infamanti*) of bankrupts had fallen into disuse and that the images that were being created were being painted "in private [*secretis*] and hidden places so that they cannot be seen." It sought to revive the practice of defaming bankrupts and ordered that the pictures be painted "on exterior walls and in the part or parts of palaces and houses most exposed [*patentibus*]."[2]

It has already been seen how an effort to unencumber streets and piazzas was part of an attempt, especially by popular governments, to promote commerce and increase market efficiency. But it was also designed to combat fraud by promoting openness. For communal legislators, the ideal commercial space consisted of broad open piazzas and wide public streets that favored visibility and surveillance. A supreme expression of the ideal derives from a 1411 ruling by Por Santa Maria defining where goldsmiths could locate their shops. After outlining the areas within Florence where shops were allowed, the rule continued that even within those areas, shops were only to be located on "public and major streets" and not in "alleys or hidden places." An exception to this latter restriction was made for the extremely congested quarters around the Mercato Nuovo. There shops could be located in alleys, but even they had to be within 150 Florentine *braccia* (87.6 meters) of "public streets."[3] The Florentine Lana guild likewise forbade its members to have shops anywhere but in a "via publica."[4] And, as has been seen, the 1296 statutes of the podestà of Pistoia declared that thenceforth bakers, wine sellers, innkeepers, and others who sold bread and wine were not to do so in their private "houses, cells, courtyards, gardens or other places" but only in "public roads and streets."[5]

Some cities, including Florence, retained something of the old Roman grid pattern. But centuries of haphazard development and building had often obscured aspects of the original orderly Roman grid. In such towns and elsewhere, civic authorities made an effort to widen and straighten streets in order to improve access and increase commerce. This occurred in Siena.[6] And the statutes of Perugia called for the appointment of five masters of the streets who were to be assisted by five notaries. Their job was to make sure that all "public" roads (*via publica*) were at least ten Perugian feet wide (3.6 meters) and "neighborhood streets" (*via vicinalis*) eight feet wide (2.9 meters).[7]

It was only in newly established towns, however, where these ideals could be most easily and fully put into effect. As David Friedman showed, Florence largely achieved this ideal in the new towns that it built in the fourteenth century – places such as San Giovanni Valdarno (fig. 91), Scarperia, Firenzuola, and Castelfranco – towns where, as he puts it, "orthogonality" ruled.[8] Friedman observed: "The physical city of the merchant commune was an open one. The uniformity of authority and jurisdiction that the government strove for translated directly into a concept of urban space, in which every part of town was to be equally accessible and all buildings, both private and public, would be visible to everyone."[9] But these ideals were already at play with the rise of popular communes. As Areli Marina has argued, in the new "vast, open, and consequently well-lit" piazzas that the commune of Parma designed in the thirteenth century, "it would have been difficult to avoid the eyes in, and of, the piazza."[10]

The openness of streets and piazzas facilitated visibility, and visibility inhibited fraud.[11] Just as vendors were warned against selling goods behind counters, away from their shops, and out of public sight, so conversely they were enjoined again and again to display their goods on the tops of counters, in public streets, and in full view of others. A 1397 addition to the rules of the Venetian vair furriers' statutes articulated this particularly well. It stated that in order to avoid "scandal, error, and fraud," members

91   San Giovanni Valdarno, central piazza with the Palazzo Pretorio.

of the guild should sell their wares only on the *ruga* of the *varoteri* at Rialto. Thereby, the rule continued, "every man being in the said *ruga* and acting in the way prescribed above, the better one will see the good and the evil adopted by everyone [of the guild]."[12] This statement captures the atmosphere of mistrust that characterized the marketplace and the corollary conviction that trust could only be generated by means of mutual surveillance.[13] It also helps to explain further the reliance on witnesses to commercial transactions, discussed in Chapter Five.

In addition to the general layout of streets and organization of shops, other features of the marketplace reinforced the values that the regimes wished to promote. Throughout this study, the infrastructure elements that many, if not all, marketplaces had in common have been noted. These included columns, fountains or wells, proclamation posts, pillories, and, most common of all, displays of measuring standards. Many of these features had a practical function: for example, fountains and wells were essential for washing counters, especially of food vendors, while standards were used to gauge and calibrate the measures used in shops. Others were clearly symbolic, as in the female abundance figures that adorned columns and fountains in Verona, Perugia, and Florence. But practicality and symbolism could conjoin, especially in the displays of standards.

It is unfortunate that most of the art that embellished marketplaces has been lost; this is especially true of frescoes which must have been ubiquitous in porticoes and loggias. There are numerous records of the *pitture infamanti*, which from at least the 1260s were painted on buildings in cities across the peninsula, that defamed those accused (or convicted) of various infractions, including commercial crimes.[14] The Sienese wool guild, for example, authorized the depiction within its hall of members who fraudulently labeled the goods of others as their own.[15] In Pisa, the particulars of

92    Modena, Duomo, North Portal (Porta della
Pescheria), early 12th century.

investigations of fraud committed in paying customs were to be written "on a public
wall" at the Customs House in the vernacular, "in order that they can be read by all."[16]
And images of those who had failed to satisfy their creditors or honor their debts
adorned the Bargello or podestà's palace in Florence. The podestà was required by law
to have these images made: the portraits were to be clearly visible and accompanied
by the first and last names of the guilty written in "large and clear letters," as well as
the names of the guilds to which they belonged.[17] None of these *pitture infamanti*
survives.[18] Nevertheless, by piecing together the few surviving remnants of decoration,
especially those found in guild halls and *mercanzie*, we can begin to understand the
fundamental role that art played in reinforcing the values of the market, promoting
commerce, and legitimizing civic regimes.

A good place to begin is Modena where three sculptural elements that adorned the
cathedral and marketplace are extant and that address, in one way or another,
the themes of fraud, truth, and justice. Modena is one of the cities where the ecclesiastical, governmental, and market centers conjoined in one space. The city's major
market occupied the piazza on the south flank of the cathedral, while the communal
palace was located near its eastern apse. The fish market utilized the space near the
church's north portal, which still goes by the name the Porta della Pescheria or Fish-
Market Door.[19]

The north flank of the cathedral virtually abuts the Via Emilia, the road running
from Piacenza to Rimini; it was Modena's primary trade and communication route.
An archivolt with scenes from Arthurian legend tops the Porta della Pescheria (fig. 92).

It is narrower than the lintel on which it rests, suggesting some change from the original plan for the portal. The lintel itself is carved with four animal scenes – a sea-nymph riding a Triton, two cocks bearing a fox on a stick (see fig. 93), two ibises attacking a snake, and a wolf and a crane – all flanking a cross embedded in an elaborate knot. On the front of the doorposts are depictions of various fables interlaced in an acanthus-leaf vine pattern, while the sides are adorned with the months of the year. Dorothy Glass notes that the portal predates the year 1135, and suggests that it can legitimately be called "the people's portal" since it "celebrates the agriculture that fed the growing commune, offers moral exempla in easily understood terms, and celebrates heroes who perhaps trod the . . . Via Emilia on which the Porta della Pescheria fronts."[20]

Several of the scenes depicted on the portal resonated with the surrounding marketplace. Five of the fables on the front of the doorposts involve the fox. These are: the fox and the eagle, the fox and the stork, the fox and the rooster-confessor, the fox and the kite-confessor, and the fox feigning death. In all but one, that of the fox and the stork, the fox successfully employs his astuteness, that is, his proclivity to defraud and deceive, to achieve his nefarious ends. The same is true of the scene on the lintel depicting the funeral of the fox; the two pall-bearer chickens are unaware that the fox is only feigning death and that they will end up attending their own funeral (fig. 93). Other scenes on the portal, including the fable of the wolf and the crane, according to which the wolf repays the crane's kindness of removing a bone from his throat by devouring the crane, reiterated themes of deception and oppression of the less powerful.[21]

The iconography of the portal has been brilliantly elucidated by Chiara Frugoni and Monica Chiellini Nari; they argue that the portal is a meditation on the consequences of sin, with the world transformed into a "receptacle of vices" in which an "immoderate affirmation of self-interest" and of the vices (represented by various animals but especially the fox) are depicted.[22] At the same time, the cross embedded in the knot at the center of the lintel opens the path to salvation by way of the church, through the portal itself.[23] As the authors also demonstrate, the humans depicted in the illustrations of the months and in the battle scene on the archivolt, show a world

93  Modena, Duomo, North Portal (Porta della Pescheria), lintel, detail,
*The Funeral of the Fox*, early 12th century.

94  Ambrogio Lorenzetti, *Allegory of Good Government*, 1338–40, Palazzo Pubblico, Siena.

divided among those who work, those who fight, and, by implication, those who pray.[24]
Given the early date of the portal (prior to 1135) and the failure to depict merchants
among the humans represented (although one *artifex* [artisan] is shown), it is by no
means certain that the images were originally intended as condemnations of marketplace fraud in particular.[25] But surely they assumed those meanings and associations
with time. The images of the fox in particular served as warnings to the practitioners
of deceit, a vice of which, as has been seen, fishmongers often stood accused.

Certainly, the most prominent and direct image of fraud is that found in Ambrogio
Lorenzetti's fresco program (dating to the last years of the 1330s) in the Sala dei Nove
of Siena's communal palace on the Campo. The representations of tyranny and of the
well-run commune along with their respective councils of advisors are the centerpieces
of Lorenzetti's depictions of good and bad government (figs 94 and 95). From left to
right, Cruelty, Treason, Fraud, Furor, Division, and War comprise the tyrant's council,
while Peace, Fortitude, Prudence, Magnanimity, Temperance, and Justice constitute the
well-run commune's advisors.

Fraud (clearly labeled *Fraus*; fig. 96) sits in a privileged position at the right hand
of the tyrant and directly under Avarice, which along with Pride and Vainglory com-
prises the trinity of deadliest sins.[26] Lorenzetti has depicted Fraud as a young man with
a benign face but clawed feet and batlike wings. There are clear affinities to Dante's
Geryon and to the batlike creature that hovers over the grain market in times of dearth

95   Ambrogio Lorenzetti, *Allegory of Bad Government*, 1338–40, Palazzo Pubblico, Siena.

in Lenzi's manuscript (see figs 8 and 85), suggesting again that not only dearth but also fraud undermine the market.[27] Unfortunately, part of this figure has been lost so it is difficult to determine what Fraud holds in his hands. Some describe it as a cudgel; others as a crosier.[28] In his late sixteenth-century treatise *Iconologia*, Cesare Ripa states that Fraud is sometimes depicted with a fishing rod and that this epitomizes fraud's character, since what appears at first to be an act of kindness (offering food to fish) results in their entrapment and death.[29] Perhaps the object in Fraud's hand is an illicit measuring rod. Regardless, Lorenzetti has chosen to assign Fraud an especially prominent place in his depiction of the vices that corrupt society, and to associate it closely with avarice.[30]

Depictions of Avarice mirrored those of its progeny Fraud since it too was usually depicted as grasping. In Herrad of Hohenbourg's *Hortus deliciarum*, Avarice holds in her hand a fork or trident, which, as the scroll indicates, symbolizes her rapacity.[31] In Lorenzetti's fresco, Avarice clutches a grapnel in her claw-like hands and wears around her neck a vice which tightly secures the openings to two moneybags (see fig. 2).[32]

If the image on the archivolt of the Porta della Pescheria offered an image of fraud as the crafty fox, another sculpture on the south flank of Modena's cathedral represented fraud as falsehood and truthfulness as its antidote.[33] It depicts truth overcoming fraud. The sculpture is located high on the south wall near the Porta dei Principi overlooking the main piazza. Unfortunately, it suffered heavy damage during the

96   Ambrogio Lorenzetti, *Allegory of Bad Government*,
detail showing *Fraud*, 1338–40, Palazzo Pubblico, Siena.

Second World War (fig. 97). It shows a bearded figure of Truth in a long flowing gown who leans over a devilish figure of Fraud. Truth uses his right foot to steady himself, while with his left, he pins Fraud to the ground. With his hands he pulls the mendacious tongue from Fraud's mouth. The accompanying inscription, which fills the space between the figures, explains precisely what is happening: "VERIDUS LINGUAM FRAUDIS DE GUTTURA STIRPAT" (truth extirpates the tongue of fraud from [its] throat).[34]

Dating to the second decade of the twelfth century, it has been argued that the sculpture (and the accompanying smaller one to its left depicting Jacob wrestling with the angel) were originally parts of a pilaster and that the subjects were inspired by the conflict in 1111 between the Holy Roman Emperor Henry v and Pope Paschal ii, with the Truth sculpture in particular referring to papal condemnations of imperial "deceit and trickery." The sculptures were created, then, in the context of the Investiture Controversy.[35] In spite of the original meaning and intention as a condemnation of the imperial side, again it is not difficult to assume that over time the sculpture took on new significance unrelated to the papal/imperial struggle but directly related to merchandising. Falsehood was, after all, like fraud, considered one of avarice's offspring; and, as San Bernardino observed, one form of fraud practiced by merchants involved lying about the quality of their goods. Overlooking as it did Modena's marketplace, it seems likely that the image was reinterpreted within a commercial (and political–juridical) context as an admonition to honest dealing.

97    Modena, Duomo, south façade, *Truth Tearing out the Tongue of Fraud*, c. 1110–20.

A later example of the same theme (unfortunately now lost) supports just such an interpretation, since it was painted in the headquarters of the Florentine Mercanzia. According to Giorgio Vasari, an allegorical painting executed by Taddeo Gaddi in 1363 once adorned the Mercanzia's ground floor. It showed the members of the Mercanzia court witnessing truth, as in the Modenese sculpture, tearing out the tongue of false-hood. An inscription below the Florentine painting read: "Pure truth, obeying holy Justice that does not delay, extracts the liar's tongue" (*La pura verità, per ubbidire/ Alla santa giustizia che non tarda/ Cava la lingua alla falsa Bugiarda*).[36] Vasari relates that Gaddi depicted truth as a naked figure under a sheer veil while falsehood was sheathed in black. The emphasis on truth and justice in the Mercanzia's dealings was further rein-forced by an inscription over the doorway of the palace that read: "Domus equitatis et veritatis" (the home of equity and truth).[37] As noted earlier, statutes in both Rome and Pisa called for those giving false testimony to have their tongues cut out in order that, as the Roman statute proclaimed, "they are no longer able to speak."[38] Here is a compelling instance of art imitating life or, perhaps, life imitating art. Those statutes, like the Modenese sculpture and Gaddi's painting, placed emphasis on truth, which served justice and engendered trust.

The statue known as *Bonissima*, the third remnant in Modena, is incontrovertibly related to the marketplace and always has been (see fig. 19). As noted in Chapter One, the statue has some affinities with the abundance figures found in the marketplaces of other cities, but its primary function was to personify the office of the officials of *bona opinione*, also known as the *officium bulletarum*, who established the official standards for weights and measures, carried out periodic inspections of the weights and measures used by merchants, and investigated accusations of bad measure.[39] As also noted before, it appears from the positioning of the figure's left hand that she once held a balance. It is not known when the statue was first sculpted. A record from 1220, when the commune purchased land to enlarge the piazza, mentions the "Bonissimam," although it is not clear if this refers to the statue or the headquarters of the officials.[40] Two later chronicles state that in 1268, "Bonissima was erected in a marble statue in the piazza of the city of Modena." The fact that these chronicles emphasize that it was erected in "marble" seems to indicate that this was when the statue was created and not simply moved from its earlier location.[41] Be that as it may, in 1468 the statue was moved to its present site on the corner of the old communal palace, where the office had been relocated; in 1498 it was placed higher up on the building in order to accommodate better the colonnade below.[42]

From the later thirteenth century until its relocation in 1468, the *Bonissima* formed one part of an ensemble in Modena's marketplace. According to the late fifteenth-century authority Jacopo dei Bianchi, the statue stood atop a ciborium which consisted of four pillars supporting a marble slab. Various standards, including for the *braccio* and for tiles and bricks, were carved onto the pillars or perhaps on a supporting base for the columns.[43] Some reconstructions suggest affinities with the Capitello that graces Verona's Piazza delle Erbe, which has standard measures carved both on the columns and along the base (see fig. 68), but these are only conjectures.[44]

What is certain is that the statue personifying the office of weights and measures stood prominently in the marketplace and that the official standards were carved on the ciborium on which it stood. As Emmanuele Lugli observes of the Verona Capitello, the ensemble monumentalized the standards, "highlighting their presence from a distance and working as a physical pivot for the concordance of the citizens' controlling gazes."[45] Lugli views the *Bonissima* ensemble, like the standards created and displayed by other communal governments, as an expression of a collective political enterprise and as an element of the commune's "tools of control."[46] When, under the Este lords of Modena, the ensemble was destroyed and the columns of the ciborium used to decorate the family's private garden, new standards were carved into the apse of the cathedral (fig. 98). But these standards are inaccessible and therefore had no practical function for gauging measuring instruments actually in use; they served instead, as Lugli notes, as "purely visual markers of power;" indeed, "their remoteness reminds the beholder of the distance that separates him or her from actual power and his or her irrelevancy in the preservation of the key tools of justice."[47]

The *Bonissima* ensemble – if indeed it dates from 1268 – served, then, as a powerful assertion by the communal popular government (in which the guilds had had representation since 1229) that justice would be rendered in the marketplace and that wrongdoers would be punished. And if, as seems likely, the figure held a balance, then this message was explicit. Even if she did not, the meaning was clear nevertheless,

98    Modena, Duomo, standards carved on apse, 16th century.

because she personified the office that enforced right measures. In this way, the *Bonis-sima* served both as the personification of justice and a warning to those who would flout the laws of the market. She was intended to reassure those coming to the marketplace that in Modena trade was licit.

Carved standards even without accompanying statues performed a similar function in other cities. Although they had a practical purpose as the official measures against which those used in shops could be compared, all standards served as symbols of justice and public authority. In fact in Florence, the authorized example of each standard was tellingly referred to in one text at least as the "iudex" or judge.[48] As Aquinas and other scholastics made clear, market relations were ultimately about justice as epitomized in the concept of the just price. In his discussion of fair or just exchanges, Henry of Ghent even compared the positions of buyers and sellers to the pans of scales which had come into balance. Furthermore, being given short measure was very likely to have been the average person's most frequent and readily discernible experience with fraud (and by extension injustice). As James Shaw notes, "the mundane crimes of economic life probably corresponded to what most ordinary people understood by 'justice'."[49] Hence it is not surprising that balances served as some of the most ubiquitous symbols of justice, as seems to have been the case with *Bonissima*. The other common piece of weighing equipment, the steelyard, also served this purpose. Indeed, a manuscript of Francesco da Barberino's *Documenti d'amore* shows Justice holding a down-turned sword in her right hand while with her left she adjusts a steelyard (fig. 99).

Balances and steelyards were not the only instruments of measure used to symbolize justice. In a sermon on the theme of justice, Bernardino of Siena relied on his

99    Francesco da Barberino, *Iustitia* (Justice with a steelyard),
from his *Documenti d'amore*, c. 1315, Vatican City, Biblioteca
Apostolica Vaticana, Ms. Barb. Lat. 4076, fol. 87v.

audience's acquaintance with market practices when he quoted the Book of Revelation
11: 1: "Then I was given a measuring rod like a staff." Bernardino translated the Latin
term used in the Vulgate *calamus* as "canna," the term used throughout much of Italy
to denote one kind of measuring stick. He went on to explain that each person would
be judged according to his worth.[50] In this way he used the image of measuring cloth,
to convey to his audience the measuring that awaited their souls. Readers will recall
the inscription over the public scales in Ragusa/Dubrovnik which reminded merchants
that as they were weighing goods, so God was also weighing them.[51] Their weighing
was like God's, only writ small.

Painters too employed measuring sticks and units of dry and liquid measure as
images of Justice; this was the case in the fresco that was painted above the bench of
the Iudex Victualium in the Salone in Padua's Palazzo della Ragione (fig. 100).[52] The
Salone was, as noted in Chapter Three, the location of Padua's courts. Here the
tribunals that handled various civil and criminal matters met. Following a tradition
common in medieval Italy, many of these courts were identified by animals (for
example, a bull or a bear); this designation served as a mnemonic device for the
unlettered seeking the proper court. To aid in this search, an image of the appropriate
animal was painted over each bench, as required by a law of June 1, 1271. When in
1306 the Salone was heightened and many of the interior partitions removed, the newly
installed ship's-hull ceiling was decorated with the signs of the Zodiac and planets by
Giotto and his workshop.[53]

Despite over-painting in later centuries, the image for the Iudex Victualium appears,
according to Eva Frojmovič, to follow the original design by Giotto.[54] The judges had

100  Anonymous, after a design by Giotto, *Tribunal of the Iudex Victualium*, depicting Justice with standards and a steelyard, 18th century, Salone, Palazzo della Ragione, Padua.

jurisdiction over cases involving violation of the *divieto*, the rules against exporting food from the city, as well as over the use of fraudulent weights and measures.[55] Their bench was located in the northeast corner of the building, at the top of the Staircase of the Birds, at the base of which, on the ground floor, were inscribed Padua's standards (see fig. 47).[56]

The fresco depicts a female figure seated at a throne behind a counter. In her right hand she holds a balance while with her left she holds a measuring rod. Another rod lies atop the counter, as do two books that could possibly be ledgers. Placed around the foot of the counter are various measures for dry and perhaps liquid volume. In the upper right corner of the image, the one section that has not been repainted, a steelyard is visible.

Many of the images in the Salone originally had accompanying inscriptions that are now lost. However, Hartman Schedel of Nuremberg, a student at Padua in the early 1460s, recorded them in his memory book. The inscription for this image, which he tellingly identified as "Ratio" or Judgment, read: "Temperoque gestus hominis ratione magistra/Pondere mensura facio cessare sinistra" (And I, mistress, temper the deeds of men by means of justice/ I bring an end to crimes involving weight and measure).[57] In this image, then, Giotto used instruments of measure simultaneously to identify the competency of this court and to symbolize the justice that it rendered.

Furthermore, although visual artists were unable to convey it, measuring bore yet another meaning: it suggested the idea of moderation or mean, a concept inherited from ancient writers.[58] This connotation depended on the double significance of the word "measure" itself, as well as related words such as *dritto*, as when the pans of the scales were said to hang "straight" or in balance. Two examples make this point: in his *Libro di buoni costumi*, the merchant-writer Paolo da Certaldo wrote: "'Misura dura': e però in ogni tuo fatto abbi misura acciò che tu non possi fallare, ché chi avrà misura ne'suoi fatti soprastarà a ogni vizio" (Measure endures; therefore in all your dealings exercise measure so that you cannot fail, for he who has measure in all his deeds will overcome every vice).[59] And for his part, Giovanni di Pagolo Morelli wrote in his *Ricordi*, "Ma sopra tutto ti misura in ogni cosa" (But above all, measure yourself in everything).[60] Here the idea of personal moderation blended with the Christian idea of the measuring of souls and the triumph over sin.

The foregoing discussion has at times ventured far from Modena, but it has done so in order to demonstrate how the three extant sculptural works that adorned its marketplace — the sculptures of the funeral of the fox, of truth tearing out the tongue of fraud, and of *Bonissima* and her standards — carried powerful meanings regarding the dangers of fraud and falsehood in the marketplace and reassurance that the authorities would use their power to guarantee justice in commercial transactions. In so doing, these works served to engender confidence, trust, and faith in the Modenese marketplace.

Further evidence of how images were used to shape market values and practices can be gleaned from other spaces that had decidedly commercial and judicial functions — guildhalls and *mercanzie*. Unfortunately, most medieval guildhalls have been destroyed, repurposed, or never fully examined; one important exception is Florence's Lana guild headquarters, centrally located close to the Mercato Vecchio and the Mercato Nuovo on a strip of land between the Via Calimala and Orsanmichele.[61] Giovanni Villani considered the site the very center of the town.[62] Plaques sporting the *Agnus dei* (the symbol of the guild), placed high up on the walls facing Via Calimala and Orsanmichele, state that the palace is the "home and court of the wool guild of the city of Florence" (*domus et churia artis lane civitatis Florentie*) and bear the date of the building's foundation — 1308 (fig. 101).[63]

Resembling a communal palace, the Lana guildhall sits on a site once occupied by the palace of the Ghibelline Compiobbesi family. The exterior consists of cleanly finished stone on the ground or first floor with more rusticated stone on the upper floors (see fig. 38). The building is topped with Guelf crenelation. The façades facing Via Calimala and Orsanmichele are pierced with three arches on the ground floors (originally open) with simple arched windows on the floors above. The interior includes

101    Florence, plaque with the symbol of the Florentine Lana Guild,
Lana Guildhall, 1308.

subterranean spaces perhaps originally used for offices or storage, ground-floor space
also used for offices and to store the guild's records, a second-floor assembly or audience hall, and a third floor that originally housed a jail where those who violated the
guild's statutes were imprisoned. A fire in 1331 destroyed much of the interior and led
to a redesign of the spaces, including elegant arched ceilings.[64]

The subterranean spaces and the ground floor (both today occupied by stores)
contain fragments of fourteenth-century frescoes. The most important appears to commemorate the investiture of Robert of Anjou by the pope in 1310 and the celebrations,
including a joust, that Florence held during Robert's visit to the city. They also depict
various stages in the production of wool. These frescoes, which would have been fairly
accessible to the public since they were located at street level, seem to have been
intended to align the guild squarely with Florence's Guelf political orientation and to
celebrate the woolen cloth industry's contribution to the Florentine economy.[65]

The most significant works, however, are found in the second-floor audience hall
or tribunal. This space consists of a rectangular room divided into two vaulted square
bays of equal size – hence the room is twice as long as it is wide.[66] The fourteenth-
century decoration for the rear bay (closest to Orsanmichele) has been lost, except for
four painted tondi occupying the space between the ribs of the vaults; they depict the
cardinal virtues Prudence, Fortitude, Temperance, and Justice, against a blue sky with
stars. In the second bay (facing Via Calimala), the four tondi depict the Evangelists,
also against a starry blue sky. All date after the fire of 1331 when the vaulting was
added; they have been attributed to the Master of the Dominican Effigies, who also
illuminated the guild's statutes.[67]

102    Anonymous, *Christ as Judge with Saints and Madonna and Child*, c. 1320,
Audience Hall, Lana Guildhall, Florence.

In the second bay, fourteenth-century frescoes adorn the tops of the three walls and
the arches of the vault; wooden benches must have been affixed to the lower portion
of the walls, which are now simply whitewashed. The focus of the room is the center
wall, pierced by two windows, which faces Via Calimala; but it is unclear how the
room was arranged in the fourteenth century. On one hand, it is hard to imagine that
the guild officials would have sat in front of the windows; most illustrations of tribunals
show the judges sitting against a solid wall; on the other hand, this wall is adorned
with the most prestigious images, those of Christ and Mary, giving it pride of place,
and it is not clear how the windows were originally configured.

In the partial lunette above the windows is a poorly preserved roundel of Christ as
Judge (he holds a sword in one hand and an open book in the other); he is flanked
by two saints also in roundels, neither of whom has ever been definitively identified,
although some suggest that the figure on the right is San Zanobio, the first bishop of
Florence and one of the city's patron saints, and that the other may be Santo Stefano,
patron of the Lana guild.[68] Below, in the space between the windows, is an image of
the Madonna and Child with saintly figures, also severely damaged, as is an inscription
below the Virgin which reads: "O dulcissima semper Virgo Maria, in te angeli recipient
laetitiam, inveniunt justi gratiam, peccatores in eternum veniam consecuntur. In gremio

103  Master of the Corsi Crucifix, *The Four Patron Saints of the Lana Guild and the Symbols of their Districts*, c. 1320, Audience Hall, Lana Guildhall, Florence.

Matris resident sapientia Patris" (O most sweet ever Virgin Mary, in you the angels receive joy, the just find grace, sinners acquire forgiveness in eternity. In the lap of the Mother resides the wisdom of the Father; fig. 102).[69] These frescoes are generally dated to c. 1320, before the fire. The image of Christ as judge, with saints and the Virgin as witnesses and advocates, would have added an aura of solemnity and seriousness to proceedings, especially trials, that took place in this room, since defendants in particular would have been reminded of the Last Judgment and the way in which their words would resonate not only with their earthly judges but with God and the saints.[70] They were reminded, in other words, to tell the truth.

In the lunette on the wall to the left, also dating in all likelihood to before 1331 and attributed to the Master of the Corsi Crucifixion, are images of the patrons of the four *conventi*, or sections, of the Lana guild (fig. 103). Readers will recall that for administrative purposes the guild was divided into four urban territorial districts – Por San Piero, San Pancrazio, San Piero a Scheraggio, and Oltrarno – and that during their supervised buying excursions, foreign merchants were taken by their broker/minders on tours of all four districts; the districts also had measurers and other staff specifically assigned to them. The saints are separated by the columns of a kind of aedicule or gothic frame, with the emblems of their "conventi" painted below them. They are from

104    Maso di Banco, *Brutus as Judge*, 1330s or 1340s, Audience Hall, Lana Guildhall, Florence.

left to right: Saint Martin representing Porta San Piero, symbolized by red keys; Saint Pancras, representing the district of the same name and with a red talon; Saint Peter representing San Piero a Scherragio and its emblem the wheel painted in green; and Saint Augustine representing Oltrarno denoted by a red bridge.[71] This fresco offered, then, an image of the guild as a corporation, made up of its constituent elements, the *conventi*, which came together like the *gonfaloni* or neighborhoods of Florence to form a whole. Addressing the tribunal that met in this hall, one was addressing figuratively the entire guild and its saintly protectors. This fresco spoke to the representative or popular aspect of the Lana guild's enterprise.[72]

On the opposite wall is a fresco dating from the 1330s or first half of the 1340s and attributed to Maso di Banco or his followers, depicting the first Roman consul Brutus as judge (fig. 104). Brutus, who led the revolution that overthrew the last Roman king and tyrant Tarquinius and later put his own sons to death for their role in a conspiracy to restore the kings, was considered a model of judicial probity.[73] In the fresco he sits isolated at the center of a massive stone bench that is raised two steps off the ground; he holds a small baton in his right hand while in his left he holds an object that may be a seal, a brand, or even one of the weights to be placed in the pans of a balance. Indeed, it seems that a scale of justice once was painted in the large void above Brutus's head but was later painted over. It was probably similar to the balance that is held above the large figure of Justice in Lorenzetti's fresco of Good Government (see fig. 116).[74]

Stern and immobile, Brutus is defended from four men by the cardinal virtues, represented as women. Scrolls at the top record the conversations between the virtues and their adversaries on the upper tier; similar scrolls, now lost, once adorned the lower-tier figures as well, and have been reconstructed from manuscripts. The four figures are seeking to corrupt justice by various means. That in red at the top left tries to approach Brutus with flattering speech, but is rebuffed by Prudence who assures him that ingratiating words and supplications (flattery and pleading, in other words) carry no weight for those who love the truth.[75] The man in the upper right who is dressed in green and holds a purse in his hand – probably a merchant – hopes to subvert justice with a bribe, but Justice brandishing a sword warns him that he is worthy of a "shameful death" and that "here sentences are not sold for gold, rather everyone gets what he deserves."[76] On the lower tier, the two figures try different tactics. The man on the left, wearing a fantastically patterned robe and clutching a glove, claims that he has been wronged and that if death does not stop him, he will have his vengeance. But Fortitude is unmoved, warning this man, the personification of arrogance, that his fury and threats will come to nothing here.[77] On the lower right, Temperance tries to prevent a man in a heavy cloak and hood who clutches a scroll from escaping. His now-missing *cartello* originally read: "I am afraid to pursue my case in front of you, because some of you may have been offended by my actions in the past."[78] But Temperance assures him that in this court, justice is fair and the scales hang true.[79] Temperance is apparently referring to the scales that once hung above Brutus's head.

Various interpretations have been put forward as to the significance of the figure fleeing Temperance. Salomone Morpurgo described him as "un uomo *occulto*," in other words a deceiver, who carries some sort of falsified document that he hopes will disqualify the judges from the case, but who then tries to flee when Temperance tells him that in this court, despite any past offense, justice will prevail.[80] His heavy cloak serves as the mantle of concealment, becoming the dark cover for fraud and falsehood.[81] The tyrant in Lorenzetti's Bad Government fresco is likewise enveloped in a heavy cloak, while at his feet a figure of Justice wearing a sheer veil lies bound (see fig. 95).[82] Scholars starting with Morpurgo have drawn parallels between this decorative program and the aphorisms of Paolo da Certaldo.[83] As has been seen, in one Certaldo warns his readers, "guard yourself from men who keep themselves hidden [in other words, hypocrites] more than from those who are open" (Dagli occulti uomini ti guarda più tosto che da' palesi).[84] Like his contemporaries, Certaldo understood that fraud flourishes in concealment and in the hidden hearts of men.

In the fresco, then, Brutus with the aid of the cardinal virtues vanquishes flattery, bribery, fury, and deception, the enemies of truth and justice. He reminds the Lana guild officials, especially in their role as judges, to take him as their model; indeed, one manuscript that records the painting's captions offers the following epigraph for the entire fresco; it derives from a commentary on "Inferno," Canto 4: "Da Bruto, primo Consol de' Romani,/ prudente, giusto, temperato, forte,/ essenpro prenda ogni rettor di corte" (Every rector of the court take an example from prudent, just, temperate, and strong Brutus, first consul of the Romans).[85]

In the audience hall of the Lana guild, where members of the guild met, where the statutes were read out, and where cases were heard before the guild's court of judges, the images on the walls came together to create an atmosphere redolent with Christian, civic, and antique values and meanings.[86] The emblems of the *conventi* and their saintly protectors reminded those in the room that they were acting for (and, by extension, in the presence of) the entire guild and indeed the entire city, while the Brutus fresco admonished them to shun, as Brutus did, the vices and cultivate instead the cardinal virtues.[87] The images of the saints and of Christ as judge reminded those present that what transpired in this room would resonate beyond earthly concerns. In this merchant guildhall, justice and truth would prevail over injustice and fraud.

The decoration of the guildhall and statutes of the Perugian guild of merchants, another extant guildhall, shared several features with the Florentine Lana hall. As discussed in Chapter Two, in 1390 the Mercanzia of Perugia was granted two rooms on the ground floor of the Palazzo dei Priori which it remodeled to serve its purposes. It visually unified the space by sheathing the walls with elaborate wooden paneling and benches. A small pulpit, from which sentences of the guild court were announced, was also added; it adorns the left-hand wall. Above it are gilded images of the cardinal virtues, as well as the symbols of Perugia (the griffin) and of the guild (the griffin atop a bale of merchandise).[88] Here, as in the Lana hall, the cardinal virtues are given special prominence.

When the miniaturist Matteo di Ser Cambio illuminated the guild's 1403 statutes, he depicted the guild's emblem (fig. 105). In the decorated border, he included as an epigraph the same commentary on "Inferno" Canto 4, invoking Brutus as a model that was used to describe the Lana guildhall fresco.[89] In this guildhall as well, the theme of justice was preeminent.

Brutus also served as a powerful model for Siena's Mercanzia. It was established in the late twelfth century and represented merchants engaged in international trade; manufacturing guilds were not included. The four consuls of the Mercanzia enjoyed a privileged place in Sienese government since they, along with the four proveditors of the Biccherna (the treasury) and the three consuls of the knights, met with the nine priors to form the Signoria or Concistoro.[90] Like its Florentine counterpart, the Sienese Mercanzia handled such matters as reprisals and bankruptcies and heard appeals of cases from guild courts. It also ran the Sienese mint.

For many years the Mercanzia of Siena met at the church of San Paolo, adjacent to its later headquarters. The church bordered the Campo, Siena's communal square and central marketplace.[91] Originally the Campo was itself divided into two parts that were separated by a stream: the lower part, called the Campo del Mercato or Campo Foris, and the upper part, the Campo di San Paolo; however, by the thirteenth century the two sections were certainly unified into a single space.[92] In 1309 work began on the Mercanzia's first headquarters. One side housed a hall that faced the Campo and was elevated above a row of shops. The other side faced the Croce del Travaglio, the

105   Matteo di Ser Cambio, *Griffon atop a Bale*,
Matriculation Book of the Perugian Mercanzia, 1403, Perugia,
Archivio del Collegio della Mercanzia, Ms. 2, fol. 66r.

city's main intersection linking the two parts of the Via Francigena (known as the Banchi di Sopra and di Sotto) and the Via di Città leading to the Duomo. That side housed the offices that dealt with the public. This first Sienese Mercanzia conformed to the other buildings on the Campo in that it had small columns defining the space between the biforate windows.[93] However, in 1417, the commune decided to rebuild the Mercanzia. The new structure reoriented the main façade from the Campo to the Croce del Travaglio and consisted primarily of a loggia that underwent an elaborate decoration program in the 1450s and 60s.[94]

According to a 1391 inventory of the furnishings of the "casa della Mercantia" (headquarters of the Mercanzia), one item in the possession of the Mercanzia was a wooden bench (*sedia*) located in the room by which one entered the palace from the Campo and at which "the officials sit." This bench was located along a wall, "at the foot of the painting of Brutus and other figures." The next three entries in the inventory further clarify the arrangement. The first reads, "a wooden counter [*bancho*] which goes in front of the said bench [*sedia*], at which counter are the notary and the trea-surer"; the second: "two wooden platforms [*predelle*], where the notary and treasurer sit"; and the third: "a pole [*stangha*] with a chain of wide iron, which is in front of the said counter and by which chain is attached [a copy of] the statutes in the volgare of the "casa" [that is, the Mercanzia] with a little iron chain." In other words, this room, like the room in the Florentine Lana hall, served judicial and administrative purposes. The arrangement of the room was in all likelihood similar to that of the

106   Vanni di Baldolo, *Tribunal of the Notaries' Guild*, c. 1333, Matriculation Book of the Perugian
Notaries, Perugia, Biblioteca Comunale Augusta, Ms. 972, fol. 3v.

tribunal depicted in the matriculation book of the notaries of Perugia by Vanni di
Baldolo (fig. 106). The image of Brutus and the "other figures" would have had functions similar to that found in the Florentine Lana guildhall: as a warrant for the activities of the Mercanzia, and as an admonition to the officials to live up to Brutus's
example by issuing just rulings.[95]

107    Bologna, *Justice*, Loggia della Mercanzia, late 14th century.

The theme of Justice was even more explicit in a second object in the Sienese Mercanzia's possession adorned with an image of Brutus. According to the same inventory, the Mercanzia also owned two silver seals that were attached by a silver chain. One seal depicted "Brutus consul of the Romans with the balance and with a bale"; the second smaller seal likewise depicted a balance and bale.[96] And when in the mid-fifteenth century, the Mercanzia was rebuilt giving it a monumental presence at the Croce del Travaglio, a sculpted image of Brutus along with other exemplars of Roman republican virtue was included on the backrest of one of the benches.[97]

In Bologna, the exterior decoration of that city's Mercanzia brought together the city's patron saints and guilds in a program that likewise emphasized justice. Again, as discussed in Chapter Two, in 1382 the commune of Bologna built a new loggia for the office for the gabelles, but when the building at the rear of the loggia was finished in 1391, it came to house the Foro dei Mercanti, a court established by the Universitas to handle disputes between guilds and other trade matters (see fig. 29).[98] The result of this building program was a magnificent two-story vaulted loggia surmounted by a third-story vaulted hall and a crenellated cornice. The front façade is adorned with an elaborate balcony protected by a baldachin between two gothic windows and by roundels that continue around the two sides of the building. The central roundel contains a sculptured figure of Justice (fig. 107) while the others have images of Saints Francis, Petronius, Florian, Ambrose, Peter, and Dominic, either patron saints of the city or saints with other associations with Bologna.[99] A frieze with the arms of the city's guilds also adorns the façade.

A similar frieze of guild emblems, but this time in stone, runs across the façade of Florence's Mercanzia and, as noted earlier, a painting of truth tearing out the tongue of the liar was painted on its interior. At least one other painting is known that also adorned the building. Around 1420 the Mercanzia commissioned the painter Giovanni Toscani to create an image of Christ and St Thomas for its headquarters (fig. 108).

108    Giovanni Toscani, *Incredulity of Saint Thomas*, c. 1420,
Florence, Galleria dell'Accademia.

Toscani's panel shows Christ raising his right arm high so that Thomas has access to the wound on his breast. The saint reaches out to touch the gash, focusing his eyes intently on the task at hand.[100]

The incredulity of Thomas was a theme that particularly resonated with Florence's Mercanzia. Some evidence suggests that the Mercanzia had patronage over the chapel of Saint Thomas in the Duomo.[101] And from 1435 on, with the impetus of Cosimo de' Medici, the Sei della Mercanzia (the Six of the Mercanzia, its executive board), along with guild officials and the Council of Eight began making an annual procession on December 21, the feast of the saint, to the church of San Tommaso located in the Mercato Vecchio.[102] Situated in the northeastern corner of the market, San Tommaso was a modest if venerable foundation that enjoyed particularly close ties to the Medici family, whose original family palaces had been located in the vicinity of the Mercato Vecchio (see fig. 6).[103] Over the doorway of the church, a fresco that Giorgio Vasari credited to Paolo Uccello depicted the Doubting Thomas theme; Uccello probably executed the painting no later than 1448. A drawing in the Codex Rustici indicates that the artist placed Christ and Thomas at the center of the grouped Apostles and showed Thomas placing his hand in the wound in Jesus's breast in order to alleviate his doubt as to the Resurrection (fig. 109). Thomas's touch became incontrovertible

109   Marco di Bartolomeo Rustici, *Mercato Vecchio, Church of San Tommaso, and the Incredulity of Saint Thomas*, from the Codex Rustici (*Dimostrazione dell'andata del Santo Sepolcro*), 1425, fol. 29v, Florence, Biblioteca del Seminario Arcivescovile Maggiore di Firenze.

proof; for this reason the theme readily pertained to matters legal, as well as to the market. As has been seen, merchants commonly used all of their senses, including touch, to determine the authenticity of goods.[104]

The Mercanzia's association with Thomas reached its artistic apogee, however, when in the mid-1460s the Six commissioned Andrea del Verrocchio to cast figures of

Thomas and Christ to adorn the niche in Orsanmichele which the Mercanzia had purchased in 1463 from the Parte Guelfa; the sculptural group was installed at Orsan-michele in 1483.[105]

This Thomas theme adorned other spaces in Florence as well. A now lost fresco executed around 1385 once graced the space above a door in the Sala dell'Udienza (Audience Hall) of the Signoria, the chief executive branch of the Florentine government. An accompanying inscription from Franco Sacchetti's *Libro delle rime* read:

> Touch the truth as I do, and you will believe
> In the high justice of the Trinity, which always
> exalts each person who makes judgments.
>
> Your hand to the truth and your eyes to
> highest heaven, your whole tongue and your every
> deed direct to the common good without hesitation.
>
> Search for the truth, following justice; [direct]
> your whole and free mind to the common good,
> for without this every government is deficient.
>
> [Toccate il vero com'io e crederete
> nella somma Iustizia in tre persone,
> che sempre essalta ognun che fa ragione.
>
> La mano al vero e gli occhi al sommo cielo,
> la lingua intera, ed ogni vostro effetto
> raguardi al ben comune sanza diffetto.
>
> Cercate il vero, iustizia conseguendo;
> al ben comune la mente intera e franca,
> perch'ogni regno sanza questo manca.][106]

In Florence, images of Thomas thus formed an axis running from the Palazzo della Mercanzia and the Palazzo della Signoria to the Mercato Vecchio by way of Orsan-michele (or a "v" if one also takes into account the chapel in the Duomo). Together they reassured merchants as to the integrity of the Florentine marketplace, government, and church (see fig. 34).[107] They brought the themes of proof, justice, and the search for truth in the marketplace together and linked them in the Palazzo della Signoria explicitly to the idea of the common good.

Many of the works examined earlier either had inscriptions (in the case of sculptures) or *cartelli* (in the case of paintings) that served to identify, admonish, reassure, or guarantee. Again, the now lost inscription over the doorway of the Florentine Mercanzia declared it to be the "Home of Equity and Truth" (*Domus equitatis et veritatis*). Inscriptions often adorned marketplaces, and even if they were incomprehensible to most passersby because they were in Latin – recall the Pisan injunction that *pitture infamanti* be labeled in the *volgare* so that could be understood by all – they served nevertheless to add an aura of legitimacy to what transpired in the marketplace. Like

110 Venice, inscription on the east end of San Giacomo di Rialto, 11th century.

the contracts drafted by notaries and the notations in personal account books that were increasingly being accepted as valid proof in courts, inscriptions authenticated and guaranteed. Indeed, the written word seems to have acquired a kind of totemic significance.

One of the earliest extant inscriptions – it dates to the eleventh century – is that found on the eastern exterior wall of the church of San Giacomo di Rialto, the church which held great significance for the Venetians (fig. 110). An inscribed Byzantine-style cross of white Istrian stone is embedded in the brick wall. The cross rests on an inscribed band of Istrian stone. On the cross itself the inscription reads: "Sit crux tua vera salus huic Christe loco" (Let your cross, oh Christ, be the true salvation of this place), while that on the supporting band states: "Hoc circa templum sit ius mercantibus aequum: pondera nec vergant nec sit conventio prava" (Around this temple let the law of merchants be equitable: let the weights not bend and the contract be not crooked).[108]

The placement of the cross and accompanying band appears to have been especially strategic, for its location high on the eastern wall of the church meant that, before the first bridge at Rialto was built sometime in the first half of the thirteenth century, it would have been visible to those disembarking at the mercantile center. And once the bridge was constructed, it would have been seen by those descending the steps of the bridge after they had crossed over from the San Marco side of the Grand Canal. Furthermore, the cross faced the loggia that stood at the foot of the bridge – the loggia where, as Jacopo d'Albizzotto Guidi observed, gentlemen gathered.[109] As for the inscriptions, they had different intentions. The one on the cross reminded merchants that true salvation should come not from making money but from the church, while

111    Lucca, inscription on the west façade of San Martino, 1111.

the one on the band sought to reassure them that in the precincts surrounding the church, that is at Rialto, trade would be conducted fairly. In these ways, the Venetians reminded both themselves and foreigners of their status as Christian merchants and of the business integrity of their city.

Another early inscription is that found on the façade of the church of San Martino, the cathedral of Lucca (fig. 111). Dated 1111, it records that all money-changers and spice dealers who located their shops in the cathedral square had sworn to engage honestly in their trade. The inscription reads:

AD MEMORIAM HABENDAM ET JUSTITIAM RETINENDAM CURTIS ECCLESIE BEATI MARTINI. SCRIBIMUS JURAMENTUM QUE QUOD CAMBIATORES ET SPECIARII OMNES ISTIUS CURTIS. TEMPORE RANGERII EPISCOPI FACERUNT UT OMNES HOMINES CUM FIDUCIA POSSINT CAMBIARE. VENDERE. ET EMERE JURAVERUNT OMNES CAMBIATORES. ET SPECIARII. QUOD AB ILLA ORA IN ANTEA. NEC FURTUM FACIENT. NEC TRECCAMENTUM. NEC FALSITATEM INFRA CURTE SANCTI MARTINI NEC IN DOMIBUS ILLIS. IN QUIBUS HOMINES HOSPITANTUR. HOC JURAMENTUM FACIUNT. QUI IBI AD CAMBIUM. AUT. AD SPECIES. STARE VOLUERINT SUNT ETIAM INSUPER. QUI SEMPER CURTEM ISTAM CUSTODIUNT. ET QUOD MALEFACTUM FUERINT. EMENDARE FACIUNT. ANNO DOMINI M.C.X.I. ADVENIENS QUISQUAM SCRIPTURAM PERLEGAT ISTAM. ET QUA CONFIDAT ET SIBI NIL TIMEAT.

[To preserve its memory and to maintain the justice of the court[yard] of the Church of Saint Martin, we shall write down the oath which was sworn by all money-changers and dealers in spices of this court[yard], in the time of Bishop Rangerio – so that all men can exchange, sell, and buy in good faith. All money-changers and dealers in spices swore that from that moment forward they would commit no theft nor trick nor falsification within the court[yard] of Saint Martin nor in those houses in which men are given hospitality. Those who shall wish to dwell there [as dealers] in exchange or spice take this oath. Moreover, there also are [officials] who always guard this court[yard] and who see to it that any wrong that may have been

112   Taddeo di Bartolo, *Last Judgment*, detail showing *The Damned*, c. 1393–1413,
Collegiate Church, San Gimignano.

done be emended. In the year of the Lord 1111. Let everyone coming peruse this
inscription, and place trust in it, and fear nothing for himself.]

By petrifying (and thereby perpetuating) the money-changers and spice dealers'
oath, the inscription sought to instill confidence or trust in this marketplace. Customers
were assured by words carved in stone that vendors had sworn not to commit
fraud and that the marketplace itself was under surveillance by both officials and by
the church.[110]

Of course, images in churches, particularly depictions of the Last Judgment, also
served to remind merchants and artisans, like the inscription at Rialto, that they should
be attentive not only to profit but also to the fate of their eternal souls. One example
will suffice – the fresco of the Last Judgment completed sometime between 1393 and
1413 by Taddeo di Bartolo for the Collegiate Church of San Gimignano (fig. 112). In

the scene illustrating the tortures of the greedy, Taddeo depicted a usurer (labeled "USURAIO"), a money-lender ("MUTATARIO"), a man labeled simply "AVARO" (the avaricious one), and another for whom the label is incomplete and no longer decipherable (it reads "M ...SI ..."). It has been suggested that he represents either a miller or a grain merchant. The condemned suffer appalling punishments: the usurer is forced to eat the excrement of a demon, the lender is pilloried; the avaricious man is strangled with a rope by two demons, while the emaciated miller or grain merchant is tantalized by the abundant grain that is close at hand but ultimately unattainable.[111]

In all these instances, then, civic officials, guildsmen, judges, and churchmen employed painters and sculptors to create works of art to embellish marketplaces, guildhalls, courts, and churches in order to exhort men to good behavior and to reinforce the values of the marketplace. Although most of the art created for marketplaces has been lost, it appears that popular regimes had a special hand in creating works that celebrated truth and justice and condemned fraud in its many forms. The very fact that the first notices of *pitture infamanti* date from the 1260s, when popular regimes were coming to the fore, supports this view.[112] As Massimo Giansante's penetrating analysis of the 1245 statutes of the Bolognese money-changers' guild makes clear, the author of the prologue, the notary Rolandino Passageri, repositioned the professional or marketplace values of trust, truth, and legality (*fides*, *veritas*, *legalitas*) as "political virtues" and, of course, as a justification for the rule of the *popolo*.[113]

By the 1390s, however, at least two cities had decided that *pitture infamanti*, which were originally intended to defame those who threatened the market and thus to reassure other merchants that they would find justice in the marketplace, were actually a liability since they could be construed as besmirching their cities' good names. During that decade, both Lodi and Milan wrote into their statutes rules calling for the removal of the images of notaries, money-changers, and merchants who committed fraudulent acts. The authorities in both cities feared that these images would bring "scandal and infamy" not only on the men who had perpetrated these acts, but also on the cities themselves, since foreigners who saw these images would believe "that the greater part of the citizens *know little trust* [*agnoschant parvam fidem*] and are involved in great falsities."[114] By this time Milan and Lodi were both under the control of the Visconti family, who had instituted a lordship over these cities. For the Visconti, defaming pictures no longer had value, as they once had had in popular regimes, as expressions of the common will to good governance, but instead represented a threat to regimes which themselves relied on great falsities and engendered little trust. The age of the marketplace as an expression of the common good, promoted by popular regimes, was rapidly passing from the scene.

# EPILOGUE

## "È IL BENE COMUNE NEL MERCATARE"

Through an examination of the representational, spatial, and architectural elements of marketplaces, as well as of the performative aspects of marketplace activities and the ethical concerns behind them, this study has shown that the marketplace was a multivalent space that touched the lives of medieval Italians in myriad ways. In so doing, it has engaged either directly or indirectly with a number of longstanding historical and art historical issues, debates, and concerns.

Regarding the question of the commercial revolution and its place in the development of the modern economy, this work joins several that challenge the long-held idea that there emerged in late medieval and Renaissance Europe the kind of internally contained, morally neutral marketplace later envisioned by Adam Smith and others, in which the competing egoistic interests of market participants resulted in a self-referential and self-determining market dynamic driven by the pursuit of profit. This debate has sometimes been framed as the evolution from a status-driven society to one regulated by contracts. To be sure, actors in the medieval Italian marketplace were motivated, at least in part, by the desire for profit. But profit was measured in many ways, not simply in monetary terms. A good reputation, the common welfare of a guild or a city, the salvation of one's eternal soul, as well as material gain, were all forms of 'profit' that influenced the way people acted in the marketplace. The marketplace was not a morally neutral space filled with wholly autonomous actors but, instead, was a sphere in which *ragion di mercatura* was just one element of a complicated marketplace calculus. Like the goods they offered for sale, actors were evaluated for their character – were they "sincere," genuine (as one document described worthy products) – or were they, as heretics were often considered, counterfeit.[1] Ideologically, this tension was framed as a contest between private interest and the common good, a struggle that took on particular weight as merchants, bankers, and, to a lesser extent, artisans gained power in the popular communes of the thirteenth and fourteenth centuries and began to determine commercial policy. Posited as a claim to universal benefit, the appeal to the common good both justified and masked the *popolo*'s own particular hold on power.

At the same time, this conflict between private interest and the common good, fueled as it was by the dynamic of bargaining in a marketplace filled with non-standardized goods, served to foster a deep attentiveness to motivation. This contributed in turn, aided by a new emphasis on writing and by the unique configuration of political power in Italy that allowed for autonomous communes to develop, to a greater awareness of human nature, the interior self, and of the capacity to deceive. This too was framed in moral terms. The minute dissection of the virtues and vices and of their 'children' was a way for people to consider the complexity of human personality and its capacity for good or evil, and thus to decide whether or not they could extend trust to others.[2] In this sense the medieval marketplace represented one stage among many in the evolution of attitudes toward the self, and in particular in the development of the early modern obsession with self-presentation and dissimulation. The ability to judge the quality of goods mirrored the dynamic of social interactions and helped to shape those dynamics.

This study has sought to contribute to these debates and issues by paying particular attention to the material and spatial aspects of the marketplace. As has been seen, the market was both a concept and a space, and efforts were made (again by popular governments in particular) to organize market space in such a way as to foster trust through openness and to inhibit fraud by containing concealment. The layout of market streets, shops, and stalls, and the inscriptions, sculptures, and paintings that adorned market squares, merchant courts, and guildhalls were intended to influence behavior and to create the ideal marketplace.

And so, additionally, this study offers a mercantile perspective on much of the art produced during this period. As Adrian Randolph has observed with regard to analyses of Donatello's *Dovizia*, "the secular, nongovernmental, mercantile element of fifteenth-century Florentine society" has traditionally been "undervalued in art historical analyses."[3] The same applies equally well, mutatis mutandis, to much of the art produced during the period examined here, although, as this study has also shown, efforts to distinguish the secular from the religious in all spheres of medieval life seems misplaced.

With this in mind and by way of conclusion, it is worth taking a final look at one of the celebrated works of the period – Ambrogio Lorenzetti's Sala dei Nove frescoes – to see what they tell about the role of the marketplace in medieval Italy, especially again, in the popular communes.[4] Scholars have long sought to uncover the textual inspiration for Lorenzetti's program. Most have looked to philosophical or theological texts. Nicolai Rubinstein believed that Aristotle, as interpreted by medieval

113    Ambrogio Lorenzetti, *Effects of Good Government in the City*, 1338–40, Palazzo Pubblico, Siena.

commentators, specifically his theories of justice and the common good, inspired Lorenzetti (or those who commissioned him) in the design of the program.[5] By contrast, Quentin Skinner looked to Cicero and the influence that the Roman statesman's writings had on the pre-humanist literature of the early communes.[6] Maria Monica Donato finds the "polarity" between Rubinstein's and Skinner's positions, that is between the supposed Aristotelianism and Ciceronianism of the frescoes, to be "exaggerated" and argues instead that the frescoes are really a *summa* of the lengthy development of the juridical and political culture of the communes, while for her part Chiara Frugoni believes that the inspiration for the frescoes derives not from juridical or philosophical texts but rather from the Bible.[7] According to Frugoni, the Book of Wisdom, especially its opening phrase in the Vulgate version, "Diligite iustitiam qui iudicatis terram" (Love Justice you who judge on earth; a phrase repeated around the figure of Justice in the Good Government tribunal fresco), served as the ultimate source for the ideas visualized in the paintings.[8]

While there is evidence for all these positions, it is clear that the mercantile element is also central to Lorenzetti's program, since the well-governed city is represented by commercial and material prosperity (fig. 113).[9] As has been seen, Lorenzetti was not unique in this regard. He simply reflected the ideas of medieval theologians and preachers who by the early thirteenth century had integrated the market economy into their vision of a Christian society, arguing as did such figures as Thomas of Chobham and Alexander of Halles that, although commerce was always potentially hazardous to the soul of the individual merchant, it was, at the same time, useful and necessary to society generally.[10] Even the Franciscans did not condemn wealth per se but, rather, its hoarding for personal nonproductive uses, as when preachers railed against the purchase of vain luxuries by women. Instead they argued that when wealth was used to help one's neighbor and for the good of society, it was a positive force.[11] As one anonymous fifteenth-century Franciscan wrote, *mercancia* (commerce) as an activity was "holy and licit and approved" (*sancta et licita et approbata*).[12] This is precisely how Lorenzetti depicts commerce; it is at once the source and symbol of the *bene comune*.[13]

Lorenzetti's fellow Sienese, San Bernardino, understood this well. In a sermon intended to warn merchants of the sins to which they were susceptible, the preacher offered, following Duns Scotus, three reasons why trade was essential to a city: first, it brought to the city products that were not available locally (he named spices in particular); second, the conservation and subsequent exchange of those items helped enrich everyone; third, the importation of materials like wool offered work to those who transformed it into something else (namely cloth).[14] In the same sermon, Bernardino declared: "nothing profits the Comune so much as the usefulness of the guilds and of the merchandise that is bought and sold."[15] Accordingly, Lorenzetti depicted the city and countryside under good government as overflowing with material benefits.

By contrast, in the part of the painting illustrating the effects of bad government, Lorenzetti depicted a city and countryside in economic ruin. Although the section of the painting showing the devastated city has suffered significant damage, still legible are buildings in disrepair, rubble-filled streets, and, most importantly, empty shops. Only one shop, the armorer's, is well stocked and occupied, while in the countryside villages are aflame and marauding soldiers commandeer roads and bridges, vital to the economic welfare of the city (fig. 114). The *cartello* below the painting proclaims that here "wars, rapines, treacheries, and deceptions [*en ganni*] gain the upper hand."[16] Accepting that war can be considered the ultimate form of violence, all four of these malevolent actions figure in at least one medieval dissection of avarice's baseborn progeny.

Furthermore, as noted in the last chapter, the personification of Fraud occupies a prominent place in the tyrant's court: he sits at the tyrant's right hand and directly under Avarice.[17] And in this council hall or tribunal, Justice lies at the feet of the black enshrouded tyrant, while the broken scales of justice are strewn about her. Sheathed in a sheer veil (like the figure of truth in Gaddi's lost Florentine Mercanzia work), she embodies openness and transparency, which are essential to justice.[18]

Some commentators have asked why the three theological virtues surrounding the head of the good ruler (from left to right Faith, Charity, and Hope) are not properly matched against their opposites among the vices surrounding the head of the tyrant (from left to right, Avarice, Pride, and Vainglory). According to most schemes of the virtues and vices, Charity is the opposite of Avarice, yet in Lorenzetti's fresco Faith occupies that position.[19] But, within the context in which Lorenzetti was working, namely a program deeply informed by mercantile practices and designed to celebrate the common good (and the rule of the merchant elite), *fides* (trust) more properly counterbalanced avarice and its underlying child *fraus* (fraud).

I SIGNORIA SOPRA OLLEI · PONGASI LA MENTE E LO INTELLETTO ·  ... TURB

114    Ambrogio Lorenzetti, *Effects of Bad Government in the City*, 1338–40, Palazzo Pubblico, Siena.

Lorenzetti chose to include two figures of Justice on the Good Government wall. One sits on the far right, as part of the Comune's tribunal (although the current figure appears to reflect Andrea Vanni's repainting in the second half of the fourteenth century[20]). She holds an upturned sword in her right hand and in her left she clutches a crown, perhaps the crown that once mistakenly graced the decapitated head that lies cradled in her lap (fig. 115). But a more prominent figure of Justice takes up the left side of the wall. In this case Justice does not actually hold the balance that dangles above her head – that task falls to Sapientia (divine wisdom), at whom Justice casts an upward gaze (fig. 116).[21] Instead, Justice balances the pans of the scales, whence descend the cords which when entwined become the rope of concord that winds through the hands of the citizens at the bottom. The pan on the left is labeled Distributive Justice. Behind it hovers an angel who is crowning the just man while preparing to decapitate the evil-doer. The pan on the right is labeled Commutative Justice. Here a second angel is offering a grain measure (the *staio*) to the man in green kneeling in front, and measuring sticks (the *canna* and the *passetto*) to the man in orange behind him.[22] Contemporary theorists, following Aristotle, understood distributive justice as "the

115   Ambrogio Lorenzetti (with significant repainting by Andrea
Vanni), *Allegory of Good Government*, detail showing *Justice*, 1338–40,
repainting between 1360 and 1385, Palazzo Pubblico, Siena.

distribution of rewards and punishments . . . to each according to what he deserved."[23]
Commutative justice, by contrast, involved exchanges and required "not cheating and
paying one's debts."[24] Accordingly, the angel offers to the kneeling merchants instruments of proper measure. As Donato has observed, it is surely no accident that "in a
city of merchants" commutative justice is depicted in this way.[25] As in Giotto's program
for the Salone in Padua, instruments of measure adorn this image of justice since
equity in both the court and the marketplace contribute to the *bene comune*. A thriving
marketplace was the sign of a just society, and the marketplace values of truthfulness
and trust became political virtues.[26]

     Finally, it is worth observing that Justice herself serves as a kind of balance between
the two halves of the entire fresco cycle, as if good government and bad government
are themselves being weighed.[27] In this way, as has been noted by scholars before, the
entire program becomes a kind of secularized Last Judgment – with the saved and the
damned corresponding to the subjects of good and bad government.[28] The saved, the
blessed, are those who live the "dolce vita" – a phrase used in the *cartello* below the
*Effects of Good Government in the City and Country* – under a government which, by

116   Ambrogio Lorenzetti, *Allegory of Good Government*, detail showing *Sapientia or Divine Justice*, 1338–40, Palazzo Pubblico, Siena.

rendering justice, ensures the rich provisioning of the city and promotes commerce by combating fraud.[29] The common good – the *bene comune*, in other words – was understood by people at the time in both material and political terms and was shaped and defined by the practices and experience of the marketplace.[30] As Bernardino stated in his sermon aimed at merchants, "è il bene comune nel mercatare" (the common good resides in trade).[31] The marketplace was where that common good was forged with trust, guaranteed by justice, and made visible through material prosperity.

# Notes

**Introduction**

1 Bernardino da Siena, 1934, 1: 3.

2 Giordano da Pisa, 2006, 591.

3 Ibid., 581–2.

4 The phrase appears to have been first used by Robert S. Lopez's *The Commercial Revolution of the Middle Ages,* 950–1350 (1971).

5 On the use of "marketplace vocabulary" by the friars and the idea of holy commerce, see Little, 1978, 195, 200–01; Iannella, 1999, 134–41; Muzzarelli, 2005, 26–33.

6 The commercialization of medieval society was not confined to Italy, although it seems to have made its appearance earliest there. For commercialization generally, see Little, 1971, 8–18; Howell, 2010; Davis, 2012.

7 Langholm, 2003, 244. This was especially the case when intellectuals considered one of the most hotly contested issues in medieval economic thought: how to determine the "just price." Most agreed that the just price was the equilibrium established in the local market by the needs and desires of buyers and the ability of sellers to supply that demand. As Langholm observes, 247, "Casting aside all modern notions, the current competitive market price served as a standard of justice in the confessional books insofar as it offered protection against economic coercion. In such a market, no one can force the price of individual transactions above or below the just market value, because there will be better alternatives."

8 Guido Carocci reports that the tabernacle in the Mercato Vecchio known as Santa Maria della Tromba was erected to commemorate where Pietro da Verona (Peter Martyr) preached against the Patarines; Carocci, 1975, 97. See also Prudlo, 2008, 44–5.

9 This study does not consider rural communes. For the terminological difficulties of the term commune, see Coleman, 1999, 375.

10 The phrase "mirror of the city" (*lo specchio della città*) appears to originate with Francesca Bocchi in reference to Bologna's Piazza Maggiore; Bocchi, 1995, 1: 105. Tuliani, 1998, 69, also uses the phrase in his work on the Campo of Siena.

11 During the past several decades, first as social and then as cultural history, both heavily influenced by the linguistic turn in literary studies, came to the fore, historians largely lost interest in the history of the economy. Two important exceptions to this trend were the growth of interest in the history of consumerism and in material culture more generally. As contemporary consumers went on a credit-driven buying spree and as material objects came more and more to define not only the well-lived life but also the very idea of selfhood, scholars sought to locate the historical origins of these phenomena. See esp. Goldthwaite, 1993 and Welch, 2005.

12 LeGoff, 1980, 29–42.

13 See the discussion in Caferro, 2011, 127–31.

14 Jones, 1997, 202.

15 Ibid., 204.

16 Davis, 2012, 25.

17 Todeschini, 1994; Todeschini, 2004; Todeschini, 2008; Todeschini, 2009.

18 Todeschini, 1994, 147–8.

19 Ibid., 153.

20 Ibid., 193. For a sophisticated analysis of the church's view of trade and commerce, see Langholm, 1992 and Langholm, 2003.

21 Prodi, 2009, esp. 18. I wish to thank Wietse de Boer for first bringing this book to my attention.

22 Ibid., 148–9.

23 Braudel, 1977.

24 Ibid., 16–17, 40.

25 Ibid., 62, 111. Also according to Braudel (63), the market economy and capitalism could advance simultaneously and not necessarily in succession.

26   Howell, 2010.

27   Ibid., 49–92. For the appearance in Italy of
     the view that land was "a marketable com-
     modity (*merces*) like any other," see Jones,
     1997, 166–8, 230. See also Witt, 2012, 231–2.

28   Howell, 2010, 29.

29   Muldrew, 1998, 94–5.

30   Molho, 1979; Weissman, 1989.

31   See Shaw and Welch, 2011, 22–3, 81, 84.

32   For the early modern period, see the works
     of Welch, 2005; Shaw, 2006; Shaw and Welch,
     2011.

33   Bec, 1967.

34   See Branca's introduction to Giovanni di
     Pagolo Morelli's *Ricordi* (Morelli, 1956,
     29–30), where he first used the term *ragion di
     famiglia*. See also Branca, 1986, xiv–xxi; Pan-
     dimiglio, 1974.

35   For general introductions, see Waley, 1969;
     Hyde, 1973.

36   De Matteis, 1977, 3. (*Bonum commune indubi-
     tanter preferendum est bono particulari*).

37   See Little, 1971.

38   Davis, 2012, 450–58, describes the economy
     of medieval England as pragmatically moral
     in that the prevailing mores "aided in modi-
     fying the degree to which participants
     engaged in unfair exchange and thus lowered
     the risks involved" (454).

39   See Burckhardt, 1954.

40   Von Martin, 1944, esp. 5–19.

41   Weissman, 1989, 269, giving a synopsis of von
     Martin's view. See also Caferro, 2011, 127–8.

42   The term "revolt of the Medievalists" was
     originally used by Ferguson, 1948; for the
     ongoing "revolt," see e.g. Morris, 1972.

43   Lapo Mazzei quoted in Origo, 1957, 224.

44   Witt, 2012, esp. 3.

45   For the contrast, see Muldrew, 1998, esp. ch.
     10. As Shaw, 2006, 6 observes, early modern
     society was a "hybrid" of the two: "Although
     justice meant treating equal persons in an
     equal manner, it did not necessarily mean
     treating *unequal* persons in the same way."

46   Stock, 1983, 86.

47   Eslami, 2010, 32.

48   Ibid., 33, 38.

49   Ibid., 24.

50   Calabi, 2004 (*Il mercato e la città: Piazze, strade,
     archittetura d'Europa in età moderna*, Venice:
     Marsilio, 1993).

51   Arnade, Howell, and Simons, 2002. See now
     also the essays in Boone and Howell, 2013.

52   Arnade, Howell, and Simons, 2002, 522, 535.

53   Ibid., 544. See also Howell, 2000.

54   My thinking has been deeply influenced by
     Henri Lefebvre's *The Production of Space*

(1974), in which he identifies three aspects of
spatiality: spatial practice, representations of
space, and representational space, which correspond, in his view, to "lived, conceived, and
perceived" spaces; and by Clifford Geertz's
study of the suq in Moroccan society where
he sets forth his own tripartite analysis: consideration of the suq must take account of its
physical form and social form, and its dynamics. See Lefebvre, 1991, 33–46, 288–9; Geertz,
1979, 123–313, esp. 175.

55   For an example from the early modern
     period, see Shaw, 2006.

56   Naso, 1985, 52–3; Grillo, 2001, 442; Shaw and
     Welch, 2011, 62.

57   Strozzi, 1997, 124–7; see also the interaction
     of women with the Giglio apothecary shop
     in Shaw and Welch, 2011, 89–92.

58   Bernardino, 1989, 2: 1131. The entire passage
     reads, "Or tolle l'ultima circustanzia, e sarà
     fine: dove si contiene ogni bene, la quale è il
     bene comune nel mercatare. Io non dico del
     bene comune de le gabelle de le mercantile;
     io dico del bene comune dell'arti; ché di
     niuna cosa partecipa tanto il Comuno, quanto
     dell'utile dell'arti e de le mercantie che si
     vendono e si comprano."

59   As Casagrande and Vecchio, 2000, 117, claim,
     "sulla compatibilità tra lucro individuale e
     bene comune si è costruita nei secoli tardo-
     medievali un'etica cristiana del commercio e
     della finanza."

*Part 1   Space and Place*

1    Fiamma, 1869.

2    My reading of the map follows closely that
     of Lucio Gambi and Maria Cristina Gozzoli,
     1982, 5–12. See also Tozzi and David, 1993,
     352.

3    Fiamma, 1869, 472–3.

4    Ibid., 724–5; for some other distances, see
     473–4.

5    According to Zupko, 1981, 190, in Milan a
     *pertica* was equivalent to 6.545 *are* (1 *are* =
     100 square meters).

6    Fiamma, 1869, 452.

7    Ibid., 453. For the Broletto as the expression
     of the popular regime, see Grillo, 2001, 657.

8    Fiamma, 1869, 452–3.

9    Grillo, 2001, 59–62; Grillo, 1998, 282; Salva-
     tori, 1994, 256.

10   Baroni, 1975, 260, 265–6.

11   See the remarks on ideal forms in Friedman,
     1988, 200–04.

12   Lefebvre, 1991, 26 (quotation), 31.

13   Ibid., 33–46, 288.

14  Ibid., 265 (quotation), 268–9.

15  Ibid., 40–41.

*Chapter 1   Marketplace as Civic Symbol*

1  For a still useful survey of this tradition, see Hyde, 1966a. See also Occhipinti, 1991.

2  Jones, 1997, 214. For the importance of the marketplace, see also Eslami, 2010, 16.

3  For the Veronese work, see Witt, 2012, 42, with bibliography.

4  Brolo, 1724, 529–36. See also Hyde, 1966a, 318–20; Witt, 2012, 300–01. Hyde noted (319) that the *Liber Pergaminus* had virtually no influence on subsequent city descriptions.

5  Anonimo Genovese, 1970, 563, 564. Romania refers to the Byzantine empire; Beyond-the-Sea to the eastern coast of the Mediterranean, i.e., parts of present-day Syria, Lebanon, Israel, and Palestine.

6  For Bonvesin da la Riva's life and works, see d'Arco, 1970.

7  Hyde, 1966a, 328.

8  Riva, 1974, 104.

9  See the introduction by Maria Corti in ibid., 4, 14–15, and Riva's text, 194–201. See also the summary of Milanese politics in Grillo, 2001, 643–74. See also Boucheron, 2003, 41–2.

10  Canistris, 2004, ix–xvi. All translations are mine unless otherwise noted. See Hyde, 1966a, 333–5; also Tozzi and David, 1993. For his biography, see Becker, 1975.

11  Canistris, 2004, 94–5; Canistris, 1984, 118–19. Piazza San Savino today is called Piazza Cavagneria; Canistris, 1984, 119 n. 156.

12  Canistris, 2004, 48–9.

13  Ibid., xv–xvi, 4, 102.

14  Villani, 1980, bk 11, chs 92–4, 178–88. On the importance of statistics in *laudes*, see Jones, 1997, 220.

15  Villani, 1980, bk 11, ch. 92, 178–81.

16  Ibid., ch. 94, 183.

17  Ibid., 183–8.

18  Ibid., 183–4.

19  Hyde, 1966a, 308–9. Bruni's work is available in English in Kohl and Witt, 1978, 121–75. The date of his *Laudatio* is uncertain: Baron famously dated it to 1402, but his dating remains contested. See Hankins, 1995, 315. Travelers' accounts also serve as witness to the commercial character of these cities; e.g. Fra Niccolò da Poggibonsi, 1990, 31–158, in his account of his journey to the Holy Land, commented (34) that Venice appeared to him to be the "most regal port in the world" and that "all the people [of Venice] are merchants."

20  Guidi, 1995, ix–xv.

21  Ibid., 3.

22  Ibid., x.

23  Ibid. and 19.

24  Ibid., 13, 16, 17, 18, 19, 21, 24.

25  Ibid., 19.

26  Ibid., 25.

27  Levin, 2004, 42–3. For Pucci's reputation as a popular poet, see also Cherubini, 1988.

28  I follow the version of Pucci's "Proprietà di Mercato Vecchio" in Sapegno, 1952, 403–10. A partial English translation is available in Dean, 2000, 121–4.

29  For a discussion of brigades in the fourteenth and fifteenth centuries, see Trexler, 1980, esp. 217–24; for brigades, known as *potenze*, in grand-ducal Florence, see Rosenthal, 1999.

30  Welch, 2005, 33–5.

31  Cherubini, 1988, 211–14.

32  It may not be coincidental that the four corner colonettes at Orsanmichele, Florence's grain market, are decorated with depictions of the four seasons. See Zervas, 1996, 1: 47.

33  Cherubini, 1988, 212.

34  For Canistris's job as a toll collector, see Canistris, 2004, ix.

35  Pinto, 1978, 17, 20.

36  Frugoni, 1991a, 109.

37  Pinto, 1978, 169 and pl. 3. See also the discussion in Branca, 1965.

38  Pinto, 1978, 169–70.

39  For the demon as a figure of *Crudelitas*, see Partsch, 1981, 43–4.

40  Pinto, 1978, 373–4 and pl. 8. According to the *Grande dizionario della lingua italiana*, "alpestre" could have the meaning of mean, arduous, difficult, or wild; see Battaglia, 1961–2002, 1: 346–7.

41  For the captions, see Pinto, 1978, pl. 9.

42  For a tumult in the grain market at Rome in 1353, see Modigliani, 1998, 12. I thank Helen Tangires for alerting me to this important book.

43  Caprioli, 2008, 220.

44  Morandini, 1961, 49.

45  Masi, 1934, 16–33. On the equation of grain abundance with peace and unity, see also Seidel, 1999, 47–51.

46  Hubert, 1993, 24. For many other examples of policies to protect food supplies, see Franco, Lanconelli, and Quesada, 1991.

47  Caprioli and Langeli, 1996, 1: 72–4, 244. For Venice, see ASVenezia, Provveditori alle biave, b. 1, capitolare, fol. 77r (Senate act dated July 30, 1411).

48  Blanshei, 1976, 61 n. 109.

49  Roberti, 1906–11, 3: 223. This rule was included in the capitulary of the Giudici del

Contrabbando. For efforts to supply Milan, see Grillo, 2001, 180–82, 535–9.

50 The much altered Bolognese Palazzo della Biada is now the Palazzo d'Accurisio; see Bocchi, 1995, 2: 105. For the dating of 1287 when the commune began to acquire property to construct the granary, see Touring Club Italiano's *Emilia Romagna*, 1991, 122. For the date of Padua's granary, see Puppi and Universo, 1982, 63.

51 Caggese, 1999b, 400–01.

52 ASParma, Diplomatico, Pergamene miniate, pergamena 50, s.d. [*senza data*] 1318. It is not clear which communal palace was the location of the work. Presumably, it was on that of San Vitale built in 1281, rather than on the older palace, known as Torello's palace, built in the 1220s. See Marina, 2012, 65–71, 90–100. For more on the parchment, see Franco, Lanconelli, and Quesada, 1991, 17, 132–3. Siena kept its salt stores in the lower levels of the Palazzo Pubblico; see Nevola, 2007, 2.

53 Pinto, 1978, 18 n. 51. For the idea that she represents the personification of grain or cereals, see Partsch, 1981, 22–3.

54 See Wieruszowski, 1944, 26, and the brief remarks in Cassidy, 2007, 115. For the importance of Chiusi in supplying Perugia with grain, see Blanshei, 1976, 15, 61–2.

55 Pope-Hennessy, 1955, 178.

56 I have not yet been able to determine when the banderole was added to the *Madonna Verona*. For the statue, see Bertolini, 1988, 255–9. See also Randolph, 2002, 51–2.

57 For a thorough and illuminating discussion of the *Bonissima* and its peregrinations, see Lugli, 2010, 86–90; "sturdy and healthy" is his description (87). For the balance she may have held, see Braglia, 1985, 49.

58 Wilkins, 1983, 414; see also Pope-Hennessy, 1993, 143–4.

59 Wilkins, 1983, 413; Wilk, 1986; Randolph, 2002, 19–75.

60 Rossi, 2007, 14.

61 On the rich associations of Mary and Saint Anne at Orsanmichele and their role as "potent fertility symbols," see Zervas, 1996, 1: 23–7, 65.

62 Miller, 2000, 113, 153.

63 Most importantly, see Rubinstein, 1958; Skinner, 1999; Starn, 1987; Frugoni, 1991a; Belting, 1989; Donato, 2003.

64 One theory has it that Lorenzetti showed Siena as if one was looking *from* the Palazzo Pubblico; see Tuliani, 81 n. 83; also Nevola, 2007, 7. For the changes by Vanni, see Gibbs, 1999a, 11–16, esp. 15.

65 Seidel, 1999, 53. For the argument that Lorenzetti's fresco was meant to be seen from the vantage point of the figure of Peace, see Greenstein, 1988, esp. 497 and figs 11 and 12.

66 Pächt, 1950, 41.

67 Seidel, 1999, 49. The peasant woman with a basket on her head also conveys some of the qualities of an Abundance figure: her heavily laden basket is not unlike a cornucopia. Moreover, her swaying stance is similar to the pose that Donatello later explored in his *Dovizia*.

## Chapter 2   Evolution of Marketplaces

1 Moriani Antonelli, 1996, 1109–10. For a similar escalation of fines for crimes committed in Perugia's main piazza, market, and major streets, see Blanshei, 1976, 63.

2 Howell, 2000, 17.

3 Bocchi, 1995, 1: 62.

4 Rauty, 1988, 237.

5 Ibid., 233–5. The diploma is reprinted in Rauty, 1981a, 280.

6 Rauty, 1981a, 39.

7 Rauty, 1988, 262–3.

8 Ibid., 344–5.

9 Ibid., 1–20. The law can be found in Rauty, 1996, 311.

10 Rauty, 1991, 270.

11 This information is derived from Cherubini, 1998, 41–87.

12 Rauty, 1991, 268–9; Moretti, 1998, 271.

13 Rauty, 1991, 270–73.

14 Ibid., 267.

15 This information derives from Neri, 1998, esp. 127 ("elemento propulsore").

16 Mazzi, 1998, 400.

17 Bocchi, 1995, 1: 54–73.

18 Ibid., 84.

19 Ibid., 94.

20 Ibid., 2: 11–16; for the *yscarii*, see Hessel, 1975, 184.

21 Bocchi, 1995, 2: 21.

22 Hessel, 1975, 148–9.

23 Bocchi, 1995, 2: 21–6; Hessel, 1975, 149; Blanshei, 2010, 15–18.

24 Bocchi, 1995, 2: 33–106.

25 Ibid., 161.

26 Hubert, 1993, 13–29.

27 Bocchi, 1995, 2: 97–8.

28 The 1288 statutes of Bologna made the penalty for giving false testimony more severe than earlier statutes (the punishment was execution), and they increased other penalties for various forms of falsifying; see Pini, 2011, 18, 22.

29 For a brief but useful summary, see ibid., 22–30. See also Blanshei, 2010, 499–508.

30  Bocchi, 1995, 3: 28–9; Frati, 1890, 68–9.

31  Frati, 1890, 204; Bocchi, 1995, 3: 36.

32  Bocchi, 1995, 3: 36; Friedman, 1998, 335.

33  Friedman, 1998, 336. See a consideration of the court in Legnani, 2005.

34  Bocchi, 1995, 3: 36. For the power of notaries in Bologna, see also Witt, 2012, 469.

35  Bocchi, 1995, 2: 95–6.

36  Miller, 1995, 175–85, quotations on 181; Miller, 1996, 27–41. On comital rights, see Tabacco, 1989, 125–36, 166–76; Miller, 2000, 55, 78–80.

37  Grillo, 1998, 282; Salvatori, 1994, 249–54.

38  Galvano de la Fiamma stated that there were three communal buildings (palatiis) in the Broletto Vecchio; Fiamma, 1869, 453–5. See also Grillo, 2001, 57.

39  Baroni, 1975, 260.

40  Salvatori, 1994, 254.

41  Ibid., 256; Grillo, 1998, 282; Grillo, 2001, 59–62.

42  Baroni, 1975, 260, 265–6.

43  Zaninoni, 1994, 268–9. For the grant of full comital rights to the bishop, see Miller, 1995, 177.

44  Zaninoni, 1994, 278.

45  Zaninoni and Spigaroli, 1998, 47–50.

46  Pancotti, 1925–29, 1: 170–72.

47  Zaninoni, 1994, 274–9; Zaninoni and Spigaroli, 1998, 52–4.

48  Zaninoni, 1994, 281–2; Zaninoni and Spigaroli, 1998, 56–61.

49  Zaninoni and Spigaroli, 1998, 85–9. For another reading of signorial interventions in urban space, see Delzant, 2013.

50  Zaninoni, 1994, 285.

51  Guidi, 1995, 13–25.

52  See Marina, 2011, 363–4.

53  These developments are nicely summarized in Lane, 1973, 103–9.

54  See e.g. the statutes of the mercers which specifically stated that stalls had to be removed from the piazza by nones; see Monticolo, 1896–1914, 2: 321.

55  Ibid., 471–2. It is not clear whether they set up shop in the atrium of the church or outside under the arches.

56  See Cessi and Alberti, 1934, 22–4; Ortalli, 1993, viii–ix.

57  Cessi and Alberti, 1934, 23–4. The Mint was later moved to be near the Palazzo Ducale.

58  Ortalli, 1993, xx; Cessi and Alberti, 1934, 25–41.

59  Agazzi, 1991, 121.

60  For a useful summary, see Schulz, 1991, 425–8.

61  Ortalli, 1993, xii–xiv.

62  Ibid., xvi–xvii.

63  Modigliani, 1998, esp. 10, 47–9, 51–5, 73–4, 83–4, 88.

64  Ibid., 73–5, 87–109.

65  For Santa Maria Rotonda, see ibid., 99; for the control of butcher stalls by churches, 80.

66  Ibid., 60–61, 262–3.

67  Sframeli, 1989, 27.

68  Rubinstein, 1995, 1–12; see also Trachtenberg, 1988, esp. 25–9.

69  Carocci, 1975, 19; for the beccaria, Sframeli, 1989, 27–8.

70  Fanelli, 1980, 58.

71  See Rubinstein, 1995, 8, and 79: "unlike the Sienese . . . the Florentines did not choose the market square, the Mercato Vecchio, as the site of their new civic palace."

72  For the piazza's few commercial uses, see Trachtenberg, 1997, 248. For the woolen cloth fair, see Fanelli, 1980, 60. In the fifteenth century the fair was moved to Piazza Santo Spirito in Oltrarno.

73  Dameron, 1991, 156–8; Miller, 2001, 92.

74  Goldthwaite, 2009, 109–10, 486.

75  Ibid., 383; for the guild-based government, see Najemy, 1982.

76  Fanelli, 1980, 60–61.

77  Goldthwaite, 2009, 287.

78  Fanelli, 1980, 59–60; see also Franceschi, 1998, 78–9.

79  Goldthwaite, 2009, 348.

80  Carocci, 1975, 97, 178–83; Sframeli, 1989, 309–17; Goldthwaite, 2009, 348; for a map locating the halls of all the guilds, see Franceschi, 1998, 78–9.

81  Zervas, 1996, 1: 125–8, 188.

82  Ibid., 211–19.

83  Astorri and Friedman, 2005, 15. See also Astorri, 1998, and the remarks in Goldthwaite, 2009, 109–14, and Zervas, 1996, 1: 213–15.

84  Astorri and Friedman, 2005, 29–32.

85  Ibid., 36–54. For the shields, see Friedman, 1998, 334 n. 17. It has been suggested that the Mercanzia may have met for a time before they constructed their palace, in the building that eventually became the guildhall of the Medici e Speziali. That would perhaps explain the elaborate painted ceiling that was found in that space depicting the arms of Florence's twenty-one guilds in a circle, with the arms of the church, the Parte Guelfa, the Republic, and the Florentine Popolo and the Commune in the center. See Sframeli, 1989, 312–13, 328, figs 213–15.

86  Astorri and Friedman, 2005, 13.

87 Goro (Gregorio) Dati cited in Rubinstein, 1995, 88.
88 For the well-known tabernacle of Santa Maria della Tromba, see Sframeli, 1989, 28–9.
89 Friedman, 1998, 336; Pini, 1962, 53; Hessel, 1975, 192 n. 43. Pini states that they did not move to the Mercanzia until the mid-fifteenth century, but that seems incorrect. According to Hessel, ibid., n. 45, it is not clear whether the church was located at an earlier fairground and then moved to the fairground established in the years 1217–19.
90 Zaninoni and Spigaroli, 1998, 53–4.
91 Paul, 1969, 222.
92 Bona, 1997, 142; Modigliani, 1998, 326 n. 27.
93 Paul, 1969, 222; Modigliani, 1998, 326.
94 Gasparini, 1988, 343, 346.
95 For Piacenza, see Zaninoni and Spigaroli, 1998, 86–8; for Parma, see Marina, 2012, 134.
96 Bocchi, 1996–98, 2: 171; see also Witt, 2012, 469.
97 Biganti and Cutini, 1997, 337. For the period up to 1340, see also Blanshei, 1976, 16–17.
98 Riess, 1981a, 17. For a time in the Middle Ages, a suburban market (probably the live-stock market) existed in Perugia in the Campo Battaglia, which took its name from the tournaments or "battles" that the magnates held there. As part of the popular regime's efforts to control noble violence, in 1294 a law was passed forbidding games there and elsewhere in the city. See Blanshei, 1976, 22, 64–5.
99 Biganti and Cutini, 1997, 339.
100 Friedman, 1998, 338.
101 Ibid., 335.
102 Ibid., 336.

Chapter 3   *Organization*
1 ASPrato, Ceppi 1322, fols 15r, 18r, 65v, 82v, 85v. Cecco's extant account book runs October 11, 1389–June 8, 1390. See Marshall, 1999, 122.
2 Pierotti, 1975, 81, 99, 103.
3 Masi, 1934, 64–5; Marri, 1955, 60–61.
4 Monticolo, 1986–1914, 1: 259.
5 Atwell, 2006, 210.
6 Ibid., 205–11.
7 For the Florentine cattle market, see Caggese, 1999b, 281–2. For Verona's, see Brugnoli, 1978, 243.
8 Caprioli and Bartoli Langeli, 1996, 1: 402; see also Grohmann, 1981, 48.
9 Lieto, 1998, 251. For the location of the hay and wood markets in Padua, see Benton, 1995, 2: 18.
10 See Carli, 1936, 269–77; Tuliani, 1998, 71–2.

11 Grohmann, 1989, 100; Castignoli and Racine, 1967, 40, 153, 156–7.
12 Carli, 1936, 276.
13 Morandini, 1961, 234–5; Betto, 1984–6, 1: 559.
14 Ghignoli, 1998, 451.
15 Ibid.; Tolaini, 1992, 64; Grohmann, 1989, 100.
16 ASBologna, Capitano del Popolo, Società d'arti e d'armi, Società d'arti, b. 5, Statutes of the Calzolarie Veteris, n.p., clause entitled "De stationibus mercati"; Frati, 1890, 67–8.
17 Ricci, 1980, 49–50.
18 Tolaini, 1992, 64.
19 Puppi and Universo, 1982, 28. See also Collodo, 1986.
20 Frati, 1890, 67–8.
21 For a fuller treatment of the Verona marker, see Modonesi, 1988, 571.
22 Fabris, 1932–39, 25 (1932): 30; for the date of composition of the trilogy, see ibid., 22, 27. The text of the *Visio* is printed in 27–8 (1934–9); page numbers in the text refer to this volume. Hyde, 1966b, 29 dates the work between 1314 and 1318.
23 Hyde, 1966a, 320–23, 330–32.
24 Frojmovič, 1996, 35–8; Carlo Guido Mor apparently misidentified this as the tribunal of the Lion; Mor, 1963, 13.
25 Hyde, 1966a, 331–2. For Padua and usury, see Hyde, 1966b, 40. The reference to usury in the *Visio Egidii* occurs on p. 3.
26 Occhipinti, 1991, 41–2.
27 Puppi and Universo, 1982, 33–5.
28 Mor, 1963, 1–3; Zaggia, 1997, 258; Rossi, 2007, 23–4.
29 Puppi and Universo, 1992, 35; Mor, 1963, 7.
30 Hyde, 1966b, 33; Bortolami, 2008, 54–5.
31 Semenzato, 1963, 27–30.
32 Ibid., 32.
33 It is unclear whether the Peronio was actually a building or just a location. While Da Nono refers to the Alodio as a "palacium," he then states, "iuxta hoc Alodium erit ordinatus locus unus, qui Peronium dicetur, intra quem vendentur omnium frutuum genera" (13).
34 Puppi and Universo, 1982, 63. The Fondaco was begun in 1302; see Semenzato, 1963, 31 n. 16.
35 Semenzato, 1963, 38–9.
36 For the question of when these additional loggias were added, see ibid., 40 n. 33.
37 Hyde, 1966b, 42.
38 Modigliani, 1998, 196.
39 Puppi and Universo, 1982, 60–3. On the difficulty of distinguishing the portico from the loggia, see Eslami, 2010, 206–7.
40 Rossi, 2007, 25.

41  Zaggia, 1997, 258 refers to them as Padua's "arti maggiori."

42  A law in Siena from 1309 banned certain trades such as tanning from the Campo; and in 1407 the grain and poultry markets were removed from the Campo so that this most prestigious site became increasingly the location for "quality retailers such as goldsmiths or cloth merchants, and professionals such as notaries and bankers." Nevola, 2007, 19; see also 96, 125.

43  Lieto, 1998, 251.

44  Geertz, 1979, 174.

45  As cited in Tuliani, 1998, 83.

46  Marri, 1955, 62–3.

*Part 2    Buying and Selling*

1  Salimbene, 1998–9, 2: 880–81. Translation modified from Joseph Baird's in Salimbene, 1986, 592.

2  Scott, 1985.

3  Geertz, 1979, 217, 221.

4  Fanselow, 1990, 251.

5  Ibid., and 263.

6  For the term "climate of mistrust," see ibid., 255. The essential distinction between a market in standardized and non-standardized goods and its contribution to the market's atmosphere is considered more fully in this section.

*Chapter 4    Market Infrastructure*

1  Piasentini, 2009, 1: doc. 242. As a preliminary to the Great Council considerations, the Council of Forty also approved the petition.

2  Carocci, 1975, 62–4.

3  Monticolo, 1896–1914, 1: 259. In 1368, a goldsmith named Antonio Vendramin was granted the right to practice his craft at his home, rather than on the Ruga since he suffered from "podagrosus"; see Piasentini, 2009, 2: doc. 1096. At the end of the fourteenth century, it seems that the Giustizieri Vecchi began enforcing the rule by prohibiting goldsmiths from also selling their wares at the markets at San Marco and in San Polo. According to a Great Council deliberation of 1394, this was causing great inconvenience to respectable women (*domine*) since they would not go to Rialto, presumably because of the danger to their reputation for being seen there. To resolve the issue, the Great Council again authorized goldsmiths to sell at San Marco and San Polo. See ASVenezia, Maggior Consiglio, Deliberazioni, reg. 21 (Leona), fols 74v–75r (April 14, 1394). The law was published in Newett, 1907, 270 n. 51.

4  See also the discussion of the layout of the meat markets of Bologna. One, the *vaso grande*, erected in the middle of the thirteenth century, extended about 165 feet (50 m) and consisted of "a long hall with entrances at both ends. The stalls would have been placed against the walls in two rows facing each other, and we can assume that the aisle between them was tight." Another, the *vaso piccolo*, dating from the fourteenth century, consisted of a meeting hall on the second floor where the butchers' guild transacted its business and a ground floor devoted to stalls. A long and narrow space, the ground floor "was probably organized in two rows of facing stalls with an aisle for customers between them"; see Dickerson, 2010, 38–48, esp. 46–7, 48.

5  As Fanselow, 1990, 262 notes, "price competition is minimised in the bazaar."

6  Monticolo, 1896–1914, 3: 405–6.

7  Todeschini, 2008, 34. See also Lugli, 2010, 82–3; Marina, 2012, 109.

8  Simeoni, 1914, 184–5.

9  The Piacentine drapers had to stay in one *bina* (*bigna*), foreign drapers in another. Castignoli and Racine, 1967, 154, 159.

10  Monticolo, 1896–1914, 2: 112, 164.

11  Branca, 1986, 34 (adage 151).

12  Piasentini, 2009, 1: doc. 791. According to one account, the spot where the bakers had their stalls stood just outside the door next to stall 16 (it describes stall 16 as "prima eundo ad panatarium penes portam"); see ASVenezia, Provveditori alle beccarie, b. 5, reg. 1, fol. 30v. See also Eslami, 2010, 212–13.

13  Castignoli and Racine, 1967, 272.

14  Ibid., 144.

15  Simeoni, 1914, 201.

16  Ibid., 262–3.

17  Gaudenzi, 1896, 250.

18  ASBologna, Capitano del Popolo, Società d'arti e d'armi, Società d'arti, b. 7 (drappieri), Statutes of 1256, n.p; b. 4 (beccai), Statuti 4 (1293), n.p.

19  E.g. in Venice where a virginal boy was selected at random to draw ballots in ducal elections; see Boholm, 1990, 123–4.

20  Princivalli and Ortalli, 1993, 46, 90; see also Princivalli, 1993, xxxviii–xxxix.

21  Mueller, 1997, 41.

22  Piasentini , 2009, 1: doc. 319. In 1304 there were apparently 59 officially sanctioned fishmongers at San Marco and Rialto; see Favaro, 1962, 115–16, doc. 497.

23  Piasentini, 2009, 1: doc. 647. For the grant of a "staçonelam" to a tailor, see ibid., doc. 874.

24 Simeoni, 1914, 434–8.

25 Morandini, 1961, 175.

26 Betto, 1984–6, 2: 102; Castignoli and Racine, 1967, 50–51; Morandini, 1961, 226.

27 Nelli and Pinto, 2002c, 132.

28 Dorini, 1934, 85–6.

29 Nelli and Pinto, 2002c, 189–90.

30 Ibid., 193–4. For a similar rule from Perugia and its concern with impediments to the movement of humans and horses, see Caprioli and Bartoli Langeli, 1996, 1: 213–14.

31 Nelli and Pinto, 2002c, 189–90.

32 Masi, 1934, 114–15.

33 ASBologna, Capitano del Popolo, Società d'arti e d'armi, Società d'arti, b. 4 (beccai), Statutes of 1408, n.p.

34 Piasentini, 2009, 1: doc. 581; 2: doc. 1063. In 1372 the "bancham in Piscaria Rivoalti" that had been awarded to Aguia (now deceased) was conceded by a *grazia* to his brother-in-law Martino Avonal; ibid., 2: doc. 1691.

35 For a good summary of the situation in Rome, see Modigliani, 1998, 47–9, and for Pisa, see Redi, 1986, 647–50.

36 For an interesting typology of shops and efforts to relate them to the kinds of business transacted, see Clark, 2000.

37 Paul, 1969, 222.

38 For the grain market in Milan, see Grillo, 1998, 282; for linen in Bologna, see ASBologna, Capitano del Popolo, Società d'arti e d'armi, Società d'arti, b. 9bis, 1287 Statutes of the Linaroli, n.p; for the butchers in Bologna, see Frati, 1890, 68.

39 Betto, 1984–6, 1: 289.

40 Paul, 1969, 222.

41 Rauty, 1991, 271.

42 Rauty, 1981a, 149, 302.

43 Grohmann, 1989, 58.

44 Lansing, 1997, 54 n. 58.

45 While the original plan called for the shops to be approximately 15 ft sq., most probably ended up being 11 × 15 ft (3.3 × 4.5 m). See Flanigan, 2008, 6–8, 12.

46 Dorini, 1934, 125–6. Shaw and Welch, 2011, 58 note that in the Quattrocento customers regularly entered pharmacies.

47 Modigliani, 1998, 48–9, 73. See also, Luzzati, 1974.

48 Piasentini, 2009, 1: doc. 132. Due to the loss, the Rosso brothers asked to be able to extend their lease on a shop for another ten years at a cost of 20 ducats a year. The Ufficiali sopra Rialto noted that a shop across from theirs paid 50 ducats a year, but agreed to the brothers' petition, given the "great loss" (*magnum dannum*) they had suffered in the fire. But the new grant was only for five years. For another "volta" used for storage, see ibid., doc. 16.

49 Fanselow, 1990, 56 notes concealment from officials in the Indian bazaar.

50 For a discussion of the Fondaco dei Tedeschi and its Middle Eastern prototypes, see Howard, 2000, 126–31. For the fondaco in general, see Constable, 2003, 306–54.

51 For some evidence of signs, though most of it from the Renaissance, see Welch, 2005, 137–40. It may well be that the medieval shops had no need of signs since in the market for non-standardized goods, as Fanselow, 1990, 256 notes (of the bazaar), "they do not compete against each other for customers, but . . . instead compete with buyers."

52 Masi, 1934, 89–90; Caggese, 1999a, 34.

53 See Poliakov, 1965, 130; Muzzarelli, 2007, 577.

54 Carocci, 1974–5, 199–200 gives the names of some of the more famous Florentine taverns in the vicinity of the Mercato Vecchio. He does not, however, identify when they were established. Some may have been founded during the Renaissance or beyond.

55 Welch, 2005, 140–41. For increasing consumer demand, see Goldthwaite, 1993.

56 Tuliani, 1998, 86. See also the rules about the setting up of stalls or counters by the shoemakers of Assisi during the weekly market in that town in Suppa, 1971, 98.

57 For lamps installed at both ends of the drapers' *bina* at the Bologna fairs, see ASBologna, Capitano del Popolo, Società d'arti e d'armi, Società d'arti, b. 7 (drappieri), Statutes of 1256, n.p.

58 Ibid.

59 Piasentini, 2009, 2: doc. 1417.

60 Masi, 1934, 121.

61 Zdekauer, 1897, 176 n. 1.

62 ASBologna, Capitano del Popolo, Società d'arti e d'armi, Società d'arti, b. 9bis (linaroli), Statutes of 1287, n.p; Gaudenzi, 1896, 292.

63 Castignoli and Racine, 1967, 165, 205–6.

64 Dorini, 1934, 85–6.

65 Sapori, 1932, 41–6, 239–41, 353–6; see also Origo, 1957, 76–7.

66 Goldthwaite, 2009, 414. See also Spallanzani, 2007, 53.

67 A good Renaissance example of a carpet is visible in Vittore Carpaccio's *The Calling of Saint Matthew* in the Scuola of San Giorgio degli Schiavoni, Venice; see Welch, 2005, 152 (fig. 147). For the counting board, see Origo, 1957, 77.

*Chapter 5    Choreography of Buying and Selling*

1   For Accursius, see Witt, 2012, 426.

2   Braunstein, 2005, 335. For the text of the dictionary/grammar book, see Pausch, 1972. See also Rossebastiano Bart, 1983.

3   For two poems that were set to music and that capture the sounds of the late Trecento Roman market, including the calls of vendors, the queries of potential buyers, and some negotiations over price, see Ugolini, 1986.

4   Simeoni, 1914, 417, 438; Castignoli and Racine, 1967, 50–51.

5   Masi, 1934, 123.

6   ASBologna, Capitano del Popolo, Società d'arti e d'armi, Società d'arti, b. 4 (beccai), Statutes of 1408, n.p; Gaudenzi, 1896, 175.

7   Sgrilli, 2003, 195.

8   ASBologna, Capitano del Popolo, Società d'arti e d'armi, Società d'arti, b. 10 (peliparii), Statutes of 1265–71, n.p; Simeoni, 1914, 264.

9   Marri, 1960, 43–5.

10  Dorini, 1934, 108.

11  Cardinali et al., 2000, 1: 70.

12  Sapori, 1932, 218–19.

13  Simeoni, 1914, 29.

14  Ibid., 325.

15  Pausch, 1972; page numbers follow in the text. See also the discussion of the dialogue in Braunstein and Franceschi, 2007, 664–9.

16  Re, 1883, 163. For a similar rule in Pisa, see Ghignoli, 1998, 268–72.

17  Monticolo, 1896–1914, 3: 399.

18  Stussi, 1967, 75–8; translation in Dotson, 1994, 127–30.

19  Ibid.

20  Gloria, 1873, 271.

21  Dorini, 1934, 418, 451. The rule of 1418 says that the original fine was 10 lire; perhaps it was raised between 1411 and 1418 from 5 to 10 lire.

22  Gatti, 1885, 44–5.

23  On the requirement to visit all shops, see Atwell, 2006, 210; Dorini, 1934, 125–6.

24  In a real-life case of bargaining, Marcus de Ponte asked 6 *grossi* per pound for some zedoary (white turmeric); the German to whom he was showing it offered 5½ *grossi* per pound. See Piasentini, 2009, 2: doc. 1266. Shaw and Welch, 2011, 127–9 suggest that in the late Quattrocento Florentine apothecary shop known as the Speziale del Giglio at least, the real bargaining occurred with regard to the payments on credit extended. This was especially true for wealthier and better connected customers. It may be that bargaining over price was more common in wholesale transactions.

25  Masi, 1934, 91.

26  In the Venetian dialogue the deposit is made before the items are weighed.

27  Fanselow, 1990, 254,

28  For weighing and measuring in the Florentine Lana guild, see Atwell, 2006, 184.

29  For Pisa, Bologna, and Verona, see Lugli, 2010, 79–81; for Bergamo, see Miller, 2000, 185, for Reggio, see Cerlini, 1933, 253. For Bologna, see Bergonzoni, 1990, 168. According to Bergonzoni, the standards in Bologna were first located on the church of Santa Maria dei Rustigani, near Piazza Maggiore; they were later transferred to a chapel that was destroyed in 1404 as work on San Petronio progressed; only in 1574 were they moved to their current location.

30  Masi, 1934, 136–7.

31  Dorini, 1934, 110–11, 418–19. The town of Bassano also required that measuring sticks there have metal tips at both ends; Fasoli, 1940, 75.

32  Gatti, 1885, 75; Castignoli and Racine, 1967, 82; Cerlini, 1933, 254.

33  Humphrey, 2007, 428–36, esp. 432.

34  Nelli and Pinto, 2002c, 248.

35  Betto, 1984–6, 101–2.

36  Ghignoli, 1998, 268–72.

37  An exception was allowed for the sale of "ceppi"; Princivalli and Ortalli, 1993, 81.

38  Dorini, 1934, 110, 418–19.

39  Morandini, 1956, 160–61.

40  For the image, see Sherman, 1995, 255, fig. 75, lower register at right.

41  Gatti, 1885, liii–liv, 19; Agnoletti, 1940, 28; Sapori, 1932, 72–4.

42  Castignoli and Racine, 1967, 38; Simeoni, 1914, 478. For the handshake securing wedding agreements in fifteenth-century Italy, see Klapisch-Zuber, 1985, 183.

43  Dorini, 1934, 116–18.

44  Gatti, 1885, liii.

45  Re, 1883, 168.

46  Marshall, 1999, 72. For the reliance on credit more generally, see Rosser, 1997, 9–10.

47  Naso, 1985, 66–7.

48  Ibid., 67; Marshall, 1999, 77.

49  The issue of trust is discussed more fully in Part Three.

50  For more on brokers, see Lattes, 1884, 105–21; Braunstein and Franceschi, 2007, 668–9.

51  For condemnations for conducting even parts of sales without a broker, see Piasentini, 2009, 2: docs 1209, 1266. For an appointment as a broker at the Fondaco, see ibid., 1: doc. 510.

52  The exceptions concern deals involving coins, bullion, grain, wine, and animals. Simeoni, 1914, 478.

53  Ghignoli, 1998, 263–4.

54  Agnoletti, 1940, 32–5, 39.

55  Sapori, 1932, 217–18.

56  Mainoni, 1975, 364–5.

57  Dorini, 1934, 493–6.

58  Boccaccio, *Decameron*, Day 8, Tale 10.

59  Gaudenzi, 1896, 2: 358–60.

60  Monticolo, 1896–1914, 3: 404; Simeoni, 1914, 478.

61  Agnoletti, 1940, 41–2.

62  Sapori, 1932, 214–15.

63  For lists of the commission rates in Verona for various objects sold, see Simeoni, 1914, 474–6. For the rates in Rome, see Gatti, 1885, 20, 137. For the pooling of money, see Agnoletti, 1940, 36.

64  On keeping good records, see Morandini, 1956, 111–12; Simeoni, 1914, 479. For prohibitions on gifts, see Ghignoli, 1998, 264–5; Dorini, 1934, 101, 340–41.

65  As Lattes, 1884, 106 noted, there was a "certain logical relationship" (*certa relazione logica*) between the notion of a broker and of a guarantor.

66  Agnoletti, 1940, 28,

67  Rossebastiano Bart, 1983, 3: xx noted the ritualized nature of the arguments between buyers and sellers.

68  For the treatise, see Gibbs, 1999b, 270–78, and Fabbri, 1999. As Fabbri, 317 notes, the image of the avaricious (and probably usurious pawnshop) is juxtaposed with an image of an orderly bank located under arcades that are emblazoned with the Genoese coat of arms.

69  Certaldo, 1945, 132, no. 179.

70  Ibid., 241–3, no. 375. For the agonistic society, see Weissman, 1982, ch. 1.

71  Certaldo, 1945, 123, no. 152.

72  This rule applied only to certain types of grain; Nelli and Pinto, 2002c, 194–5. A Venetian rule required that the grain measure be held "straight and not tilted" (*rectam et non stortam*). Tilting would also have given less than a full measure; Monticolo, 1896–1914, 2: 392–3.

73  Even in this case, Certaldo followed up his advice by advocating moderation, what he called "la via del mezzo e la ragione"; Certaldo, 1945, 123, no. 152.

74  Marshall, 1999, 44, 64.

75  Origo, 1957, 95.

76  Naso, 1985, 65.

77  Sapori, 1932, 134.

78  "Se pigli a trafficare di lana o panni franceschi, fa da te medesimo e non volere arricchire in due dì…" Giovanni di Pagolo Morelli, *Ricordi* in Branca, 1986, 177.

79  Braudel, 1977, 62–3, 112–13.

80  Masi, 1934, 114–15.

81  Caprioli and Bartoli Langeli, 1996, 1: 242.

82  Masi, 1934, 153–4.

83  ASBologna, Capitano del Popolo, Società d'armi e d'arti, Società d'arti, b. 10 (guainai, spadai, scudai, pittori, and sellai), n.p; b. 8 (fabbri), notebook with 1397 on cover, fol. 19r.

84  Dorini, 1934, 153–4.

85  Fanselow, 1990, 254–5. At the same time (and this was certainly true in medieval Italy), buyers and sellers tend to develop "enduring credit relationships." As Fanselow, 260 observed, "by giving credit to a buyer, a seller tries to monopolise the former's future demand."

86  See also ibid., 1990, 236.

87  Giordano da Pisa cited in Lesnick, 1989, 123.

88  On the growing importance of the idea of choice in medieval society, see Roach, 2005.

89  Strata, 1852, 3: 314.

*Chapter 6   Regulating and Controlling*

1  Salimbene, 1998–9, 2: 880–81.

2  Rauty and Savino, 1977; Rauty, 1996; Nelli and Pinto, 2002a, 2002b, and 2002c. All of these statutes are also available online at http://www.societapistoiesestoriapatria.it/P_ListaLibri.aspx.

3  There are statutes for Genoa for 1143 and for Pisa from 1162–4. See Rauty, 1996, 43.

4  Rauty and Savino, 1977, 43, 52, 56–9.

5  Rauty, 1996, 304–5.

6  Ibid., 302–3.

7  Ibid., 310–11.

8  Ibid., 272–3.

9  As Carli, 1936, 125 observed, "the conquest of the street," by which he meant the acceptance of streets as public rather than as private property, "was the great preoccupation of the mercantile commune."

10  Rauty, 1996, 146–7. Other clauses tried to protect the city's walls and ditches (moats); ibid., 158–9, 222–5.

11  Ibid., 81–2, 99, 166–9.

12  Ibid., 84, 95–6, 198–201.

13  Ibid., 93; Herlihy, 1967, 216–19; Cherubini, 1998, 51–2.

14  Herlihy, 1967, 172.

15  Nelli and Pinto, 2002b, 70–71; ibid., 2002c, 191–2.

16  Ibid., 2002b, 72. In the statutes of the podestà, a rule forbade the selling of leeks, onions, and cooked foods under, next to, or within four feet of the ciborium located in front of San Zeno facing the market next to the episcopal palace; ibid., 2002c, 185.

17  Ibid., 2002b, 71. The same rule was included in the statutes of the podestà; ibid., 2002c, 195–6.

18  Ibid., 2002c, 143.

19  Ibid., 167.

20  Ibid., 167–8.

21  Ibid., 157. For the *congio* or *cogno*, see Edler, 1934, 319.

22  Nelli and Pinto, 2002b, 70–71; see also ibid., 2002c, 162, 192.

23  Ibid., 2002c, 162–3.

24  For the preponderance of regulations of the food trade in seventeenth-century Venice, see Shaw, 2006, 105.

25  The popular regime would even take on the responsibility for the provisioning of wine and salt; see Cherubini, 1998, 78; see also Grillo, 2001, 535–9.

26  Jones, 1997, 246–7. For the situation in England, see Davis, 2012, 233.

27  Morandini, 1956, 160–61.

28  Nelli and Pinto, 2002c, 161.

29  Ibid., 165–6. See also the discussion in Neri, 1998, 138–9. According to Herlihy, 1967, 172–3, the statutes of 1330 show that, by that time, there was a guild of butchers, leather workers, and furriers in Pistoia.

30  On the clearly subordinate position of the wine sellers and hostel keepers and the charge that they were often to blame for high prices and were prevented from forming guilds, see Neri, 1998, 153.

31  Nelli and Pinto, 2002c, 132. For the efforts to encourage immigration from Verona and Lombardy, see 239.

32  Ibid., 244.

33  Ibid., 124, 162.

34  Ibid., 194–5.

35  Ibid., 140. On the iron trade, see Neri, 1998, 127–32.

36  Nelli and Pinto, 2002c, 163–4. See also Rauty, 1981b, 370–71.

37  Nelli and Pinto, 2002b, 70.

38  For this "mensurator," see ibid., 2002c, 164.

39  Ibid., 161. For the office of "judge on damage caused," see Herlihy, 1967, 215.

40  Nelli and Pinto, 2002c, 35.

41  Ibid., 141–2.

42  The commune also expressed concern for the maintenance of the well in the Piazza della Sala, which would have been an essential piece of infrastructure for the daily market there; see Cherubini, 1998, 79.

43  Nelli and Pinto, 2002c, 272.

44  Ibid., 160.

45  Ibid., 193.

46  Ibid., 132–3.

47  Ibid., 275.

48  Ibid., 131, 138.

49  Ibid., 189–90.

50  Ibid., 132, 190. One clause in the law regarding butchers and fishmongers seems to indicate that the best spots would be given to those who could pay the most, but how this fit with the set fee of 40 soldi is unclear.

51  Ibid., 190.

52  Ibid., 124.

53  Ibid., 275.

54  Ibid., 249.

55  Ibid., 2002b, 70–71; ibid., 2002c, 194–5.

56  Ibid., 2002c, 279, 280.

57  Ibid., 2002b, 72, 83.

58  Ibid., 2002c, 138, 140–41.

59  Ibid., 193–4.

60  For a discussion of the preacher Remigio dei Girolami's understanding of *utilitas*, see Kempshall, 1999, 325–6.

61  Rauty, 1996, 253; for other examples, see 131, 155, 175, 213, 235.

62  Ibid., 183, 277, 295.

63  Ibid., 253; for an exception in which *utilitas* is used without the accompanying word *honor*, see 197.

64  Banti, 1997; Ghignoli, 1998. All of these statutes are included in Bonaini, 1854.

65  For the twelfth century, see Banti, 1997, 60, 62–64, 80, 81, 93, 99, 100. The relevant thirteenth-century rules are too numerous to list but see e.g. Ghignoli, 1998, 69–70, 173–4, 259–62, 268–74, 319–22, 343–55, 438, 447–8.

66  For Pisa's market landscape, see Redi, 1986; Redi, 1991; Tolaini, 1992.

67  Boniani, 1854, 62–3.

68  For similar policies pursued by the merchant-dominated regime in Piacenza between 1271 and 1290, see Castignoli, 1984, 290–94.

69  ASBologna, Capitano del Popolo, Società d'armi e d'arti, Società d'arti, b. 7 (drappieri), Statutes of 1256, n.p.

70  Dorini, 1934, 112–13.

71  Stevenson, 1893, 35, 37–8.

72  Masi, 1934, 103–5; Caggese, 1999a, 32; Caggese, 1999b, 365.

73  ASBologna, Curia del Podestà, Ufficio delle acque, strade, ecc, b. 10, notebook labeled "1304–1," fols 7v, 14v; notebook labeled "1305," fols 7r, 13r. For the courts of the podestà and capitano, see Blanshei, 2010, 511–25.

74  Caggese, 1999a, 280–81; Princivalli and Ortalli, 1993, 68–71.

75  Monticolo, 1896–1914, 1: 125, 3: 389–90.

76  Masi, 1934, 64–5, 120–21.

77 ASBologna, Capitano del Popolo, Società d'armi e d'arti, Società d'arti, b. 9bis (linaroli), Statutes of 1307, n.p; Marri, 1955, 60–61.

78 Castignoli and Racine, 1967, 184.

79 Monticolo, 1896–1914, 3: 126–7.

80 Morandini, 1961, 77.

81 Pancotti, 1925–29, 3: 42.

82 Monticolo, 1896–1914, 2: 321; 3: 163.

83 Lanconelli, 1985, 117. The stated reason was so that the guilds' scribes would not have to write by candlelight. For Venice, see Monticolo, 1896–1914, 1: 194–5.

84 Naso, 1985, 53.

85 Marshall, 1999, 30.

86 See Brucker, 1967, 124.

87 Cardinali et al., 2000, 1: 21–2.

88 Monticolo, 1896–1914, 2: 322–3. Similarly, the statutes of the Florentine oil and cheese sellers allowed them to keep their shops open on feast days if they fell on a Friday or Saturday. But, like the mercers of Venice, they could not display goods outside their shops; see Morandini, 1961, 33–4.

89 See e.g. the cases listed in Piasentini, 1992, app., cases 797, 1023, 1058, 1066, 1109.

90 Zdekauer, 1897, 290.

91 Domenico Lenzi cited in Pinto, 1978, 315–16; see also 301–2. For cut-purses at Rialto, see Piasentini, 1992, app., cases 24, 57, 101, 146, 171, 182, 227, 235, 237, 245, 269, 435, 441, 1021, 1140.

92 Bianchi and Granuzzo, 1992, 185.

93 Ghignoli, 1998, 415–16.

94 Dorini, 1934, 422–3.

95 Princivalli and Ortalli, 1993, 20–22; 38–9. See also ASVenezia, Compilazione delle leggi, b. 326 "Rialto," fols 67r, 81r, 83r, 85r, 87r, 93r.

96 In his poem, Jacopo d'Albizzotto Guidi states that the space below the loggia at Rialto "è per gente più vile: si giuoca a zara, tavole, e carte, secondo che cciascuno è più sottile"; Guidi, 1995, 16. Verona tried to control gambling by prohibiting it anywhere except around the column in the marketplace; see Bianchi and Granuzzo, 1992, 494–5.

97 Favaro, 1962, 111, doc. 477.

98 See Bec, 1967, 78–9. Giovanni di Pagolo Morelli, by contrast, was strongly opposed to gambling; see Pandimiglio, 1974, 562.

99 Pinto, 1978, 302; see also 297.

100 Ibid., 294, 297, 299, 314, 329, 331–3, 370, passim. According to Davidsohn, 1956–68, 4: pt 1 (1962), 148, as a notary with the title of "knight," Ser Villano was in charge of a force of policemen; their job was to patrol the city.

101 Pinto, 1978, 297, 299.

102 Cessi and Alberti, 1934, 47, 85–91.

103 Carocci, 1975, 56.

104 Compagni, 2000, 97; translation by Daniel Bornstein in Compagni, 1986, 71.

105 Betto, 1984–6, 1: 325–8; see also 470–71.

106 The positions were to be announced and rewarded to those who agreed to sweep at the lowest price; Caprioli and Bartoli Langeli, 1996, 445.

107 Morandini, 1961, 202, 219; see also 231–2.

108 Castignoli and Racine, 1967, 108, 213.

109 For Verona, see Bianchi and Granuzzo, 1992, 242. For the covering of a gutter in the market square in Piacenza, see Castignoli and Racine, 1967, 113.

110 For Siena, see Zdekauer, 1897, 288; for Florence, see Caggese, 1999b, 321–2.

111 Princivalli and Ortalli, 1993, 73.

112 See e.g. Bianchi and Granuzzo, 1992, 241–2.

113 Ibid., 543.

114 Morandini, 1961, 48–50. For other techniques and materials used in substandard candles, see Roberti, 1902, 237 n. 2.

115 Castignoli and Racine, 1967, 58.

116 Morandini, 1961, 231.

117 Tirelli, 1991, 213.

118 Ibid., 104; Zdekauer, 1897, 175–6.

119 Liberali, 1950–55, 1: 280–1; Betto, 1984–6, 1: 276; for Verona, see Bianchi and Granuzzo, 1992, 555. For a long series of Veronese regulations concerning the recipes and prices for bread, see Bianchi and Granuzzo, 1992, 557–65.

120 For a fuller discussion, see Atwell, 2006, 196.

121 Re, 1883, 167–8.

122 Atwell, 2006, 196.

123 The regulation of measurers contained several other directions as well; Agnoletti, 1940, 64–6. See also Atwell, 2006, 184. For the official measurers for Por Santa Maria, see Dorini, 1934, 486–7.

124 Castignoli and Racine, 1967, 73 (see also the definition of *tiratorium* on 560).

125 Ibid., 159.

126 Ghignoli, 1998, 438.

127 Agnoletti, 1940, 28.

128 Ibid., 201–2.

129 Pozza, 1988, 298–9, 303.

130 Betto, 1984–6, 1: 269–72. For these locations, see Marchesan, 1990, 1: 24, 262.

131 Liberali, 1950–55, 1: 293–4.

132 Castignoli and Racine, 1967, 162.

133 Fersouch, 1993, lxxii–iii. Many of the weighers received their jobs as governmental favors; see Guidi, 1995, 21; Piasentini, 2009, 1: docs 400, 678, 867; 2: docs 1051, 1125, 1302.

134 For the Dubrovnik inscription, see Harris, 2003, 304–5. The building was constructed

between 1516 and 1520. I thank Stanko Kokole for bringing this to my attention.

135   Princivalli and Ortalli, 1993, 54–5.

136   Betto, 1984–6, 1: 567–8.

137   Ortalli, 1993, xii–xiv; Cessi and Alberti, 1934, 233–44.

138   Nelli and Pinto, 2002b, 72.

139   Ibid., 176–80.

140   For examples of retail space granted as *grazie*, see Piasentini, 2009, 1: docs 319, 456.

141   Princivalli, 1993, xxxviii–xxxix.

142   Ghignoli, 1998, 273–4. Shops were not added to the Rialto bridge until the fifteenth century and were expected to bring in an annual revenue of 500 lire; see Cessi and Alberti, 1934, 169–70.

143   Betto, 1984–6, 1: 281, which states, "Item quod piscarie comunis fiant per comune Trevisii secundum quod per consilium Trescentorum fuerit ordinatum." For the payment due from the Paduan butchers to the commune, see Hyde, 1966b, 53.

144   Flanigan, 2008, 4, 7.

145   Tuliani, 1998, 73–5.

146   Ibid., 76–81.

147   Ibid., 90–91. Used-article dealers were classified as either "rigrettieri" or "treccole" – it is unclear what the distinction between the two represented. Battaglia, 2002, 21: 295 defines "trecco" as a "rivendugliolo"; the word *treccola* also referred to an itinerant woman seller of fruit and vegetables, but that cannot be the meaning in this instance.

148   Tuliani, 1998, 92–6.

149   Ibid., 98–100.

150   Monticolo, 1896–1914, 3: 363–4.

151   Ibid., 406–7.

152   Sercambi, 1995, 2: 1239, 850.

153   Ibid., 850 n. 13. See Boccaccio, *Decameron*, Day 3, Tale 3.

154   Certaldo, 1945, 241–3, no. 375.

*Part 3   Marketplace Ethics*

1   Monticolo, 1896–1914, 3: 328; for the phrase "badly worked" (*male laborata*), see 279. For an explanation of the process and the quality standards, see Mazzaoui, 1981, 74–6, 185–6 n. 104. The merchant members of the guild "included doublet and quilt makers who maintained workshops for the beating of cotton"; Mazzaoui, 1981, 207 n. 12.

2   Monticolo, 1986–1914, 3: 38.

3   Tirelli, 1991, 206–7, 208–10, 213.

4   Castignoli and Racine, 1967, 58, 311.

5   Bianchi and Granuzzo, 1992, 614; Ghignoli, 1998, 319.

6   Morandini, 1961, 222–3; Masi, 1934, 126–7; Dorini, 1934, 128–9. Straw and hay could be counterfeited by putting good material on the outside of bales and defective materials on the inside.

7   Morandini, 1961, 22–3; Dorini, 1934, 128–9.

8   Ghignoli, 1998, 273–4.

9   See n. 1 above but see also Simeoni, 1914, 15.

10   For the destruction of houses in Venice following the Querini-Tiepolo conspiracy of 1310, see Romano, 1987, 151; for Florence and the destruction of the Uberti family homes, see Trachtenberg, 1997, 92–3; for the destruction of the properties of those exiled from Reggio d'Emilia, see Cerlini, 1933, 202. On the close connection between the burning of counterfeit coins and heresy, see Roach, 2005, 137–9.

11   Origo, 1957, 70–72.

12   Caggese, 1999b, 40.

13   For the column at Rialto, see Cessi and Alberti, 1934, 39, 46. The *colonna del malefizio*, however, was moved from Rialto to San Marco; ibid.

14   Muzzarelli, 2005, 152–8. According to Muzzarelli, 158, when Bernardino da Feltre was preaching in Venice in 1481, he did not begin his sermon on Saturday, market day, until late in the day, after the market had concluded.

15   Rigobello and Autizi, 2008, 76–7; Mueller, 1997, 124–5. For the ritual in Treviso, see Marchesan, 1990, 2: 95–7. For a humiliating ritual in Florence's Mercato Nuovo, see Masi, 1931, 2: 639.

16   Mor, 1964, 8–9; Edgerton, 1985, 65.

17   Bianchi and Granuzzo, 1992, 495.

18   Bocchi, 1995, 2: 105; Frati, 1890, 82–3. See also Terpstra, 2008, 127–30, for sixteenth-century Bolognese practice.

19   Trexler, 1980, 262–3, and map on endpaper.

20   Friedman, 1988, 77–8.

21   The doge did make a visit to the church of San Giacomo di Rialto on Maundy Thursday; see Muir, 1981, 118.

22   Cessi and Alberti, 1934, 5–7; Muir, 1981, 70–72.

23   Pazzi, 1998, 779; Howard, 2000, 119.

24   Cessi and Alberti, 1934, 49–51.

25   For the placement of Italy and Siena at the center of the world in Lorenzetti's *mappamondo* in Siena's Palazzo Comunale, see Kupfer, 1996, 301.

26   Cessi and Alberti, 1934, 39, 67, 259, 317–18. See also Brown, 1988, 261, 268.

27   Cessi and Alberti, 1934, 259. See also Cattaneo, 2011, 116, 209, 210, 224.

*Chapter 7   Bona fide*

1   See e.g. Nelli and Pinto, 2002c, 249.

2   Béaur et al., 2006; Shaw, 2006; Davis, 2012.

3   Roland of Cremona quoted in Langholm, 1992, 92.

4   These ideas found their way to the wider public via sermons. For example, in a set of sermons presented in 1309, Giordano da Pisa, 1997, 52–3 affirmed precisely the same idea: merchants had the capacity when selling to sin in substance, quality, and measure.

5   www.sacred-texts.com/chr/aquinas/summa/sum333.htm.

6   Langholm, 1992, 235.

7   Saint Bonaventure quoted in ibid., 158.

8   www.sacred-texts.com/chr/aquinas/summa/sum333.htm.

9   Gerald Odonis quoted in Langholm, 1992, 516–17; translation modified.

10   Montenach, 2006, 516.

11   Abraham-Thisse, 2006, esp. 456.

12   Montenach, 2006, 533.

13   For the rock-crystal carvers, see Monticolo, 1896–1914, 3: 124; for the Florentine chandlers, see Caggese, 1999b, 172; for the goldsmiths, see Dorini, 1934, 399–400. Also in Venice, the spice dealer Bonaventura, known as Fana, was fined by the Giustizieri Vecchi and forbidden to practice the trade when pepper in his shop was found to be adulterated. He apparently claimed that it had been done by his shop-boys and that he was unaware of it. He was granted a *grazia* that allowed him to resume practicing his trade; see Favaro, 1962, 97–8, doc. 420.

14   For the Roman furriers, see Re, 1883, 162; for the Veronese metalworkers, see Simeoni, 1914, 255.

15   Betto, 1984–6, 1: 278. In his *Libri della famiglia*, Leon Battista Alberti wrote that "the world is amply supplied with fraudulent, false, perfidious, bold, audacious, and rapacious men. Everything in the world is profoundly unsure. One has to be far-seeing, alert, and careful in the face of frauds, traps, and betrayals"; Alberti, 1969a, 350; translation modified from Alberti, 1969b, 266.

16   See e.g. Betto, 1984–6, 1: 273–4; Morandini, 1961, 231; Caprioli and Bartoli Langeli, 1996, 344–6; Simeoni, 1914, 418. For the *fraudem magnam*, see Nelli and Pinto, 2002c, 143. Apparently, butchers were able to make meat look fresher by somehow "inflating" it between the skin and the meat underneath; see Cerlini, 1933, 211.

17   Monticolo, 1896–1914, 1: 63.

18   Masi, 1934, 126–7; Lanconelli, 1985, 119.

19   Agnoletti, 1940, 105–6. For another kind of fraud, see Sapori, 1932, 131–2.

20   Bernardino da Siena, 1989, 2: 1116.

21   Ibid., 1116–17.

22   Ibid., 1122–3. For the thirteenth-century Dominican, Gulielmus Peraldus's discussion of the kinds of fraud perpetrated by merchants, see Peraldo, 1546, 201–4.

23   ASBologna, Curia del Podestà, Ufficio delle acque, strade, ecc, b. 10, 1304–11, fol. 23r.

24   Piasentini, 2009, 1: doc. 362. For some cases in which men took items to be weighed at the public scales but got caught in the clutches of overzealous officials, see ibid., 127, 129.

25   Dorini, 1934, 537–8.

26   For *falsità* or *falsitas*, see Cardinali et al., 2000, 17; for *malizia*, see Polidori and Banchi, 1863–77, 2: 243; for *dolo*, see Stevenson, 1893, 125; for *male*, as in the expression *res falsa et mala*, see Monticolo, 1896–1914, 3: 226.

27   For both of these terms, see Monticolo, 1896–1914, 3: 363–4.

28   Ibid., 355, 356 n. 1. In a *grazia* awarded by the state, giving short measure was associated with sin (*peccandi*); see Piasentini, 2009, doc. 362.

29   Ghignoli, 1998, 319. The terms *sophisticus* and *sophisticatus* were used in Padua to describe goods that had been falsified or counterfeited. See Roberti, 1902, 237 n. 2; 241 n. 1. Apparently, saffron could be adulterated by treating it with almond oil; see Cattaneo, 2011, 208.

30   Zdekauer, 1897, 231.

31   Dorini, 1934, 112–13.

32   For *bonas et idoneas* and *sincerus*, see Masi, 1934, 126–7; for *legittimas*, see Caprioli, 2008, 233; for *rectum*, see Tirelli, 1991, 213; for *recentes*, see Roberti, 1902, 241 n. 1; for *pura et vera*, see Caprioli, 2008, 239.

33   Monticolo, 1896–1914, 3:166; Stevenson, 1893, 125.

34   The wool merchants of Rome pledged to observe their statutes *bona fide et puro animo*; see Stevenson, 1893, 125. For the term *simpatia*, see Morandini, 1961, 206. In Treviso, the weighers at the communal scales had to swear to weigh goods "with all purity and truth" (*cum omni puritate et veritate*); see Liberali, 1950–55, 1: 244.

35   Siddons, 1999, 335, 405. According to Siddons, 335, Gulielmus Peraldus offered the same example.

36   Bianchi and Granuzzo, 1992, 568. For the watering down of wine, see Liberali, 1950–55, 1: 158.

37  Masi, 1934, 176–7.

38  Dorini, 1934, 147–8.

39  ASBologna, Capitano del Popolo, Società d'arti e d'armi, Società d'arti, b. 9, Statutes of the Speziali 1303, n.p. but see esp. preface to new statutes.

40  Dorini, 1934, 128–9, 537–8. The rule regarding trade in various items was annulled in 1440; ibid., 551.

41  Monticolo, 1896–1914, 3: 406–7.

42  Morandini, 1961, 54–5.

43  For scholastic debates on the common good, see Kempshall, 1999.

44  Huizinga, 1924, 18–19; Little, 1971; Little, 1978.

45  Casagrande and Vecchio, 2000, 97.

46  Baschet, 2000, 235.

47  Casagrande and Vecchio, 2000; Saint Augustine quoted on 101.

48  Ibid., 103–8.

49  Ibid., 116.

50  Ibid., 183.

51  For his part, Henry of Rimini repeated Gregory's and Aquinas's list; see Siddons, 1999, 399.

52  Langholm, 1992, 450.

53  Saxl, 1942, 107–15.

54  Sandler, 1999, 48 and pl. 8.

55  Giamboni, 1968. For biographical information on Giamboni, see Foà, 2000.

56  Giamboni, 1968, 52–3.

57  Ibid., 92–3. See also Prudentius, 1949–53, 1: 296–7, lines 253–71.

58  Casagrande and Vecchio, 2000, 188.

59  Ibid., 188–9.

60  Herrad of Hohenbourg, 1979, 2: 334, image 282.

61  See Flinn, 1963, esp. chs 11 and 12.

62  Branca, 1989, 9–37.

63  Ibid., 107–10.

64  Riess, 1981a, 62.

65  Branca, 1989, 165–8.

66  Ibid., 203–6.

67  Ibid., 169–70.

68  Ibid., 140–42.

69  Latini, 1981, 136–9. I have largely followed Holloway's translation but have translated *parole bianche* as "pure words." For *bianco* as meaning "clean" and therefore "pure," see Battaglia, 1961–2002, 2: 207.

70  I have followed, with some modifications, the Allen Mandelbaum translation found at the World of Dante website: www.worldofdante.org/about.html.

71  The literature is vast: see esp. Boyde, 2000, 67–9. For Remigio de'Girolami's argument that usurers sin against nature and law, see Langholm, 1992, 459–60.

72  Chevigny, 2001, 788–93.

73  For illustrations of the Geryon, see Friedman, 1972.

74  For the Vatican manuscript, see Brieger, Meiss, and Singleton, 1969, 327–31.

75  As Edwin S. Hunt and James M. Murray, 1999, 56 observe, "merchant reputation and trust were the foundation of the commercial revolution of western Europe." However, in the iconography current in churches near Strasbourg, Fraus is juxtaposed to Simplicitas (innocence); see Norman, 1988, 67–70.

76  Caprioli, 2008, 237.

77  However, see the stimulating discussion in Giansante, 1998, 40–43. Also, the iconography of faith (*fede*) is of little help in this regard.

78  See Inglese, 2005, 7. Latini attributed the *Rhetorica ad Herennium* to Cicero.

79  Latini, 1968, 26.

80  For some general remarks, see Brucker, 2005.

81  Betto, 1984–6, 2: 320–21.

82  Branca, 1989, 165–8.

83  For more on the sculpture, see Rizzi, 1987, 485.

84  Branca, 1989, 82–4.

85  Loyalty was also important to Giovanni Sercambi; see his story "De perfecta societate," in Sercambi, 1995, 2: 1077–83.

86  Paolo da Certaldo in Branca, 1986, 16, no. 92.

87  Rossebastiano Bart, 1976, 560.

88  Certaldo in Branca, 1986, 77, no. 337.

89  Re, 1883, 163. For a similar rule in Pisa, see Ghignoli, 1998, 269.

90  Monticolo, 1896–1914, 2:105.

91  Roberti, 1902, 249.

92  Rosser, 1997 emphasizes the importance of confraternities in establishing trust relations.

93  See the remarks in Weissman, 1989, 272.

94  Certaldo in Branca, 1986, 91–2, no. 375.

95  Giovanni di Pagolo Morelli in ibid., 177–8. For the date of the *Ricordi*'s composition, see xxxvi, n. 6.

96  Sercambi, 1995, 1: 616–19.

97  Certaldo in Branca, 1986, 42, no. 205.

98  Salimbene, 1998–9, 2: 828–9; Salimbene, 1986, 558.

99  On the importance of *fama*, see Ortalli, 1979, 151–66. See also the essays in Fenster and Smail, 2003, esp. those by Chris Wickham and Thomas Kuehn.

100  Corti, 1952, 118.

101  Morelli in Branca, 1986, 188.

102  Ibid., 177. Branca explained that "sieno creduti" means "have credit," but it surely means that they have a credible character.

103  Todeschini, 2008, esp. 21–2, 26–8, 34. See also the remarks on the importance of reputation in Iannella, 1999, 72–84; Pini, 2011, 56–8.

104 Certaldo in Branca, 1986, 21, no. 108. In another instance, 45, no. 239, he wrote that a factor needed to be "humble, loyal, industrious, steadfast, and honest and orderly."

105 Stock, 1983, 41.

106 Ibid., 41, 86. See also Petrucci, 1958, 25–6; Jed, 1989, 74–120.

107 Subbioni, 2003, 1: 157.

108 Betto, 1981, 128.

109 Franco Sacchetti quoted in Frugoni, 1991a, 86.

110 Gaudenzi, 1896, 2: 104, 108–9.

111 Salvatori, 1994, 256.

112 Ghignoli, 1998, 320.

113 Re, 1883, 105.

114 Betto, 1984–6, 1: 43; for the Venetian example, see ASVenezia, Consiglio dei Dieci, Deliberazioni, Miste. reg. 8, fol. 146v, August 31, 1407; for that from Frignano, see Ortalli, 1979, 17 n. 13, 39. For examples of Bolognese notaries whose images were painted, see Ortalli, 1979, 55 n. 66. And for two Bolognese notaries who had their right hands amputated and received a fine for tearing some sheets from a book of judgments, see Pini, 2011, 47–8.

115 For a more general consideration of the problem of falsified documents, both public and private, see Pertile, 1966, 5: 547–51. For prosecution of notaries in Bologna, see Blanshei, 2010, 331–2.

116 Betto, 1984–6, 1: 386. For another example, see Stevenson, 1893, 155.

117 Agnoletti, 1940, 113–14.

118 ASBologna, Capitano del Popolo, Società d'arti e d'armi, Società d'arti, b. 6, Statutes of the Cambiatori dated 1377, fols 8v–9r.

119 Dorini, 1934, 98; Nelli and Pinto, 2002b, 70.

120 For recording immediately, see Dorini, 1934, 119–20; for cancelling debts, see Nelli and Pinto, 2002c, 124; for no erasures, see Marri, 1955, 28.

121 Marri, 1955, 72–3; ASBologna, Capitano del Popolo, Società d'arti e d'armi, Società d'arti, b. 6, Statutes of the Cambiatori dated 1377, fols 8v–9r. In Treviso, notaries were warned not to use abbreviations for sums of money; see Liberali, 1950–55, 1: 284. On the interplay of merchant arithmetic and reasoning, see Swetz, 2002, 404–5.

122 Dorini, 1934, 148.

123 Re, 1883, 104; Ghignoli, 1998, 320–21. See also Pertile, 1966, 5: 560–67.

124 Pini, 2011, 48–9.

125 Braunstein, 2005, 335.

126 Rebhorn, 1988, x.

127 Ibid., 15.

128 For the translation of Mark's relics, see Geary, 1990, 88–94; Muir, 1981, 78–84.

129 My description follows Demus, 1984, pt 2, 1: 199–200; for the date of the mosaics, see 205. For the San Clemente mosaic and the inscription "Kanzir, Kanzir," see ibid., pt 1, 1: 67; as Demus notes, 326 n. 79, *khinzir* is the Arabic word for pork or swine.

130 For Mark's *praedestinatio*, see Pincus, 2000, 68–9.

131 On *furberia* in the tales of Giovanni Sercambi, see the introduction by Giovanni Sinicropi in Sercambi, 1995, 1: 22–4.

132 On the all-encompassing nature of avarice, as not simply an uncontrolled love of money, see Casagrande and Vecchio, 2000, 100–03.

133 See e.g. several of the tales told on the third day in Boccaccio's *Decameron*.

134 As Sinicropi notes, craftiness (*furberia*) was admired more than intelligence; Sercambi, 1995, 1: 24. But see also Langer, 1999.

135 Boccaccio, 1980, 890–94; trans. in Boccaccio, 2002, 555–7.

136 Boccaccio, 2002, 555.

137 Ibid.

138 See Branca, 1999, 1: 5–14. Branca suggests, 7, that Boccaccio himself supervised the illustrations. See also Castelli, 1999, 2: 66–72.

139 See e.g. Boccaccio, *Decameron* Day 8, Tale 3; Day 9, Tales 3 and 5. For urban attitudes to country-dwellers, see Jones, 1997, 245–6. But see also Plaissance, 1985, 61–7.

140 For accounts of some of Sercambi's business dealings, see Nelli and Trapani, 1991, esp. 81–92.

141 Sercambi, 1995, 1: 24 ("la vita reale della città medievale"). Later, 30, he says that the stories reflect "infinite aspects of the life of a medieval city governed by a signorial [i.e. princely] regime."

142 Ibid., 252–9.

143 The statutes of Bologna of 1288 included a clause about those who changed their names as a form of falsification (*dolo vel fraude*); see Fasoli and Sella, 1937, 214, rubric 54. See also Pini, 2011, 22.

144 Sercambi, 1995, 1: 262–7.

145 Ibid., 2: 733–6.

146 Ibid., 1239–42.

147 These cases are found in Brucker, 1971, 156–9.

148 See Rebhorn, 1988, 23, 28, 31.

149 See also the 10th story on Day 8 of the *Decameron*, the story of Salabaetto and Jancofiore. When Jancofiore defrauded Salabaetto, he had no recourse since "he had neither a written receipt of the loan nor a witness to the transaction"; Boccaccio, 2002, 644.

150 Burckhardt, 2004.

151   Weissman, 1989, 271; for the phrase "communal self," see Martin, 2002, 211–14.

152   Weissman, 1989, Martin, 2002; Greenblatt, 1980.

153   Despite Weissman's claims to the contrary, the marketplace did offer a first-stage venue for these developments; Weissman, 1989, 278–9. Of course, judgments in the marketplace were not made in the absence of other information. That was why, for example, Sercambi's tricksters Guida, Ghisella, and Basino sought to give the appearance of social prominence. On the problem of trust, see Muldrew, 1998; Greif, 2006.

154   Morris, 1972. For a critique of Morris, see Gurevich, 1995, 4–12.

155   Witt, 2012, 4, 181, 267, 381.

156   Hall, 1980, 128.

157   Ibid., 128–9.

158   Sercambi, 1995, 1: 263–4.

159   There was the danger of the loss of face, which also served to increase self-awareness. In Boccaccio's tale of Jancofiore and Salabaetto, Salabaetto "was ashamed to complain about it [his defrauding by Jancofiore] to anyone, both because he had been forewarned and also because of the well-earned ridicule awaiting him because of his stupidity"; Boccaccio, 2002, 644.

160   Naso, 1985, 64–5.

161   Certaldo in Branca, 1986, 39, no. 178.

162   Boccaccio, 2002, 648. The original reads, "Chi ha a far con Tosco, non vuole esser losco"; Boccaccio, 1980, 1024.

163   Sercambi, 1995, 2: 1239.

164   Stussi, 1967, 111. For the same phrase in Venetian–German vocabularies, see Rossebastiano Bart, 1976, 561.

165   Howell, 2010, 245. Nevertheless, since negotiating was an aspect of trade everywhere, and perhaps especially in the Mediterranean world, the question remains why this new consciousness of self seems to have developed most precociously in north and central Italy. Although the question warrants a detailed examination, a tentative answer might be that the relative autonomy of the Italian communes – an autonomy derived at least in part from these cities' ability to play off the competing powers of the papacy and empire – offered an opportunity for the development of merchant citizens, who were responsible for both the prosperity and reputation of their cities. This sense of responsibility made merchants very aware of the importance of their economic decisions and transactions. For the different political situation in northern and southern Italy and the development of the "merchant-citizen," see Eslami, 2010, 38.

166   Da Strata, 1852, 3: 314.

## Chapter 8   *Combatting Fraud*

1   It may be no accident that avarice was especially identified with concupiscence of the eyes; see Casagrande and Vecchio, 2000, 97.

2   The law is printed in Masi, 1931, 654–7.

3   Dorini, 1934, 416.

4   Agnoletti, 1940, 116–17.

5   Nelli and Pinto, 2002c, 195–6.

6   Zdekauer, 1897, 295–6.

7   Caprioli and Bartoli Langeli, 1996, 180–83.

8   Friedman, 1988, 51. See also Seidel, 1999, 30–32.

9   Friedman, 1988, 205.

10   Marina, 2012, 132.

11   See also the remarks in Lugli, 2010, 82–3.

12   Monticolo, 1896–1914, 3: 405–6.

13   Todeschini, 2008, 34.

14   Ortalli, 1979, 184–7 dated the phenomenon to the second half of the thirteenth century and to the regions of Emilia and Tuscany, seeing it as part of a new "logica urbanocentrica." He also believed that it was most in use in Guelf-leaning cities, "con decisa connotazione di 'popolo'." It then became more diffuse in the Trecento, only to fade after that, although the practice lingered in Florence until the 1530s.

15   Polidori and Banchi, 1863–77, 1: 273; see also Ortalli, 1979, 45. Also in Siena, the Mercanzia threatened those who committed any "falsity" in their court with loss of their shop, a heavy fine, and a *pittura infamante* to be painted "ne la casa de la Mercantia col nome e sopranome suo et colla spetie de la falsità scritto"; Ortalli, 1979, 148.

16   Ghignoli, 1998, 128–31, esp. 129.

17   Caggese, 1999a, 115. See also Edgerton, 1980, 30.

18   The painted-over portrait of Doge Marino Falier in the Sala del Maggior Consiglio in the Ducal Palace in Venice is in many respects a *pittura infamante*. Falier was deposed for conspiring against the state, and his portrait was effaced and a black curtain painted in its place with a notice that he had been decapitated for his crimes.

19   On the use of this piazza as the marketplace, see Biondi, 1984, 573–5.

20   Glass, 2010, 190; she suggests (167) a date c. 1120–30. I am baffled, however, as to why she describes the portal as "secular rather than sacred" (133), especially in light of the

readings of the portal by Frugoni, 1991b and Nari, 1991.

21   Nari, 1991, esp. 37.

22   Ibid., 49 and 50; Frugoni, 1991b.

23   Nari, 1991, 52–4; Frugoni, 1991b, 27–8, who notes (27) that the depictions of the seasons emphasize the growing of grain and grapes (bread and wine).

24   Frugoni, 1991b, 21–3, 26.

25   For the *artifex*, see ibid., 23.

26   Fraud has received little consideration in previous discussions of the fresco. It should go without saying that fraud was not confined to economic issues; it could also be (and was) a political vice.

27   See also the depiction of famine in a copy of Sercambi's chronicle of Lucca in which winged devils shoot arrows at piles of dead bodies; Franco, Lanconelli, and Quesada, 1991, 6–9, 122–3.

28   For the idea of it being a cudgel, see Rowley, 1958, 1: 105. Frugoni, 1991a, 157 sees it as a crozier. In her view, Treason holding a lamb with a scorpion's tail and Fraud with a crozier "allude to those who cloak themselves to act, adopting attributes that are not theirs."

29   Ripa, 1976, 188. See also Ripa's description of "Inganno" or deceit (248–9) as a man with a serpent's tail and holding fish hooks. Another image of fraud may perhaps be found in the fresco *The Fall of the Duke of Athens* completed c. 1360 on a wall of the Stinche, the Florentine prison. In his hand, Walter of Brienne, the duke, holds "a small but outlandish monster with a curled scorpion's tail and a benign Socrates-like human head"; Edgerton, 1985, 84, who hypothesizes (83–4) that this figure may have derived from the *pittura infamante* of the duke that was executed at the Bargello in 1344 and in which the duke was shown surrounded by, in Vasari's words (81), "rapacious animals and other sorts signifying the nature and quality of the man," in other words, his vices.

30   Rowley, 1958, 1: 105 has argued that Lorenzetti "departed so radically from the vices traditionally coupled with Magnanimity and the four Cardinal Virtues" in order to emphasize "new political aspects." For his part, Starn, 1987, 15 observes that the vices on the tyrant's left represent "vices of deceit," those on the right "vices of violence," although it is difficult to see how cruelty fits that scheme.

31   Herrad of Hohenbourg, 1979, 1: 195; 2: 334, image 282.

32   See Frugoni, 1991a, 139, for the description of the hook as a grapnel. But she is wrong when she writes (156) that Avarice holds "in her clawed hands a purse from which overflow packets of money." Avarice clearly holds a vice.

33   As Birgit van den Hoven, 1996, 231 observes, in her discussion of virtues and vices in medieval *sermones ad status*, "the opposite of any form of deception (*fraus* or *usura*) is of course honesty . . ."

34   For images from both before and after the War, see *Lanfranco e Wiligelmo*, 1984, 386, 784. See also Donato, 1988, 1203–4; Donato, 1994, 499.

35   Glass, 2010, 181–4; "deceit and trickery" on 183.

36   See Astorri and Friedman, 2005, 23. As they also observe (23), when the Mercanzia later adorned its niche at Orsanmichele, it commissioned Verrocchio's *St Thomas* that also, as they note, "interprets the themes of evidence and proof in the concrete terms on which the court insisted."

37   Ibid., 22 n. 39.

38   Re, 1883, 104; Ghignoli, 1998, 320–21. See also, Pertile, 1966, 5: 343.

39   Bertoni and Vicini, 1941, 28–9.

40   Ibid., 20; Lugli, 2010, 88.

41   One of the chronicles states, "Dicto tempore die ultimo Aprilis erecta fuit Bonissima in statua marmorea in plateis civitatis Mutine, ante officium bullettarum"; Bertoni and Vicini, 1941, 19; Lugli, 2010, 88. All of these authors argue that the statue existed already in 1220.

42   Bertoni and Vicini, 1941, 23–4; Lugli, 2010, 89.

43   Lugli, 2010, 86; Bertoni and Vicini, 1941, 23, 26.

44   Lugli, 2010, 87–8.

45   Ibid., 88; he also uses the word "monumentalizes."

46   Ibid., 77.

47   Ibid., 89.

48   Masi, 1934, 136–7.

49   Shaw, 2006, 19.

50   Bernardino da Siena, 1989, 735–6. In another case, Henry of Ghent stated, when trying to judge the terms of a just exchange, that the needs and desires of buyers had to come into equilibrium like the bar of the steelyard; quoted in Langholm, 1992, 255–6.

51   Of course, many images of the Last Judgment also used images of scales and balances. In the pulpit that he carved for the cathedral of Pisa, Giovanni Pisano depicted Christ as Judge by

showing him holding a balance. And the right-hand panel in the predella of Orcagna's Strozzi altarpiece in Santa Maria Novella, Florence, shows demons and angels fighting over the soul of Emperor Henry II by trying to tip the scales of the balance to their side. According to Jacopo da Voragine's *Golden Legend*, the emperor's fate hung in the balance, but his gift of a golden chalice to a church tipped the scales in his favor.

52 For this discussion, I largely follow Frojmovič, 1996.

53 Ibid., 26–7.

54 Ibid., 26–7, 35.

55 Fabris, 1932–9, n.s. 27–8: 16.

56 Frojmovič, 1996, 37–8.

57 Ibid., 29, 36, 46–7. Frojmovič's translations are somewhat different. She offers (36) two readings of the first line: "And I, the mistress, temper the actions of men by means of reason" or "And I, by means of *ratio* the mistress of men, regulate actions." She also notes, and I concur, that *ratio* has the meaning of justice. Bernardino of Siena, 1989, 735–6 used the Italian *ragione* in that sense, when, in his commentary on Revelation 11: 1 he said, "cioè che si misura ciascuno la sua ragione, e tanta ragione li dà quanta tu ne gli trovi."

58 However, the virtue of Temperance may have visually conveyed a sense of measure. In his *Tesoretto*, Latini wrote: "Qui stae la temperanza,/ cui la gente talora/ Suole chiamare misura." Latini, 1981, 67.

59 Paolo da Certaldo in Branca, 1986, 5, no. 3.

60 Giovanni di Pagolo Morelli in ibid., 195.

61 Fanelli, 1980, 60–61. For evidence about the guildhalls destroyed when the Piazza della Repubblica was constructed in Florence, see Sframeli, 1989, 309–41.

62 See Friedman, 1988, 201.

63 Fossi, 2009, 14.

64 Ibid., 12–16.

65 Montagnani, 2009, 45–9; Lusanna, 2001, 126; Boskovits, 1984, 19–20.

66 I have not found the dimensions of this hall, but it is narrowly rectangular. For a discussion of the significance of square halls as less hierarchical than long, narrow halls, see Miller, 2000, 117, 173. Several other guildhalls in Florence (now destroyed) were also vaulted spaces; see Sframeli, 1989, 310–11, 315, 326 fig. 211.

67 Montagnani, 2009, 51–2.

68 Spagnesi, 1992, 8–9. As Spagnesi notes, in a statute book of the Arte della Lana dated 1333, one illustration shows Christ holding a

sheet of paper on which are written the words "fa misericordia, fa iustitia."

69 As reported by Morpurgo, 1933, 163; Slepian, 1987, 82.

70 The 1333 statutes of the Lana guild include a miniature with Santo Stefano and Christ holding an upturned sword in his right hand, while with his left he holds a scroll with the words "fa misericordia, fa iustitia" (do mercy, do justice); see Partsch, 1981, 66, 123, and pl. 64. For her remarks on the judging Christ, see Miller, 2000, 197.

71 Montagnani, 2009, 56. Slepian, 1987, 83 suggests the fourth figure is San Frediano, but that seems unlikely. The major Augustinian church of Florence, Santo Spirito, was located in Oltrarno.

72 For parallels, see Miller, 2000, 208.

73 Montagnani, 2009, 67 n. 15.

74 Morpurgo, 1933, 147–8.

75 The man says, "Non tenner questo luogo mai alcuni/per vertu come voi degni di loda/ onde il ver mio da voi prego che s'oda"; to which Prudence responds, "Lusinghe e prieghe nelle menti folli/operan molto et entran di leggero/ma come tu non parla chi ama il vero." See ibid., 14–3; Slepian, 1987, 84.

76 The man, "Io posso meritar ben chi mi serve/ onde se giudicate quel ch'io cheggio/ non ne verrà alcun di voi di peggio," to which Justice responds, "Tu se' di morte vergognosa degno!/ qui giudicio per oro non si vende,/ ma quel ch'è suo a ciaschedun si rende." Morpurgo, 1933, 144, who suggests he is a merchant; Slepian, 1987, 84–5; Montagnani, 2009, 59.

77 The man, "Io veggio ben com'io ricevo torto;/ ma se per caso Morte non m'affretta/ questo non passerà senza vendetta!" Fortitude responds, "Se tu sapessi come fa per nulla/ qui ogni furia e ogni minaccia,/ sapresti che'l dir tuo te solo impaccia." Morpurgo, 1933, 145–6; Slepian, 1987, 85; Montagnani, 2009, 59–61.

78 The man, "Io temo di seguir dinanzi a voi/ la ragion mia, perchè già forse avvenne/ ch'offeso alcun di voi da me si tenne." Morpurgo, 1933, 146; Montagnani, 2009, 61.

79 Temperance responds, "Non temer torto qui ricever mai/ ben che ci fosse singulare offesa/ ché quel, bilancia dritta mai non pesa." Morpurgo, 1933, 147; Slepian, 1987, 86.

80 Morpurgo, 1933, 146–7. See also Slepian, 1987, 86; Ruck, 1989, 117; Atwell, 2006, 192–3; Donato, 2002, 216–17.

81 In his *ricordi*, Giovanni di Pagolo Morelli warns of hypocrites who cover themselves with the "cloak" (*mantello*) of religion; see Branca, 1986, 178.

82 For this connection, see Slepian, 1987, 103 n. 17.

83 Morpurgo, 1933, 143 n. 1; Slepian, 1987, 86 n. 79.

84 Branca, 1986, 39, no. 178. The second half reads, "però che sono di maggiore pericolo quando vogliono nuocere al loro nimico."

85 Morpurgo, 1933, 148–9. The other manuscripts offer variations; see ibid., 148, 150.

86 A clause in the statutes of the Lana guild required the guild consuls to have a translation of the statutes made in the vulgar tongue and to have the statutes read to members so that no one would have a pretext for claiming ignorance of the rules. See Agnoletti, 1940, 198–9. What is known about the decoration (both sculptural and painted) of several other Florentine guildhalls indicates that many of them attempted to associate themselves with the civic government by incorporating the arms of, among others, the Republic, the Florentine *popolo*, and the Parte Guelfa. See Sframeli, 1989, 314, 315, 316–17 n. 84.

87 Brutus appeared elsewhere in Florence too. He was included in the cycle, probably painted shortly after 1385, of Famous Men in the Saletta in the Palazzo della Signoria. This cycle is entirely secular; as Rubinstein, 1995, 52–3 notes, "no biblical or Christian heroes are included in it."

88 Fidanza, 1997, 351–62.

89 Morpurgo, 1933, 152–3. When in 1459 Benedetto Bonfigli decorated the dining hall of the priors of Perugia, he included an image of Brutus; see ibid., 152.

90 Bowsky, 1981, 23.

91 Tuliani, 1998, 66–7 sees the creation of the Campo market space as a reaction against the bishop of Siena and argues that control of the market represented the passage of power from the bishop to merchants and aristocrats.

92 Bortolotti, 1982, 34–6; for the Campo as one space, see Tuliani, 1998, 64.

93 Friedman, 1998, 326–8; Bortolotti, 1982, 36; Braunfels, 1953, 250.

94 That program emphasized saintly protectors, the cardinal virtues, and heroes of the Roman Republic; see ibid., 335–7.

95 For the inventory, see Hansen, 1987, 213–19, esp. 215–16.

96 Ibid., 217; see also Morpurgo, 1933, 152.

97 Hansen, 1987, 81–93; Friedman, 1998, 335. Brutus's image was also included in the antechapel of the Palazzo Comunale in a work by Taddeo di Bartolo; see Morpurgo, 1933, 152; see also Rubinstein, 1958, esp. 195–6.

98 Friedman, 1998, 336.

99 All of these saints had special significance for the city. Ambrose visited the city on several occasions and set up the four crosses; Petronius was the bishop who established Santo Stefano; he also acquired the relics of Florian, another patron saint of the city; the cathedral is dedicated to Peter. Francis visited Bologna, and Dominic is buried in the city. For Ambrose, see Bocchi, 1995, 1: 51–2. For Florian, see Kaftal, 1978, 322. According to Pancotti, 1925–9, 1: 171, the *Palatium nuxii* (the palace where the consuls of the Nuxium in Piacenza met) was adorned with a statue of justice with the inscription *Huius in auspiciis – recta hic justitia floret – iurgia mos est – primo sedare – sine qua reddere jus statim cuique suum*. Pancotti does not offer a possible date for the statue or the inscription.

100 See Butterfield, 1992a, 230; Paoletti, 1993, 231.

101 Paoletti, 1993, 231, 245–6 n. 47. See also Poggi, 1988, 1: 215, doc. 1075.

102 Paoletti, 1993, 235–6; Butterfield, 1992a, 231.

103 Sframeli, 1989, 27.

104 See Paoletti, 1993, 232–5.

105 For the chronology, see Butterfield, 1992a, 225–8.

106 The translation is from Zervas, 1996, 1: 216. Here in the civic palace, as Rubinstein, 1995, 51 observed, Sacchetti invested "the biblical theme of the Incredulity of St Thomas with a civic meaning . . ." See also Sacchetti, 1990, 374.

107 In the 1440s Bicci di Lorenzo painted a *Christ and Thomas* for the Tribune of Florence's Duomo; he also painted the same theme in a now lost fresco on the façade of Santa Croce; see Butterfield, 1992b, 67. See also Zervas, 1996, 1: 215–19.

108 For the inscriptions and dating, see Dorigo, 2003, 1: 398.

109 Guidi, 1995, 15.

110 See Ridolfi, 1882, 11–12; Blomquist, 1979, 55–7. The translation, with one slight modification, is from Lopez and Raymond, 1955, 418–19. In 1425 Gentile da Fabriano painted an image in Siena's Campo that came to be known as the *Madonna dei Banchetti*. It marked the notaries' location in the Campo and no doubt served to instill trust in their activities. See Nevola, 2007, 19. For other

remarks on the role of the church and especially of arcades in legitimizing market activities, see McLean, 2008, 79–83.

111 Baschet, 1993, 636–9. In a Last Judgment created by Tommaso and Matteo Biazachi in 1483 for the Santuario della Madonna in Montegrazie in Liguria, the place in Hell reserved for the avaricious includes corrupt judges (labeled "FALSI JUDICES") who are being roasted on a fire that is fed by the bodies of corrupt notaries (labeled "NOTARI FALSI"); ibid., 655.

112 Ortalli, 1979, 184–5.

113 Giansante, 1998, 1–49, esp. 17, 44.

114 Ortalli, 1979, 50–53, esp. n. 63; my emphasis. The phrase reads in part, "reditur scandalum et jnfamia, ymo totaliter civitati in conspectu maxime forasteriorum ipsas figuras plerumque spectantium, qui cum vident ymaginantur et quasi firmiter credunt quod maior pars civium parvam fidem agnoschant et magnis falsitatibus involuti sint . . ."

### Epilogue

1 For *sincerus*, see Masi, 1934, 126–7. For *ragion di mercatura*, see Branca, 1986, xvi, xlii–xliii. For counterfeiting and heresy, see Roach, 2005, 137–9.

2 I thank Katherine Jansen for this insight.

3 Randolph, 2002, 57.

4 Giotto's frescoes in the Scrovegni Chapel in Padua (c. 1306) served as important precedents for Lorenzetti's depictions of good and bad government. Giotto's figure of Injustice in particular, who holds a sword and a barbed snare in his claw-like hands, served as a model for the figure of the tyrant. And the effects of Injustice on the economy are clear: behind him the gate through which merchandise should enter his city is crumbling, and in the foreground cultivated fields have given way to a forest. The scenes at his feet show a merchant being robbed of his horse and left for dead, a woman about to be raped, and a band of soldiers. The reading of these figures is not entirely clear. Frugoni, 1991a, 141–2 says they show "a rider who has been thrown from his horse, a girl forced to disrobe, two warriors armed to the teeth." If they are intended precisely to serve as counterparts of the scenes under the figure of Justice, then it may be that the rider has been thrown from his horse; but if so, the soldiers serve as the counterpart to the merchants on the right of the Injustice scene, in which case the merchants are soon to be robbed. Donato, 2002, 215–17; Edgerton, 1980, 33.

5 Rubinstein, 1958, esp. 179–89.

6 Skinner, 1986; for a restatement see Skinner, 1989.

7 For her criticism of Rubinstein and Skinner, see Donato, 1988, 1271–2; for her own view, see Donato, 2003, esp. 398–400.

8 Frugoni, 1991a, 124.

9 This is not to say that the secular, and especially the mercantile, elements of the Sienese frescoes have been entirely ignored in previous scholarship. Many years ago Otto Pächt, 1950, 13–47 called attention to the affinity between Lorenzetti's painting and depictions of the labors of the months as found in painted calendars and deemed Lorenzetti's work, especially the depiction of the Sienese countryside, to be "the first landscape portrait of modern art" (41). And in an important and much cited essay, Uta Feldges-Henning, 1972, 145–62 argued that Lorenzetti illustrated in this fresco the seven mechanical arts that included, according to Hugh of St. Victor, *lanificium* (wool and other kinds of textile manufacturing) and *navigatio* or trade. She too compares (162) the program to a literary work, in her case to an encyclopedia that encompasses "the whole accumulated knowledge of the time." Most appositely, Max Seidel, 1999 has seen in the frescoes a reflection of actual Sienese life, as evidenced by laws, statutes, and other governmental directives, as has, more briefly, Donato; see also Seidel, 1997. Donato, 1993, 339–40 notes that the vices in the tyrant's court "incarnano terrori radicattissimi nell'esperienza di ogni comune."

10 Langholm, 1992, 54–5, 135; Todeschini, 1994, 195–6.

11 Prodi, 2009, 60–61; Todeschini, 1994, 167, 218–19, 225–6 n. 10.

12 Anonymous Franciscan quoted in Todeschini, 1994, 227 n. 11. The writer gave six reasons why this was the case, concluding, "itaque est propter hoc necessaria mercancia."

13 As Starn, 1987, 23 observes, "the reader of texts [he is referring to the captions and labels in the cycle] is transformed into a viewer of a painted world whose obvious moral – that the virtuous republic secures a harmonious plenitude of productive activity in the city and country – is naturalized in a panorama of seemingly commonplace details." Lorenzetti appears to have had Paduan precedents. As Frojmovič, 1996, 45 notes, the inscription below Giotto's depiction of Justice in the Arena Chapel states that under Justice's reign 'the worthy knight hunts, people sing and trade, the merchant

travels . . ." All of these figures are included in the Good Government frescoes.

14 Bernardino da Siena, 1989, 2: 1131–8.

15 Ibid., 1131. The entire passage reads, "Or tolle l'ultima circustanzia, e sarà fine: dove si contiene ogni bene, la quale è il bene comune nel mercatare. Io non dico del bene comune de le gabelle de le mercantie; io dico del bene comune dell'arti; ché di niuna cosa partecipa tanto il Comuno, quanto dell'utile dell'arti e de le mercantie che si vendono e si comprano."

16 Translation by Rowley, 1958, 1: 128; my emphasis.

17 In many respects, Domenico Lenzi's image of the grain market at Orsanmichele in times of dearth, in his *Specchio umano* (see fig. 8), perfectly captures a marketplace where individual interests have overcome any impulse toward the common good, a theme that was also explored by Giotto and others in paint and stone in images of the commune under assault. Lenzi's malevolent creature with batlike wings who sends God's angel fleeing echoes the virtually contemporary winged figure of fraud created by Lorenzetti. In addition, the demon clutches bags – containing either money or grain – and in this way also becomes a personification of avarice or cupidity. In the market below, the forces of order (and justice) are unable to contain the situation as people look out only for themselves, ignoring the shrine of the Madonna and the chandler behind his counter who offers candles for sale, candles that should be lit to honor the Virgin. For the theme of the commune under assault, see Donato, 1988, 1179–88; Frojmovič, 1996, 31–4.

18 Again in Lenzi's image (see fig. 8), at the base of the counter below the altar dedicated to Mary sit three figures, who appear dazed or in a torpor. They remain impassive, oblivious to the chaos around them. Some have identified them as beggars, or perhaps they represent the powerless poor resigned to their unhappy fate. At their feet in turn sits a naked male figure, who has also been identified possibly as a condemned criminal. Although male, his placement at the base of the painting and his nakedness seem to echo that of Lorenzetti's bound figure of Justice, while his nudity may identify him in some way with Truth, certainly with innocence. What is clear

is that in this marketplace gone terribly awry, piety, justice, trust, truth, and concern for the common good have all taken their leave. See Partsch, 1981, 47.

19 Frugoni, 1991a, 156.

20 Gibbs, 1999a.

21 This point is made by Polzer, 2002, 77.

22 For my interpretation, I follow the reading of Donato, 1993, esp. 335–9. As to the instruments themselves, Polzer, 2002, 80 suggests that the round object is a sieve. For more on the measuring sticks, see Donato, 2002, 218. See also Frojmovič, 1996, esp. 35–8, 45.

23 Donato, 1993, 336, quoting the Dominican Domenico Cavalca.

24 Ibid., 337, again quoting Cavalca.

25 Ibid., 339. Frugoni, 1991a, 121–4, believes, by contrast, that the labels were at some point (possibly during a repainting) mistakenly inverted; see Donato, 1993, 337 n. 91. Polzer, 2002, 80 concurs with Donato. The evidence from the writings of Peter of LaPalu in Langholm, 1992, 489 supports Donato's position.

26 Giansante, 1998, 17, 44.

27 As Gibbs, 1999a, 14 notes, "Justice and government by the processes of legal order are strong visual as well as symbolic features of Ambrogio's design, in which balance is fundamental both visually and as a familiar metaphor for the judicial process." In his view, ibid., legal manuscripts are the "most demonstrable of his [Lorenzetti's] sources."

28 Frugoni, 1991a, 127, 136. As Frugoni observes, 141, "entering the hall of Peace . . . one feels genuine astonishment at the unaccustomed liberty with which Ambrogio has treated secular subjects while making massive use of figurative schemes proper to the world of religion." One could also compare the entire fresco to a triptych with the figure of justice serving as the central panel.

29 The inscription below the fresco of the *Effects of Good Government* reads in part, "Guardate quanti ben vengan da lei [Justice] e come e dolce vita eriposata quella dela citta dve servata . . ." See Rowley, 1958, 1: 127.

30 At the same time, I believe that too much emphasis has been placed on the frescoes as statements of republican principles. Donato, 1994, 517 sees them as "uno proclama strenuamente repubblicano."

31 Bernardino da Siena, 1989, 2: 1131.

# BIBLIOGRAPHY

*Archival Sources*

AS = Archivio di Stato

AS Bologna, Capitano del Popolo, Società d'arti e d'armi; Curia del Podestà; Ufficio abbondanza e grascia.

AS Parma, Diplomatico, Pergamene miniate.

AS Prato, Ceppi.

AS Venezia, Compilazione delle leggi; Consiglio dei Dieci, Deliberazioni; Maggior Consiglio, Deliberazioni; Provveditori alle beccarie; Provveditori alle biave.


*Websites*

www.sacred-texts.com/chr/aquinas/summa/sum333.htm

www.societapistoiesestoriapatria.it

www.worldofdante.org/about.html


*Printed Works*

Abraham-Thisse, Simone. 2006. "La fraude dans la production des draps au moyen-âge: Un délit?" In Gérard Béaur, Hubert Bonin, and Claire Lemercier, eds. *Fraude, contrefaçon et contrebande de l'antiquité à nos jours*, 431–56. Geneva: Librairie Droz.

Agazzi, Michela. 1991. *Platea Sancti Marci: I luoghi marciani dall'xi al xiii secolo e la formazione della piazza*. Venice: Comune di Venezia.

Agnoletti, Anna Maria E., ed. 1940. *Statuto dell'arte della lana di Firenze (1317–1319)*. Florence: Felice Le Monnier.

Alberti, Leon Battista. 1969a. *I libri della famiglia*, ed. Ruggiero Romano and Alberto Tenenti. Turin: Giulio Einaudi Editore.

—. 1969b. *The Family in Renaissance Florence*. Trans. Renée Neu Watkins. Colombia, S.C.: University of South Carolina Press.

Anonimo Genovese. 1970. *Poesie: Edizione critica, introduzione, commento e glossario*, ed. Luciana Cocito. Rome: Edizioni dell'Ateneo.

Arnade, Peter, Martha Howell, and Walter Simons. 2002. "Fertile Spaces: The Productivity of Urban Space in Northern Europe." *Journal of Interdisciplinary History* 32: 515–48.

Astorri, Antonella. 1998. *La mercanzia a Firenze nella prima metà del Trecento: Il potere dei grandi mercanti*. Florence: Olschki.

—, and David Friedman. 2005. "The Florentine Mercanzia and its Palace." *I Tatti Studies: Essays in the Renaissance* 10: 11–68.

Atwell, Adrienne. 2006. "Ritual Trading at the Florentine Wool-Cloth *Botteghe*." In Roger J. Crum and John T. Paoletti, eds. *Renaissance Florence: A Social History*, 182–215. Cambridge University Press.

Banti, Ottavio, ed. 1997. *I brevi dei consoli del comune di Pisa degli anni 1162 e 1164: Studio introduttivo, testi e note con un'appendice di documenti*. Rome: Istituto Storico Italiano per il Medio Evo.

Barbieri, Gino. 1988. "Economia, finanza e tenore di vita nella Verona scaligera." In Gian Maria Varanini, ed. *Gli scaligeri, 1277–1387*, 329–41. Verona: Mondadori.

Baroni, Maria Franca. 1975. "Il consolato dei mercanti a Milano nel periodo comunale." *Nuova Rivista Storica* 59: 257–87.

Baschet, Jérôme. 1993. *Les justices de l'au-delà: Les représentations de l'enfer en France et en Italie (xiie–xve siècle)*. Rome: École Française de Rome.

—. 2000. "I peccati capitali e le loro punizioni nell'iconografia medievale." In Carla Casagrande and Silvana Vecchio. *I sette vizi capitali: Storia dei peccati nel medioevo con un saggio di Jérôme Baschet*, 225–60. Turin: Einaudi.

Battaglia, Salvatore. 1961–2002. *Grande dizionario della lingua italiana*. 21 vols. Turin: UTET.

Béaur, Gérard, Hubert Bonin, and Claire Lemercier, eds [Béaur et al.]. 2006. *Fraude, contrefaçon et contrebande de l'antiquité à nos jours*. Geneva: Librairie Droz.

Bec, Christian. 1967. *Les marchands écrivains: affaires et humanisme à Florence, 1375–1434*. Paris: Mouton and Co.

Becker, Hans Jürgen. 1975. "Canistris, Opicino de." *Dizionario biografico degli italiani* 18: 116–19.

Belting, Hans. 1989. "Das Bild als Text: Wandmalerei und Literatur in Zeitalter Dantes." In Hans Belting and Dieter Blume, eds. *Malerei und Stadt-kultur in der Dantezeit: Die Argumentation der Bilder*, 23–64. Munich: Hirmer Verlag.

Benton, Tim. 1995. "The Three Cities Compared: Urbanism." In Diana Norman, ed. *Siena, Florence, and Padua: Art, Society and Religion, 1280–1400*, 2 vols. 2: 7–27. New Haven and London: Yale University Press.

Bergonzoni, Franco. 1990. "Note sulle unità di misura bolognesi." In Francesca Bocchi, ed. *I portici di Bologna e l'edilizia civile medievale*, 161–70. Casalecchio di Reno: Grafis Edizioni.

Bernardino da Siena. 1934. *Le prediche volgari: Predicazione del 1425 in Siena*, ed. Ciro Cannarozzi. 2 vols. Pistoia: Alberto Pacinotti.

—. 1989. *Prediche volgari sul campo di Siena, 1427*, ed. Carlo Delcorno. 2 vols. Milan: Rusconi.

Bertolini, Virginio. 1988. "Cansignorio e la città marmorina." In Gian Maria Varanini, ed. *Gli scaligeri: 1277–1387*, 255–9. Verona: Mondadori.

Bertoni, G., and E. P. Vicini. 1941. "La 'Bonissima'." *Studi e documenti: Periodico trimestrale pubblicato a cura della R. Deputazione di Storia Patria per l'Emilia e la Romagna*. 5: 17–29.

Betto, Bianca, ed. 1981. *I collegi dei notai, dei giudici, dei medici e dei nobili di Treviso (sec. xiii–xvi): Storia e documenti*. Venice: Deputazione Editrice.

—. 1984–6. *Gli statuti del comune di Treviso (sec. xiii–xiv)*. 2 vols. Rome: Istituto Storico Italiano per il Medio Evo.

Bianchi, Silvana Anna, and Rosalba Granuzzo, eds. 1992. *Statuti di Verona del 1327*. 2 vols. Rome: Jouvence.

Biganti, Tiziana, and Clara Cutini. 1997. "Le arti nel Palazzo: I collegi della mercanzia e del cambio." In Francesco Federico Mancini, ed. *Il Palazzo dei Priori di Perugia*, 337–50. Perugia: Quattroemme.

Biondi, Albano. 1984. "Tra duomo e palazzo: La piazza." In *Lanfranco e Wiligelmo: Il duomo di Modena*, 573–6. Modena: Panini Edizioni.

Blanshei, Sarah Rubin. 1976. *Perugia, 1260–1340: Conflict and Change in a Medieval Italian Urban Society*. Transactions of the American Philosophical Society, n.s., 66, part 2. Philadelphia: American Philosophical Society.

—. 2010. *Politics and Justice in Late Medieval Bologna*. Leiden and Boston: Brill.

Blomquist, Thomas W. 1979. "The Dawn of Banking in an Italian Commune: Thirteenth Century Lucca." In *The Dawn of Modern Banking*, 53–75. New Haven and London: Yale University Press.

Boccaccio, Giovanni. 1980. *Decameron*, ed. Vittore Branca. Turin: Einaudi.

—. 2002. *The Decameron*, trans. Mark Musa and Peter Bondanella. New York: Penguin.

Bocchi, Francesca, ed. 1995. *Bologna*. 4 vols. Bologna: Grafis Edizioni.

Boholm, Asa. 1990. *The Doge of Venice: The Symbolism of State Power in the Renaissance*. Gothenburg: Institute for Advanced Studies in Social Anthropology.

Bona, Andrea. 1997. "Brescia: xv secolo. Acque e mercati nella formazione del nuovo centro politico." In Donatella Calabi, ed. *Fabbriche, piazze, mercati: La città italiana nel rinascimento*, 130–58. Rome: Officina Edizioni.

Bonaini, Francesco, ed. 1854. *Statuti inediti della città di Pisa dal xii al xiv secolo raccolti ed illustrati*. 3 vols. Vol. 1. Florence: G. P. Vieusseux.

Boone, Marc, and Martha C. Howell. 2013. *The Power of Space in Late Medieval and Early Modern Europe: The Cities of Italy, Northern France and the Low Countries*. Turnhout: Brepols.

Bortolami, Sante. 2008. "'Spaciosum, immo speciosum palacium': Alle origini del Palazzo della Ragione di Padova." In Ettore Vio, ed. *Il Palazzo della Ragione di Padova: La storia, l'architettura, il restauro*, 39–73. Padua: Signumpadova Editrice.

Bortolotti, Lando. 1982. *Siena*. Rome and Bari: Laterza.

Boskovits, Miklós. 1984. *The Fourteenth Century: The Painters of the Miniaturist Tendency. Corpus of Florentine Painting*. Section III, Vol. IX. Florence: Giunti Barbèra.

Boucheron, Patrick. 2003. "De l'urbanisme communal à l'urbanisme seigneurial: Cités, territoires et édilité publique en Italie du nord (xiiie–xve siècle)." In Élisabeth Crouzet-Pavan, ed. *Pouvoir et édilité: Les grands chantiers dans l'Italie communale et seigneuriale*, 41–77. Rome: École Française de Rome.

Bowsky, William M. 1981. *A Medieval Italian Commune: Siena under the Nine, 1287–1355*. Berkeley: University of California Press.

Boyde, Patrick. 2000. *Human Vices and Human Worth in Dante's Comedy*. Cambridge University Press.

Braglia, Graziella Martinelli. 1985. "L'ufficio della 'Bona Stima': La Bonissima." In Gabriella Guandalini, ed. *Il Palazzo Comunale di Modena: Le sedi, la città, il contado*, 48–9. Modena: Edizioni Panini.

Branca, Vittore. 1965. "Un biadaiuolo lettore di Dante nei primi decenni del '300." *Rivista di cultura classica e medioevale* 7: 200–15.

—. 1999. "Introduzione: Il narrar boccacciano per immagini dal tardo gotico al primo rinascimento." In Vittore Branca, ed. *Boccaccio visualizzato: Narrare per parole e per immagini fra medioevo e rinascimento*, 3 vols. 1: 3–37. Turin: Einaudi.

—, ed. 1986. *Mercanti scrittori: Ricordi nella Firenze tra medioevo e rinascimento*. Milan: Rusconi.

—, ed. 1989. *Esopo toscano: Dei frati e dei mercanti trecenteschi*. Venice: Marsilio Editore.

Braudel, Fernand. 1977. *Afterthoughts on Material Civilization and Capitalism*, trans. Patricia M. Ranum. Baltimore and London: Johns Hopkins University Press.

Braunfels, Wolfgang. 1953. *Mittelalterliche Stadt-baukunst in der Toskana*. Berlin: Gebr. Mann Verlag.

Braunstein, Philippe. 2005. "Imparare il tedesco a Venezia intorno al 1420." In *La trasmissione dei saperi nel medioevo (secoli xii–xiv): Pistoia, 16–19 maggio 2003*, 321–36. Pistoia: Centro Italiano di Studi di Storia e d'Arte.

—, and Franco Franceschi. 2007. "'Sapersi governar': Pratica mercantile e arte di vivere." In Franco Franceschi, Richard A. Goldthwaite, and Reinhold C. Mueller, eds. *Il rinascimento italiano e l'europa*, vol. 4: *Commercio e cultura mercantile*, 655–77. Treviso: Angelo Colla Editore.

Brieger, Peter, Millard Meiss, and Charles S. Singleton. 1969. *Illuminated Manuscripts of the Divine Comedy*. 2 vols. Princeton University Press.

Brolo, Moses de. 1724. *Carmen de laudibus bergomi* [also known as the *Liber Pergaminus*]. In Antonio Muratori, ed. *Rerum italicarum scriptores*. 25 vols. Vol. 5: 529–36. Milan: Societatis Palatinae.

Brown, Patricia Fortini. 1988. *Venetian Narrative Painting in the Age of Carpaccio*. New Haven and London: Yale University Press.

Brucker, Gene. 2005. "*Fede* and *Fiducia*: The Problem of Trust in Italian History, 1300–1500." In *Living on the Edge in Leonardo's Florence: Selected Essays*, 83–113. Berkeley and Los Angeles: University of California Press.

—, ed. 1967. *Two Memoirs of Renaissance Florence: The Diaries of Buonaccorso Pitti and Gregorio Dati*, trans. Julia Martines. New York: Harper Torchbooks.

—, ed. 1971. *The Society of Renaissance Florence: A Documentary Study*. New York: Harper and Row.

Brugnoli, Pierpaolo. 1978. "Il trionfo cortese: la città scaligera." In Lionello Puppi, ed. *Ritratto di Verona: Lineamenti di una storia urbanistica*, 209–68. Verona: Banco Popolare di Verona.

Bruni, Leonardo. 1978. "Panegyric to the City of Florence," in Benjamin G. Kohl and Ronald G. Witt, eds. *The Earthly Republic: Italian Humanists on Government and Society*, 121–75. Philadelphia: University of Pennsylvania Press.

Burckhardt, Jacob. [1860] 1954. *The Civilization of the Renaissance in Italy: An Essay*, trans. S. G. C. Middlemore. New York: Modern Library.

Butterfield, Andrew. 1992a. "Verrocchio's Christ and St Thomas: Chronology, Iconography and Political Context." *Burlington Magazine* 134: 225–33.

—. 1992b. "The Christ and St. Thomas of Andrea del Verrocchio." In Loretta Dolcini, ed. *Verrocchio's Christ and St. Thomas: A Masterpiece of Sculpture from Renaissance Florence*, 53–79. New York: Metropolitan Museum of Art.

Caferro, William. 2011. *Contesting the Renaissance*. Chichester: Wiley-Blackwell.

Caggese, Romolo, ed. 1999a. *Statuti della repubblica fiorentina*. Vol. 1: *Statuto del capitano del popolo degli anni 1322–25*, new ed., eds. Giuliano Pinto, Francesco Salvestrini, and Andrea Zorzi. Florence: Leo S. Olschki.

—. 1999b. *Statuti della repubblica fiorentina*. Vol. 2: *Statuto del podestà dell'anno 1325*, new ed., eds. Giuliano Pinto, Francesco Salvestrini, and Andrea Zorzi. Florence: Leo S. Olschki.

Calabi, Donatella. 2004. *The Market and the City: Square, Street, and Architecture in Early Modern Europe*. Aldershot and Burlington, Vt: Ashgate.

Canistris, Opicino de. 1984. *Il libro delle lodi della città di Pavia* [with Latin text], trans. and ed. Delfino Ambaglio. Pavia: Logos International.

—. 2004. *Le lodi della città di Pavia*, ed. Dino Ambaglio. Pavia: Edizioni Antares.

Caprioli, Maria, ed. 2008. *Lo statuto della città di Rieti dal secolo xiv al secolo xvi*. Rome: Istituto Storico Italiano per il Medio Evo.

Caprioli, Severino, and Attilio Bartoli Langeli, eds. 1996. *Statuto del comune di Perugia di 1297*. 2 vols. Perugia: Deputazione di Storia Patria per l'Umbria.

Cardinali, Cinzia, Andrea Maiarelli, Sonia Merli, and Attilio Bartoli Langeli [Cardinali et al.]. 2000. *Statuti e matricole del collegio della mercanzia di Perugia*. 2 vols. Perugia: Nobile Collegio della Mercanzia di Perugia and Deputazione di Storia Patria per l'Umbria.

Carli, Filippo. 1936. *Storia del commercio italiano. II: Il mercato nell'età del comune*. Padua: CEDAM.

Carocci, Guido. [1884] 1975. *Il mercato vecchio di Firenze: Ricordi e curiosità di storia e d'arte*. Reprint. Florence: Istituto Professionale Leonardo da Vinci.

Casagrande, Carla, and Silvana Vecchio. 2000. *I sette vizi capitali: Storia dei peccati nel medioevo, con un saggio di Jérôme Baschet*. Turin: Einaudi.

Cassidy, Brendan. 2007. *Politics, Civic Ideals, and Sculpture in Italy, c. 1240–1400*. London and Turnhout: Harvey Miller.

Castelli, Maria Cristina. 1999. "I codici: scheda 7." In Vittore Branca, ed. *Boccaccio visualizzato: Narrare per parole e per immagini fra medioevo e rinascimento*, 3 vols. 2: 66–72. Turin: Einaudi.

Castignoli, Piero. 1984. "Dalla podesteria perpetua di Oberto Pallavicino al governo dei mercanti." In *Storia di Piacenza*. 6 vols. Vol. 2: *Dal vescovo conte alla signoria (996–1313)*, 277–98. Piacenza: Cassa di Risparmio di Piacenza.

—, and Pierre Racine, eds. 1967. *Corpus statutorum mercatorum placentiae (secoli xiv–xviii)*. Milan: Giuffrè.

Cattaneo, Angelo. 2011. *Fra Mauro's Mappa Mundi and Fifteenth-Century Venice*. Turnhout: Brepols.

Cerlini, Aldo, ed. 1933. *Consuetudini e statuti reggiani del secolo xiii*. Milan: Ulrico Hoepli.

Certaldo, Paolo da. 1945. *Libro di buoni costumi*, ed. Alfredo Schiaffini. Florence: Felice Le Monnier.

Cessi, Roberto and Annibale Alberti. 1934. *Rialto: L'isola, il ponte, il mercato*. Bologna: Nicola Zanichelli Editore.

Cherubini, Giovanni. 1988. "Rileggendo Antonio Pucci: Il "Mercato Vecchio" di Firenze." In *Cultura e società nell'Italia medievale: Studi per Paolo Brezzi*, 2 vols. 1: 197–214. Rome: Istituto Storico Italiano per il Medio Evo.

—. 1998. "Capitolo ii: Apogeo e declino del comune libero." In Giovanni Cherubini, ed. *Storia di Pistoia*. 4 vols. Vol. 2: *L'età del libero comune: Dall'inizio del xii alla metà del xiv secolo*, 41–87. Florence: Felice Le Monnier.

Chevigny, Paul. G. 2001. "From Betrayal to Violence: Dante's Inferno and the Social Construction of Crime." *Law and Social Inquiry* 26 (2001): 787–818.

Clark, David. 2000. "The Shop Within? An Analysis of the Architectural Evidence for Medieval Shops." *Architectural History* 43: 58–87.

Coleman, E. 1999. "The Italian Communes: Recent Work and Current Trends." *Journal of Medieval History* 25: 373–97.

Collodo, Silvana. 1986. "Il Prato della Valle nel medioevo." In Lionello Puppi, ed. *Prato della Valle: Due millenni di storia di un'avventura urbana*, 51–67. Padua: Signum Edizioni.

Compagni, Dino. 1986. *Dino Compagni's Chronicle of Florence*, trans. Daniel E. Bornstein. Philadelphia: University of Pennsylvania Press.

—. 2000. *Cronica*, ed. Davide Cappi. Rome: Istituto Storico Italiano per il Medio Evo.

Constable, Olivia Remie. 2003. *Housing the Stranger in the Mediterranean World: Lodging, Trade, and Travel from Late Antiquity and the Middle Ages*. Cambridge University Press.

Contini, Gianfranco, ed. 1976. *Poeti del Duecento: Poesie cortese toscana e settentrionale*. Milan and Naples: G. Einaudi.

Corti, Gino. 1952. "Consigli sulla mercatura di un anonimo trecentista." *Archivio Storico Italiano* 110: 114–19.

Cunningham, Colin. 1995. "For the Honour and Beauty of the City: The Design of Town Halls." In Diana Norman, ed. *Siena, Florence, and Padua: Art, Society and Religion, 1280–1400*, 2 vols. 2: 29–53. New Haven and London: Yale University Press.

Dameron, George. 1991. *Episcopal Power and Florentine Society, 1000–1320*. Cambridge, Mass: Harvard University Press.

d'Arco, Silvio Avalle. 1970. "Bonvesin da la Riva." *Dizionario biografico degli italiani* 12: 465–9.

Davidsohn, Robert. 1956–68. *Storia di Firenze*. 4 vols in 8. Florence: Sansoni.

Davis, James. 2012. *Medieval Market Morality: Life, Law and Ethics in the English Marketplace, 1200–1500*. Cambridge University Press.

Dean, Trevor. 2000. *The Towns of Italy in the Later Middle Ages*. Manchester University Press.

Delzant, Jean–Baptiste. 2013. "Instaurator et fundator: Édification de la seigneurie urbaine et présence monumentale de la commune (Italie centrale, fin du Moyen Âge)." In Marc Boone and Martha C. Howell, eds. *The Power of Space in Late Medieval and Early Modern Europe: The Cities of Italy, Northern France and the Low Countries*, 97–122. Turnhout: Brepols.

Demus, Otto. 1984. *The Mosaics of San Marco in Venice*. 4 vols. University of Chicago Press.

Dickerson iii, C. D. 2010. *Raw Painting: The Butcher's Shop by Annibale Carracci*. New Haven and London: Yale University Press.

Donato, Maria Monica. 1988. "Un ciclo pittorico ad Asciano (Siena), Palazzo Pubblico e l'iconografia 'politica' alla fine del medioevo." *Annali della scuola normale superiore di Pisa, Classe di lettere e filosofia*. ser. 3, 18: 1105–272.

—. 1993. "Testi, contesti, immagini politiche nel tardo Medioevo: Esempi toscani: In margine a una discussione sul 'Buon governo.'" *Annali dell'Istituto storico italo-germanico in Trento / Jahrbuch des italienisch-deutschen historischen Instituts in Trient* 19: 305–55.

—. 1994. "'Cose morali, e anche appartenenti secondo e' luoghi': Per lo studio della pittura politica nel tardo medioevo toscano." In Paolo Cammarosano, ed. *Le forme della propaganda politica nel Due e nel Trecento*, 491–517. Rome: École Française de Rome.

—. 2002. "Il pittore del *Buon Governo*: Le opera 'politiche' di Ambrogio in Palazzo Pubblico." In Chiara Frugoni, ed. *Pietro e Ambrogio Lorenzetti*, 201–55. Florence: Le Lettere.

—. 2003. "Il *princeps*, il giudice, il 'sindacho' e la città: Novità su Ambrogio Lorenzetti nel Palazzo Pubblico di Siena." In Francesca Bocchi and Rosa Smurra, eds. *Imago Urbis: L'immagine della città nella storia d'Italia. Atti del convegno internazionale (Bologna 5–7 settembre 2001)*, 389–407. Rome: Viella.

Dorigo, Wladimiro. 2003. *Venezia romanica: La formazione della città medioevale fino all'età gotica*. 2 vols. Sommacampagna: Cierre Edizioni.

Dorini, Umberto, ed. 1934. *Statuti dell'arte di Por Santa Maria del tempo della repubblica*. Florence: Leo S. Olschki.

Dotson, John E., trans. 1994. *Merchant Culture in Fourteenth Century Venice: The Zibaldone da Canal*. Binghamton, N.Y: Medieval and Renaissance Texts and Studies.

Edgerton, Samuel Y. Jr. 1980. "Icons of Justice." *Past and Present* 89: 23–38.

—. 1985. *Pictures and Punishment: Art and Criminal Prosecution during the Florentine Renaissance*. Ithaca and London: Cornell University Press.

Edler, Florence. 1934. *Glossary of Mediaeval Terms of Business: Italian Series 1200–1600*. Cambridge, Mass: Mediaeval Academy of America.

*Emilia Romagna*. 1991. Milan: Touring Club Italiano.

Eslami, Alireza Naser. 2010. *Architetture del commercio e città del mediterraneo: Dinamiche e strutture dei luoghi dello scambio tra Bisanzio, l'Islam e l'Europa*. Milan and Turin: Pearson Italia.

Fabbri, Francesca. 1999. "Il 'Cocharelli': Osservazioni e ipotesi per un manoscritto genovese del XIV secolo." In A. R. Calderoni Masetti, C. di Fabio, and M. Marcenaro, eds. *Tessuti, oreficerie, miniature in Liguria xiii–xv secolo*, 305–20. Bordighera: Istituto Internazionale di Studi Liguri.

Fabris, Giovanni, ed. 1932–9. "La cronaca di Giovanni da Nono." *Bollettino del museo civico di Padova* n.s. 25 (1932): 1–33, n.s. 26 (1933): 167–200; n.s. 27–8 (1934–39): 1–30.

Fanelli, Giovanni. 1980. *Firenze*. Bari: Laterza.

Fanselow, Frank S. 1990. "The Bazaar Economy or How Bizarre is the Bazaar Really?," *Man* n.s. 25: 250–65.

Fasoli, Gina, ed. 1940. *Statuti del comune di Bassano dell'anno 1259 e dell'anno 1295*. Monumenti storici pubblicati dalla R. deputazione di storia patria per le Venezie. n.s. Vol. 2. Venice: Reale Deputazione di Storia Patria per le Venezie.

—, and Pietro Sella, eds. 1937. *Statuti di Bologna dell'anno 1288*. Vatican City: Biblioteca Apostolica Vaticana.

Favaro, Elena, ed. 1962. *Cassiere della bolla ducale: Grazie – Novus Liber (1299–1305)*. Venice: Comitato per la Pubblicazione delle Fonti Relative alla Storia di Venezia.

Feldges-Henning, Uta. 1972. "The Pictorial Programme of the Sala della Pace: A New Interpretation." *Journal of the Warburg and Courtauld Institutes* 35: 145–62.

Fenster, Thelma S., and David Lord Smail, eds. 2003. *Fama: The Politics of Talk and Reputation in Medieval Europe*. Ithaca, N.Y: Cornell University Press.

Ferguson, Wallace K. 1948. *The Renaissance in Historical Thought: Five Centuries of Interpretation*. New York: Houghton Mifflin.

Fersouch, Lidia. 1993. "I luoghi del Capitolare degli ufficiali sopra Rialto." In Alessandra Princivalli and Gherardo Ortalli, eds. *Il capitolare degli ufficiali sopra Rialto: Nei luoghi al centro del sistema economico veneziano (secoli xiii–xiv)*, lxxii–iii. Milan: Editrice La Storia.

Fiamma, Galvano de la (Galvaneo Flamma). 1869. *Chronicon extravagans et chronicon maius*, ed. Antonio Ceruti. Miscellanea di Storia Italiana, 7: 439–784. Turin: Stamperia Reale.

Fidanza, Giovanni Battista. 1997. "La sala dell'udienza nel collegio della mercanzia." In Francesco Federico Mancini, ed. *Il Palazzo dei Priori di Perugia*, 351–62. Perugia: Quattroemme.

Flanigan, Theresa. 2008. "The Ponte Vecchio and the Art of Urban Planning in Late Medieval Florence." *Gesta* 47: 1–15.

Flinn, John. 1963. *Le Roman de Renart dans la littérature française et dans les littératures étrangères au moyen âge*. University of Toronto Press.

Foà, S. 2000. "Giamboni, Bono." In *Dizionario biografico degli italiani* 54: 302–4.

Fossi, Elena. 2009. "Architettura e forma del palagio: Interventi e trasformazioni fino ai nostri giorni/ The Form and the Architecture of the Palace: Developments and Changes up to Our Time." In *Il palagio dell'Arte della lana dalle origini ad oggi/ The Wool Guild Palace Since its Origins*, 9–41. Florence: Società Dantesca Italiana.

Franceschi, Franco. 1998. "La parabola delle corporazioni nella Firenze del tardo medioevo." In *Arti fiorentine: La grande storia dell'artigianato*. 6 vols. Vol. 1: *Il medioevo*, 77–101. Florence: Giunti.

Franco, Vincenzo, Angela Lanconelli, and Maria Antonietta Quesada, eds. 1991. *Pane e potere: Istituzioni e società in Italia dal medioevo all'età moderna*. Rome: Ministero per i Beni Culturali e Ambientali/Ufficio Centrale per i Beni Archivistici.

Frati, Ludovico. 1890. *La vita privata di Bologna dal secolo xiii al xvii*. Bologna: Nicola Zanichelli.

Friedman, David. 1988. *Florentine New Towns: Urban Design in the Late Middle Ages*. Cambridge, Mass: MIT Press.

—. 1998. "Monumental Urban Form in the Late Medieval Italian Commune: Loggias and the Mercanzie of Bologna and Siena." *Renaissance Studies* 12: 325–40.

Friedman, John Block. 1972. "Antichrist and the Iconography of Dante's Geryon." *Journal of the Warburg and Courtauld Institutes* 35: 108–22.

Frojmovič, Eva. 1996. "Giotto's Allegories of Justice and the Commune in the Palazzo della Ragione in Padua: A Reconstruction." *Journal of the Warburg and Courtauld Institutes* 59: 24–47.

Frugoni, Chiara Settis. 1974. "La mala pianta." In *Storiografia e storia: Studi in onore di Eugenio Duprè Theseider*. 2 vols. 2: 651–9. Rome: Bulzoni.

—. 1991a. *A Distant City: Images of Urban Experience in the Medieval World*, trans. William McCuaig. Princeton University Press.

—. 1991b. "Il ciclo dei mesi nella 'Porta della Pescheria' del duomo di Modena." In *La Porta della Pescheria nel duomo di Modena*, 13–31. Modena: Franco Cosimo Panini.

Gambi, Lucio, and Maria Cristina Gozzoli. 1982. *Milano*. Bari: Laterza.

Gasparini, Roberta. 1988. "La *Domus mercatorum* e le arti veronesi nel Trecento scaligero: Il codice degli statuti delle arti del 1319 e le sue aggiunte." In Gian Maria Varanini, ed. *Gli scaligeri, 1277–1387*, 343–50. Verona: Mondadori.

Gatti, Giuseppe, ed. 1885. *Statuti dei mercanti di Roma*. Rome: Tipografia della Pace di Filippo Cuggiani.

Gaudenzi, Augusto, ed. 1896. *Statuti delle società del popolo di Bologna*. 2 vols. Vol. 2: *Società delle arti*. Rome: Istituto Storico Italiano per il Medio Evo.

Geary, Patrick J. 1990. *Furta Sacra: Thefts of Relics in the Central Middle Ages*. Rev. ed. Princeton University Press.

Geertz, Clifford. 1979. "Suq: The Bazaar Economy in Sefrou." In Clifford Geertz, Hildred Geertz, and Lawrence Rosen. *Meaning and Order in Moroccan Society: Three Essays in Cultural Analysis*, 123–313. Cambridge University Press.

Ghignoli, Antonella, ed. 1998. *I brevi del comune e del popolo di Pisa dell'anno 1287*. Rome: Istituto Storico Italiano per il Medio Evo.

Giamboni, Bono. 1968. *Il libro de' vizî e delle virtudi e il trattato di virtú e di vizî*, ed. Cesare Segre. Turin: Einaudi.

Giansante, Massimo. 1998. *Retorica e politica nel Duecento: I notai bolognesi e l'ideologia comunale*. Rome: Istituto Storico Italiano per il Medio Evo.

Gibbs, Robert. 1999a. "In Search of Ambrogio Lorenzetti's Allegory of Justice: Changes to the Frescoes in the Palazzo Pubblico." *Apollo* 149, no. 447:11–16.

—. 1999b. "Antifonario N: A Bolognese Choirbook in the Context of Genoese Illumination between 1285 and 1385." In A. R. Calderoni Masetti, C. di Fabio, and M. Marcenaro, eds. *Tessuti, oreficerie, miniature in Liguria xiii–xv secolo*, 247–78. Bordighera: Istituto Internazionale di Studi Liguri.

Giordano da Pisa. 1997. *Prediche inedite (dal ms. Laurenziano, Acquisti e Doni 290)*, ed. Cecilia Iannella. Pisa: Edizioni ETS.

—. 2006. *Avventuale fiorentino 1304*, ed. Silvia Serventi. Bologna: Il Mulino.

Glass, Dorothy F. 2010. *The Sculpture of Reform in North Italy, ca. 1095–1130: History and Patronage of Romanesque Façades*. Farnham and Burlington, Vt: Ashgate.

Gloria, Andrea. 1873. *Statuti del comune di Padova dal secolo xii all'anno 1285*. Padua: Sacchetto.

Goldthwaite, Richard A. 1993. *Wealth and the Demand for Art in Italy, 1300–1600*. Baltimore and London: Johns Hopkins University Press.

—. 2009. *The Economy of Renaissance Florence*. Baltimore and London: Johns Hopkins University Press.

Greenblatt, Stephen. 1980. *Renaissance Self-Fashioning: From More to Shakespeare*. University of Chicago Press.

Greenstein, Jack M. 1988. "The Vision of Peace: Meaning and Representation in Ambrogio Lorenzetti's *Sala della Pace* Cityscapes." *Art History* 11: 492–510.

Greif, Avner. 2006. *Institutions and the Path to the Modern Economy: Lessons from Medieval Trade*. Cambridge and New York: Cambridge University Press.

Grillo, Paolo. 1998. "Spazi privati e spazi pubblici nella Milano medievale." *Studi storici* 39: 277–89.

—. 2001. *Milano in età comunale (1183–1276): Istituzioni, società, economia*. Spoleto: Centro Italiano di Studi sull'Alto Medioevo.

Grohmann, Alberto. 1981. *Perugia*. Rome and Bari: Laterza.

—. 1989. *Assisi*. Rome and Bari: Laterza.

Guidi, Jacopo d'Albizzotto. 1995. *El sommo della condizione di Vinegia*, ed. Marta Ceci. Rome: Zauli Arti Grafiche.

Gurevich, Aaron. 1995. *The Origins of European Individualism*, trans. Katharine Judelson. Oxford and Cambridge, Mass: Blackwell.

Hall, Edward T. [1959] 1980. *The Silent Language*. Reprint. Westport, Conn: Greenwood Press.

Hankins, James. 1995. "The 'Baron Thesis' after Forty Years and Some Recent Studies of Leonardo Bruni." *Journal of the History of Ideas* 56: 309–38.

Hansen, Sabine. 1987. *Die Loggia della Mercanzia in Siena*. Worms: Wernersche Verlagsgesellschaft.

Harris, Robin. 2003. *Dubrovnik: A History*. London: Saqi.

Herlihy, David. 1967. *Medieval and Renaissance Pistoia: The Social History of an Italian Town, 1200–1430*. New Haven and London: Yale University Press.

Herrad of Hohenbourg. 1979. *Hortus deliciarum*, ed. Rosalie Green et al. 2 vols. London: Warburg Institute.

Hessel, Alfred. [1910] 1975. *Storia della città di Bologna dal 1116 al 1280*, ed. Gina Fasoli. Bologna: Edizioni ALFA.

Hoven, Birgit van den. 1996. *Work in Ancient and Medieval Thought: Ancient Philosophers, Medieval Monks and Theologians and their Concept of Work,*

*Occupations and Technology*. Amsterdam: J. C. Gieben.

Howard, Deborah. 2000. *Venice and the East: The Impact of the Islamic World on Venetian Architecture, 1100–1500*. New Haven and London: Yale University Press.

Howell, Martha. 2000. "The Spaces of Late Medieval Urbanity." In Marc Boone and Peter Stabel, eds. *Shaping Urban Identity in Late Medieval Europe/ L'apparition d'une identité urbaine dans le bas moyen-âge*, 3–23. Leuven-Apeldoorn: Garant.

—. 2010. *Commerce before Capitalism in Europe, 1300–1600*. Cambridge and New York: Cambridge University Press.

Hubert, Hans W. 1993. *Der Palazzo comunale von Bologna: Vom Palazzo della Biada zum Palatium Apostolicum*. Cologne: Böhlau Verlag.

Huizinga, J. 1924. *The Waning of the Middle Ages: A Study of the Forms of Life, Thought and Art in France and the Netherlands in the XIVth and XVth Centuries*. London: Edward Arnold.

Humphrey, Lyle. 2007. "The Illumination of Confraternity and Guild Statutes in Venice, ca. 1260–1550: Mariegola Production, Iconography, and Use." Ph.D. Dissertation, New York University.

Hunt, Edwin S., and James M. Murray. 1999. *A History of Business in Medieval Europe, 1200–1550*. Cambridge and New York: Cambridge University Press.

Hyde, J. K. 1966a. "Medieval Descriptions of Cities." *Bulletin of the John Rylands Library* 48: 308–402.

—. 1966b. *Padua in the Age of Dante*. Manchester University Press.

—. 1973. *Society and Politics in Medieval Italy: The Evolution of Civil Life, 1000–1350*. New York: St. Martin's Press.

Iannella, Cecilia. 1999. *Giordano da Pisa: Etica urbana e forme della società*. Pisa: Edizioni ETS.

Inglese. G. 2005. "Latini, Brunetto," in *Dizionario biografico degli italiani* 64: 4–12.

Jed, Stephanie H. 1989. *Chaste Thinking: The Rape of Lucretia and the Birth of Humanism*. Bloomington and Indianapolis: Indiana University Press.

Jones, Philip. 1997. *The Italian City-State: From Commune to Signoria*. Oxford: Clarendon Press.

Kaftal, George (with Fabio Bisogni). 1978. *Iconography of the Saints in the Painting of North East Italy*. Florence: Sansoni.

Kempshall, M. S. 1999. *The Common Good in Late Medieval Political Thought*. Oxford: Clarendon Press.

Klapisch-Zuber, Christiane. 1985. *Women, Family, and Ritual in Renaissance Italy*, trans. Lydia G. Cochrane. Chicago and London: University of Chicago Press.

Kupfer, Marcia. 1996. "The Lost Wheel Map of Ambrogio Lorenzetti." *Art Bulletin* 78: 286–310.

Lanconelli, A. 1985. "Gli *Statuta pescivendulorum Urbis* (1405): Note sul commercio del pesce a Roma fra XIV e XV secolo." *Archivio della società romana di storia patria* 108: 83–131.

Lane, Frederic C. 1966. "At the Roots of Republicanism." *American Historical Review* 71: 403–20.

—. 1973. *Venice: A Maritime Republic*. Baltimore: Johns Hopkins University Press.

*Lanfranco e Wiligelmo: Il duomo di Modena*. 1984. Modena: Edizioni Panini.

Langer, U. 1999. "The Renaissance Novella as Justice." *Renaissance Quarterly* 52: 311–41.

Langholm, Odd. 1992. *Economics in the Medieval Schools: Wealth, Exchange, Value, Money and Usury according to the Paris Theological Tradition, 1200–1350*. Leiden and New York: E. J. Brill.

—. 2003. *The Merchant in the Confessional: Trade and Price in the Pre-Reformation Penitential Handbooks*. Leiden and Boston: Brill.

Lansing, Carol. 1997. "Gender and Civic Authority: Sexual Control in a Medieval Italian Town." *Journal of Social History* 31: 33–59.

Lattes, Alessandro. 1884. *Il diritto commerciale nella legislazione statutaria delle città italiane*. Milan: Ulrico Hoepli.

Latini, Brunetto. 1824. *Il Tesoretto e il Favoletto di ser Brunetto Latini*, ed. Giovanni Battista Zannoni. Florence: Giuseppe Molini.

—. 1968. *La rettorica*, ed. Francesco Maggini. Florence: Felice Le Monnier.

—. 1981. *Il Tesoretto (The Treasure)*, ed. and trans. Julia Bolton Holloway. New York and London: Garland.

Lefebvre, Henri. [1974] 1991. *The Production of Space*, trans. Donald Nicholson-Smith. Oxford: Blackwell.

Legnani, Alessia. 2005. *La giustizia dei mercanti: L'universitas mercatorum, campsorum et artificium di Bologna e i suoi statuti del 1400*. Bologna: Bononia University Press.

LeGoff, Jacques. 1980. *Time, Work, and Culture in the Middle Ages*, trans. Arthur Goldhammer. Chicago and London: University of Chicago Press.

Lesnick, Daniel R. 1989. *Preaching in Renaissance Florence: The Social World of Franciscan and Dominican Spirituality*. Athens and London: University of Georgia Press.

Levin, Joan. 2004. "Antonio Pucci." In Christopher Kleinhenz, ed. *Medieval Italy: An Encyclopedia*. 2 vols. Vol. 2, 42–3. New York and London: Routledge.

Liberali, Giuseppe, ed. 1950–55. *Gli statuti del comune di Treviso*. 3 vols. Venice: Deputazione di Storia Patria per le Venezie.

Lieto, Alba di. 1998. "Una piazza comunale e scaligera: Piazza delle Erbe." In Gian Maria Varanini, ed. *Gli scaligeri, 1277–1387*, 245–54. Verona: Mondadori.

Little, Lester K. 1971. "Pride goes before Avarice: Social Change and the Vices in Latin Christendom." *American Historical Review* 76: 16–49.

—. 1978. *Religious Poverty and the Profit Economy in Medieval Europe*. Ithaca, N.Y.: Cornell University Press.

Lopez, Robert S. 1971. *The Commercial Revolution of the Middle Ages, 950–1350*. Englewood Cliffs, N.J.: Prentice-Hall.

—, and Irving W. Raymond. 1955. *Medieval Trade in the Mediterranean World*. New York and London: Columbia University Press.

Lugli, Emmanuele. 2010. "Hidden in Plain Sight: The *Pietre di Paragone* and the Preeminence of Medieval Measurements in Communal Italy." *Gesta* 49: 77–95.

Lusanna, Enrica Neri. 2001. "Interni fiorentini e pittura profana tra Duecento e Trecento: Cacce e giostre a Palazzo Cerchi." In Klaus Bergdolt and Giorgio Bonsanti, eds. *Opere e giorni: Studi su mille anni di arte europea dedicati a Max Seidel*, 123–30. Venice: Marsilio.

Luzzati, Michele. 1974. "S. Martino alla Pietra di Pesce e le pescherie o piazze del pesce di Pisa." *Antichità pisane* 1: 21–4.

Mainoni, Patrizia. 1975. "Un mercante milanese del primo Quattrocento: Marco Serraineri." *Nuova rivista storica* 59: 331–77.

Marchesan, Angelo. [1923] 1990. *Treviso medievale: Istituzioni, usi, costumi, aneddoti, curiosità*. 2 vols. Reprint. Bologna: Atesa Editrice.

Marina, Areli. 2011. "From the Myth to the Margins: The Patriarch's Piazza at San Pietro di Castello in Venice." *Renaissance Quarterly* 64: 353–429.

—. 2012. *The Italian Piazza Transformed: Parma in the Communal Age*. University Park: Pennsylvania State University Press.

Marri, Giulia Camerani, ed. 1955. *Statuti dell'arte del cambio di Firenze (1299–1316) con aggiunte e correzioni fino al 1320*. Florence: Leo S. Olschki.

—. 1960. *Statuti delle arti dei correggiai, tavolacciai e scudai, dei vaiai e pellicciai di Firenze (1338–1386)*. Florence: Leo S. Olschki.

Marshall, Richard K. 1999. *The Local Merchants of Prato*. Baltimore and London: Johns Hopkins University Press.

Martin, Alfred von. [1932] 1944. *Sociology of the Renaissance*. New York: Oxford University Press.

Martin, John Jeffries. 2002. "The Myth of Renaissance Individualism." In Guido Ruggiero, ed. *A Companion to the Worlds of the Renaissance*, 208–24. Oxford: Blackwell.

—. 2004. *Myths of Renaissance Individualism*. Houndmills and New York: Palgrave Macmillan.

Masi, Gino. 1931. "La pittura infamante nella legislazione e nella vita del comune fiorentino (sec. XIII–XVI)." In *Studi di diritto commerciale in onore di Cesare Vivante*. 2 vols. 2: 625–57. Rome: Società Editrice del Foro Italiano.

—, ed. 1934. *Statutum bladi reipublicae florentinae (1348)*. Milan: Società Editrice Vita e Pensiero.

Matteis, Maria Consiglia de. 1968. "Il *De bono communi* di Remigio de' Girolami (†1319)." *Annali dell'università di Lecce: Facoltà di lettere e filosofia e di magistero* 3: 13–86.

—. 1977. *La "teologia politica comunale" di Remigio de' Girolami*. Bologna: Pàtron Editore.

Mazzaoui, Maureen Fennell. 1981. *The Italian Cotton Industry in the Later Middle Ages, 1100–1600*. Cambridge and New York: Cambridge University Press.

Mazzi, Maria Serena. 1998. "La vita in città giorno dopo giorno." In Giovanni Cherubini, ed. *Storia di Pistoia*, 4 vols. Vol. 2: *L'età del libero comune: Dall'inizio del xii alla metà del xiv secolo*, 386–415. Florence: Felice Le Monnier.

McLean, Alick M. 2008. *Prato: Architecture, Piety, and Political Identity in a Tuscan City-State*. New Haven and London: Yale University Press.

Miller, Maureen C. 1995. "From Episcopal to Communal Palaces: Places and Power in Northern Italy (1000–1250)," *Journal of the Society of Architectural Historians* 54: 175–85.

—. 1996. "Vescovi, palazzi e lo sviluppo dei centri civici nelle città dell'Italia settentrionale, 1000–1250." In Franco Spinelli, ed. *Albertano da Brescia: Alle origini del razionalismo economico, dall'umanesimo civile, della grande Europa*, 27–41. Brescia: Grafo.

—. 2000. *The Bishop's Palace: Architecture and Authority in Medieval Italy*. Ithaca, N.Y. and London: Cornell University Press.

—. 2001. "The Medici Renovation of the Florentine Arcivescovado." *I Tatti Studies: Essays in the Renaissance* 9: 89–117.

Modigliani, Anna. 1998. *Mercati, botteghe e spazi di commercio a Roma tra medioevo ed età moderna*. Rome: Roma nel Rinascimento.

Modonesi, Denise. 1988. "Iscrizioni di epoca scaligera del Museo del Castelvecchio: Scipione Maffei e la riscoperta del medievo." In Gian Maria Varanini, ed. *Gli scaligeri, 1277–1387*, 567–78. Verona: Mondadori.

Molho, Anthony. 1979. "Cosimo de Medici: *Pater Patriae* or Padrino?" *Stanford Italian Review* 1: 5–33.

Montagnani, Katiuscia. 2009. "Il patrimonio artistico del palagio dell'Arte della lana/The Wool Palace Artwork." In *Il palagio dell'Arte della lana dalle origini ad oggi/The Wool Guild Palace Since its*

*Origins*, 45–67. Florence: Società Dantesca Italiana.

Montenach, Anne. 2006. "Une économie de l'ombre? La fraude dans le commerce alimentaire à Lyon au XVIIe siècle." In Gérard Béaur, Hubert Bonin, and Claire Lemercier, eds. *Fraude, contrefaçon et contrebande de l'antiquité à nos jours*, 515–38. Geneva: Librairie Droz.

Monticolo, Giovanni, ed. 1896–1914. *I capitolari delle arti veneziane*. 3 vols. Rome: Forzani e c. Tip. del Senato.

Mor, Carlo Guido. 1963. "Il Palazzo della ragione nella vita di Padova." In *Il Palazzo della ragione di Padova*, 1–20. Vicenza: N. Pozza.

Morandini, Francesca, ed. 1956. *Statuti delle arti dei fornai e dei vinattieri di Firenze (1337–1339) con appendice di documenti relativi alle arti dei farsettai e dei tintori (1378–1379)*. Florence: Leo S. Olschki.

—, ed. 1961. *Statuti delle arti degli oliandoli e pizzicagnoli e dei beccai di Firenze (1318–1346)*. Florence: Leo S. Olschki.

Morelli, Giovanni di Pagolo. 1956. *Ricordi*, ed. Vittore Branca. Florence: Felice Le Monnier.

Moretti, Italo. 1998. "Le pietre della città." In Giovanni Cherubini, ed. *Storia di Pistoia*. 4 vols. Vol. 2: *L'età del libero comune: Dall'inizio del xii alla metà del xiv secolo*, 227–74. Florence: Felice Le Monnier.

Moriani Antonelli, Margherita. 1996. *Statuto di Spoleto del 1347 con additiones del 1348 e del 1364*. Spoleto: Ed. dell'Accademia Spoletina.

Morpurgo, Salomone. 1933. "Bruto, 'il buon giudice,' nell'Udienza dell'Arte della lana in Firenze." In *Miscellanea di storia dell'arte in onore di Igino Benvenuto Supino*, 141–63. Florence: L. S. Olschki.

Morris, Colin. 1972. *The Discovery of the Individual, 1050–1200*. Reprint 1987. University of Toronto Press.

Mueller, Reinhold C. 1997. *The Venetian Money Market: Banks, Panics, and the Public Debt 1200–1500*. Baltimore and London: Johns Hopkins University Press.

Muir, Edward. 1981. *Civic Ritual in Renaissance Venice*. Princeton University Press.

Muldrew, Craig. 1998. *The Economy of Obligation: The Culture of Credit and Social Relations in Early Modern England*. Houndmills, Basingstoke: Palgrave.

Muzzarelli, Maria Giuseppina. 2005. *Pescatori di uomini: Predicatori e piazze alla fine del medioevo*. Bologna: Società Editrice il Mulino.

—. 2007. "Il credito al consumo in Italia: Dai banchi ebraici ai Monti di pietà." In Franco Franceschi, Richard A. Goldthwaite, and Reinhold C. Mueller, eds. *Il rinascimento italiano e l'europa*. vol. 4: *Commercio e cultura mercantile*, 567–89. Treviso: Angelo Colla Editore.

Najemy, John. 1982. *Corporatism and Consensus in Florentine Electoral Politics*. Chapel Hill: University of North Carolina Press.

Nari, Monica Chiellini. 1991. "Le favole, i simboli, il 'ciclo di Artù': Il fronte istoriato nella 'Porta della Pescheria'." In *La Porta della Pescheria nel duomo di Modena*, 32–59. Modena: Franco Cosimo Panini.

Naso, Irma, ed. 1985. *Una bottega di panni alla fine del Trecento: Giovanni Canale di Pinerolo e il suo libro di conti*. Università di Genova, Istituto di Medievistica.

Nelli, Renzo, and Giuliano Pinto, eds. 2002a. *Statuti pistoiesi del secolo xiii: Studi e testi*. Vol. 1: *Studi*. Pistoia: Società Pistoiese di Storia Patria.

—. 2002b. *Statuti pistoiesi del secolo xiii: Studi e testi*. Vol. 2 [1891]: *Breve et ordinamenta populi pistorii (1284)*, ed. Lodovico Zdekauer. Reprint. Pistoia: Società Pistoiese di Storia Patria.

—. 2002c. *Statuti pistoiesi del secolo xiii: Studi e testi*. Vol. 3 [1888]: *Statutum potestatis comunis pistorii (1296)*, ed. Lodovico Zdekauer. Reprint. Pistoia: Società Pistoiese di Storia Patria.

Nelli, Sergio, and Maria Trapani. 1991. "Giovanni Sercambi: Documenti e fatti della vita familiare." In *Giovanni Sercambi e il suo tempo: Catalogo della mostra (Lucca, 30 novembre 1991)*, 33–100 Lucca: Nuova Graffica Lucchese.

Neri, Francesco. 1998. "Attività manifatturiere, mercato ed arti." In Giovanni Cherubini, ed. *Storia di Pistoia*. 4 vols. Vol. 2: *L'età del libero comune: Dall'inizio del xii alla metà del xiv secolo*, 121–53. Florence: Felice Le Monnier.

Nevola, Fabrizio. 2007. *Siena: Constructing the Renaissance City*. New Haven and London: Yale University Press.

Newett, M. Margaret, 1907. "The Sumptuary Laws of Venice in the Fourteenth and Fifteenth Centuries." In T. F. Tout and James Tait, eds. *Historical Essays*, 245–78. Manchester University Press.

Niccolò da Poggibonsi. 1990. "Libro d'oltramare." In Antonio Lanza and Marcellina Troncarelli, eds. *Pellegrini scrittori: Viaggiatori toscani del Trecento in Terrasanta*, 31–158. Florence: Ponte alle Grazie.

Norman, Joanne S. 1988. *Metamorphoses of an Allegory: The Iconography of the Psychomachia in Medieval Art*. New York: Peter Lang.

Occhipinti, Elisa. 1991. "Immagini di città: Le 'laudes civitatum' e le rappresentazioni dei centri urbani nell'Italia settentrionale." *Società e storia* 51: 23–52.

Origo, Iris. 1957. *The Merchant of Prato: Francesco di Marco Datini, 1335–1410*. New York: Alfred A. Knopf.

Ortalli, Gherardo. 1979. *"Pingatur in palatio": La pittura infamante nei secoli xiii–xvi*. Rome: Jouvence.

—. 1993. "Introduzione." In Alessandra Princivalli and Gherardo Ortalli, eds. *Il capitolare degli ufficiali sopra Rialto: Nei luoghi al centro del sistema economico veneziano (secoli xiii–xiv)*, vii–xxvi. Milan: Editrice La Storia.

Pächt, Otto. 1950. "Early Italian Nature Studies and the Early Calendar Landscape." *Journal of the Warburg and Courtauld Institutes* 13: 13–47.

Pancotti, Vincenzo, ed. 1925–29. *I paratici piacentini e i loro statuti*. 3 vols. Piacenza: Tipografia Editrice A. del Maino.

Pandimiglio, Leonida. 1974. "Giovanni di Pagolo Morelli e la ragion di famiglia." In *Studi sul medioevo cristiano offerti a Raffaello Morghen*, 2 vols, 2: 553–608. Rome: Istituto Storico Italiano per il Medio Evo.

Paoletti, John T. 1993. "'. . . ha fatto Piero con voluntà del padre . . .': Piero de'Medici and Corporate Commissions of Art." In Andreas Beyer and Bruce Boucher, eds. *Piero de' Medici, "Il Gottoso" (1416–1469): Kunst im Dienste der Mediceer/ Art in the Service of the Medici*, 221–50. Berlin: Akademie Verlag.

Partsch, Susanna. 1981. *Profane Buchmalerei der bürgerlichen Gesellschaft im spätmittelalterlichen Florenz: Der Specchio Umano des Getreidehändlers Domenico Lenzi*. Worms: Werner'sche Verlagsgesellschaft.

Paul, Jürgen. 1969. "Commercial Use of Mediaeval Town Halls in Italy." *Journal of the Society of Architectural Historians* 28: 222.

Pausch, Oskar. 1972. *Das älteste italienisch–deutsche Sprachbuch: Eine Überlieferung aus dem Jahre 1424 nach Georg von Nürnberg*. Vienna: Böhlau in Komm.

Pazzi, Piero, ed. 1998. *Dizionario biografico degli orefici, argentieri, gioiellieri . . . della repubblica aristocratica di Venezia*. Treviso: Grafiche Crivellari.

Peraldo, Guilielmo. 1546. *Summae virtutum, ac vitiorum, tomus secundus*. Lyon: Sub Scuto Coloniensi.

Pertile, Antonio. 1966. *Storia del diritto italiano dalla caduta dell'impero romano alla codificazione*. 6 vols. 2nd ed. Bologna: Arnaldo Forni Editore.

Petrucci, Armando, ed. 1958. *Notarii: Documenti per la storia del notariato italiano*. Milan: Editrice Dott. A. Giuffrè.

Piasentini, Stefano. 1992. *"Alla luce della luna": I furti a Venezia, 1270–1403*. Venice: Il Cardo.

—, ed. 2009. *Cassiere della Bolla ducale: Grazie, Registro n. 16 (1364–1372): Anticamente Liber gratiarum XIII*. 2 vols. Venice: Il Comitato Editore.

Pierotti, Romano. 1975–76. "Aspetti del mercato e della produzione a Perugia fra la fine del secolo xiv e la prima metà del xv: La bottega di cuoiame di Niccolò di Martino di Pietro." *Bolletino della deputazione di storia patria per l'Umbria* 72 (1975): 79–185; 73 (1976): 1–131.

Pincus, Debra. 2000. *The Tombs of the Doges of Venice*. New York: Cambridge University Press.

Pini, Antonio Ivan. 1962. "L'arte del cambio a Bologna nel xiii secolo." *L'archiginnasio* 57: 20–81.

Pini, Raffaella. 2011. *Le giustizie dipinte: La raffigurazione della giustizia nella Bologna rinascimentale*. Argelato (Bologna): Minerva Edizioni.

Pinto, Giuliano, ed. 1978. *Il libro del biadaiolo: Carestie e annona a Firenze dalla metà del '200 al 1348*. Florence: L. S. Olschki.

Plaissance, Michel. 1985. "Les rapports ville-campagne dans les nouvelles de Sacchetti, Sercambi et Sermini." In *Culture et société en Italie du moyen-âge à la renaissance: Hommage à André Rochona*, 61–73. Paris: Université de la Sorbonne Nouvelle.

Poggi, Giovanni, ed. [1909] 1988. *Il duomo di Firenze: Documenti sulla decorazione della chiesa e del campanile tratti dall'archivio dell'opera*, ed. Margaret Haines. 2 vols. Reprint. Florence: Edizioni Medicea.

Poliakov, Léon. 1965. *Les banchieri juifs et le saint-siège du xiiie au xviie siècle*. Paris: École Pratique des Hautes Études.

Polidori, Filippo Luigi, and Luciano Banchi, eds. 1863–77. *Statuti senesi scritti in volgare ne' secoli xiii e xiv*. 3 vols. Bologna: G. Romagnoli.

Polzer, Joseph. 2002. "Ambrogio Lorenzetti's *War and Peace* Murals Revisited: Contributions to the Meaning of the *Good Government Allegory*." *Artibus et historiae* 45: 65–105.

Pozza, Marco. 1988. "Podestà e funzionari veneziani a Treviso e nella Marca in età comunale." In Gherardo Ortalli and Michael Knapton, eds. *Istituzioni, società, e potere nella marca trevigiana e veronese (secoli xii–xiv): Sulle trace di G. B. Verci*, 291–303. Rome: Istituto Storico Italiano per il Medio Evo.

Pope-Hennessy, John. 1955. *Italian Gothic Sculpture*. New York: Phaidon.

—. 1993. *Donatello Sculptor*. New York: Abbeville Press.

Princivalli, Alessandra. 1993. "Il capitolare degli ufficiali sopra Rialto." In Alessandra Princivalli and Gherardo Ortalli, eds. *Il capitolare degli ufficiali sopra Rialto: Nei luoghi al centro del sistema economico veneziano (secoli xiii–xiv)*, xxvii–lx. Milan: Editrice La Storia.

—, and Gherardo Ortalli, eds. 1993. *Il capitolare degli ufficiali sopra Rialto: Nei luoghi al centro del sistema economico veneziano (secoli xiii–xiv)*. Milan: Editrice La Storia.

Prodi, Paolo. 2009. *Settimo non rubare: Furto e mercato nella storia dell'occidente*. Bologna: Società Editrice il Mulino.

Prudentius, Aurelius Clemens. 1949–53. *Prudentius*, trans. H. J. Thomson. 2 vols, vol. 1: *Psychomachia*.

Loeb Classical Library. Cambridge, Mass: Harvard University Press.

Prudlo, Donald. 2008. *The Martyred Inquisitor: The Life and Cult of Peter of Verona (†1252)*. Aldershot: Ashgate.

Puppi, Lionello and Mario Universo. 1982. *Padova*. Bari: Editori Laterza.

Randolph, Adrian W. B. 2002. *Engaging Symbols: Gender, Politics, and Public Art in Fifteenth-Century Florence*. New Haven and London: Yale University Press.

Rauty, Natale. 1981a. *L'antico palazzo dei vescovi a Pistoia*. Vol. 1: *Storia e restauro*. Florence: L. S. Olschki.

—. 1981b. "Intervento del comune nel controllo delle misure a Pistoia (secoli xii–xv)." In *Civiltà ed economia agricola in Toscana nei sec. xiii–xv: Problemi della vita delle campagne nel tardo medioevo*, 357–77. Pistoia: Centro Italiano di Studi di Storia e d'Arte.

—. 1988. *Storia di Pistoia*. 4 vols. Vol. 1: *Dall'alto medioevo all'età precomunale*, 406–1105. Florence: Felice Le Monnier.

—. 1991. "Schede storiche dei palazzi pistoiesi." In Nori Andreini Galli, ed. *Palazzi pistoiesi*, 265–311. Lucca: Maria Pacini Fazzi Editore.

—. 1998. "Capitolo 1: Società, istituzioni, politica nel primo secolo dell'autonomia comunale." In Giovanni Cherubini, ed. *Storia di Pistoia*. 4 vols. Vol. 2: *L'età del libero comune: Dall'inizio del xii alla metà del xiv secolo*, 1–40. Florence: Felice Le Monnier.

—, ed. 1996. *Statuti pistoiesi del secolo xii: Breve dei consoli (1140–1180), statuto del Podestà (1162–1180)*. Pistoia: Società Pistoiese di Storia Patria.

—, and Giancarlo Savino, eds. 1977. *Lo statuto dei consoli del comune di Pistoia: Frammento del secolo xii*. Pistoia: Società Pistoiese di Storia Patria.

Re, Camillo, ed. 1883. *Statuti della città di Roma del secolo xiv*. Rome: Tipografia della Pace.

Rebhorn, Wayne A. 1988. *Foxes and Lions: Machiavelli's Confidence Men*. Ithaca, N.Y., and London: Cornell University Press.

Redi, Fabio. 1986. "Le strutture produttive e distribuzione nell'edilizia e nel tessuto urbano di Pisa medievale: Fonti documentarie, iconografiche, materiali." In *Mercati e consumi: Organizzazione e qualificazione del commercio in Italia dal xii al xx secolo*, 647–70. Modena: Istituto Formazione Operatori Aziendali.

—. 1991. *Pisa com'era: Archeologia, urbanistica e strutture materiali (secoli v–xiv)*. Pisa: GISEM.

Ricci, Giovanni. 1980. *Bologna*. Bari: Laterza.

Ridolfi, E. 1882. *L'arte in Lucca studiata nella sua cattedrale*. Lucca: B. Canovetti.

Riess, Jonathan B. 1981a. *Political Ideals in Medieval Italian Art: The Frescoes in the Palazzo dei Priori, Perugia (1297)*. Ann Arbor: UMI Research Press.

—. 1981b. "Uno studio iconografico della decorazione ad affresco del 1297 nel Palazzo dei Priori a Perugia." *Bollettino d'arte* ser. 6, 66: 43–58.

Rigobello, Maria Beatrice, and Francesco Autizi. 2008. *Palazzo della ragione di Padova: Simbologie degli astri e rappresentazioni del governo*. Padua: Il Poligrafo.

Ripa, Cesare. 1976. *Iconologia (Padua 1611)*. New York and London: Garland.

Riva, Bonvesin de la. 1974. *De magnalibus Mediolani/ Le meraviglie di Milano* (1288), trans. Maria Corti. Milan: Bompiani.

Rizzi, Alberto. 1987. *Scultura esterna a Venezia: Corpus delle sculture erratiche all'aperto di Venezia e della sua laguna*. Venice: Stamperia di Venezia.

Roach, Andrew P. 2005. *The Devil's World: Heresy and Society 1100–1300*. Harrow: Pearson Longman.

Roberti, Melchiorre, ed. 1902. *Le corporazioni padovane d'arti e mestieri: Studio storico-giuridico con documenti e statuti inediti*. Memorie del Reale Istituto Veneto di Scienze, Lettere ed Arti, 26: 8. Venice: Officine Grafiche di Carlo Ferrari.

—, ed. 1906–11. *Le magistrature giudiziarie veneziane e i loro capitolari fino al 1300*. 3 vols. Padua: Deputazione Veneta di Storia Patria.

Romano, Dennis. 1987. "The Aftermath of the Querini-Tiepolo Conspiracy in Venice." *Stanford Italian Review* 7: 147–59.

Rosenthal, David. 1999. "The Genealogy of Empires: Ritual Politics and State Building in Early Modern Florence." *I Tatti Studies: Essays in the Renaissance* 8: 197–234.

Rossebastiano Bart, A. 1976. "Serie di proverbi in lessici italiano-tedeschi del sec. xv." *Giornale storico della letteratura italiana* 153: 549–65.

—, ed. 1983. *Vocabolari veneto–tedeschi del secolo xv*. 3 vols. Savigliano: Edizioni l'Artistica.

Rosser, Gervase. 1997. "Crafts, Guilds, and the Negotiation of Work in the Medieval Town." *Past and Present* 154: 3–31.

Rossi, Elisabetta Antoniazzi, ed. 2007. *Palazzo della Ragione a Padova*. Milan: Skira.

Rowley, George. 1958. *Ambrogio Lorenzetti*. 2 vols. Princeton University Press.

Rubinstein, Nicolai. 1958. "Political Ideas in Sienese Art: The Frescoes by Ambrogio Lorenzetti and Taddeo di Bartolo in the Palazzo Pubblico." *Journal of the Warburg and Courtauld Institutes* 21: 179–207.

—. 1995. *The Palazzo Vecchio, 1298–1532: Government, Architecture, and Imagery in the Civic Palace of the Florentine Republic*. Oxford: Clarendon Press.

Ruck, Germaid. 1989. "Brutus als Modell des guten Richters: Bild und Rhetorik in einem Florentiner Zunftgebäude." In Hans Belting and Dieter Blume, eds. *Malerei und Stadtkultur in der Dantezeit: Die Argumentation der Bilder*, 115–31. Munich: Hirmer Verlag.

Sacchetti, Franco. 1990. *Il libro delle rime*, ed. Franca Brambilla Ageno. Florence: Leo S. Olschki.

Salimbene de Adam. 1986. *The Chronicle of Salimbene de Adam*, trans. Joseph L. Baird, Giuseppe Baglivi, and John Robert Kane. Binghamton, N.Y.: Medieval and Renaissance Texts and Studies.

—. 1998–9. *Cronica*, ed. Giuseppe Scalia. 2 vols. Turnhout: Brepols.

Salvatori, Enrica. 1994. "Spazi mercantili e commerciali a Milano nel medioevo: La vocazione del centro." In A. Grohmann, ed. *Spazio urbano e organizzazione economica nell'Europa medievale*, 243–66. Naples: Edizioni Scientifiche Italiane.

Sandler, Lucy Freeman, ed. 1999. *The Psalter of Robert of Lisle in the British Library*. London: Harvey Miller Publishers.

Sapegno, Natalino, ed. 1952. *Poeti minori del Trecento*. Milan and Naples: Riccardo Ricciardi Editore.

Sapori, Armando. 1932. *Una compagnia di Calimala ai primi del Trecento*. Florence: L. S. Olschki.

Saxl, Fritz. 1942. "A Spiritual Encyclopaedia of the Later Middle Ages." *Journal of the Warburg and Courtauld Institutes* 5: 82–134.

Schulz, Juergen. 1991. "Civic Urbanism in Medieval Venice." In Anthony Molho, Kurt Raaflaub, and Julia Emlen, eds. *City States in Classical Antiquity and Medieval Italy*, 419–45. Ann Arbor: University of Michigan Press.

Scott, James. 1985. *Weapons of the Weak: Everyday Forms of Peasant Resistance*. New Haven and London: Yale University Press.

Seidel, Max. 1997. "Vanagloria: Studien zur Ikonographie der Fresken des Ambrogio Lorenzetti in der 'Sala della Pace.'" *Städel-Jahrbuch*. ser. 2, 16: 35–90.

—. 1999. *Dolce vita: Ambrogio Lorenzettis Porträt des Sienseser Staates*. Basel: Schwabe and Co.

Semenzato, Camillo. 1963. "L'architettura del Palazzo della Ragione." In Carlo Guido Mor, ed. *Il Palazzo della ragione di Padova*, 21–44. Vicenza: N. Pozza.

Sercambi, Giovanni. 1995. *Novelle*, ed. Giovanni Sinicropi. 2 vols. Florence: Editrice Le Lettere.

Sframeli, Maria, ed. 1989. *Il centro di Firenze restituito: Affreschi e frammenti lapidei nel Museo di San Marco.* Florence: Alberto Bruschi.

Sgrilli, Paola, ed. 2003. *Testi viterbesi dei secoli xiv, xv, e xvi*. Viterbo: Sette Città.

Shaw, James E. 2006. *The Justice of Venice: Authorities and Liberties in the Urban Economy, 1500–1700*. Oxford University Press.

—, and Evelyn Welch. 2011. *Making and Marketing Medicine in Renaissance Florence*. Amsterdam and New York: Rodopi.

Sherman, Claire Richter. 1995. *Imaging Aristotle: Verbal and Visual Representation in Fourteenth-Century France*. Berkeley, Los Angeles, and London: University of California Press.

Siddons, Hilary. 1999. "The *Tractatus de Septem Vitiis Capitalibus* by Henry of Rimini O.P." *Medioevo* 25:313–440.

Simeoni, Luigi., ed. 1914. *Gli antichi statuti delle arti veronesi secondo la revisione scaligera del 1319 con una notizia sull'origine delle corporazioni a Verona.* Venice: A Spese della Società.

Skinner, Quentin. 1986. "The Artist as Political Philosoper." *Proceedings of the British Academy* 72: 1–56.

—. 1989. "Ambrogio Lorenzetti: The Artist as Political Philosopher." In Hans Belting and Dieter Blume, eds. *Malerei und Stadtkultur in der Dantezeit: Die Argumentation der Bilder*, 85–103. Munich: Hirmer Verlag.

—. 1999. "Ambrogio Lorenzetti's Buon Governo Frescoes: Two Old Questions, Two New Answers." *Journal of the Warburg and Courtauld Institutes* 62: 1–28.

Slepian, Marcie Freedman. 1987. "Merchant Ideology in the Renaissance: Guild Hall Decoration in Florence, Siena, and Perugia." Ph.D. dissertation, Yale University.

Spagnesi, Annalisa Bricoli. 1992. "Su alcune pitture nella sala d'udienza del palazzo dell'Arte della lana a Firenze." *Antichità viva* 31, 2: 5–10.

Spallanzani, Marco. 2007. *Oriental Rugs in Renaissance Florence*. Florence: Studio per Edizioni Scelte.

Starn, Randolph. 1987. "The Republican Regime of the 'Room of Peace' in Siena, 1338–40." *Representations* 18: 1–32.

Stevenson, Enrico, ed. 1893. *Statuti delle arti dei merciai e della lana di Roma*. Rome: Tipografia Poliglotta.

Stock, Brian. 1983. *The Implications of Literacy: Written Language and Models of Interpretation in the Eleventh and Twelfth Centuries*. Princeton University Press.

Strata, Zanobi da. 1852. *I morali di San Gregorio Magno Papa volgarizzati nel secolo xiv da Zanobi da Strata.* 3 vols. Verona: Stabilimento Tipografico Eredi di Marco Moroni.

Strozzi, Alessandra Macinghi. 1997. *Selected Letters of Alessandra Strozzi*, trans. Heather Gregory. Berkeley, Los Angeles, and London: University of California Press.

Stussi, Alfredo, ed. 1967. *Zibaldone da Canal: Manoscritto mercantile del secolo xiv*. Venice: Comitato per la Pubblicazione delle Fonti Relative alla Storia di Venezia.

Subbioni, Marina. 2003. *La miniatura perugina del Trecento: Contributo alla storia della pittura in Umbria nel quattordicesimo secolo.* 2 vols. Perugia: Guerra Edizioni.

Suppa, Nicola, ed. 1971. *Lo statuto dell'arte dei calzolai di Assisi (1377).* Assisi: Tipografia Porziuncola.

Swetz, Frank J. 2002. "*Figura mercantesco:* Merchants and the Evolution of a Number Concept in the Later Middle Ages." In John J. Contreni and Santa Casciani, eds. *Word, Image, Number: Communication in the Middle Ages*, 391–412. Florence: Sismel/Edizioni del Galluzzo.

Tabacco, Giovanni. 1989. *The Struggle for Power in Medieval Italy: Structures of Political Rule,* trans. Rosalind Brown Jensen. Cambridge University Press.

Terpstra, Nicholas. 2008. "Theory into Practice: Executions, Comforting, and Comforters in Renaissance Italy." In Nicholas Terpstra, ed. *The Art of Executing Well: Rituals of Execution in Renaissance Italy*, 118–158. Kirksville: Truman State University Press.

Tirelli, Vito, ed. [1867] 1991. *Statutum Lucani Communis an. MCCCVIII.* Reprint. Lucca: Maria Pacini Fazzi Editore.

Todeschini, Giacomo. 1994. *Il prezzo della salvezza: Lessici medievali di pensiero economico.* Rome: La Nuova Italia Scientifica.

—. 2004. *Ricchezza francescana. Dalla povertà volontaria alla società di mercato.* Bologna: Il Mulino.

—. 2008. "Theological Roots of the Medieval/ Modern Merchants' Self-Representation." In Margaret C. Jacob and Catherine Secretan, eds. *The Self-Perception of Early Modern Capitalists*, 17–46. New York: Palgrave.

—. [2004] 2009. *Franciscan Wealth: From Voluntary Poverty to Market Society,* trans. Donatella Melucci. St. Bonaventure, New York: Franciscan Institute.

Tolaini, Emilio. 1992. *Pisa.* Rome and Bari: Laterza.

Tozzi, Pierluigi, and Massimiliano David. 1993. "Opicino de Canistris e Galvano Fiamma: L'imagine della città e del territorio nel Trecento lombardo." In *La pittura in Lombardia: Il Trecento*, 339–61. Milan: Electa Lombardia.

Trachtenberg, Marvin. 1988. "What Brunelleschi Saw: Monument and Site at the Palazzo Vecchio in Florence." *Journal of the Society of Architectural Historians* 47: 14–44.

—. 1997. *Dominion of the Eye: Urbanism, Art, and Power in Early Modern Florence.* Cambridge and New York: Cambridge University Press.

Trexler, Richard C. 1980. *Public Life in Renaissance Florence.* New York: Academic Press.

Tuliani, Maurizio. 1998. "Il Campo di Siena: Un mercato cittadino in epoca comunale." *Quaderni medievali* 46: 59–100.

Ugolini, Francesco A. 1986. *Voci di venditori in un mercato romano alla fine del Trecento.* Perugia: Opera del Vocabulario Dialettale Umbro.

Villani, Giovanni. [1823] 1980. *Cronica di Giovanni Villani.* Reprint. 8 vols. Rome: Multigrafica Editrice.

Waley, Daniel Philip. 1969. *The Italian City-Republics.* New York: McGraw-Hill.

Weissman, Ronald F. E. 1982. *Ritual Brotherhood in Renaissance Florence.* New York: Academic Press.

—. 1989. "Importance of Being Ambiguous: Social Relations, Individualism , and Identity in Renaissance Florence." In Susan Zimmerman and Ronald F. E. Weissman, eds. *Urban Life in the Renaissance*, 269–80. Newark: University of Delaware Press.

Welch, Evelyn. 2005. *Shopping in the Renaissance: Consumer Cultures in Italy, 1400–1600.* New Haven and London: Yale University Press.

Wieruszowski, Helene. 1944. "Art and the Commune in the Time of Dante." *Speculum* 19: 14–33.

Wilk, Sarah Blake. 1986. "Donatello's *Dovizia* as an Image of Florentine Political Propaganda." *Artibus et historiae* 14: 9–28.

Wilkins, David G. 1983. "Donatello's Lost *Dovizia* for the Mercato Vecchio: Wealth and Charity as Florentine Civic Virtues." *Art Bulletin* 65: 401–23.

Witt, Ronald. 2012. *The Two Latin Cultures and the Foundation of Renaissance Humanism in Medieval Italy.* Cambridge and New York: Cambridge University Press.

Zaggia, Stefano. 1997. "Padova: xv–xvii secolo: Trasformazione e continuità negli spazi urbani centrali." In Donatella Calabi, ed. *Fabbriche, piazza, mercati: la città italiana nel rinascimento*, 255–93. Rome: Officina Edizioni.

Zaninoni, Anna. 1994. "Piazze e mercati a Piacenza (secoli ix–xv)." In A. Grohmann, ed. *Spazio urbano e organizzazione economica nell'Europa medievale*, 267–85. Naples: Edizioni Scientifiche Italiane.

—, and Marcello Spigaroli. 1998. "Il secondo medioevo." In Marcello Spigaroli, ed. *Piacenza: La città e le piazze*, 39–89. Piacenza: Tep Edizioni d'Arte.

Zdekauer, Lodovico, ed. 1897. *Il constituto del comune di Siena dell'anno 1262.* Milan: Ulrico Hoepli.

Zervas, Diane Finiello, ed. 1996. *Orsanmichele a Firenze/Orsanmichele Florence.* 2 vols. Modena: Franco Cosimo Panini.

Zupko, Ronald Edward. 1981. *Italian Weights and Measures from the Middle Ages to the Nineteenth Century.* Philadelphia: American Philosophical Society.

# Index

abundance, 20–41, 83, 107, 227; artistic depictions of, 27–41, 193, 199–200, 223, 231n67; and divine approbation, 20, 27–32, 41; as sign of good governance, 30–31, 36, 40–41, 136–38
Accursius, 109–10, 112–13, 118, 179
Aesop's fables, 167–68, 173–74
aesthetics, markets and, 96, 137, 139, 144, 150. *See also* embellishment, market
agriculture, 20, 39–41, 104, 149
Aguia, Donato, 96
Alberti, Leon Battista, 241n15
Alegri, Pietro, 162
Alexander of Halles, 223
*Allegory of Bad Government* (Lorenzetti), 8, 197–98, 209, 245n26, 245n30
*Allegory of Good Government* (Lorenzetti), 196, 208, 225–27, 248n13
Ambrose, Saint, 160
animals, symbolic, 167–68, 173–74, 195–96, 204
Anonimo Genovese, 20
Antonino of Pistoia, 45
*anziani* (elders), 46, 51, 130
Aquinas, Thomas, 159–60, 165, 201
architecture, 10, 44, 64, 68–69, 78–81, 148, 157, 163
Aristotle, 120, 160, 222–23, 225–26
Arnade, Peter, 10
artisans, 3, 7, 25, 58, 127, 130
Assisi, 73, 98–99
Atwell, Adrienne, 72
*Augusta Perusia* (statue), 34–35, 193
Augustine, Saint, 164
avarice, 7, 164–70, 174, 188, 196–97, 224, 244n1, 248n111, 249n17

banking. *See* money-changers
Barbarigo, Andrea, 125
Barberino, Francesco da, 201–2
Barcelona, 9
bargaining, 115–16, 180, 188–90, 222, 236n24. *See also* buying and selling
*Bartering/Bargaining* (illustration; workshop of Boccardino il Vecchio), 115
Bec, Christian, 6

*Beffa del Gulfardo* (illustration, *Decameron*), 183–84
Bella, Gabriele, 103
Berengario I, 44
Bergamo, 20, 54, 73, 116
Bergonzoni, Franco, 236n29
Bernardino da Feltre, 240n14
Bernardino da Siena, 1–3, 6, 11, 155, 246n57; on commerce, 224, 227; on fraud, 161–62, 198; on justice, 201–2
Bertalia, 44
Bianchi, Jacopo dei, 200
Biazachi, Matteo, 248n111
Biazachi, Tommaso, 248n111
Bicci di Lorenzo, 247n107
Biganti, Tiziana, 68–69
Boccaccio, Giovanni, 122, 151, 182, 190, 244n159
Boccardino il Vecchio, 115
Bocchi, Francesca, 49–50
Boethius, 165
Bologna, 30, 49–54, 61, 73, 98, 122, 162, 234n4, 236n29, 243n143; Asinelli tower, 33, 51, 101; Beccharia Magna (Great Meat Market), 51; Campo del Mercato (today Piazzolo), 51; Carrobbio, 45, 52, 54; Foro dei Mercanti, 52, 213; Garisenda tower, 33, 51, 101; guilds of, 50–54; Loggia della Mercanzia, 53, 213; market regulation in, 94, 96–97, 111, 116–18, 121, 126, 138–40, 163, 179; Mercanzia, 53, 67, 70, 213, 247n99; Mercato del Mezzo, 49, 51; Palazzo d'Accursio, 51–52, 116–17; Palazzo dei Notai, 68–69; Palazzo della Biada, 31, 51; Palazzo del Podestà, 49–50, 51; Palazzo del Re Enzo, 51; Pescheria, 51; Piazza Maggiore, 31, 45, 49–51, 53, 68, 177; Porta Ravegnana/Carrobbio market complex, 33–35, 45, 49–52, 54, 58, 103–4, 177; Reno fairgrounds, 67; San Petronio church, 53; San Pietro cathedral, 45, 49; Santa Maria di Porta Ravegnana church, 67; textile industry in, 33–35, 100, 104–7, 117, 138, 140; Universitas Mercatorum, 52, 54, 213
Bon, Piero, 154
*bona fide, sine fraude* (in good faith and without fraud), 157, 171, 190

Bonaventura of Bagnoregio (Saint Bonaventure), 160

Bonfigli, Benedetto, 247n89

*Bonissima* (statue), 36, 199–201, 204

Bono, Ermolino, 94

Branca, Vittore, 6

Braudel, Fernand, 5, 125, 228n25

Braunstein, Philippe, 111, 180

bread, 102, 105, 116, 128, 131–34, 136, 145, 192

Brescia, 54, 68

brokers, 120–23, 145, 179, 237n65

Bruni, Leonardo, 22

Brustoloni, Giovanni Battista, 91

Brutus (Roman consul), 208–13, 247n87, 247n89

*Brutus as Judge* (Maso di Banco), 208–10, 246nn75–79

Burckhardt, Jacob, 8, 188

butchers, 106, 131, 132, 174; in Bologna, 51, 98, 234n4; in Florence, 62, 144, 145, 163; in Venice, 59, 74, 90, 93, 147–48

buyer-seller relationships, 86–87, 108, 123–26, 150, 160, 180, 237n85

buying and selling, 72, 109–26, 130–31, 180, 188–90, 222, 236n26, 237n67; customer approach, 111–12; customer inspection, 112–14; negotiation, 115–16, 236n24; weighing and measuring, 116–20, 237n72; exchange, 120–23

Calabi, Donatella, 9–10, 67

*Calling of Saint Matthew* (Carpaccio), 235n67

*Calling of Saint Matthew* (Matteo di Ser Cambio), 107–8

*Campo San Giacomo di Rialto/Ruga dei Oresi* (Brustoloni), 91

Canale, Giovanni, 121, 125, 140, 189–90

candles, 144–45

Canistris, Opicino de, 20–22, 26, 82

capitalism. *See under* economy

Carocci, Guido, 228n8

Carpaccio, Vittore, 235n67

Carrara regime (Padua), 68, 70, 75, 173

Casagrande, Carla, 164

Castelfranco, 98, 192

Cecco, Stefano di, 71

Ceci, Marta, 23

Celsi, Bortolamio, 153

*Centiloquio* (Pucci), 24

Certaldo, Paolo da, 125–26, 151, 174–75, 190, 209, 237n73, 243n104; *Libro di buoni custumi* of, 93, 125, 204

charity, Christian, 4, 9, 30, 132, 190, 224

*Cheese-Monger* (painting), 99

Cherubini, Giovanni, 26

Chioggia, 162

*Christ and Thomas* (Bicci di Lorenzo), 247n107

*Christ as Judge with Saints and Madonna and Child* (fresco), 206

Christianity: and charity, 4, 9, 30, 132, 190, 224; and commerce, 4–5, 67, 147, 223–24; and fraud, 164–67, 171, 175; and Last Judgment, 207, 219–20, 226, 245n51, 248n111; and marketplace metaphors, 1–3; and public art, 180–82, 206–7, 210, 214–16, 218–20, 223, 247n106; and salvation, 195–96, 217–18, 221. *See also* morality

*Chronicon extravagans de antiquitatibus mediolani* (Appended Chronicle Concerning the Antiquities of Milan; Fiamma), 13–17, 19

*Chronicon maius* (Great Chronicle; Fiamma), 13

church authority, 7, 44–46, 61, 98

Cicero, 172–73, 223

Ciompi Revolt (1378; Florence), 70, 73

civic *laudes*, 19–20, 22, 24–30, 39, 40–41, 76, 83

Clement V, 165

*Cocharelli Treatise on the Virtues and Vices*, 123, 237n68

Codex Rustici, 214–15

Collegiate Church (San Gimignano), 219

columns, 25, 27, 36–38, 61, 112, 193, 200

*Comedy* (Dante), 168–71

commerce: and Christianity, 4–5, 67, 147, 223–24; and civic prosperity, 11, 136–38; and common good, 6, 39, 224, 226–27; and communal governments, 41, 136–38, 224; and politics, 4–5; promotion of, 53–54, 136–38, 192, 194, 226

commercial revolution, 2–6, 9, 164, 221, 242n75

common good (*bonum commune; bene commune*), 3, 7, 30, 70, 83, 89, 136–37, 144, 216, 222–24; and commerce, 6, 39, 224, 226–27; and communal politics, 190, 222, 226–27; and fraud, 163–64, 171, 180, 182, 188, 190; in Lorenzetti frescoes, 249nn17–18; vs. self-interest, 10–11, 40–41, 87–88, 126, 151, 157, 164, 180, 188, 190, 222, 249n17

communes, Italian. *See* governments, communal

Compagni, Dino, 142

competition, 5, 91–92, 126

conflicts, marketplace, 86–87, 125–26, 132, 138–39, 151, 164–65, 190

*Consolation of Philosophy* (Boethius), 165

*contado* (countryside), 30, 46, 49, 51, 127, 139

Contarini, Stefano, 94

counterfeiting, 154, 161, 172, 184–86

courts, guild and civic, 76, 179, 202–3, 210–12

credit, 5–6, 121, 125, 136, 236n24, 237n85

Cremona, 54

Cristofalo of San Salvador, 153–54

Cutini, Clara, 68–69

da la Riva, Bonvesin, 20–22, 26, 40

Dandolo, Giovanni, 59

Dandolo, Marino, 146

Da Nono, Giovanni, 70, 74–82, 233n33

Dante Alighieri, 168–71, 196

Dati, Goro, 66, 140–41

Datini, Francesco di Marco, 9, 125

Davis, James, 4, 229n38

"De amicitia probata" (Sercambi), 175

de' Barbari, Jacopo, 24, 39, 102

*Decameron* (Boccaccio), 122, 182–84, 190, 243n149

"De Falsario: Di Guida d'Ascoli" (On the counter-feiter: of Guida d'Ascoli; Sercambi), 184–85

*De generatione aliquorum civium urbis Padue* (On the families of some citizens of the city of Padua; Da Nono), 75

de Guioldis, Petrus, 14–17

*De hedificatione urbis Patholomie* (On the building of the city of Padua; Da Nono), 75

"De inganno et falsitate: di Ghisello da Racanati" (On deception and falsity: of Ghisello of Racanati; Sercambi), 185–86, 189–90

*De Inventione* (Cicero), 172

Della Scala, Cansignorio 35

Della Scala, Mastino, 22

Della Scala regime (Verona), 68

*De magnalibus urbis Mediolani* (On the Marvels of Milan; da la Riva), 20–22, 40

Demus, Otto, 181

de Roover, Raymond, 4

*Dickering in the Pawnbroker's Shop* (in *Cocharelli Treatise*), 123

display of market goods, 104–8; and fraud, 161, 163, 192–93

disturbances, public, 30, 120, 132, 142

*Documenti d'amore* (da Barberino), 201–2

*Domina Clusii* (statue), 34–35, 193

*Domina Laci* (statue), 34–35, 193

Donatello, 36–38, 61, 65, 231n67

Donato, Maria Monica, 223, 226, 248n9

*Dovizia* (statue; Donatello), 25, 36–38, 61, 193, 222, 231n67

Dubrovnik (Ragusa), 147, 202

earnest money (*denarius dei*), 120–21, 173

economy: capitalist (modern), 4–5, 8, 125, 221, 228n25; history of, 3–4, 228n11; market, 5, 125, 223–24, 228n25

*Effects of Bad Government in the City* (Lorenzetti), 224–25

*Effects of Good Government in the City and Countryside* (Lorenzetti), 39–41, 92, 104, 231n67, 248n13, 249n29

elite merchants, 3, 7, 39, 55, 66, 68–70, 82, 178, 234n42; and market regulation, 132–33

embellishment, market, 191–220, 222, 224, 230n32, 245n36, 247n86, 247n99, 247n110; and market values, 191, 194, 204, 210, 220

England, 6–7, 229n38

Eslami, Alireza Naser, 9, 10

ethics, market, 153–57. *See also* charity, Christian; fraud; morality; values, market

European marketplaces, 6–7, 9–10

evolution, marketplace, 43–70; in Bologna, 45, 49–54; in Florence, 61–66; in Milan, 54–55; in Piacenza, 54–58, 60; in Pistoia, 45–49; in Rome, 60–61, 66; in Venice, 58–60, 66

Ezzelino da Romano, 75, 76, 78

Fabbri, Francesca, 237n68

fables, 167–68, 173–74

fairs and fairgrounds, 51, 58–59, 67, 73–75, 83, 103, 139

Falier, Doge Marino, 244n18

*Fall of the Duke of Athens* (fresco), 245n29

Famous Men in the Saletta cycle (paintings), 247n87

Fanselow, Frank, 87, 126, 237n85

Feldges-Henning, Uta, 248n9

Fiamma, Galvano de la, 13–17, 16, 19, 27, 55, 232n38

Firenzuola, 156, 192

fires, marketplace, 142

*Fishmonger* (painting), 84

fishmongers, 61, 85–88, 127, 131, 132, 148, 234n22

Florence, 1–3, 44, 47, 54, 61–68, 71–74, 151, 201; Bargello, 61–63, 194; Calimala (guild of wool merchants), 63–64, 66, 120, 122; Carnival, 25–26; Ciompi Revolt in, 70, 73; in civic *laudes*, 22, 24–30; *Dovizia* (Donatello statue), 25, 36–38, 61, 193, 222, 231n67; Duomo, 62–63; Francesco del Bene and Company of, 108, 112, 122, 125; Ghibelline Uberti family of, 62; and international trade, 36, 62–63, 66; Lana guild of, 72, 114, 120–25, 145–46, 161, 179, 192, 204–10, 246n70, 247n86; Loggia del Grano, 64; map of, 63; market regulation in, 95–96, 105, 111–17, 120–26, 137–40, 144–46, 163–64, 179, 192, 238n88; Mercanzia, 65–66, 70, 199, 213–16, 224, 232n85, 233n89; Mercato Nuovo, 27, 62–64, 144, 155, 156, 192; Mercato Vecchio (today Piazza della Repubblica), 3, 22, 24–27, 61–63, 67, 83, 90, 139, 142, 144, 154–56, 216, 228n8; Orsanmichele, 27–31, 39, 62–65, 71, 74, 108, 139–44, 155, 215–16, 230n32, 245n36; Palazzo della Mercanzia, 66–67, 216; Palazzo della Signoria (today Palazzo Vecchio), 62–63, 68, 98, 155, 216, 247n87; Parte Guelfa, 64–65; Piazza della Signoria, 63; Ponte Vecchio, 100, 101, 144, 149; Por Santa Maria (guild of cloth retailers and silk manufacturers), 64–66, 96, 112–14, 117, 120–22, 126, 138, 141, 154, 162–64, 179, 192; Santa Croce, 73; Santa Maria della Tromba, 228n8; Santa Maria Novella, 245n51; San Tommaso church, 214; St. Thomas chapel, 214; textile industry in, 63, 100, 145, 205

*Florentia* (Massaio), 27, 29, 37, 66

Foggini, Giovanni Battista, 36

food, provision of, 30–31, 41, 89, 128, 132, 150, 226, 238n25

foreign merchants, 72, 75, 89, 122–23, 139, 146, 207, 234n9

Fortune, 26–27, 35, 76

*Four Patron Saints of the Lana Guild and the Symbols of their Districts* (Master of the Corsi Crucifix), 207

*Fox and the Crow, The* (painting), 167

*Fox and the Stork, The* (sculpture), 173

foxes, 167–68, 173–74, 195–96, 204

Francesco, Antonio di, 153

Francesco del Bene and Company (Florence), 108, 112, 122, 125

Francis, Saint, 4

fraud, 3, 7, 30, 87, 140, 157, 159–90, 241n28; Aquinas on, 159–60; artistic depictions of, 195–98, 204, 220, 224, 245n26, 245n29, 248n111; Bernardino da Siena on, 161–62, 198; in Bologna, 162, 243n143; and common good, 163–64, 171, 180, 182, 188, 190; and concealment, 163, 190, 209, 222; and display of market goods, 161, 163, 192–93; Giordano da Pisa on, 241n4; Leon Battista Alberti on, 241n15; in literature, 164–71; and marketplace layout, 91, 163, 191; prevention of, 91, 145, 150, 163, 176–77, 191–220, 226–27, 241n34; in Rome, 161, 241n34; and trust, 171, 180, 224; in Venice, 161–62, 192–93. *See also* trickery

Friedman, David, 70, 192

Frignano, 177

Frojmovič, Eva, 202, 246n57, 248n13

Frugoni, Chiara, 195, 223, 249n28

*Funeral of the Fox* (sculpture), 195, 204

furriers, 91–93, 139


Gaddi, Taddeo, 199, 224

Galegata, Martino de, 179

Galegata, Tommaso de, 179

gambling, 141–42, 239n96, 239n98

Geertz, Clifford, 83, 87, 229n54

Genoa, 20, 58

Gentile da Fabriano, 247n110

*Geography* (Ptolemy), 27, 29

*Geryon* (Dante's *Comedy*), 172

Ghini, Giovanni di Lapo, 66

Giamboni, Bono, 165

Giano della Bella, 130

Giansante, Massimo, 220

Giordano da Pisa, 1–3, 126, 241n4

Giotto, 76, 78, 103, 202–4, 226, 248n4, 248n13, 249n17

Giovanni degli Eremitani, 78

Gisalba, 73

Glass, Dorothy, 195

*Golden Legend* (Jacopo da Voragine), 245n51

goldsmiths, 71, 90–91, 105, 139, 192, 234n3

Goldthwaite, Richard, 64, 108

governments, communal, 4–5, 7, 59–60, 93–95, 105, 178, 191; and commerce, 41, 136–38, 224; and guilds, 68–69, 247n86; magnate-controlled, 128–30, 137–38; and provision of food, 30–31, 41, 89, 128, 132, 150, 226, 238n25; and public art, 194, 220; and weights and measures, 116–20. *See also* politics

*Grain Market at Orsanmichele in a Time of Abundance* (illustration, *Specchio umano*), 28, 31–32, 39

*Grain Market at Orsanmichele in a Time of Dearth* (illustration, *Specchio umano*), 28, 40, 142–43, 171, 196–97, 249nn17–18

grain markets, 27–32, 62–65, 71, 74, 98, 120, 124–25, 133, 139–42

granaries, public, 31, 51, 76, 78

Gregory I (Gregory the Great), 126, 165, 190

*Griffon atop a Bale* (Matteo di Ser Cambio), 211

Gubbio, Palazzo dei Consoli, 68

Guidi, Jacopo D'Albizzotto, 22–23, 58, 217, 239n96

guildhalls, 64, 72; decoration of, 204–10, 247n86

guilds, 3, 26, 61–66, 87, 122–23, 144, 176–79, 232n85; and communal governments, 68–69, 247n86; courts of, 179, 210–12; and fraud, 164, 176–77, 191; and market regulation, 91, 93–95, 106, 117, 127, 138; and member protection, 96, 114, 120, 126, 139, 150; and promotion of commerce, 53–54; and reputation, 163–64, 191. *See also under particular towns and cities*

Hall, Edward T., 189

Henry of Ghent, 201, 245n50

Henry of Rimini, 163

Henry V (emperor), 45, 49, 199

Herrad of Hohenbourg, 167, 197

honor, 137–38

*Hortus deliciarum* (Herrad of Hohenbourg), 167, 197

Hoven, Birgit van den, 245n33

Howell, Martha, 5, 10, 43, 190

Huizinga, Johann, 164

humanism, 6

human personality, understanding of, 9, 11, 180; and character evaluation, 188–90, 221–22, 244n153, 244n159. *See also* selfhood

Hunt, Edwin S., 242n75

Hyde, J. K., 20, 22, 76


*Iconologia* (Ripa), 197

identity, civic, 10, 39, 41, 43

idolatry, 164–65

*Incredulity of Saint Thomas* (painting; Toscani), 213–14

India, 87, 126

individualism. *See* selfhood

infrastructure, market, 89–108, 193; regulation of, 129, 130, 135, 139–41

inscriptions, public, 147, 191, 216–19

inspections, 92, 134, 145–46, 164

instruments of measure: measuring sticks, 108, 116–18, 146, 197, 202–3, 225, 236n31; scales (in artwork), 32, 36, 118, 200–204, 208–9, 213, 224–25, 245n51; scales (public), 98, 116, 133–34, 145–47, 179, 202, 241n34; steelyards, 118–20, 133–34, 147, 201–3, 245n50; symbolizing justice, 201–4, 208, 213, 225–26, 245nn50–51; symbolizing moderation, 204, 246n58. See also weights and measures

international trade, 7, 20, 70, 125; in Florence, 36, 62–63, 66; in Milan, 16, 55; in Pisa, 138; in Siena, 40, 210; in Venice, 44, 63, 148, 157

Investiture Controversy, 199

Isidore of Seville, 165

itinerant sellers, 71, 87, 104, 138–39

*Iustitia* (Justice with a steelyard; da Barberino), 201–2

Jacopo da Voragine, 245n51

Jones, Philip, 4, 19

jurisdiction, market, 44–46, 49, 54–61, 77, 98, 130, 133. See also governments, communal; guilds

justice, 3, 173, 180, 199–213, 216, 229n45, 245n50, 248n4; artistic depictions of, 201–13, 220, 223–27, 245n51, 246n57, 246n68, 246n70, 248n13, 249n18, 249nn27–29; Bernardino da Siena on, 201–2; and Last Judgment theme, 207, 219–20, 226, 245n51, 248n111; in Lorenzetti frescoes, 249n27, 249nn17–18. See also courts

*Justice* (sculpture), 213

Lane, Frederic C., 4

Langholm, Odd, 3, 4, 160, 228n7

*Last Judgment* (Taddeo di Bartolo), 219–20

Latini, Brunetto, 168–69, 172, 174

*Laudatio Florentinae urbis* (Panegyric to the City of Florence; Bruni), 22

*laudes*, civic, 19–20, 22, 24–30, 39, 40–41, 76, 83

layout, marketplace, 48–49, 74–83, 90–94, 222, 234n4, 234n9; and prevention of fraud, 91, 163, 191

Lefebvre, Henri, 17, 39, 229n54

LeGoff, Jacques, 4, 17

Lenzi, Domenico, 27–32, 40, 76, 141–43, 171, 197, 249nn17–18

*Liber ludi fortunae* (The Book of the Play of Fortune; Da Nono trilogy), 76

*Liber Pergaminus* (Moses del Brolo), 20

*Libro delle rime* (Sacchetti), 216

*Libro de' vizî e delle virtudi* (Giamboni), 165

*Libro di buoni costumi* (Book of Good Practices; Certaldo), 93, 125, 204

Liguria, 248n111

Lisle, Robert de, 165, 166

literacy. See writing

Little, Lester, 164

livestock markets, 48, 51, 54, 73, 112, 140, 233n98

Lodi, 54, 220

Lombard, Peter, 159

Lopez, Robert S., 4

Lorenzetti, Ambrogio, 10, 222–27, 231n64, 248n9, 249nn17–18, 249nn27–30; *Allegory of Bad Government*, 8, 197–98, 209, 245n26, 245n30; *Allegory of Good Government*, 196, 208, 225–27, 248n13; *Effects of Bad Government in the City*, 224–25, 248n4; *Effects of Good Government in the City and Countryside*, 39–41, 92, 104, 231n67, 248n13, 249n29; *mappamondo*, 240n25

lotteries, stall assignment, 93–94, 234n19

Louis the Pious, 55

loyalty, 173, 176

Lucca, 145, 154; San Martino church, 218–19

Lugli, Emmanuele, 200

Machiavelli, Niccolò, 180

*Madonna dei Banchetti* (Gentile da Fabriano), 247n110

Madonna Master, 165–66

*Madonna Verona* (statue), 35–36, 193

Maestro della Madonna della Misericordia, 105

magnates, 7, 44–46, 49, 51, 53, 128–30, 137–38

maintenance, marketplace, 134–35, 142–44, 150, 238n42

maps: Florence, 63; *Map of Milan and Surrounding Territory* (de Guioldis), 14–17; *mappamondo* (in Venice), 157; *mappamondo* (Lorenzetti), 240n25; Padua, 77, 81; Piacenza, 56; Pistoia, 46, 48; *Woodcut Map of Venice* (de' Barbari), 24, 39, 102

Marina, Areli, 192

Mark, Saint, 180–82

*Market and the City, The* (Calabi), 9

*Market at Porta Ravegnana* (in Matriculation Book of the Bolognese Drapers), 33–35, 100, 103–4, 106–7, 148

*Market Scene* (Master of 1328), 109–10, 118

Marseille, 9

Marshall, Richard, 121, 125

Martinengo, 73

Martino di Pietro, Niccolò di, 71

Masio da Fano, 177

Maso di Banco, 208

Massaio, Piero di Jacopo del, 27, 29, 37, 66

Master of 1328 (Bolognese illuminator), 109–10, 112–13, 121, 179

Master of the Dominican Effigies, 205

materialism, 20–22, 40, 228n11

Matteo di Ser Cambio, 107, 210–11

Mazzei, Lapo, 9

*Measuring Cloth* (painting), 118

*Measuring Grain and the Grain Merchant in his Office Surrounded by Sieves and Measures* (in *Specchio umano*), 124

measuring standards. See standards, public

Medici family, 65, 214

mercantile theme: in public art, 196, 198, 215–18, 222–26, 245n36, 248n9, 248n13; in trickster tales, 183–84, 188–89

*Mercato Vecchio* (School of Vasari), 37

*Mercato Vecchio, Church of San Tommaso, and the Incredulity of Saint Thomas* (in Codex Rustici), 214–15

merchandise: descriptions of, 13, 16, 20–21, 23, 24–26, 80–82; organization of, 81–83

*Merchant in the Confessional* (Langholm), 3

Mercury (Roman god of commerce), 38–39

metaphor, marketplaces as, 1–3, 26

Milan, 54–55, 122; Broletto Nuovo, 14–17, 27, 47, 55, 80, 98, 177; Broletto Vecchio, 16, 55, 232n38; da la Riva's description of, 20–22, 40; Fiamma's description of, 13–17, 19; map of, 14–17; Santa Maria Maggiore cathedral, 55; Sant'Ambrogio monks, 44–45, 55; Santa Tecla cathedral, 55; Universitas Mercatorum, 55; Visconti of, 20, 52, 55, 57, 68, 220

Miller, Maureen, 54

*Mirabilia urbis Romae* (literary work), 76

Modena, 54; Duomo, 194–96, 201; Porta della Pescheria, 194; public sculptures in, 100, 194–201, 204

moderation, 204, 237n73, 246n58

Modigliani, Anna, 61, 68

Molho, Anthony, 6

money-changers (bankers), 7, 44, 48, 62–69, 71, 108; and fraud, 171–72; and market regulation, 133, 140, 178–79

monopolies, 5, 96, 125–26

Montenach, Anne, 160

*Moralia* (Gregory I), 126, 165, 190

morality: and fraud, 160, 162–64; and marketplace, 4, 6, 26–29, 35, 41, 102, 157, 180, 221–22, 229n38

Morelli, Giovanni di Pagolo, 125, 175, 204, 239n98

Morocco, 83, 87, 229n54

Morpurgo, Salomone, 209

Morris, Colin, 188

Moses del Brolo, 20

Muldrew, Craig, 5–6

Murray, James M., 242n75

Nari, Monica Chiellini, 195

Niccolò da Poggibonsi, 230n19

*Nicomachaean Ethics* (Aristotle), 160

non-standardized goods, 86–87, 112, 126, 150, 161, 222, 234n6, 235n51

notaries, 68–69, 121, 136, 148, 177–78, 247n110, 248n111

*novelle* (short stories), 7, 151, 180, 182

Occhipinti, Elisa, 76

Odonis, Gerald, 160

"On the condition of the city of Genoa" (Anonimo Genovese), 20

openness and transparency, 191, 192, 222, 224

Orcagna, 64, 245n51

*Ordinary Gloss of Justinian's Digest* (Accursius), 109–10, 112–13, 118, 179

organization, marketplace, 3, 6, 43–44, 71–83, 87, 150; in Florence, 90; in Padua, 75–83, 90; in Venice, 90–93

Origo, Iris, 125

Orvieto, 99

Otto I, 44, 55

Otto III, 45

Pächt, Otto, 248n9

Padua, 44, 54, 73, 75–83, 90, 116, 149, 155–56, 174; Alodio, 77–78, 81, 233n33; Carrara regime of, 68, 70, 75, 173; Domus Communis, 77; Fondaco delle Biade (public granary), 31, 76, 78; maps of, 77, 81; Palazzo degli Anziani, 76–78, 80–81; Palazzo del Consiglio, 76–78, 80; Palazzo della Ragione, 37, 76–82, 98, 99, 202–4; Palazzo del Podestà, 76–78, 80–81; Peronio, 37–38, 77–78, 81, 156, 233n33; Porciglia, 76; Prato della Valle, 73–74; Salone (Palazzo della Ragione), 78, 80, 84, 156, 202–3, 226; Scrovegni Chapel, 103, 248n4; Stone of Vituperation, 156; Torre Bianca, 78; Torre Rossa, 78; in *Visio Egidii*, 70, 74–82

palaces, communal, 76; market spaces in, 14–16, 51, 80–82, 97–99, 148. *See also under particular towns and cities*

Parigi, Giulio, 64

Parma, 31–32, 68, 192

Paschal II, 199

Passageri, Rolandino, 220

Paul, Jürgen, 68, 97–98

Pavia, 20–21, 54; Piazza Atria, 82

"La Penetanza" (Latini; *Tesoretto*), 168–69

Peronio Column (Padua), 37–38

*Personification of Abundance* (in *Specchio umano*), 32

Perugia, 24, 30–31, 61, 71, 126, 192, 210–12, 247n89; Campo Battaglia, 233n98; Collegio del Cambio (guild of money-changers), 68–69; Fontana Maggiore statues, 34–35, 193; Matriculation Book of the Perugian Notaries, 176–77, 212; Mercanzia, 68–69, 112, 210–11; Palazzo dei Priori, 69, 167–68, 177, 210

Piacenza, 54–58, 60, 68, 73, 117; College of Merchants (Nuxio), 56–58, 67; map of, 56; market regulation in, 92–95, 107–8, 111, 120, 140, 144–47, 234n9; Palatium Nuxii, 56; Palazzo Gotico, 57, 98; Piazza del Borgo, 56, 58, 67, 108, 144, 154; San Francesco church, 57; San Sisto monastery, 67; Santa Brigida monastery, 67; Torrazzo, 57

pillories, 156, 193

Pinerolo, 121, 125, 140

Pinto, Giuliano, 27

Piranesi, Francesco, 74

Pisa, 73, 141, 149, 162, 245n51; market regulation in, 116, 120, 122, 138, 146; punishment for crimes in, 154, 177, 179, 193–94, 199

Pisano, Giovanni, 35, 245n51

Pisano, Nicola, 35

Pistoia, 45–49, 142, 161; guilds of, 129, 133, 238n29; maps of, 46, 48; market regulation in, 96, 120, 128–38, 145, 148, 179, 192, 237n16; Opera di San Jacopo, 133–34; Palazzo degli Anziani, 47, 130; Palazzo del Podestà, 98; Piazza della Sala, 45, 48, 101, 134, 238n42; Piazza Maggiore (Piazza del Duomo), 45, 145; San Zeno cathedral, 128–30, 237n16

Pitti, Buonaccorso, 141–42

*pitture infamanti* (defamatory pictures), 191, 193–94, 216, 220, 244nn14–15, 244n18, 245n29

politics, 3, 4–5; and civic spaces, 7, 9, 41, 44, 49, 58, 68, 127; communal, 6, 190, 220, 222–23, 226–27, 244n165. *See also* governments, communal

*Politics* (Aristotle), 120

Polo, Marco, 157

Pope-Hennessy, John, 35

*popolo*, 44, 50–51, 53, 63, 78, 86, 127–32; *grasso*, 7, 132; *minuto*, 7, 24, 58, 132; of Pistoia, 46, 128–32, 137–38; of Venice, 58, 89–90

porters, 148

Prato, 44, 71, 121, 125, 140

*Prato della Valle* (Piranesi), 74

pricing, 116, 131, 228n7

*Procession in Piazza San Marco; Saint Mark's Relics Taken from his Tomb* (Bellini), 181

*Procession of the Notaries* (Vanni di Baldolo), 176–77

proclamation posts, 155, 193

Prodi, Paolo, 4–5, 6

*Production of Space* (Lefebvre), 17, 229n54

profit, pursuit of, 4, 6, 7, 9, 125–26, 190, 221

"Proprietà di Mercato Vecchio" (Pucci), 24–27, 67, 76

Prudentius, 165–66

*Psychomachia* (Prudentius), 165

Ptolemy, 27, 29

*Public Treasurer and his Scribe in their Office* (illustration), 178

Pucci, Antonio, 22, 24–27, 67, 76, 83

punishment for crimes, 43, 145, 161, 179, 193–94, 199, 219–20, 231n28; and public humiliation, 153–57, 177; and ritualized destruction of goods, 153–55. *See also pitture infamanti*

Querini family (Venice), 59

Querini-Tiepolo conspiracy (1310), 59

Ragusa (Dubrovnik), 147, 202

Randolph, Adrian, 222

Rauty, Natale, 45, 133

Ravenna, Platea Mercurii (Piazza of Mercury), 38

Rebhorn, Wayne, 180

Reggio, 85–88, 116–17, 127

regulation, market, 5–7, 30–31, 71, 88–89, 96–97, 127–51; and bread, 102, 105, 116, 128, 131–34, 136, 145, 192; and buying and selling, 111, 130–31; and display of goods, 105; and elite merchants, 132–33; enforcement of, 112, 126, 140–42, 144, 177, 191, 234n3; and fairs, 74, 139; growth of, 127–38; and guilds, 91, 93–95, 106, 117, 127, 138; and magnate-controlled regimes, 128–30, 137–38; and market infrastructure, 129, 130, 135, 139–41; and material abundance, 136–38; and money-changers, 133, 140, 178–79; and *popolo*, 127–32, 137–38; and pricing, 116, 131; and protection of public space, 96, 100, 103, 107, 129–30, 135, 192, 237n9; and textile industry, 132–33, 178; and weights and measures, 116–20, 133–34, 145–47, 200. *See also under particular towns and cities*

Remigio de' Girolami, 7

Renaissance, Italian, 6, 188

rents. *See under* revenue, market

republicanism, 4, 6, 249n30

reputation: civic, 72, 88–90, 96, 120, 137, 150–51, 154, 163–64, 220; guild, 163–64, 191; individual, 9, 175–76, 180, 188, 221, 242n75

*Rettorica, La* (Latini), 172

revenue, market: from gabelles, 74, 139, 148; from market spaces, 127, 135–36, 148–50, 240n142

*Rhetorica ad Herennium* (Cicero), 172

*Ricordi* (Morelli), 175, 204

Rieti, 30, 171

Rigaud, John, 165

riots, market, 30, 142

Ripa, Cesare, 197

Robert of Anjou, 205

Roland of Cremona, 159

*Roman de Renart*, 167

Rome, 60–61, 66, 161, 179, 199, 241n34; L'Abbondanza, 78–80; Campidoglio, 61; Campo de' Fiori, 61, 78; market regulation in, 112–14, 117, 120–21, 139, 140, 144–45, 163; Piazza Giudea, 61; San Celso, 61; Santa Maria Rotonda, 61–62; Sant'Angelo, 61

Rosso brothers (Venetian cheese-mongers), 101, 235n48

Rowley, George, 245n30

Rubinstein, Nicolai, 222–23, 247n106

Rustici, Marco di Bartolomeo, 214–15

Sacchetti, Franco, 177, 182, 216, 247n106

*Saint Eligius as Goldsmith* (Maestro della Madonna della Misericordia), 105

Sala dei Nove frescoes (Lorenzetti; Palazzo Pubblico, Siena), 10, 39–41, 222–27, 231n64, 248n9, 249nn17–18, 249nn27–30. *See also particular paintings*

*Sale of a Horse* (Master of 1328), 37, 112–13

Salimbene de Adam of Parma, 86–86, 88, 127, 173

*Salt Deposits Controlled by the Commune of Parma* (painting), 32

salt trade, 31, 59, 125

salvation, eternal, 195–96, 217–18, 221

Salvatori, Enrica, 55

*San Bernardino Preaching in the Campo of Siena* (Sano di Pietro), 2

Sandler, Lucy Freeman, 165

San Gimignano, 54, 219

San Giovanni Valdarno, 192–93; Palazzo Pretorio, 193

Sano di Pietro, 2

Sapori, Armando, 125

Saragoni, Manno, 122

Scarperia, 192

Schedel, Hartman, 203–4

scholastics, 159–60

Scott, James, 86

seals, 132, 133, 145–46

security, market, 134, 141–42, 150, 191

Sefrou (Morocco), 83

Seidel, Max, 248n9

selfhood, 4, 8, 11, 126, 180, 228n11, 244n159, 244n165; and fraud, 160; and introspection, 6, 9–10, 188–90, 222

self-interest. *See under* common good

*Seller of Dried Meat* (painting), 106

*Sentences* (Lombard), 159

Sercambi, Giovanni, 151, 175, 182, 184–87, 189–90, 244n153

Serraineri, Marco, 122

Shaw, James, 229n45

shops and stalls: in communal palaces, 14–16, 51, 80–82, 97–99, 148; location of, 51, 71, 74, 93–95, 108; physical description of, 97–103, 108, 235n45

short measure, 11, 116, 125–26, 145, 150, 201, 241n28

Siena, 1–3, 11, 24, 54, 141, 149–50, 162, 192, 244n15; Campo, 2, 103, 136, 144, 149, 155, 210–11, 234n42, 247n91, 247n110; and Lorenzetti's *mappamondo*, 240n25; market regulation in, 83, 105, 136, 144, 145; Mercanzia, 70, 210–13; Palazzo Pubblico, 98, 231n64; Palio (horse race), 156; San Paolo, 210. *See also* Sala dei Nove frescoes

signs, shop, 102, 235n51

*Silent Language* (Hall), 189

Simons, Walter, 10

Skinner, Quentin, 223

Smith, Adam, 221

social relations, 5–6, 54, 86–88, 126, 127, 132, 175, 180, 188, 222; and class, 3, 21, 25, 39, 68–69, 88, 123, 164–65; and fraud, 150, 162

*Sociology of the Renaissance* (von Martin), 8

*Sommo della condizione di Vinegia, El* (The Summation of the Situation of Venice; Guidi), 22–23, 58

spaces, civic, specialization and overlapping of, 9, 16–17, 44, 49, 53–56, 58, 60–63, 67–68, 70

spaces, market, 10, 17, 23, 48, 66, 240n14; as city center, 19, 39, 155–56; as civic symbol, 19, 26, 36–37, 40–41, 70, 224; in communal palaces, 14–16, 50–51, 80–82, 97–99, 148; location of, 21, 44, 51, 54–55, 71, 73–74; in medieval Italian art, 27, 33–35; revenue from, 127, 135–36, 148–50, 240n142

Spagnesi, Annalisa Bricoli, 246n68

*Specchio umano* (*Libro del biadaiolo*; Book of the Grain Seller; Lenzi), 27–32, 39, 76, 141–43, 171, 197, 249nn17–18

spices, 113–14, 145, 218–19, 241n13

Spigaroli, Marcello, 57

Spoleto, 43

*St. Thomas* (Verrocchio), 245n36

standardization. *See* non-standardized goods; weights and measures

standards, public, 36, 82, 117, 133–34, 193, 200–201, 203–4, 236n29. *See also* weights and measures

Starn, Randolph, 245n30, 248n13

Stock, Brian, 9, 177

storage, market, 101–2

*Storia di Sant'Eligio*, 105

Subbioni, Marina, 177

*Summa Theologica* (Aquinas), 159–60, 165

supervision, market, 92, 127–28, 133–34, 141–47, 200, 219


Taddeo di Bartolo, 219–20

*Tesoretto* (Latini), 168–69

textile industry, 7, 48, 56, 66, 117–18, 132–33, 145–46, 178, 241n34. *See also under* Bologna; Florence

theft, 5, 141–42, 182

Thomas, Saint, 213–16, 247n106, 247n107

Thomas of Chobham, 223

Three Maries acquiring perfumes for Jesus's body (Modena capital), 100

time and marketplace, 21, 25–26, 73

Todeschini, Giacomo, 4, 6, 92, 176

Toscani, Giovanni, 213–14

Toschi, Giuseppe, 50

traffic flow, 51–52, 83, 96, 107–8, 135, 139, 144

*Tree of Vices* (Madonna Master), 166

Treviso, 54, 73, 142, 149, 161, 241n34; market regulation in, 95, 98, 120, 145–48, 173, 177

*Tribunal of the Index Victualium* (after Giotto), 202–4, 246n57

*Tribunal of the Notaries' Guild* (Vanni di Baldolo), 212

trickery, 151, 180–88; in *novelle*, 7, 180, 182–87, 190, 244n153, 244n159. *See also* fraud

trust, 3, 5–6, 9, 87, 123–25, 141, 171–77, 193, 226, 242n75; and character evaluation, 188–90, 221–22, 244n153; and fraud, 171, 180, 224; promotion of, 150, 180, 201, 204, 216, 218–19, 222, 247n110; in trickster tales, 183–84; and truthfulness, 173–74, 199; and written records, 179

truth, 3, 173–74, 197–99, 226–27, 245n33
*Truth Tearing out the Tongue of Fraud* (sculpture), 199, 204
Tuliani, Maurizio, 103, 149–50

Uberti family (Florence), 62
Uccello, Paolo, 214
usury, 4, 7, 76, 159, 165, 170, 174

values, market, 193, 226; and market embellishment, 191, 194, 204, 210, 220. *See also* common good
Vanni, Andrea, 39, 225
Vanni di Baldolo, 176–77, 212
Vasari, Giorgio, 199, 214, 245n29
Vatican, Mercatello in, 61
Vecchio, Silvana, 164
Vendramin, Antonio, 234n3
Venice, 31, 66–68, 89–93, 151, 163, 177, 230n19; Beccarie, 59, 74, 90, 93, 147–48; Campo San Polo, 58; in *El sommo della condizione di Vinegia*, 22–23, 58; Fondaco dei Tedeschi (German merchants' warehouse), 102, 111, 122, 142, 148, 154; Fondaco della Farina, 148; fraud in, 161–62, 192–93; Giustizieri Vecchi (Old Justices), 58, 97, 153–54, 234n3; guilds of, 58, 153–54; and international trade, 44, 63, 148, 157; map of, 24, 39, 102; *mappamondo* in, 157; market regulation in, 94–97, 113, 120, 122, 139, 140, 144, 146–49, 237n72, 241n13; Merceria, 58; Murano, 105; Pescheria, 61, 148, 234n22; Piazza San Marco, 23, 58, 63, 89, 92–93, 103, 155; Pietra di Bando (Proclamation Stone), 155; Querini family of, 59; Rialto market, 23–24, 58–60, 67, 70–71, 93, 142, 153–57, 240n142; Ruga dei Oresi (Street of the Goldsmiths), 90–91, 234n3; San Giacomo di Rialto church, 67, 156–57, 217, 240n21; San Marco church, 180–81; San Pietro di Castello, 58; Scala dei Giganti, 39; Sensa Fair, 58–59, 73, 103; Ufficiali sopra Rialto, 59, 139, 141, 235n48
Verdili, Zanin di, 154
Verona, 19, 54, 61, 72–75, 82–83, 141, 154, 156, 161; Campo Marzo, 74–75, 83; Capitello, 116–17, 200; Della Scala regime of, 68; Domus

Mercatorum, 68, 83, 97–98; Fair of Saints Michael and Giustina, 74; *Madonna Verona*, 35–36, 193; market regulation in, 92, 94–95, 111–12, 116–17, 120, 122, 236n52, 239n96; Piazza Bra, 73; Piazza delle Erbe, 35, 116–17, 200
Verrocchio, Andrea del, 65, 215–16, 245n36
*View of the Pantheon* (painting), 62
Villani, Giovanni, 22, 24, 72, 148, 204
Villano da Gubbio, 142–43
Virgin, miraculous image of (Florence), 64
Visconti of Milan, 52, 57, 68, 220; Giangaleazzo, 55; Ottone, 20
*Visio Egidii regis Patavie* (Vision of Egidius, king of Padua; Da Nono), 70, 74–82
Viterbo, 111
von Martin, Alfred, 8

Walter of Brienne, 245n29
*Weighing Wool with a Steelyard* (painting), 118–20
weights and measures, 36, 44–45, 48, 50, 57, 59, 76, 81–82, 128–29; during buying and selling, 116–20, 237n2; and fraud, 161–62; regulation of, 116–20, 133–34, 145–47, 200; standardization of, 6, 44, 88, 116, 164, 191, 200. *See also* instruments of measure; standards, public
Weissman, Ronald, 6, 188
Welch, Evelyn, 26
wholesale trade, 11, 236n24
wine sellers, 120, 131–34, 163, 192, 238n25
witnesses to commercial exchange, 121, 179, 193
Witt, Ronald, 9
women, 11
*Woodcut Map of Venice* (de' Barbari), 24, 39, 102
writing: and inscriptions, 216–17; and introspection, 6, 9, 189, 222; merchant-writers (*mercanti scrittori*), 6; and record keeping, 9, 177–79

Zaninoni, Anna, 57
Zanobi da Strata, 126, 190
*Zibaldone da Canal* (Venetian merchant manual), 113–14, 190
Ziliulo, Cabrin di, 154
Zorzi da Norimburgo, 111, 112, 123, 180, 189

# ILLUSTRATION CREDITS